PRENTICE HALL
Encyclopedic Dictionary
of
BUSINESS TERMS

WILBUR CROSS

PRENTICE HALL
Englewood Cliffs, New Jersey 07632

Prentice-Hall International, Inc., *London*
Prentice-Hall of Australia Pty., Ltd., *Sydney*
Prentice-Hall Canada, Inc., *Toronto*
Prentice-Hall Hispanoamericana, S.A., *Mexico*
Prentice-Hall of India Private Ltd., *New Delhi*
Prentice-Hall of Japan, Inc., Tokyo
Prentice-Hall of Southeast Asia Pte., Ltd., *Singapore*
Editora Prentice-Hall do Brasil, Ltda., *Rio de Janeiro*

© 1995 by
PRENTICE HALL

10   9   8   7   6   5   4   3   2   1

Special thanks to Alice Richey, Editorial Coordinator

Library of Congress Cataloging-in Publication Data

Cross, Wilbur.
   Prentice Hall encyclopedic dictionary of business terms / Wilbur
Cross.
      p.   cm.
   Other title: Encyclopedic dictionary of business terms.
   ISBN 0–13–026221–8
   1. Business—Dictionaries.   2. Management—Dictionaries.
I. Prentice Hall, inc.   II. Title.
HF1001.C68   1995
650'.03—dc20   95–23813
                                           CIP

ISBN 0-13-026221-8

PRENTICE HALL
Career and Personal Development
Englewood Cliffs, NJ 07632
A Simon & Schuster Company

PRINTED IN THE UNITED STATES OF AMERICA

CONTENTS

Alphabetical listings of words, phrases, and names, from A to Z, cross-referenced, and encompassing:

- ▓ Concise definitions in dictionary format.
- ▓ Comprehensive explanations of key words and phrases applicable to business, commercial, and professional dialogue.
- ▓ Compact essays on major topics.

Concise evaluations of key topics and issues in five selected categories:

— Part 1 —

MANAGEMENT—393

The nature and scope of management and administration in business, industry, and commercial enterprises of all types and sizes, public and private.

– Part 2 –

RESOURCES—403

An overview of the many resources available to an organization, whether profit or nonprofit, including manpower, capital, communications, research, inventory, production capability, and intangibles such as social acceptability and corporate image.

– Part 3 –

PROCEDURES AND REGULATIONS—413

The legal agenda and regulatory procedures that formalize the composition and operations of an organization, regardless of its size, areas of function, or financial structure.

– Part 4 –

MONEY—423

The nature and usages of money and its many related components and derivatives, from hard cash and currency to commodities, liquid assets, securities, and intangibles such as credit ratings, appreciation, and deductibles.

– Part 5 –

COMMUNICATIONS—431

The broad range of methods, equipment, and state-of-the-art research that make it possible to communicate more quickly and effectively and reliably than ever before in the history of business and industry.

PREFACE

NATURE AND SCOPE OF THE
ENCYCLOPEDIC DICTIONARY

The Encyclopedic Dictionary of Business Terms is a compact, ready-to-use reference source for information on words, phrases, and meanings that particularly relate to business, commerce, industry, and associated fields. As a practical guide to more than 500 subject areas, it covers everything you need to know, from historical and traditional language to popular idioms and the latest terminology in state-of-the-art technological communications. In this single volume, you will find immediate, comprehensive information about business language and phraseology, from A to Z, with the latest spellings, definitions, and reference to related words, phrases, and concise bodies of information.

Equally important, *The Encyclopedic Dictionary of Business Terms* is organized alphabetically, providing not only definitions but encyclopedic coverage of major subject areas, to make it easier for you to focus on the exact field(s) in which you are most interested. This advanced reference guide has been written for professionals in all fields of business, large and small, for managers and entrepreneurs, for authors and editors, and for everyone who wants a better understanding of professional terms and meanings, whether for writing texts or for reading books, periodicals, and other literature with greater understanding.

As a new breed of reference work, this compact volume is more than a dictionary, more than an encyclopedia. It is both of these, combined for easy reference. It also provides guidance in the areas of management, communications, resources, money, and industrial procedures, as well as cross-references to current terms and phrases that apply to all business-related disciplines and theme areas. Cross-indexing makes it possible for readers to locate synonyms and equivalent terms, analogues, related subject matter, and antonyms at will. Thus, the book serves as an aid to memory in the location of subject matter. For those who desire to use the encyclopedic dictionary as a study guide, it can be a ready, valuable, and authoritative vocabulary builder as well.

INTRODUCTION

HOW TO USE THIS REFERENCE WORK

The A to Z sections provide information, alphabetically arranged on subjects particularly related to business and industry. They extend from very brief entries, with definitions and cross-references, to comprehensive coverage of major subjects. In many instances, the latter are further subdivided into related topics or elements, arranged alphabetically, chronologically, or sequentially. In all cases, the entries have been selected because of their practical application to business, whether they are single words, abbreviations, acronyms, phrases, titles, degrees, theories, formulas, equations, proper names, foreign words, initialisms, organizations, institutions, or otherwise.

Readers can locate references as easily as when using a standard dictionary, but will not find either nonbusiness entries or business words and phrases that are so familiar as to require no definitions. Some common words, however, are included when they have special business meanings not normally associated with the term. An example is *uttering,* which is generally connected with speech, but which in business terminology means "making use of a counterfeit document for personal gain."

The *A* to *Z* sections include mini-essays—also arranged in alphabetical sequence—for more comprehensive coverage of major subjects that are business-oriented, such as *accounting, advertising, business law, career education,* and *marketing.* Most entries in the alphabetical sections, whether long or short, are cross-referenced so that readers can obtain information about related, or supplementary, subjects.

Encyclopedic attention is given to five major business disciplines, in article formats, which not only cover a broad range of pertinent subject areas and help readers to grasp the nature and spirit of the business world, but provide ready references to other fields of coverage that are related. These essays cover management, administration, and leadership; the wide scope of resources available to business and industry; the legal, regulatory, and functional procedures that mandate many of the operations and decisions of a business organization; the nature and extent of money, funds, and assets that nourish and sustain the business and industrial world; and the many vehicles and media of communication that facilitate the conduct of commercial and professional transactions throughout the world.

In all divisions and supplements of this compact work, references are also made to lists, charts, graphs, statistics, tabulations, and graphics. These can be found in the Appendix, as well as in the A to Z and the essay sections. They are identified by subject and location for quick and easy cross-reference and examination.

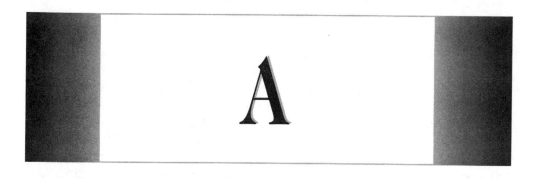

ABSENTEE OWNERSHIP

Property that the owner does not actively use or personally occupy.

ACCEPTANCE SAMPLING

In quality control procedures and research, the use of samples, selected at random, to determine the quality, components, and acceptability of a larger quantity of the units being sampled.

ACCESS

In data processing, the manner in which information files are referred to by the computer. *See* Direct Access.

ACCESS METHOD

A technique for moving data between the main storage unit in a computer and its input/output devices. *See* Access.

ACCOUNTING

The accumulation and preparation of financial data for the management of organizations of all sizes and types. Accounting programs and records start with simple, day-to-day bookkeeping, which provides pertinent information to establish the basic accounting system. These records include routine entries about such subject areas as income from the sale of products or services, expenses of business operations, cost of merchandise produced, and overhead expenses such as employee compensation, rent, and transportation. Accounting principles determine which financial events and transactions should be recorded in the bookkeeper's ledgers, journals, and computer disks. The review and evaluation of these records is the primary function of accounting. Financial statements produced by accountants then furnish business and other types of organizations with the basis for their financial planning and control and provide outside investors and government agencies with data they

1

can use to make decisions about these organizations. Accounting systems provide statistical access to a firm's financial condition for three broad interest groups: (1) management, which needs such information to evaluate financial performance over given periods of time and to make decisions regarding the future; (2) the general public, especially stockholders or dealers in securities, who cannot make investment decisions without knowing the financial status of a company over the previous quarter or year; (3) regulatory departments of the various levels of government that are concerned with taxes and regulations. Accountants also perform similar functions for government agencies and nonprofit organizations.

Accounting is a centuries-old profession, going back at least to the fourteenth century when Italian merchants evolved the practice of double-entry bookkeeping, the basis for modern-day accounting, to record commercial trade that might last for months, or even years, in which private investors had bought shares. The historic Italian system resembled its modern counterpart in that it consisted of a balance sheet with two sections, one listing assets and the effect of sales, purchases, and investments on assets, and the other recording shares and various liabilities incurred. Thus, owners who had originally bought shares could claim their proportion of the profits when and if the venture succeeded. By the end of the seventeenth century, as trade grew more widespread and financing became more complex, the profession of the accountant was a reality, and by the late nineteenth century, regulations controlled the chartering of accountants in both Europe and America. Today's system of accounting matured in response to changes in the legal structure of companies, as well as to rising needs for accurate financial reports, as well as reports to government regulations. In the field of law, the development of the corporation has had the greatest impact because it allowed public scrutiny of internal financial affairs, something unheard of in earlier forms of business ownership. The rise of the multinational corporation has also increased accounting responsibilities, to meet such mandates as foreign-currency conversion, reporting under many new legal structures, and the adjustment of financial reporting to attain the least costly payments in regard to taxes, tariffs, and jurisdictional controls. Equally significant, increases in the quantity and kinds of financial instruments that has taken place just in the past generation has escalated the professional demands placed upon accountants. *See* Accounting Industry, Auditing, Financial Accounting, Tax Accounting.

ACCOUNTING INDUSTRY

The discipline comprised of public accountants who are available to the business world and the public at large for such functions as periodic bookkeeping and tax preparation. Although most states do not regulate the performance of public accountants, the only ones permitted to offer opinions about financial statements are Certified Public Accountants (CPAs), who have passed rigorous national examinations and must also fulfill the requirements of the state in which they practice, including specified periods of practical experience within the profession. CPAs are expected to maintain a relationship of strict independence and professionalism with the firms for whom they work and avoid any conflicts of interest, such as stock acquisitions in client firms, so that the objectivity of their opinions may not be questioned. By and large, most accounting firms are small and local, serving clients within narrow geographical areas. While there are six very large accounting firms, these tend to be multilateral, offering a range of services that often includes, for example, executive searching and management consulting.

ACCOUNTING STANDARDS

Accounting regulations are strict and come under the scrutiny of the Financial Accounting Standards Board (FASB), which prepares advisory statements that are widely accepted as accounting principles. The Securities and Exchange Commission (SEC) also has a strong hand in the establishment of accounting principles, as do federal, state, and local authorities in this field. One of the ongoing dilemmas has been the matter of review of the accounting problems of individual industries, to resolve the question of how accounting theory should respond to current economic conditions, such as inflation, fraud, and large-scale financial scandals such as the savings and loan failures of the late 1980s. The accounting industry is largely responsible for disciplining itself to ensure the independence of its professionals, to set standards, and to establish workable reporting and accounting principles. In this respect, the American Institute of Certified Public Accountants (AICPA) has developed standards of performance designed to ensure objectivity and prevent conflicts of interest among its members. *See* Accounting, American Institute of Certified Public Accountants, Auditing, Securities and Exchange Commission.

ACCRUAL

In financial record keeping a system for recording grievances and expenses as they are earned or incurred during a predetermined period rather than when they are received or paid. This method is also known as accrual basis.

ACCRUE

To be gained or obtained, such as profit, credits. or other benefits. The term can also be applied to a loss, such as an accrued obligation to a lender.

ACCUMULATION

In commercial practice, the purchases of goods made in advance or contracts for services negotiated earlier in anticipation of rising prices and wages.

Example: The ABC Company negotiated an accumulation of steel bearings when it was announced by the steel industry that the price of ore would rise within three months.

ACE/SCORE PROGRAM

Valuable services provided by the Small Business Administration (SBA) through the Active Corps of Executives and the Service Corps of Retired Executives. Members of the two organizations are volunteers who are capable, seasoned business advisers who provide counseling to entrepreneurs and other small business managers. Except for minor costs, both ACE and SCORE services are free. *See* SCORE.

ACHIEVEMENT TEST

A measure of skills and proficiency determined by testing performance displayed in specific fields of work.

ACLU

American Civil Liberties Union, a nonpartisan organization devoted to the preservation of the basic rights set forth in the United States Constitution. Founded in 1920, ACLU maintains a program that is directed toward three major areas of civil liberties: (1) Freedom of speech press, assembly, and religion; (2) Equality before the law for everyone, regardless of race, nationality, political opinion, or religious belief; (3) Due process of law for all individuals. The ACLU has participated directly or indirectly in almost every civil liberties case contested in American courts, including many involving business and commerce. For example, the ACLU was involved in the landmark *Brown vs. Board of Education* school desegregation case in 1954. *See* Civil Rights, Discrimination.

ACQUISITION

In corporate finance, the act of taking over one organization by another; usually accomplished by the purchase of a controlling portion of the acquired company's common stock. *See* Merger.

ACROSS-THE-BOARD

In personnel administration, that which applies to all employees, groups, members, or categories. An across-the-board pay increase, for example, would be a uniform raise for all employees of an organization. *See* compensation.

ACTUARY

A mathematician or other individual trained in the fields of mathematics and statistics who is assigned the responsibility for determining insurance rates and risks from accumulated data and analysis. *See* Insurance.

ADD-ON

A clause in an installment contract that permits new purchases to be added to the contract in a specified manner in the future.

ADDRESSOGRAPH

Trademarked name for a machine designed for the rapid, automatic addressing of mail for mass distribution. This machine and similar ones are most frequently used in mailing multiple promotions to many individuals at one time.

ADHESION CONTRACT

A legal agreement that benefits a company or other organization in a superior bargaining position, while leaving the weaker party to the agreement in a situation of having to accept the stipulations on a take-it-or-leave-it basis.

AD HOC

Latin term that translates "for this purpose or end presently under consideration" and is used mainly for legal documents.

ADJUDICATION

In law, the act of a court in making an order, decree, or judgment. Also, a judicial decision or sentence, or a court decision in bankruptcy. *See* Business Law.

ADJUSTABLE RATE MORTGAGE (ARM)

In business and industry, an ARM is a mortgage that provides for periodic changes in the interest rate over the life of the loan, based on changing market conditions. ARMs commonly feature low starting interest rates and/or monthly payments, but can rise substantially under certain market fluctuations. Generally, ARMs are more readily available and their processing time is more prompt than is the case of fixed-rate mortgage. Under many business circumstances, ARMs are assumable by new borrowers, which can be advantageous to a company wishing to sell the business before the mortgage has been completely paid. Many ARMs also allow the borrower to prepay the loan without penalty. *See* Fixed Rate Mortgage, Flexible Rate Mortgage.

ADJUSTED BASIS

For tax purposes, the basis used to figure depreciation of fixed or non-inventory assets, or gains and losses on sales.

ADJUSTMENT BOARD

An established body composed of both union and management members, with the responsibility of dealing with labor/management problems within a company, particularly after other acts of negotiation and arbitration have failed to settle grievances. *See* Arbitration, Labor Unions, Management.

AD REFERENDUM

Latin term that translates "to be considered" and is used most commonly in business or legal documents, indicating that although an agreement has been made, specific details remain to be finalized. Example: "The sanction between the two parties was signed with the exception of the assignment of an ethics committee, which is being acted upon *ad referendum.*"

ADULT EDUCATION

The expression relates specifically to programs aimed at improving the skills, knowledge, or sensitivity of men and women after their formal schooling is completed. Business organizations and professional associations as well as public and private colleges sponsor adult education, often in the form of on-the-job training and self-education programs. Adult education has traditionally served practical, more than theoretical purposes, but not infrequently curricula have been sponsored on the premise that they would alleviate some major problem of concern to society. For example, in times of high unemployment, adult education has often been offered as one of the solutions to finding a decent position by making its students more competitive in the job market. Free-enterprise nations are using adult education more and more often to prepare women for jobs that have traditionally been considered suitable only for men and to assist the underprivileged. In Third World countries, adult education is an important part of modernization and industrialization, where business can never be upgraded without increasing knowledge and literacy. "In all countries," says the National Education Foundation, "adult education is used to bring about a more equitable distribution of the opportunities of the society. It has traditionally emphasized the practical rather than the academic, the applied rather than the theoretical, the acquisition of skills rather

AFFILIATE

A company or division that is owned or largely controlled and managed by a parent company. *See* Subsidiary.

AFFIRMATIVE ACTION

A committed movement to provide increased employment opportunities for women and minorities, to overcome discriminatory practices of all kinds, including those related to business opportunities and employment. Under the Equal Opportunity Act, federal contractors and subcontractors, state governments, state educational institutions, and local governments are obligated to increase the proportions of their female and minority personnel until they are equal to the proportions existing in the available labor market. Following a rash of controversies over the nature and extent of these obligations, a bipartisan coalition in Congress mediated the Civil Rights Act of 1991, reaffirming and strengthening the protections afforded minorities by earlier acts. *See* Civil Rights, Equal Employment Opportunity Act.

AGRIBUSINESS

A business venture or enterprise involved with agriculture, including not only farming, but the storage, distribution, marketing, and processing of farm produce. *See* Subsidies.

AIDED RECALL

A technique used by interviewers making a survey in which they show an article, ad, or other sample to aid the memory of the person being interviewed. *See* Advertising.

ALPHANUMERIC

In data processing, a character set that contains letters, digits, and usually other characters such as punctuation marks. *See* Computers, Data Processing.

AMERICAN ASSOCIATION FOR THE ADVANCEMENT OF SCIENCE

The largest scientific organization in the United States devoted to all fields of science, AAAS was founded in 1848 to further the goals and commitments of scientists and to foster scientific freedom and responsibility. With a membership of over 140,000 individuals and some 300 scientific and technological societies, the association promotes a range of specialized and professional educational programs, publishes the weekly magazine, *Science,* and in 1992 launched the first electronic medical journal. *See* Technology.

AMERICAN BANKERS ASSOCIATION

Founded in 1875, the ABA promotes "the general welfare and usefulness of banks" and continuously distributes to bankers the latest information on activities in their field. It publishes the monthly journal, *Banking,* and news bulletins, conducts educational programs for bankers and bank employees through schools such as the Stonier Graduate School of Banking and the American Institute of Banking, and sponsors seminars and conferences. Its membership includes more than 90 percent of the banks in the United States. *See* Banking.

AMERICAN BAR ASSOCIATION

Founded in 1878, the ABA is the largest professional association of U.S. lawyers, with some 280,000 members from all states. Along with promoting professional activities, the association helps to maintain high standards within the legal profession, advances the practice of law, promotes the administration of justice by securing uniform laws and judicial decisions nationwide and publishes legal periodicals. Its goals are achieved through some 27 committees that review the legal aspects of a broad range of subjects such as labor legislation, legal education, and maritime law. *See* Business Law.

AMERICAN BUSINESS WOMEN'S ASSOCIATION (ABWA)

An association of business women with some 1,900 chapters in the United States, whose stated mission is "to bring together business women of diverse backgrounds and to provide opportunities for them to help themselves and others grow personally and professionally through leadership, education, network support and national recognition." Since its founding in 1949, ABWA has provided workplace skills and career-development training for more than 500,000 members.

AMERICAN CIVIL LIBERTIES UNION

The ACLU is an organization dedicated to "the protection of constitutional rights and liberties in the United States," founded in 1920 by a group of noted civil libertarians including Jane Addams, Helen Keller, and Norman Thomas. The ACLU provides legal counsel in cases involving civil liberties and has been active in cases relating to academic freedom, separation of church and state, the right to privacy, due process of law, desegregation, freedom of speech, and other freedoms guaranteed in the Bill of Rights. Opposed to capital punishment, censorship, and loyalty oaths, the ACLU has often stirred controversy by supporting unpopular causes or assailing widely accepted practices. *See* Civil Liberties, Civil Rights.

AMERICAN INSTITUTE OF CERTIFIED PUBLIC ACCOUNTANTS (AICPA)

This widely recognized association performs a multitude of services for the accounting profession. It prepares and administers semi-annual three-day CPA examinations, publishes newsletters, and a monthly journal summarizes important changes in government regulations and law, conducts conferences and training seminars for members, and represents the profession before Congress, the courts, and various other legislative bodies. *See* Accounting, CPA, Ledgers.

AMERICAN MANAGEMENT ASSOCIATION (AMA)

Founded in 1923, this association is composed of managers in industry, commerce, government, and nonprofit organizations, teachers of management, administrators, and others concerned with organizational management. The AMA's basic objectives are to broaden management knowledge and skills, further the cause of ethics in business, and provide training and orientation for members. The AMA makes awards for distinguished achievements in the field of management, maintains an extensive library and resource center, publishes books and other literature on all phases of management, operates the Extension Institute, a private, self-paced study program, and conducts numerous seminars, both internal and external. The Association also sponsors young-adult programs at the high school and college level, publishes management periodicals, and hosts annual and regional conventions. *See* Leadership, Management, Supervisors.

THE AMERICAN NEWSPAPER PUBLISHERS ASSOCIATION

Formed in 1887, the ANPA is the trade association of daily newspapers created by their publishers and business managers to represent the industry to the public and to participate in legislative lobbying. Major areas of activity have included technological research, labor union negotiations, adjusting newsprint prices, trying to maintain low postal rates, and supporting education for journalism. ANPA has a membership of more than 1,200. *See* Communications, Media.

AMERICANS FOR DEMOCRATIC ACTION

The ADA is a political-action organization dedicated to the advancement of liberal causes and was created in the late 1940s by a group of prominent leaders in government, labor, academia, politics, and journalism, with the stated objective to "map a campaign for restoring the influence of liberalism in the national and international policies of the United States," stressing also that the campaign was to be "free of totalitarian influence from either the Left or the

Right." Besides endorsing candidates, generally liberal Democrats, the ADA publishes a yearly appraisal of the performance of many members of Congress, and formulates comprehensive liberal positions on national issues.

AMORTIZATION

A gradual and methodical apportionment of a monetary amount or balance over a designated period of time.

ANNUAL REPORT

An organizational report, required for public corporations but prepared by many other organizations for informational purposes. The report for the former contains the audited financial statements for the fiscal period, specific data for stockholders, and usually a formal letter from the chief executive officer with comments about the year's operations and plans for the future. In recent years, the trend has been away from stark, statistical types of reports to publications that embellish this information with illustrations, charts, and general information about the organization. In this respect, annual reports are often useful vehicles for distribution by public relations staff members, the advertising department, and others whose assignments are to build a better public image of the organization. *See* Accounting, Financial Reporting, Management, Public Relations.

ANTITRUST ACTS

Legislation enacted at federal and state levels to prevent individual corporations, combinations of companies, or consortiums from establishing monopolies or otherwise limiting free trade and commerce. *See* Cartel, Monopoly.

APPRAISED VALUE

A monetary valuation based on the opinion of an expert qualified to judge the worth of property, antiques, art, jewelry, or other assets. *See* Assets.

APPRECIATION

In real estate, the increase in value because of a number of economic factors such as inflation, neighborhood improvement, or the increasing popularity of an area. *See* Real Estate.

ARBITRAGE

Purchasing something in one market and selling it in another in order to profit on a situation in which there are price differences in the two markets. *See* Investments.

Arbitration

In labor/management relations, the submission of a dispute to an impartial third party for a decision. Although the acceptance of the decision is voluntary, the usual practice is to make acceptance compulsory. Two types of labor/management arbitration are most commonplace: (1) arbitration of rights, providing ways to settle disputes over the interpretation of the terms in a collective-bargaining agreement; (2) arbitration of interests, used far less often, since it is a last step after a deadlock develops in negotiations. Laws often compel arbitration in industries involving public utilities or municipal services, where public safety or convenience is involved. Commercial arbitration has been used for some 500 years to settle disputes outside the courts in such a manner that the parties concerned agree to abide by a decision, often referred to as an *award,* made by skilled arbitrators who are often educators, attorneys, or other professionals familiar with a particular area of business. The American Arbitration Association, founded in the 1920s, offers the services of numerous experts. *See* Labor/Management.

Articles of Incorporation

The provisos stipulated by the framers of a corporation that state, among other data, the objectives of the organization, principal place of business, amount of capitalization, names of the directors, and business policies. *See* Corporation, Incorporation.

ASAP

A common abbreviation marked on a document that is somewhat urgent, meaning "as soon as possible."

Assessed Valuation

The monetary worth that a tax authority or agency places upon real or personal property for the purpose of computing taxes. *See* Taxation.

Assets

The term refers to anything of value that is legally owned by an organization that is due on the financial records or that would substantially make the business more attractive and marketable were it put up for sale. Total assets include all net values, which are the amounts derived when you subtract depreciation and amortization from the original costs of acquiring and maintaining the assets. The following relate directly or indirectly to the assets of an organization:

Accounts Receivable. Sums due from individuals and organizations for goods supplied or services rendered. The expression usually relates to short-term moneys due rather than long-term debts such as loans and mortgages.

Accrued Assets. A receivable that is accumulating with the passage of time or the rendering of services, but that is not yet collectible.

Asset-based Financing. A method of financing that relies on a facility or equipment as the main source of credit support for a project's funding and that commonly does not require the credit support of an institution in order to complete the transaction.

Asset Depreciation. A sanction under the Internal Revenue Code that permits tax depreciation life for longer or shorter periods than normal. Under certain circumstances, capital assets may be depreciated over a period that may differ from the applicable class life. Often referred to as an *accelerated cost-recovery system.*

Betterments. Improvements to existing assets that increase the value of the assets in question. Ordinary repairs and maintenance are not considered as betterments. However, completing additions, such as adding an extension to an assembly line, would meet this requirement.

Cash. Resources, as well as actual cash, that can be converted into cash within an established time cycle of operations (12 months, for example, for an annual balance sheet). Included are checking accounts, savings accounts, and demand deposits in a bank.

Current Assets. Assets that will be realized or converted into the accounting cycle of a business. The cycle is most commonly one year. Accounts receivable is a current asset, for example, since it is generally due in 30, 60, or 90 days.

Deferred Assets. Assets that are not readily convertible into cash or are subject to current settlement.

Fixed Assets. This category includes all resources a business owns or acquires for use in operations and not intended for immediate resale, although they can be leased without jeopardizing their status. Factories and machinery are common examples of fixed assets.

Intangible Assets. The most common intangible assets are privileges or rights acquired or developed at a cost that can be identified and recognized. Typical examples are patents, trademarks, franchises, copyrights, licenses, royalty contracts, leaseholds, and even good will. Most intangible assets have a limited life, depending on their nature and contractual stipulations.

Inventory. The total quantity of goods, materials, and supplies held by an organization and having values that can be ascertained as assets. The term also includes work in progress, as well as all finished products available for purchase.

Long-term Investments. Also called *long-term assets,* these are holdings that an organization intends to keep for at least one year and that typically yield investor dividends. Examples are stocks, bonds, and savings accounts earmarked for special purposes.

Petty Cash. Funds commonly kept on hand as cash and used for miscellaneous expenditures. The total sum on hand is considered an asset.

Prepaid Expenses. Goods, services, or benefits that an organization has purchased, rented, or subscribed to in advance and not yet used.

Temporary Investments. Include interest- or dividend-yielding holdings that are to be converted into cash within one year, such as stocks, bonds, time-deposit savings accounts, and certificates of deposit (CDs).

See also Accounting, Depreciation, Financial Management, Property Taxes.

Assigned Risk

A risk that underwriters do not wish to insure, but for which there must be an applicable policy in order to meet local regulations or comply with a state law. *See* Insurance, Risk Management.

Association of Managing Consultants (AMC)

This association is composed of professional managers, mainly in consulting firms that are engaged in counseling administrators and managers in all fields of business, commerce, industry, the government, and nonprofit programs. The goals of the AMC are to improve the quality of management, upgrade professional practice, and promote better ethics. The Association operates a client referral service, sponsors seminars dealing with professional development, and publishes *The Journal of Management Consulting* and a periodic newsletter. *See* Management.

Assumed Liability

An obligation that is assumed by an individual or organization for payment accepted by another party.

ATTACHMENT

A legal seizure of property or other assets, or an official claim for the purpose of acquiring jurisdiction over the units attached. *See* Real Estate.

ATTITUDE

Defined in general terms as "a state of mind or feeling with regard to some matter, a disposition and way of behaving," the word has special significance in personnel relations and employee morale. In a 1994 Census Bureau survey of 3,000 employers nationwide, the question was asked, "When you consider hiring a non-supervisory or production worker, how important are the following in your decision to hire?" Ranked on a scale of 1 (not important) to 5 (very important), the following opinions were obtained:

```
Attitude. . . . . . . . . . . . . . . . . . . . . . . . . . . 4.6
Communication skills . . . . . . . . . . . . . . . . . . 4.2
Previous work experience . . . . . . . . . . . . . . . 4.0
Recommendations from current employees . . . . . 3.4
Recommendations from previous employer . . . . . 3.4
Industry-based credentials certifying skills . . . . . . 3.2
Years of schooling completed. . . . . . . . . . . . . . 2.9
Score on tests administered as part of interview . . 2.5
Academic performance (grades) . . . . . . . . . . . . 2.5
Experience or reputation of applicant's school . . . 2.4
Teacher recommendations. . . . . . . . . . . . . . . . 2.1
```

See also Career Education, Employee Relations, Management, Personnel Administration, Training.

ATTORNEY IN FACT

See Power of Attorney.

AUDIT

The formal and official confirmation and documentation of an organization's financial accounts for the purpose of providing verified figures and proof of adequate accounting controls. An audit may be completed by public accountants hired for that specific purpose (external audit), by an organization's own personnel (internal audit), or by a combination thereof. Lending institutions traditionally require audited financial statements before making a major loan. The same is true in the case of a company that is to merge with, or be acquired by, another company. *See* Auditor, Business Law, Financial Management.

AUDITOR

An experienced and qualified specialist who performs an audit by examining the records and supporting documents of the organization being audited. In summation, the auditor is required to provide an auditor's report, sometimes called an *auditor's certificate.* Auditors are accountants who review financial statements, and their responsibility is to verify the accuracy of company reporting. Internal auditors, those who are hired by and work within the company itself, help identify accounting weaknesses and correct them before significant errors occur. They are often systems-oriented people who make flowcharts of accounting systems and evaluate these flowcharts to suggest improvements in division of labor, paper flow, cash control, or other accounting responsibilities. They usually work under the company's treasurer or controller, who can thus provide a check and balance on the accounting department. Independent auditors are hired by a company's board of directors to represent the stockholders by reviewing financial statements, in order to reassure outsiders that annual reports are fair representations of the financial position of the company.

Independent auditors may qualify their opinion with a clause describing any variance they may have found. An opinion may also be disclaimed if the auditor finds some reason that prevents the completion of an audit. Auditors are not as concerned as bookkeepers about minor discrepancies in dollars-and-cents entries. Rather, they report in rounded figures and reflect judgments about what kinds of depreciation, expense accruals, and other data should be included. To the auditor, whose certification will be based on reports involving rounded thousands, or even millions, of dollars, a number may not be considered off track if it can be identified within 5 percent of actuality. *See* Accounting, Audit, Financial Management.

AUTHORIZED DEALER

In sales and merchandising, an individual or dealership granted the exclusive right to sell a product, or group of products, in a specified marketing territory. An automobile dealership is a common example. *See* Dealer.

AUTOCRACY

A government or governing body in which one person has power over all others. *See* Dictatorship.

Automated

The term for any mechanical or electronic system that, no matter how simple or complex, is organized to function without human intervention or control. *See* Automation, Data Processing.

Automation

The installation and application of principles, equipment, and controls to render a process or operation automatic, self-functioning, and self-controlling. The term automation, coined by computer pioneer John Diebold, refers to a wide variety of systems and processes that operate with little or no human intervention. Control is exercised by the system itself, through command devices that sense changes in such conditions as pressure, temperature, rate of flow, and volume and then order the mechanisms to make adjustments to counterbalance these changes. The applications of automation are universal, in part because most state-of-the-art industrial operations are too complex and sophisticated to be controlled manually, or even with instrumentation under physical control. Automation developed as a result of advances in the design of machines. Although early machines were often complicated, most of them were designed to operate under a specific set of external conditions; when these conditions changed, a manual adjustment was necessary to assure proper operation. Automation was quickly recognized as a valuable way to assure efficiency and accuracy in manufacturing processes. The chemical industries developed the technology to regulate variables such as pressure and temperature that are involved in the production of chemicals. The food industries found that packaging, bottling, and sealing operations, as well as the production of food products, could be accomplished more efficiently by the use of automated systems. The methods of automation were refined with the development of aircraft guidance systems and automatic pilots. The development of digital computers, which can monitor external conditions and make appropriate adjustments to a system, added further impetus to the applications of automation. Today, through automation, an entire oil refinery can be operated by just four persons. Industrial robots perform numerous functions on assembly lines, and automated spacecraft on deep-space probes are programmed to make automatic adjustments in operations. An automated system responds to its physical expectations by measuring the variables that exist and is programmed to exert controls and react to changing situations. Automated functions involve feedback, data that are fed back to the system's input and then used to exercise continuing, often changing, control. The measured information is evaluated in order to determine if corrective action must be initiated. Thus, if a spacecraft evaluates its position and finds itself to be off course, a course correction must be made. The evaluation function also determines exactly what kind of corrective action is necessary in any given situation. Thus, the three major steps, in sequence, are measurement, evaluation, and control.

Automation has become essential in almost all major industries worldwide, although some industries have become more automated than others, and some devices could not work at all without automated features. In many cases, applications of the principles of automation have led to entirely new fields of operation. One of the most vital aspects of automation is process control, particularly in continuous manufacturing operations. A prime example is the petrochemical industry, where gaseous and liquid temperatures, internal pressure, reaction rates, and many other characteristics must be regulated. As a result of high-tech developments, some plants have become so automated that human control is needed only to monitor nonroutine circumstances. Many industrial operations require devices called *servomechanisms* to control routine functions through the feedback process their variations activated by changes in mechanical, electrical, or electronic conditions.

Robotics, the use of automated machines that can be programmed to perform different jobs under various operating conditions is an operational innovation that has escalated in the past few years. These devices are simply robots, employed to take over a wide range of human jobs, such as using ordinary tools, assembling products, and completing routine production-line chores. Robots can function vast distances from any human controls, even in outer space. As technology continues to be improved, more and more of the routine activities of business and industry will be taken over by automation, particularly with the development of microcomputers. Recent advances in durable miniature systems for computing, mobility, and energy storage have made the robot of science fiction a near reality, and it is likely that future societies will see the first practical robot capable of interacting with human beings. *See* CAD, Computer-Aided Design, Computer-Aided Manufacturing, Computers, Data Processing, Robotics.

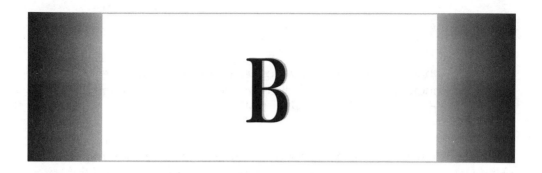

B

BABY BOND

A United States government bond of small denomination generally with a face value of $50 or less. *See* Bond.

BACKDOOR FINANCING

The practice that enables a government agency to borrow funds from the U.S. treasury directly, instead of having to apply for congressional appropriations. *See* Government.

BACKLOG

Orders for goods or services that either have not or cannot be filled and hence are backing up. *See* Marketing.

BACK ORDER

That portion of an order for goods or services that has been as yet unfilled. *See* Supply and Demand.

BACK SPREAD

The condition that exists when the price for identical items or utilities in two or more separate markets is less than the normal difference. *See* Marketing.

BACK-TO-BACK

In broadcasting, the term used to describe adjacent time slots for commercials or programs. *See* Broadcasting.

BACK-UP PROCEDURE

Any secondary system that is established to provide service or fulfillment in the event that the primary system fails or malfunctions. *See* Production.

BAD DEBT

Any debt, whether related to money or valuables, that is uncollectible. Such debts are generally accepted as deductible aggregates in the computation of business or personal taxes. *See* Debit, Debt.

BAILMENT

The act of delivering personal property or goods in trust to another person or organization for a stated purpose. The action is usually taken with the implication that the goods or property will be returned when the specified purpose has been fulfilled. *See* Guarantee, Trust.

BAIT AND SWITCH

A deceptive retail practice, now largely outlawed, whereby a low-priced product is advertised to lure customers into a store only so that the clerks can switch them to higher-priced products that are more profitable. *See* Better Business Bureau, Consumer Protection.

BALANCE OF PAYMENTS

The relationships between all payments going out of and coming into a nation currently, or within a given period of time. The concept of this condition is an outgrowth of the mercantile balance of trade and embraces the flow of public and private capital between nations. *See* Balance of Trade, Currency, Exports, Imports.

BALANCE OF TRADE

The positive and negative relationships between the exports and imports of merchandise in a country or group of countries. This concept first became significant in the sixteenth and seventeenth centuries with the growth and expansion of *mercantilism* in western Europe and the belief that the economic health of a nation depended upon its capacity to generate an excess of exports and limit its imports. *See* Exports, Foreign Trade, Free Trade, Imports, Mercantilism, Trade.

BALANCE SHEET

A statement of the assets, liabilities, and capital of a business organization on a specific date or over a period of time. Most businesses enter data regularly by computer, using a standard formula. The balance sheet is a statement of the total assets owned at a specified time, the value that the firm owes to others, and the value that is clear of debt. It is basically a statement of the accounting equation: Assets equal liabilities plus equity. All asset accounts are listed as shown on the trial balance, with any accumulated depreciation taken from the value of the asset. Usually, assets that can be readily converted into cash, known as current assets, are shown first.

All liability accounts are also recorded. The equity section states the owners' investment, as shown in the proprietorship or capital account, plus any net income earned. This net income is taken from the income-and-expense statement and is the excess of the revenue accounts over the expense accounts. If the income-and-expense statement had resulted in a net loss, this would be deducted from the owners' investment. Any withdrawals made by the owners are deducted, since they take from their equity remaining in the firm. *Closing the books* is the process of transferring the balances of income, expenses, and withdrawals into the capital account, after which the owners' capital account will show the balance indicated at the end of the equity section of the balance sheet. All other equity accounts will be at a zero balance, since their amounts have been transferred into capital. After closing entries are posted to the ledger accounts, the books are then ready to begin a new accounting period. *See* Accounting, Bookkeeping, Financial Statement.

BANK DRAFT

An order from one bank to another in writing, authorizing payment on demand to the person or organization named on the draft. *See* Banking.

BANK OF CREDIT AND COMMERCE INTERNATIONAL (BCCI)

An international banking consortium, founded with capital from the Middle East, whose assets were seized in 1991, when the bank was charged with illegal operations, including the concealment of huge losses, bribery, fraud, larceny, and money laundering. *See* Fraud.

BANKRUPTCY

In law, a state of insolvency in which the properties and/or assets of a debtor are taken over by creditors through appointed receivers or trustees. The purpose of a legal bankruptcy is to distribute as evenly as possible to creditors whatever assets are available. There are two basic forms of bankruptcy: (1) *voluntary,* in which the debtor files a petition in order to have the assets equitably distributed and thus free the company from debt, and (2) *involuntary,* in which the creditors take the action against an insolvent debtor in order to salvage at least part of the debt owed. *See* Business Law, Bankruptcy Act.

BANKRUPTCY ACT

Federal legislation providing for the relief and rehabilitation of insolvent organizations and individuals, with the intent of restoring them to a viable entity through practicable and equitable reorganization. *See* Bankruptcy.

BANKS AND BANKING

Commercial banks are institutions that provide checkable accounts to the public and have a substantial proportion of their assets invested in loans to consumers and business firms. Banks provide checking accounts, checkable deposits, and Negotiable Order of Withdrawal (NOW) accounts, as well as time deposits, and they use depositors' funds to make loans, including mortgages, and invest in securities. Banks, which function as intermediaries and are heavily regulated, pool their loans in order to reduce the risk of failure and they coordinate their actions with other depository institutions to become experienced in finding responsible borrowers and lenders and in appraising the quality of loans.

Banking in the United States goes back to 1791, when Congress established a national bank, the First Bank of the United States, which existed for two decades and was followed by the Second Bank, equally short-lived, and ultimately a system of nationally chartered banks that were required to back their notes by government securities. This led to the establishment of the Federal Reserve System in 1913, under which all national banks must be chartered, as well as joining the Federal Deposit Insurance Corporation (FDIC), which both regulates and insures their business operations. When a bank fails, the FDIC, instead of paying off depositors, usually merges the failing institution with another bank.

In recent years, competition in banking has been keen, with commercial banks competing with other institutions that offer some of the same services, such as savings and loan associations (S&Ls), savings banks, mutual banks, finance companies, and credit unions. They also compete with money market funds, which invest in short-term, consistently safe securities, and which allow customers to write checks against their accounts. *See* Federal Reserve System, Investments, Loans, Mortgages.

BANK STATEMENT

A regular statement of account, usually monthly, that a bank makes available to depositors. The statement includes credits and debits, with the dates of each transaction. *See* Banking.

BAR CHART

A chart used in business to provide a quick, visual impression of related data and statistics. The name derives from the format, using vertical and/or horizontal bars. *See* Graphics, Presentations.

BARRON'S CONFIDENCE INDEX

A listing of corporate bond yields, as reported weekly by Barron's, using a ratio as a measure of investor confidence in the economy and thus revealing whether optimism or pessimism dominates current opinions in the investment world. *See* Investments.

BARTER

The ancient (and present) practice of trading goods and/or services for other things of similar value without using any form of currency. Instead of being the lost art that comes to the minds of most people, barter has emerged from a period of inactivity to become one of today's most popular business-to-business trends. It has come a long way from the days of the Indians and the colonists, nurtured by more than $15 billion worth of surplus merchandise currently in the warehouses of many diverse industries throughout the United States alone. This unique form of business has jumped from an annual trade of some $930 million in the mid-seventies to more than $8 billion in the mid-nineties. It even has its own *Glossary of Terms for the International Barter Industry,* as well as guideline for trading without the use of money. *See* Trade.

BEAR

One who believes that the stock market will decline. *See* Securities, Stocks.

BEARER BOND

Popularly known as a *coupon bond,* this type of financial instrument has coupons attached to it that can be redeemed for interest at specified periods during the life of the bond. Each of these certificates represents an obligation by the issuer to pay interest regularly, usually every six months. *See* Bond, Investments.

BEAR MARKET

A stock market that is in decline. *See* Stock Market, Stocks.

BENCH MARK

The term used to indicate a touchstone, a point of reference. It derives from a traditional disk, often in bronze, that serves as an indicator of a precise elevation that has been determined by a geologic survey and that is inscribed with detailed information about the location of the site. Bench marks are used as reference points by surveyors and engineers in the field. *See* Cartography.

BENEFICIARY

In legal terminology, the recipient, or recipient-to-be, of funds, real property, or other valuables and benefits from an insurance policy, will, or similar settlement. *See* Inheritance, Wills.

BEST'S RATINGS

Financial ratings of securities that are evaluated and published periodically. *See* Investments.

BETTER BUSINESS BUREAU

An association of local organizations designed to protect consumers and businesses from questionable practices. The first bureau was established in Minneapolis in 1912 through the work of business leaders troubled by deceptive promotional techniques and advertising abuses. Later, a BBB network was established throughout the United States, Canada, and Mexico, linked by the Council of Better Business Bureaus, with headquarters in New York City. The bureaus cooperate with local authorities to inform the public about frauds and swindles, expose con artists, and promote high ethical standards. *See* Con Artist, Boiler Rooms, Consumer Protection, Fraud.

BIBLIOGRAPHY

The system for distributing information, in print or otherwise, about writings or publications, including the author, title, publisher, place and date of publication, number of pages, and the like. Some entries also include an abstract or other description of the entry's format and content, or a physical description of such components as the typeface, illustrations, and binding. Bibliographies are commonly used to list books compiled for a specific purpose, as in the case of the reference in the back of this encyclopedic dictionary. *See* Communications, Publishing, Research.

BIG BOARD

Popular name for the New York Stock Exchange.

BILL OF EXCHANGE

A financial order in writing, signed by the issuing party and requiring the addressee to pay a specified sum of money to a third party. A BOE is a negotiable written order for payment of a specified sum to a designated person and is commonly used in international trade, stating that the person receiving a shipment of goods must pay a certain sum before taking title to the goods. Bills of exchange, also referred to as *bank drafts,* are often purchased by banks at a discount and thus may pass through several hands before redemption. *See* Banks, Currency, Money.

BILL OF LADING

A written contract or agreement between a shipper of goods and a transportation firm that defines the terms under which the latter agrees to carry the shipment. It may also serve as a receipt and assurance of title to the shipment. Some bills of lading stipulate also the specific individual to whom the shipment is to be made. *See* Shipping, Transportation.

BILL OF SALE

A written certificate presented by a seller to a buyer as evidence that goods or entitlements have been transferred from the former to the latter for a specified sum of money or other consideration. *See* Sales.

BINARY NUMBER

A number written in base two, which means that each position in a numeral represents a power of two, rather than the ten common to the *decimal* system. Binary numbers leaped into prominence with the development of automation and computers because of the way data-processing machines function. In computers, for example, a positive integer is represented in base two by a string of zeros and 1s, such as 1101001, with each digit standing for a place value: The first represents the number of units, the second the number of twos, the third, the number of fours (2×2), the fourth, the number of eights ($2 \times 2 \times 2$) and so on. In this example, the first four decimal places represent, respectively, the number of units (10 to the power of 0), tens (10 to the power of 1), hundreds (10 to the power of 2), and thousands (10 to the power of 3). Electronic devices lend themselves to the use of binary numbers because "on/off," or "go/no-go" circuits are functioning. In computers and other electronic-processing equipment these two-state systems utilize and represent the binary digits zero and 1. One of the states represents zero; the other state represents 1. *See* Computers, Data Processing.

BINDER

An agreement, usually in writing, under which a down payment is made as evidence of good faith in the purchase of real property, goods, or services, the balance to be paid upon completion of the obligations stated. The initial sum paid is also known as the binder, or earnest money. *See* Agreement, Guarantee.

BLACKMAIL

The extraction of money or other valuables or assets from another individual or organization through the use of threats. In legal usage it implies the means the appropriation of money or something of worth in exchange for remaining silent about a person's unlawful conduct or immoral acts. In some cases, instead of monetary payments, victims may be coerced into revealing information of a confidential or possibly harmful nature. The word *extortion* is often associated with blackmail, particularly when related to demands on a public official in return for performing favors. *See* Business Law, Extortion.

BLANKET POLICY

A comprehensive insurance policy for a business, which is written to cover a wide range of problems, such as fire, theft, flooding, and liability, and often for a number of different company facilities in different locations. *See* Insurance.

BLIND TESTING

See Advertising Research.

BLUE CHIP

The term used to categorize stocks or other items of value relating to companies that are favorably regarded for their stability and earning potential. *See* Investments, Securities, Stocks.

BLUE SKY LAWS

Laws enacted by various states to protect the public against securities frauds and other financial ripoffs. *See* Better Business Bureau, Consumer Protection.

BOARD OF DIRECTORS

The body of individuals selected or elected by stockholders to manage a corporation. Some members of the board are officers of the company, while others are outsiders with particular interest in the affairs of the company they are helping to manage. Corporate statutes and bylaws specify minimum and maximum number of directors, terms of office, powers, liabilities, responsibilities, compensation, frequency of meetings, locations of meetings, and other factors pertinent to board service. *See* Annual Report, Business Administration, Corporation, Management.

BOARD OF TRADE

A council, generally privately organized and funded, and regional in nature, to generate new trade and improve existing trade through cooperative programs. *See* Associations, Trade.

BOILER ROOM

Slang term for a securities sales operation, usually unethical, if not unlawful, that coerces customers into buying low-grade stocks and charges high commissions, with multiple turnovers of sales. *See* Penny Stocks.

BOND

In finance, a formal certificate of indebtedness issued in writing by business corporations or governments in return for loans. Bonds bear interest and guarantee purchasers that they will be paid certain sums of money in the form of regular interest and/or final payments at maturity, commonly ten to twenty years from the purchase date. Some bonds are convertible upon maturity into the stock of the issuing organization. Bonds have traditionally been issued by governments as money-raising instruments during times of crisis, as in the case of the war bonds that were heavily marketed in America during World War II.

Bonds are considered conservative investments and may be either *secured* or *unsecured*. In the corporate world, bonds are secured by a pledge of assets, such as real property or equipment, the title for which would be transferred to bondholders in the event of default on the part of the issuer. A bond, in finance, is a written promise to pay a specified sum of money on a fixed future date. As a form of debt financing, the issuance of bonds has been a long-standing means of supporting the development of cities and corporations, providing maximum financial security to lenders while offering a steady income in the form of interest. Several kinds of corporate bonds are used. Mortgage, or secured, bonds are backed by specific company assets, such as land, buildings, machinery, or furniture. Debentures, on the other hand, have no specific asset pledged as security. There are two categories of municipals: general obligation bonds and revenue bonds. The security for the general obligation is the taxing power of the state or local government. Revenue bonds are payable solely from revenues derived from projects financed by the bonds, such as airports and toll roads. Investors rely on independent credit analysis to help them determine the investment risk involved in purchasing bonds, while bond ratings are assigned by rating firms, such as Standard and Poor's Corporation and Moody's Investors Service, which evaluate the issuer's capacity to pay principal and interest. Bonds are registered, requiring issuers to keep records of ownership. *See* Bond Ratings, Bond Redemption, Securities.

Bond Ratings

Ratings that reflect the possibility of a bond issue going into default and thus provide guidelines to influence prospective investors' perception of the risks involved. Such ratings have an impact on the interest rates of bond issues. *See* Bond.

Bond Redemption

Refunding by the issuing organization prior to maturity, either through the issuance of a serial bond or the exercise of a call privilege, prior to the expiration date, on a straight bond. *See* Calls.

Bond Transaction

The purchase or sale of a bond. *See* Bond.

Bookkeeping

Bookkeeping is the basic record-keeping phase of accounting, the methodical recording of the monetary value of business transactions in a book of accounts. A bookkeeping procedure called *double entry* enables an organization to know at any time the value of each item that is owned, how much of this value is owed to creditors, and how much belongs to the business, free of debt. Double entry is also evidence of the proportion of ownership that stems from the initial investment in the company and the portion, if any, amassed from profits. Information in a typical double-entry system is so comprehensive that it can be referred to in a realistic way when managers make business decisions, knowing that any monetary errors can be readily detected, since the entries result in two—hence "double-entry"—equations that must balance. The book of accounts is known as a *general ledger* and usually has a separate page for each account. A separate book showing the name and balance owed for each account payable may be kept. This is called a subsidiary ledger, with the total of the balances owed as shown in the accounts-payable ledger identical to the balance of the accounts-payable account in the general ledger. Transactions are not entered directly in the accounts, but are first recorded in a book known as a *journal,* or *book of original entry.* Several kinds of journals are used, the most common being the *general journal,* which shows accounts, debits, credits, transactions, and other relevant data. If more than one account is to be debited or credited, a separate line is used for each, listing debits first and then credits.

In corporate bookkeeping, the key elements to be examined and compared on a month-to-month and year-to-year basis are:

Assets. Everything of value that is owned by the business, or that is legally due the business and feasible to collect.

Current Assets. Cash and resources that could be readily converted into cash within 60 days (preferably 30) with few, if any, financial penalties.

Long-term Investments. Holdings that an organization expects to retain for at least one year and that typically yield interest or dividends—such as stocks, bonds, and special savings accounts.

Fixed Assets. Land, real estate, plant equipment, and other resources that have been acquired for a company's stated operations and are not intended to be sold in the near future. The entries customarily use purchase prices as a base, with deductions, if necessary, for depreciation or damage.

Additional Assets. Tangibles that are not entered in any other lists of assets, which might include scrap metal or used tools, with monetary worth, or intangibles such as copyrights, royalties, and trademarks that would be of value to prospective purchasers of the business.

Liabilities. Accounts payable, short-term notes for borrowed funds, current portions of long-term notes, interest payable (including any accrued fees), taxes, and unpaid payrolls.

Equity. The net worth of the company, after valid withdrawals by partners or other principals, or the issuance of dividends or bonuses.

Total Liabilities and Equity. The sum computed for these two amounts must always match the sum for *total assets*.

See Accounting, Double-Entry, Financial Statements.

BOOKS IN PRINT

Directories of books of all classifications that are currently in print. Separate directories, published annually, list authors, titles, and subjects. *See* Communications, Publishing, Research.

BOOK VALUE

The current value of products of substantial worth, that are commonly sold in a "second-hand" or "used" category, such as automobiles, boats, and farm machinery. *See* Supply and Demand.

BOYCOTT

The conventional act by individuals, organizations, or groups to refuse to do business with the object of the boycott in order to coerce change. The practice was named after Captain Charles Boycott, an English land agent whose ruthlessness in evicting tenants led his employees to refuse any further dealings with him or his family. *See* Business Law.

BRAILLE

A tactile system of writing for the blind, invented by Louis Braille in 1829, which utilizes dots embossed on paper or other surface to represent printed letters and numbers. The "braille cell" consists of six dominolike dots arranged in vertical columns that are identifiable to the touch by a blind person as letters of the alphabet, numbers, punctuation signs, and a few common short words, such as "and," "for," "of," and "the." A standard English braille system was inaugurated in 1932. *See* Artificial Language, Communications.

BREACH OF CONTRACT

The failure, whether deliberate or unintentional, of one party in a contract to honor the terms of the agreements and understandings that were specified without any legal justification. *See* Business Law, Contract.

BREAK-EVEN POINT

The point at which profits and losses are in balance. See Assets, Profits.

BRETTON WOODS CONFERENCE

The name commonly given to the United Nations Monetary and Financial Conference held at Bretton Woods, New Hampshire, in July, 1944, which resulted in the creation of the International Monetary Fund, to promote worldwide coordination and cooperation on financial matters. *See* International Monetary Fund.

BRIBERY

The illegal offering, giving, receiving, or soliciting of money or something of value with the intention of influencing a person or organization to perform an unlawful or immoral act. In legal matters, both the givers and receivers of bribes are guilty of the offense, the former as a perpetrator of "active" bribery and the latter as a "passive" participant. In business and industry, bribery is most frequent in labor/management relationships and in international dealings with countries where bribery is more or less accepted as a stratagem for conducting trade. *See* Better Business Bureau, Business Law, Fraud.

BRIEF

In law, a written statement, often filed in court, which summarizes the argument of the writer in a lawsuit or other case. *See* Business Law.

BROCHURE

A printed publication, generally larger than a leaflet, describing an organization's objectives, services, fields of activity, and other related information of interest to the intended recipients. *See* Advertising, Merchandising, Promotion.

BROKER

A person who acts as an agent or intermediary in a sale or other business transaction between two parties. Brokers are most commonly associated with the sale of securities, commodities, and real property and are remunerated in the form of commissions based on the monetary value of the transaction that is successfully completed. *See* Investments, Real Estate, Securities.

BROOKINGS INSTITUTION

A private, nonprofit organization committed to research in economics, government, and public affairs, which also provides objective evaluations and critiques of public policies. Its social scientists have been described as "serving as a bridge between the world of scholarship, where new knowledge is formulated, and that of policy-making, where it is applied." Founded in 1927, Brooking is funded largely by endowment and private support, for the continued programs of research, fellowships in economics and business, and its professional publications. *See* Foundations, Research.

BUDGET

In business, a formal document prepared in detail, listing the past financial history and estimating expenses and income, credits and debits, and related figures for a specified period, generally the calendar year. *See* Accounting, Bookkeeping, Financial Management.

BULL

One who believes the stock market will rise. *See* Investments, Stock Market.

BULL MARKET

An advancing stock market. *See* Investments, Stock Market.

BUREAUCRACY

Any major system for administering large organizations that are authoritative in nature and have installed clearly defined sets of regulations, as might be the case with governments, penal institutions, religious bodies, and certain kinds of corporations. Although defenders of bureaucracies contend that such systems are essential for expediting large-scale operations, the public generally associates the term with red tape, indecisiveness, and exorbitant paperwork. Some people even equate bureaucracy with threats to freedom and a domination of commercial, political, and social life. One critic stated that the problem with bureaucracy was that "the rules and procedures created to achieve certain ends may become ends in themselves," while another asserted that "bureaucratic training may produce persons who are unable to act outside of the procedural rules to which they are accustomed." Basically, there are two classes of bureaucracy:

1. *Public.* The governmental types, which provide services to the general public, paid for through taxes and assessments. These have expanded in size and scope in recent years, primarily in such areas as taxation, military operations, and welfare. However, the growth has been accompanied by restraints on the powers of bureaucratic officials, generally by legislators, who also control the purse strings. The courts have also entered into the picture in the effort to stall galloping bureaucracy and correct some of the ills. One of the problems, for example, was the vast accumulation of records, which gave rise to public fears that they could be misused, but which were alleviated in part by the *Freedom of Information Act,* which permits access to the files by private individuals.

2. *Private.* The large corporate type, which sells products and services in the marketplace, but whose management staffs may parallel the administrative bodies of government agencies. A significant dissimilarity is that private companies are owned by stockholders, their decision making is not under the thumb of legislators, and they are not fettered by rigid personnel agenda like those of the Civil Service. Bureaucratic systems in private industry have been the subject of many management research programs, going back as far as the end of the last century, in an effort to isolate the benefits from the disadvantages. These have resulted in numerous major improvements in managerial formats and styles, particularly in planning, organizing, and controlling. *See* Business Administration, Freedom of Information Act, Management.

BUREAU OF LABOR STATISTICS

The federal agency charged with maintaining and reporting on all data pertinent to labor and labor/management relations. *See* Labor/Management Relations.

BUSINESS ADMINISTRATION

The art and techniques of running a business, which is both an independent unit in the economy, run for profit, and part of a complex political and legal system whose managers must not only satisfy customers, but must also comply with government regulations, satisfy their employees, remain competitive, and make a good impression on the public. To operate under these often conflicting demands and pressures, businesses have divisions and departments and employees who specialize in particular functions. There are three distinct forms of business ownership:

Proprietorship. A sole proprietorship is a business owned by one person in which all the profits belong to the owner. The major disadvantage of the sole proprietorship is that the assets of the business are treated in law as part of the owner's personal assets. In case of bankruptcy, all the personal assets of the owner, including home and car, can be sold to settle the debts of the business. Unless the owner has personal wealth, the business may experience trouble borrowing money in times of need. A sole proprietorship may also have difficulty recruiting and keeping good employees, because the business will terminate when the owner retires or dies.

Partnership. An affiliation of two or more persons who own a business jointly. Partners may, individually and jointly, possess knowledge, skills, or resources that give the business a better chance of success than a sole proprietorship would. Partnerships are relatively easy to establish, and their profits are not subject to national corporation taxes. Financing is generally easier to obtain because the personal assets of the group are generally larger and the chances of success are higher. The major disadvantage of the partnership is that each partner is liable for the debts of the business. Also, partners who wish to retire may find it difficult to recover their investments without dissolving the partnership and the business.

Corporation. A legal entity chartered by the state in which it is incorporated and owned by its stockholders. A corporation is a separate legal entity that limits personal liability. A significant advantage of the corporate form of ownership is that investors can limit their personal liability to the amount of money they have invested. If the corporation goes bankrupt, they can lose no more than they have put in. Another advantage is that funds to operate the business are customarily obtained by the public sale of stock, which makes the obtaining of loans easier and enables the corporation to exist independently of its owners. Equally important, the very size of most corporations allows them to hire professional managers or officers. The major disadvantage of the corporate form of ownership is that business corporations must pay taxes on their income, while the stockholders also must pay taxes on the income they receive as dividends on their stock. This means double taxation of profits that are distributed to the owners. Generally, corporations cost more to found because of the legal fees involved, and they are usually required to file more reports with federal and state regulatory agencies.

Business enterprises of eleven kinds, large and small, are comprised of three major components: production, marketing, and finance.

Production. The evolution of raw materials into goods and services that are sold to other businesses or to consumers. In a wholesale or retail business, "production" is actually the purchase of articles for resale that takes the place of production. In essence, the way to make production efficient and profitable was found to be through operations research and management technology, both of which utilize complex mathematical techniques to analyze the way organizations function. On the production line itself, a specialty called production management is concerned with planning and routing materials so that time and energy will not be wasted, while the design of complex machines and procedures relies on the science of systems engineering.

Marketing. This function is basically the sale and distribution of goods or services to the public. Most product lines are aimed at sales to numerous types and groups of potential customers, and each may want a product that is different in some way. One of the major functions of marketing is advertising.

Finance. Business administration in this functional area includes the search for adequate sources of capital as well as the management of the capital already invested. It requires estimating the amount of cash the company will need in its operations, deciding whether to use short-term or long-term credit, issuing securities, budgeting, and planning all types of expenditures. Business loans can be for either the short term or the long term. The former, obtained usually through bank loans or credit extended by other companies, is used to purchase merchandise that will be sold and paid for in less than one year. As for the latter, the most common long-term debt is the mortgage, which is a loan given by a bank or other lending institution to purchase a specific asset, such as a building or an expensive piece of equipment. Corporations can also raise debt capital by issuing bonds, contracts in which the corporation agrees to pay lenders a specified rate of interest and to return the principal within a specified amount of time. Failure to pay the annual interest on its bonds can have dire results, since bondholders can take legal action forcing the corporation to sell some or all of its assets in order to meet its obligations. The issuance of stock to raise funds is called equity financing and requires that the company convince prospective purchasers that its management and its long-range plans are sound. A corporation receives direct financial benefits from the sale of stock only when it is offered to the public for the first time, since further trading merely changes ownership of the stock and is not a source of new capital. Although additional stock can be issued to raise more capital, stockholders are entitled to be consulted on any action that will change the financial structure of the company. Corporations issuing stock must give the Securities and Exchange Commission (SEC) complete statements covering their operations as well as making this information available to the public.

A vital component of successful business administration is personnel management, the selection and training of employees, which is a continuing function, under the direction of the personnel department, now most often referred to as the department of human resources. In large companies the responsibilities also include recruiting, training supervisors and administrators, and negotiating with labor unions. Labor/management contracts are also drawn up in the department, in conjunction with the legal division, to provide for grievance procedures to handle employee complaints and for arbitration to settle disputes between management and labor.

Sound management includes planning, administering, and controlling, which, though separate functions, must be handled competently and continuously if a company is to achieve its objectives. The planning function includes all managerial activities since, at the highest levels of business, planning involves establishing company strategies to determine how the resources of the business will be used profitably. Planning also involves the establishment of policies, day-to-day guidelines used by managers to accomplish their individual and collective goals. The administration must also consider what resources the organization has available and how they can best be employed particularly in getting ahead of the competition.

No business administration can be successful without a really major component: *organization*. After plans, policies, and strategies have been established, managers must organize the company to attain its stated mission. The blueprint for this, the internal structure of any company, is the organization chart, which displays the relationship of the various components of the organization, as well as indicating the chains of command. Management determines and communicates the functions to be performed, the sequence for accomplishing each goal, and the job classifications that are to be established. It is common to distinguish between staff departments and line departments. The former provide counsel to the latter. The legal department is an example of a staff function, while a production department is an example of a line function. Some employees, however, may perform both staff and line functions: giving advice (a staff function) and supervising others (a line function). Some organizations have numerous levels of management. In general, the larger the organization, the more levels of management are required.

In the long run, no business administration is likely to be prosperous if it does not exercise complete *control,* which implies also those steps necessary to keep top management informed as to how well the company is meeting its goals. Experienced administrators know they must always be ready to meet new problems, whether internal or posed by competitors, labor unions, regulatory agencies, a changing business climate, or public opinion. Essentially,the control process requires establishing clear standards of performance, measuring actual accomplishments against the standards, and making the necessary improvements. Control administration includes such functional areas as budgets, schedules, charts, statistics, and personal observation so that managers may keep as well informed as possible about the performance of their departments and are equipped to make modifications to bring performance into line with objectives.

Finally, experienced business administrators keep pace with government regulations and maintain cordial working relationships with government agencies at all appropriate levels. They are particularly concerned about laws affecting labor such as pensions, Social Security, safety, health, wages and hours, and labor/relations; laws protecting consumers such as pure food and drug, fair packaging and labeling, and health and sanitation; laws affecting competition, such as antitrust and monopolies; laws protecting investors; and laws protecting the environment and the avoidance of pollution. Depending upon their fields of operation, administrators must also be knowledgeable about government regulations and restrictions affecting public utilities, transportation, homeowners, agriculture, shipping, and many other subjects. Some large business corporations file hundreds of reports a year to federal, state, and local agencies. *See* all *Business* classifications.

BUSINESS CLIMATE

The conditions that prevail in a business or industry, either in a broad spectrum or in regard to a specific locale. See other *Business* entries.

BUSINESS COMMUNICATIONS

See the following terms that relate to this subject area: Advertising, Answering Services, Associations, Audiences, Broadcasting, Charts, Company Histories, Computers, Consumer Surveys, Employee Communications, Films, Graphics, Investor Relations, Logos, Media Relations, Memoranda, Newsletters, Press Releases, Publicity, Public Relations, Workshops.

BUSINESS COUNCIL

Any agency or official organization established to monitor either a broad or restricted field of business, provide information to the public, and assist business and industry in its field of operations. *See* Associations.

BUSINESS CYCLE

Any periodic or seasonal cycle in which business is conducted, accounted for, or reported. Although fluctuations in the level of business activity are also called *business cycles,* the term is inaccurate because it suggests that business ups and downs occur at regular intervals. Economists cite four phases in a typical cycle: (1) an expansion, marked by increasing employment and rising income; (2) a peak period; (3) a tightening, or recession, in which business declines, sales fall off, and unemployment rises; and (4) a new bottom, known as a *trough.* Cycles, and their phases, are often murky and difficult to detect until after a passage of time and a review of the economic pattern. *See* Depression, Economics, Recession.

BUSINESS EDUCATION

As early as the late eighteenth century, business education curricula in the United States were established in response to needs created largely by the Industrial Revolution. The beginnings were seen in secretarial schools and vocational schools that sought to train young men and women in specific disciplines such as bookkeeping, stenography, and office records, not unlike the simpler forms of such schooling that exist to the present day. The growing sophistication of industrial society encouraged the development of business education at the college level, where instructors would apply the principles of economic theory to business problems, typically in finance. The first formal business college was the Wharton School of Finance and Commerce, opened in 1881 at the University of Pennsylvania. By the turn of the century, several other universities had entered the field, notably Harvard, which established its School of Business in 1908. Today more than 1,300 American colleges and universities offer degrees in business, some 250 of them accredited by the American Assembly of Collegiate Schools of Business. The curriculum, however, has undergone a substantial evolution, particularly following World War II. Up until mid-century, business education tended to prepare specialists in public accounting, corporation finance, investments, marketing, management, and aspects of business law. As one reference explained, "The curriculum consisted of a core of business courses supplemented by required studies in the liberal arts. The techniques of instruction were descriptive and not quantitative, stressing the procedures involved rather than inquiry into those procedures. Moreover, business faculties were rarely research-oriented and relied on the conventional lecture method of instruction." After that era, broad curriculum changes were initiated in a new approach that softpedaled specialization, stressed the disciplines essential to decision making, such as psychology, economics, and organization theories, cultivated instruction by the case method, encouraged research, and upgraded faculty qualifications. The new educational look was dressed in an executive management perspective, stressing analysis instead of the routine learning of techniques. Although business education is most prevalent in the United States, the economic resurgence of Europe in the late twentieth century has motivated a growing number of business programs at the university level in Western European countries.

Today's business education makes extensive use of computers for both instruction and research. The new technologies have reinforced the trend toward quantitative methods and integrated simulation problems. Other trends include increased emphasis on the behavioral sciences, information systems, business ethics, and faculty/student exchange programs in both domestic and foreign institutions. *See* Career Education, Training.

BUSINESS INDEX

A microfilm listing containing a cumulative three-year index to more than 800 regional business newspapers and periodicals and a few national newspapers with substantial business sections. *See* Periodicals, Publishing.

BUSINESS LAW

This specialized legal field encompasses those branches of jurisprudence that concern the formation, operation, and termination of a business firm. The legal system regulates the way a firm is founded and organized, the character of its transactions with other firms, management/personnel relationships, environmental health, responsibilities to consumers, and obligations to society. Specific subjects in the field of business law cover contracts, sales, affiliates, bankruptcy, insurance, negotiable documents, and forensic industrial structures, plus many other actions.

One of the most active instruments covered by law is the *commercial contract,* a vehicle by which managers establish rules to govern a particular enterprise or personnel relationships. Contract law determines which contracts are enforceable in court and defines what must be done to comply with implicit judicial obligations. To be enforceable, a commercial contract must meet certain stringent conditions. There must be, for example, a valid offer to begin with, proper acceptance, sufficient time and duration considerations, participation by parties with legal qualifications, an absence of fraud or force, and consistency with acceptable public policy.

Another cornerstone of business jurisprudence is *agency law,* concerned primarily with the legal relationships of agents to companies and their principals. The agency structure enables managers to handle multitudes of transactions at the same time, to extend their marketing spheres, to function in many places, and to make use of professional expertise when needed. For their part, agents must be loyal to their principal, adhere to professional standards, be ethical in all respects, and be accountable for their transactions. Professional agents must perform according to the standards of their profession.

Business law is an absolute necessity in the field of sales, particularly through the Uniform Commercial Code (UCC), which covers regulations governing merchandising, selling, commercial paper, and sellers' security interests, holding all participants to high standards of conduct. Written sales contracts specify the dual obligations of both buyer and seller. The seller's minimum obligation is to put suitable goods at the buyer's disposition and give proper notice. If the contract obliges the seller to deliver the goods to the buyer or to a carrier, the seller must do so, obtaining the necessary documents and delivering them to the buyer. In the conduct of buying and selling, an important legal instrument is the *warranty,* a written guarantee by a seller that the goods will be of a certain quality. If they are below that quality, the buyer may sue for the difference in value. The effect of these UCC warranties is to negate the old doctrine of *caveat emptor* ("let the buyer beware") by requiring that the goods be of suitable quality or that the buyer be warned that the goods may not be up to standard. In some cases, secured transactions will be drawn up legally, to ensure that the buyer will pay as promised, especially if there is any extension of credit.

One of the most important fields of business law involves insolvency and *bankruptcy,* methods by which debtors may be discharged from claims held by creditors. In a typical bankruptcy proceeding, the bankrupt party lists all assets and debts, and the creditors are then paid on a pro-rata basis out of the debtor's available assets, after which the debtor is released from responsibility to pay any remaining claims.

Last, but far from least, business law is directly concerned with the manner in which a commercial enterprise is formulated and made into a legal entity. The three principal ways of organizing a business are as a *sole proprietorship,* as a *partnership,* or as a *corporation.* Other less well-known forms of business organization include the limited partnership and the unincorporated association. The corporation is the most formal classification, since it must be chartered by the state in which it is located. The partnership is more casual and may be formed by the independent action of the partners with the rights and responsibilities of each partner well defined. The sole proprietorship involves an individual acting on his or her own behalf in a business context and is the least intricate form. The limited partnership, regulated by the state, involves one or more investing partners and at least one operating partner. *See* Agent, Contract, Corporation, Partnership, Sole Proprietorship, Warranty, and other *Business* entries.

BUSINESS MACHINES

Devices and inventions designed and developed to expedite the performance of routine clerical work in offices and other places of business. Major examples include the typewriter, adding machine, calculator, word processor, computer, mail-handling equipment, photocopying machine, electrostatic printing, dictating instruments, and facsimile (FAX) equipment. *See* Data Processing, Office Management.

BUSINESS PLAN

As an entity, rather than a procedure, a *business plan* is a formal statement that describes in great detail an enterprise that is about to be launched, substantially reorganized, or expanded, and is most commonly prepared and presented in order to obtain financing and secure necessary permits and approvals for legalizing the venture. It is also useful for such secondary purposes as recruiting managers, partners, employees, suppliers, and others who might be essential to the successful operation of the business. As has been emphasized by the experts and professionals, most business beginners seriously underestimate both the importance of planning and the time it takes to research and prepare a competent plan and a well-documented presentation.

A sound business plan contains the following basic components, among other essential ingredients: description of the venture, nature of products and/or services, the market (both geographical and consumer), competition, location, management, personnel, current financial condition, and financing needed, both short term and long term.

The importance of planning cannot be overlooked and must be carried out in an objective manner, realistically, and with attention to the weaknesses, as well as the strengths, of the organization. A sound business plan for an untried venture can not only prepare for the future, but can help to avoid even starting an enterprise that is doomed to failure. If the proposed venture is marginal, a business plan can indicate why this is so and may help the proposers to avoid the expense and frustrations of learning about business failure. As has been pointed out by the experts, it is far less traumatic to scrap plans for an ill-fated business than to take the hard knocks of learning by experience how a sensible business plan could have saved all that grief at the cost of nothing more than a couple of days or so of concentrated planning and evaluation. *See* Business Administration, Management.

OUTLINE OF A BUSINESS PLAN

A business plan is designed to provide information and statistics required by others who are evaluating a proposed venture, most often to determine its potential for financing and support. A well structured, thoroughly documented business plan can serve not only as a guide to a company's future development, but as a financing proposal that will satisfy the criteria and conditions of banks and other lending institutions. The following components are requisites of an effective business plan:

Section 1: Basic Data

- Cover sheet, with the proposed name of the business, names of principals, addresses, and phone numbers
- Statement of purpose
- Table of contents
- Illustrations and graphics, if any

Section 2: The Business

- Description of the venture and related operations
- Classification of the business
- Products and/or services involved

- Location(s) of the business
- Economic environment
- The market for products and services
- Description of the management
- Personnel, on hand or to be recruited
- Nature, strength, and extent of the competition
- Application for loan, or alternate types of financing, if applicable

Section 3: Financial Data

- Source(s) of financial support
- List of capital equipment
- Existing inventory(ies), if any
- Balance sheet
- Evaluation of break-even figures
- Income projections for profits and losses
    - Monthly projections for first year
    - Details, by quarter or month, for second year
    - Three- to five-year summary
- Cash flow projection
    - Figures by month for first year
    - Projections by quarter for next two years

Section 4: Financial Reports for Existing Business

- Balance sheets for past two to five years
- Income statements for the same period

Section 5: Supporting Documents

- Tax returns for the previous two years
- Management résumés
- Credit reports or other financial backup
- Leases, contracts, and other legal documents
- Newspaper and trade clippings about the business and/or managers and personnel
- Letters of reference

BUSINESS PROCESS ENGINEERING

See Reengineering.

BYTE

In electronic processing, a grouping of bits of data, typically six or eight, treated as a unit in a computer procedure. Bytes may be used to represent characters, or binary data, and in some systems one of the bits in a byte is used as a unit to judge whether the number of high bits in the byte is odd or even, thus detecting any errors in the grouping. The size of a computer memory is usually measured in kilobytes (1,000) or megabytes (1,000,000). *See* Binary, Computers, Data Processing.

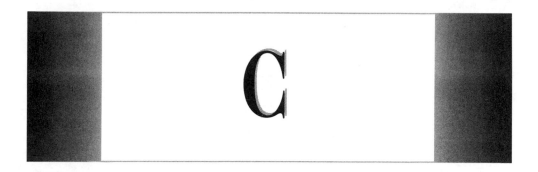

CAD (COMPUTER-ASSISTED DESIGN)

Any kind of design, whether in industrial, financial, creative arts, or other fields, that is formulated in whole or in part by computer. In this state of the art, the designers apply special types of computer software to create electronic models that represent the characteristics of physical objects or systems, thus making it possible to study these subjects on computers without having to undergo the time, work, and expense of constructing the actual objects or systems. *See* Computers, Programming, Software.

CALCULATING MACHINES

Devices, now largely electronic and computerized, that perform arithmetic functions at the command of an operator. *See* Office Machines.

CALL

A stock option to buy a certain security at a specified price and at a specified time. *See* Securities.

CALLABLE BONDS

Those for which the issuer reserves the right to pay the obligation prior to the maturity date. *See* Bonds.

CALLIGRAPHY

Lettering rendered in artistic shapes, formerly created only by hand, but now readily available in computer fonts. *See* Printing.

CAM (COMPUTER-ASSISTED MANUFACTURING)

A system of manufacturing or processing that uses computers and other data-processing equipment for quality control, speed of operation, and reduction of manpower. This concept is also referred to as *computer-integrated manufacturing (CIM)*. *See* CAD, Computers, Data Processing, Manufacturing, Production.

CAMERA-READY

In publishing, texts and illustrations that have been assembled on sheets of paper or boards and are ready to be photographed for production and publication. *See* Advertising.

CAO (CHIEF ADMINISTRATIVE OFFICER)

The title often given to the chief executive officer (CEO)—executive director— in a nonprofit organization. *See* Chief Executive Officer (CEO).

CAPABILITY PROFILE

In personnel administration, biographies of employees prepared in order to determine their proficiencies and skills and match them to jobs. *See* Personnel Administration.

CAPACITY BUILDING

Any program designed to strengthen or improve the capabilities of officers and top managers in a corporation to administer operations, or evaluate policies, strategies, and basic functions. *See* Management.

CAPACITY PLANNING

Administering for the future in such a way as to be able to measure the volume of work that can be processed with given resources and manpower. *See* Production.

CAPITAL

Any type of material wealth, such as money, real estate, or precious metals, accumulated by individuals or organizations. In economic theory, capital is one of the major factors of production, the others being labor and property. Distinctions are made between circulating capital, such as raw materials, finished goods, and wages, and fixed capital, which refers to railroads and other transportation facilities and major installations, such as factories and machinery. In financial markets, capital is associated with investments in productive assets that yield income. In accounting, capital relates to those parts of the net worth of an organization that represent claims on assets. In this sense, for tax records, the gain on capital, or capital gain, is the value of assets computed over an extensive period of time. See other *Capital* entries.

CAPITAL ACCOUNT

The section that records the fluctuations in liabilities and assets for both long and short-term monetary flows. *See* Accounting.

CAPITAL ASSET

That form of asset whose resources are to be utilized over a period of time, rather than at the time of acquisition. The term refers to almost all property owned by an individual or organization other than goods held for sale. *See* Assets.

CAPITAL BUDGETING

Systematically planning capital outlays and proposed outlays and the means of financing them for a stated time period. *See* Accounting, Annual Reports.

CAPITAL DEPRECIATION

The depreciation of capital property, installations, and equipment over given periods of time. The rate and amount of depreciation can be calculated by a variety of different systems. *See* Accounting.

CAPITAL GAIN

The surplus of proceeds that exists after the sale of a capital asset. *See* Capital Asset.

CAPITAL GOODS

Any substantial machinery or equipment used in the manufacturing of other goods, generally of the type not consumed in the normal course of production.

CAPITAL-INTENSIVE

Said of a corporation or other business organization that requires and utilizes extraordinarily large amounts of capital assets in relation to its labor force. *See* Capital, Production.

CAPITALISM

An economic system characterized by private ownership of property and the means of production. Known also as *private enterprise,* this system, the opposite of socialism, embodies the concepts of individual initiative, competition, profit motive, and supply and demand. Capitalism dates basically from the Industrial Revolution, which began in the eighteenth century when merchants and industrialists began to displace farmers and landowners in importance in Europe, and later in America. By the early twentieth century, capitalism had created vast credit, manufacturing, and distributing institutions, and the social and economic effects of the system had largely transformed world culture. *See* Capital, Free Enterprise, Labor, Nationalization, Unions.

CAPITALIZATION

In finance, the sum of the par value of an organization's stocks and bonds that are outstanding. *See* Accounting, Annual Reports.

CAPITAL LEASE

A lease whose ownership is generally transferred to the lessee at the end of the stated term and that contains an option to purchase capital property at a discounted price. *See* Leasing.

CAPITAL MARKET

The market comprised of the buyers, sellers, and issuers of securities, commonly composed of banks, governments, corporations, and individual public investors. *See* Investments, Securities.

CAPITAL PROGRAM

A plan for expenditures of capital over a period of years to meet annual and long-term needs for company projects and operations. *See* Corporations.

CAPITAL SURPLUS

Capital over and above the legal requirement that is invested in a business by the owners or stockholders; the difference between the par value of stock and the issuing price.

CAPITATION

A style of payment for health and medical services in which an individual or company is paid a fixed amount, per capita, for each person served, without regard to the actual number or type of services performed. *See* Personnel Administration.

CAPTIVE AUDIENCE

Any audience, whether in person or in a communications network that is, for one reason or another, obliged to receive the messages imparted. *See* Broadcasting.

CAPTIVE MARKET

Consumers who have little choice or freedom in purchasing merchandise, materials, or services. *See* Marketing.

CAREER COUNSELING

Guidance provided to employees to assist them in scheduling occupational training and developing enhanced, but realistic, goals. *See* Career Management.

CAREER EDUCATION

An educational effort or trend, the focus of which is on training for the professions or formal careers through conventional school and college curricula, rather than under the sponsorship of a business or industry. This category of education, though not new, came into its own in the 1960s in the United States as a reaction to what was later described as "the feeling engendered in educators that an unproductive relationship existed between the campus and that element of society representing the young." A major purpose of career education, especially at its lower levels, has been to solve some of the increasing educational/occupational problems, which included school dropouts, high rates of youth unemployment, graduates or near-graduates leaving high school without marketable skills or ambitions, and foggy personal goals. It became evident, too, during this transitionary period, that far too many high school graduates were aiming at college-degree programs that would provide few job-seeking capabilities and were shunning vocational or technical schooling that might be far better roads to satisfying and remunerative employment. *See* Career Management, Education.

CAREER MANAGEMENT

Personnel administration, which not only attempts to place the right people in the right positions, but undertakes a number of educational services that include:

- assessing skills, abilities, interests, and attitudes
- determining qualifications needed for different occupations and assignments
- defining career goals and developing plans for attaining them
- identifying and evaluating educational and training opportunities
- isolating factors that might impair career development
- pinpointing resources, both internal and external, where additional help is available.

Effective career management has become more and more reliant on external education programs, as well as an internal training. *See* Career Education.

CARGO INSURANCE

Insurance covering freight being transported by rail, water, or highway, whether in transit or temporarily in storage. *See* Insurance.

CARRIER

A transporter of goods and materials, whether by ship, plane, truck, or other mode of conveyance. *See* Transportation.

CARRY BACK

To apply a loss in one year's fiscal statement in order to lessen a previous year's listed profit and thus to minimize taxes. *See* Accounting, Bookkeeping.

CARRYING CHARGE

An expected, generally repetitive, charge that stems from asset ownership, such as interest or storage. *See* Financial Management.

CARTEL

A group of individuals and/or organizations banding together with the objective of fixing prices, cornering a market, or establishing a monopoly in a certain field. *See* Monopoly.

CARTOGRAPHY

The specialized field of mapping, charting, and map making, including the creation of atlases and other geographical guides.

CASE ADVOCACY

An argument on behalf of an individual's, group's, or organization's attempts to find a solution to existing problems or servicing needs. *See* Industrial Management.

CASE STUDY

The scientific application of management and administrative techniques to study individual business cases and problems and develop practical solutions. *See* Management.

CASH BASIS ACCOUNTING

That form of accounting by which revenues are recorded when they are received as cash, and expenditures are recorded when paid. *See* Accounting.

CASH DISCOUNT

The amount reduced from an announced price when a buyer makes a payment within a stated time limit. *See* Marketing.

CASH DIVIDEND

Dividends that have been declared by a corporation and are payable to stockholders by currency or check.

CASH FLOW

All business, no matter how large or small function on cash and the orderly flow, or use of, that cash. Many businesses become insolvent because they do not have enough cash to meet their short-term obligations. It is rare that bills can be paid in profits instead of in cash. Since sufficient cash is one of the keys to maintaining a successful enterprise, managers must understand how cash moves or flows through the business and how planning can remove some of the uncertainties about requirements for the future.

Cash flow depends substantially on cash cycle, which is the continual course and frequency of events and functions that may increase or decrease the cash balance.

Cash is decreased in the acquisition of materials and services to produce the finished goods. It is reduced in paying off the amounts owed to suppliers, that is, accounts payable. Then inventory is sold and these sales generate accounts receivable, that is, money owed from customers. When customers pay their bills, accounts receivable is reduced and the cash account increases. However, the cash flows are not necessarily related to the sales in that period because some customers may pay in a later period.

Managers must be alert to changes in working capital accounts to keep the business healthy and must be guided by the net working capital, which is the balance of current assets and current liabilities. Current assets are those resources of cash and those assets that can be converted to cash within one year of the organization's normal business cycle. They may include marketable securities, cash on hand, accounts receivable, and inventories. Current liabilities are obligations that become due within one year of the normal business cycle and may include notes payable, accounts payable, and accrued expenses.

One way to measure the flow of cash and the organization's ability to maintain its cash (liquid assets) is to compute working capital: the difference between current assets and current liabilities. The change in this value from period to period is called the net working capital. For example:

	19 × 1	19 × 2
Current assets	$ 100,000	$ 200,000
Less current liabilities	– 70,000	–112,000
Working capital	$ 40,000	$ 88,000
		40,000
Net working capital increase (decrease)		$ 48,000

While net working capital shows only the changes in the current position, a cash flow statement can be developed to explain the changes that have occurred in any account during any time period. The cash flow statement is an analysis of the cash inflows and outflows. *See* Accounting, Assets, Cash Management, Money Management, Short-Term Financing.

CASHIER'S CHECK

Type of check that a bank draws against itself rather than against a customer's account. *See* Banking.

CASH MANAGEMENT

Sound management of cash and cash flow has been described as one of the major functions for keeping an organization solvent and successful. By comparison, poor management is one of the most common causes for a cash crisis and ultimately the failure of a business. Reliable and judicious management must be practiced, too, if loans or other types of financial support are to be obtained and used profitably. Such management includes (1) knowing the firm's cash flow at all times, (2) forecasting cash needs for both short-term and long-term operations, (3) planning to implement cash at the appropriate time, and (4) knowing and substantiating the firm's payback capacity.

The following sub-topics are directly and indirectly related to cash management:

Cash Budgeting. The first essential in budgeting is to know accurately what the anticipated expenses are going to be for the organization in question, Following this, a reliable estimate must be made to determine realistically what income must be generated from one or more available sources to meet these expenses. Finally, an analysis must be made to record the high and low income time periods from the past and a chronological forecast for the future. Cash Crisis. This predicament—a lack of readily available money—is too often diagnosed as financial when in reality the problem is actually managerial. Although money can ease the crisis temporarily, further indebtedness will only magnify the current problem. Short of an illegal raid on the till, a crash crisis can almost always be traced to poor, or short-sighted, planning.

Equity Funding. This type of money is never repaid, but is obtained when management relinquishes a portion of its organization's profits to an investor, as in a sale of an interest in the business.

Long-Term Credit. Such loans, for periods of more than a year, are commonly used for the modernization or expansion of a business. They are generally repaid out of accumulated profits.

Short-Term Credit. Banks and other lenders provide this type of money to finance purchases of inventory for special reasons, such as stocking up for seasonal sales promotions. Such loans are self-liquidating within a short period of time (traditionally less than one year) because they generate sales volume and, in turn, a good cash flow.

Trade Credit. This type of credit is not borrowed as cash, but is money owed by a business to suppliers who permit them to carry fast-moving inventories on an open account, or a deferred payment plan. Such credit is generally approved only when a firm has established its ability to remunerate suppliers within an agreed-upon time frame. *See* Accounting, Assets, Cash Flow, Inventory Management.

Cash Position

The fiscal situation that exists in a company and can be presented as a percentage of cash to the total net assets. *See* Cash Flow, Cash Reserves.

Cash Reserves

The aggregate amounts of cash and/or liquid assets that can readily be converted into cash. Also, cash sums kept in reserve for stated purposes or to be used in financial emergencies. *See* Cash Management, Cash Position.

Cash Settlement

In the money market, the transaction made if the securities purchased are delivered against payment in federal funds on the same day a trade is completed. *See* Investments, Securities.

Cash Surrender Value

The cash value of an insurance policy, computed continuously prior to the due date of the policy, less any amount deducted for a surrender charge. *See* Insurance.

Casual Labor

Part-time labor, often related to seasonal job markets. *See* Human Resources, Personnel Management.

Casualty Insurance

Policies written to cover loss or liabilities that arise from accidents, with the exception of loss customarily covered by other types of insurance, such as fire or flood. *See* Insurance.

CASUALTY LOSS

A loss occurring from a casualty. *See* Casualty Insurance.

CATASTROPHIC HEALTH INSURANCE

A policy that is underwritten by an insurance agent to protect the holder against illnesses and accidents that would be financially devastating. Such policies generally contain rather large deductible terms. *See* Deductible, Insurance.

CATCH-22

An unreasonable combination of otherwise reasonable precepts that are frustrating because they prevent the accomplishment of a seemingly sensible objective. *See* Murphy's Law.

CAUSE-AND-EFFECT EVALUATION

A form of operational analysis whose objective is to determine which factors in a program or organizational function affect the end results and outcomes and to what extent. *See* Program Evaluation.

CAVEAT EMPTOR

Latin for "let the buyer beware."

CEASE-AND-DESIST ORDER

An order by a court of law or other authority to cease a practice or an operation that has been proven to be harmful or aggravating to others, over and beyond the essentials of doing business. Cease-and-desist orders are commonplace, for example, against a company engaged in operations that pollute the environment, are noisy, emit unbearable odors, or cause excessive traffic tie-ups. *See* Business Law.

CEILING

A limit, as in an individual's maximum borrowing allowance for loans or other obligations. *See* Banking, Loans.

CELLULAR RADIO

A radiotelephone communications system that, in effect, is a small-scale adaptation of broadcasting networks, divided into calling regions, each of which has its own transmission capabilities and equipment. Computerized switching enables users to continue phone communications without interruptions while moving from one transmission zone to another. *See* Microprocessors.

CENSUS

As applied in industrial research, a tabulation of data regarding personnel and facilities and equipment to determine labor concentration strengths and deficiencies. *See* Industrial Management.

CENTRAL BANK

A banking institution established by federal authorities largely to transact government business, as well as to support the nation's monetary policies. *See* Banking.

CENTRALIZATION

A form of decision making and control in an organization that is reserved for a few top administrators and not spread over a wide range of managers. *See* Business Management, Industrial Management.

CERTIFICATE OF DEPOSIT

In finance, an instrument attesting to a bank deposit by an individual or organization, rather than in passbook form. CDs are generally payable on certain dates or after a lapsed period of time, bearing interest at rates specified in advance. *See* Banking.

CERTIFICATE OF INCORPORATION

The legal document that certifies that an organization has been established as a corporation. *See* Corporation.

CERTIFICATE OF SALE

An instrument issued to a purchaser following a judgmental sale, as in the case of a mortgage foreclosure authorized by a court of law. *See* Business Law.

CERTIFICATE OF TITLE

The legal document furnished by an attorney or title company that states that an owner holds title to a particular piece of property. *See* Title Insurance.

CERTIFICATION MARK

A symbol affixed to merchandise to authenticate the quality of the goods, as well as other vital data, such as contents or materials, place of origin, or manufacturing process. *See* Trademark.

CERTIFIED CHECK

The bank check of a depositor that is recognized and accepted by a banking official, is drawn against funds in the bank, and is as valid as cash. *See* Banking.

CERTIFIED FINANCIAL STATEMENT

A declaration of financial standing that has been attested to by an independent certified public accountant. *See* Accounting, Annual Reports.

CERTIFIED FUNDS

See Certified Financial Statement.

CERTIFIED PUBLIC ACCOUNTANT (CPA)

An accountant who has not only qualified educationally, but meets certain prescribed requirements, including the successful passing of an examination sponsored by the American Institute of Certified Public Accountants. *See* Accounting.

CHAIN OF TITLE

In real estate, a document that has recorded all the transfers of title that have taken place in regard to a property, starting with the earliest transaction and continuing to the present. *See* Real Estate.

CHANNEL OF DISTRIBUTION

The course taken by a product from the manufacturer to the ultimate consumer purchaser. *See* Marketing.

CHAPTER 7

A conventional form of bankruptcy, particularly for smaller companies, regulated under the Bankruptcy Reform Act. *See* Chapter 11.

CHAPTER 11

The legal terminology for a business enterprise that has gone into bankruptcy, but which is permitted by law to continue to do business for a specified time period as long as it pays current obligations. *See* Bankruptcy.

CHARITABLE CONTRIBUTIONS LAW

A law that establishes the nature of charitable contributions that can be deducted for tax purposes. *See* Deductible, Taxation.

CHARTER

An instrument of incorporation. *See* Corporation.

CHATTELS

Personal property other than real property.

CHIEF ADMINISTRATIVE OFFICER (CAO)

The officer of a company who is directly under the chief executive officer (CEO) and in charge of administration. *See* Management.

CHIEF FINANCIAL OFFICER (CFO)

The top executive in a corporation responsible for its financial administration and reporting. *See* Business Administration, Management.

CHILLING EFFECT

Any employment practice, act, or condition that unlawfully inhibits the free employment of individual job rights, as in denying ready access to employment because of sex, age, color, ethnic background, religion, or physical appearance. *See* Civil Rights.

CHRONIC UNEMPLOYMENT

Unemployment that lasts in any given area for a long time, commonly any period over six months. *See* Recession, Unemployment.

CHURNING

In securities trading, fabricating an excessive number of transactions in order to make more commissions and/or give the misleading impression that a slow market is very active. *See* Boiler Room.

CIRCUIT COURT OF APPEALS

See Court of Appeals.

CIRCULATION

In advertising, the total number of people reached by a newspaper, magazine, or other periodical, including subscribers, purchasers at the point of sale, and nonpaying or pass-along readers. *See* Advertising.

CITATION

In law, the notification that the recipient has been charged in a legal matter. *See* Business Law.

CITY MANAGER

The chief executive of a city that has adopted the city-manager or council-manager system of municipal government, an individual who is appointed by the council and is responsible for administering the municipal government and advising the council. In contrast to a mayor, a city manager does not engage in politics, but is expected to carry out the policies of the elected council. The council may not, however, interfere with the manager's administrative functions or delegate them to others. The city manager is generally recruited, much like any business executive, selected on the basis of experience and education, which may include curricula in city management. *See* Government.

CIVIL ACTION

A lawsuit or other legal action that does not involve a criminal charge. *See* Civil Law.

CIVIL LAW

Law relating to civil suits and legal matters other than felonies. *See* Business Law, Civil Action.

CIVIL RIGHTS

The privileges and protection provided for all citizens by the U.S. Constitution, and also those positive acts of government that seek to guarantee constitutional rights to all. *See* Civil Rights Acts, Constitutional Rights.

CIVIL RIGHTS ACTS

A number of laws enacted during the last 150 years in the United States to ensure the equality of individuals in the eyes of the law and prevent the denial of rights and privileges. Although such rights were guaranteed in the Fourteenth and Fifteenth amendments after the Civil War, they were largely ineffectual in many regions of America until the Civil Rights movement of the 1960s forced new legislation to abolish local and state obstructions to the citizenships rights of blacks and other minority groups. *See* Constitutional Rights, Fifteenth Amendment.

CIVIL SERVICE COMMISSION

The name for what is now the *Office of Personnel Management,* a federal agency charged with "recruiting, examining, training, and promoting employees of government agencies without regard to their race, religion, sex, political beliefs, or other factors not related to merit." *See* Civil Rights.

CLASS ACTION

A lawsuit or legal proceeding in which the plaintiff is not an individual but a group representing a large number of persons with a common grievance. The Federal Rules of Civil Procedure define this class in court proceedings:

> One or more members of a class may sue or be sued as representative parties on behalf of all only if (1) the class is so numerous that joinder of all members is impractical, (2) there are questions of law or facts common to the class, (3) the claims or defenses of the representative parties are typical of the claims or defenses of the class, and (4) the representative parties will fairly and adequately protect the interests of the class.

Class-action suits are common in cases where legal claims and charges affect the well being or future of many people at the same time. *See* Business Law.

CLASS ADVOCACY

A legal argument on behalf of a group or class of constituents attempting to find solutions to problems or who require services to overcome denials or prohibitions by the party against whom the action is directed. *See* Business Law, Class Action.

CLASSIFIED ADVERTISING

Small advertisements, popularly known as "want ads," which are grouped in a special section of a newspaper or magazine under a variety of classifications. *See* Advertising.

CLEAN AIR ACT

A federal statute enacted to protect public health from the effects of air pollution and that establishes national air quality standards, most notably those relating to vehicle and factory emissions. *See* Ecology, Environment.

CLEARINGHOUSE

An alliance of banking institutions, geographically situated, to facilitate financial needs by exchanging checks and other forms of indebtedness with member banks and coordinating financial services. *See* Banking.

CLEAR TITLE

A title, as to property, that is free from encumbrances, liens, or other limitations. *See* Title.

CLOSED CORPORATION

A company in which the officers and directors are empowered to make decisions and fill vacancies from their own internal group without having to go to the stockholders to vote. *See* Corporation.

CLOSED END

Said of stock shares that are transferable but cannot be redeemed or canceled other than by the resolution of stockholders or by special legislation. *See* Stocks.

CLOSED SHOP

A situation that exists in management/labor relations when employees must be members of the appropriate union before they can be hired or continue employment. *See* Open Shop.

CLOSE OUT

In marketing, a sale to unload large quantities of a product or material that will no longer be produced. *See* Retailing.

CLOSING COSTS

In real estate, the costs assumed by the buyer and seller individually during the purchase, sale, or financing of property, such as taxes, title-insurance, and recording fees. *See* Real Estate.

CLUSTERING

The situation that exists when similar, but not identical, products are marketed in a mutual selling area, but tend to attract buyers to all, rather than being competitive. *See* Consumers, Marketing.

CODE OF PROFESSIONAL ETHICS

Any code or standards formulated and expressed as a statement of professional conduct to which it is hoped the practitioners of the profession will subscribe. *See* Ethics.

CODICIL

In the modification of an existing will, a document legally executed to reflect the desired revisions. *See* Business Law.

CODIFICATION

The process of compiling and arranging such things as laws, policies, regulations, policies, and accounts into one comprehensive and cohesive system. *See* Business Law.

COEFFICIENT OF DETERMINATION

In processing and production, the proportion of the variation in one step or phase that is caused by the variation in some other step. *See* Manufacturing, Production.

COLD CANVASSING

In marketing, sales, and research, an act of identifying potential customers and patrons without using outside data or references. *See* Sales.

COLLATERAL

Valuables, such as securities, real estate, or precious metals pledged by a borrower to secure the repayment of a loan. *See* Banking, Loans.

COLLECTIBLE

In financial accounting, any asset that can be converted into cash. *See* Financial Accounting.

COLLECTION AGENCY

An outside financial agency hired by a business to collect debts from customers and clients who have delinquent bills and have resisted efforts by the managers of the business to discharge their obligations. *See* Retailing, Small Business.

COLLECTIVE BARGAINING

In labor/management transactions, the situation that pertains when union members bargain collectively through a spokesperson, rather than individually, on their behalf. Many companies have a unit or department that is staffed with specialists who are experienced in negotiating with labor unions and coming to agreements on collective bargaining issues. *See* Labor/Management.

COLLUSION

An illegal agreement between parties to engage in a business procedure or act that would be mutually beneficial to the participants, but injurious to other businesses. *See* Agreement, Business Law.

COMAKER

A party signatory to a loan who becomes jointly responsible with the primary borrower for the obligation. *See* Loans.

COMMAND ECONOMY

A national economy, such as a dictatorship, in which an authoritarian government exercises major control over business and industrial operations. *See* Dictatorship.

COMMERCE CLEARING HOUSE

A professional publisher of a variety of periodical reports and summaries covering taxes, laws, regulations, administration, and many other business-related subjects. *See* Periodicals.

COMMERCE DEPARTMENT

See United States Department of Commerce.

COMMERCIAL

In advertising, the message transmitted by an advertiser on radio or television programs. *See* Advertising, Broadcasting.

COMMERCIAL ACCOUNT

A basic checking account, for an individual or an organization. *See* Banking.

COMMERCIAL PAPER

Promissory notes, usually short-term, issued by public agencies, municipalities, and corporations through authorized brokers. *See* Money.

COMMISSION

That percentage of a selling price that is paid to an agent, broker, or salesperson under the terms of a mutual agreement. *See* Sales.

COMMISSION BROKER

An agent who fills orders for the sale or purchase of securities and who is reimbursed on a commission basis. *See* Investments.

COMMISSION ON CIVIL RIGHTS

The federal body, created by an act of Congress, that oversees all activities related to Constitutional rights and that moves to encourage constructive steps toward equal opportunity on behalf of women, minority groups, the aging, and others in need of assistance. The Commission investigates complaints, holds public hearings, underwrites research studies, and makes official recommendations. *See* Civil Rights, Civil Rights Acts.

COMMITTEE

A body made up of individuals who are appointed or elected to form a subsidiary group in an organization for the purpose of studying a situation or circumstance or issue of mutual interest, make conclusions, and report to the parent organization.

COMMITTEE FOR ECONOMIC DEVELOPMENT (CED)

A nonpartisan body of business leaders and scholars who undertake research studies and circulate procedural recommendations relating to economic and public-policy issues. *See* Economics.

COMMITTEE FOR INDUSTRIAL ORGANIZATION (CIO)

A body founded within the American Federation of Labor (AFL) in the 1930s that grew to be the Congress of Industrial Organizations (CIO). *See* Labor/ Management, Labor Unions.

COMMODITIES

In the investment field, the term used for raw materials, farm products, and sometimes semi-finished materials traded in designated quantities and prices for future delivery. *See* Futures, Investments.

COMMODITY CREDIT CORPORATION

An agency of the federal government established to support prices of agricultural products through subsidies and the purchase of loans, in order to help sell these products in domestic and foreign markets alike. *See* Futures.

COMMON BUSINESS-ORIENTED LANGUAGE (COBOL)

A computer language that is procedure-oriented and resembles standard business English. *See* Artificial Language, Communications, Computers.

COMMON LAWS

Unwritten laws of the land that originated largely in the United Kingdom and have come into international usage through common acceptance. *See* Business Law.

COMMON MARKET

An alliance of nations joined together by uniform trading agreements on international regulations, such as those relating to tariffs and duties. *See* Foreign Trade, Free Trade.

COMMON STOCK

That class of stock whose holders have residual claims on the assets of a corporation after debts have been paid and the demands of preferred stockholders have been met. *See* Investments, Securities, Stock.

COMMUNITY PROPERTY

Property owned and administered jointly by two or more parties. *See* Property.

COMPACT

A mutual agreement between two or more parties. *See* Agreement, Contract.

COMPARABLES

In real estate, those properties that can be used for comparisons with properties that are similar in value and characteristics and that are up for sale, during their appraisal for prospective customers. *See* Real Estate.

COMPARISON ADVERTISING

The use of advertisements that compare the advertiser's product line or brand with competing merchandise that is clearly identified. *See* Advertising, Competition.

COMPENSATION

Salaries, wages, employee benefits, and other financial advantages granted to employees for services rendered. Also, sums paid to employees for injuries or illnesses incurred on the job. *See* Personnel Management.

COMPETITION

In marketing and sales, the individuals and companies that threaten to seize a significant share of a given market for products and services. *See* Marketing.

COMPETITIVE ADVANTAGE

Any situation, price structure, or customer convenience that gives one marketer an advantage over another. *See* Marketing.

COMPETITIVE BIDDING

A system mandating that two or more firms be invited to make bids on a job, each one of which will be considered equally in regard to cost estimates, scheduling, and other pertinent factors. *See* Proposal.

COMPETITIVE LEVEL

The stage in the development of a product when it has been tested and readied for market and is now to be distributed and sold in competition with similar products. *See* Competition, Marketing.

COMPETITIVE WAGE

Any wage, including related compensation, that a company must offer its personnel and prospective employees in order to keep them from being hired by competitors. *See* Compensation, Personnel Administration.

COMPLEMENTARY PRODUCT LINES

Lines of products that supplement or tie in with other lines produced by the same manufacturer. *See* Merchandising, Retailing.

COMPONENT

An integral element, segment, or ingredient of a piece of equipment, product, data-processing system, or other unit that is composed of multiple parts. *See* Production.

COMPTROLLER

The officer of a company or government official who supervises and regulates monetary and fiscal matters. *See* Business Administration, Corporation. *See* Controller.

COMPTROLLER GENERAL

In the federal government, the head of the General Accounting Office (GAO), an arm of the legislative branch, who reports directly to Congress on the financial status and accounting programs of government agencies. *See* General Accounting Office.

COMPULSORY ARBITRATION

Mediation that has been made mandatory by the government in order to forestall a strike and that requires the intervention of an appointed third party to resolve the dispute. *See* Labor Relations.

COMPULSORY RETIREMENT

Retirement of an individual employee that is mandated by one or more factors, including age, disability, or unlawful behavior on or off the job. *See* Personnel Administration.

COMPUTER

An integrated electronic unit that can program and store information in large quantities, reveal it when requested, and otherwise expedite data-processing functions with speed, reliability and ease. The three basic types are (1) *digi-*

tal, which function internally and perform operations exclusively with discrete numbers, (2) *analog,* which use continuously variable components for the internal representation of magnitudes and to facilitate their built-in operations, and (3) *hybrid,* which use both continuously variable techniques and discrete digital techniques in their functions. All three types are theoretically alike in that they depend on external commands, but they differ in the means they provide for accepting new programs to accomplish new instructions and programs. While digital computers receive new programs quite easily via manual or automated procedures, analog or hybrid computers cannot always be reprogrammed without the internal alignment of mechanisms and components. *See* Hardware, Software, and other *computer* references. *See also* Back-of-the-book Supplement, "Computer Terms and Phrases," page 442.

COMPUTER-AIDED DESIGN

See CAD.

COMPUTER-AIDED MANUFACTURING

See CAM.

COMPUTER GRAPHICS

The application of computers to the creation of pictorial representations of data, a science that has advanced to a stage where almost any graphic image may be stored in a computer and arranged in accordance with the operator's needs. While computer graphics capabilities can be enjoyed with almost any state-of-the-art computer, the procedure does require the application of a graphics software program and input/output command devices attuned to the kinds of images desired. A common personal-computer system, for instance, with a keyboard and graphics monitor, can execute fairly intricate visual factory production line. The process can be greatly enhanced with the installation of a number of devices, including color printers, color plotters, electronic sketch pads, and video cameras. Sophisticated graphics capability requires high-density computer memory and complex input-output devices, however, since pictorial images may contain substantial access to data, transposed by the computer into a digital code and stored in memory. Whenever single images are just part of a series of images, as in the case of an animated simulation, the amount of data that must be stored and processed may be huge, requiring highly advanced power capacities. For this reason, the kinds of computers owned and used by private individuals are generally capable of creating only simple images or graphic presentations such as charts and maps and blueprints. *See* Computer.

COMPUTER HARDWARE

The physical parts of a computer. *See* Computer, Hardware.

COMPUTER LANGUAGE

The combinations of symbols, icons, words, and phrases that, individually and collectively, can dictate a computer's performance. The power of any computer lies in the rapidity with which it can, through its *language* capabilities, execute many commands. Language systems function by responding to differences in electrical voltages, represented by the binary digits zero and one. Personal computers generally use a language referred to as *basic,* while more complex mainframe computers use the language named *Fortran. See* Artificial Language, Fortran, other *Computer* references.

COMPUTER NETWORK

An alliance of computers joined so they interact in ways that are preplanned upon being alerted by given signals and commands. The objective of such a network is to tie together a conglomeration of computers, whether in a single location (LANS, for "Local Area Network") or geographically far apart, to provide instantaneous information and statistics that are centrally located. A computerized banking system is a common example, through which depositors can take actions or obtain information in many convenient locations, rather than having to visit a specific bank or customer office. *Computer networking* is a popular term describing the interconnection of many computers for the purpose of sharing databases and input\output devices, reducing costs, and enhancing productivity. *See* Computers, Internet, other *Computer* entries.

COMPUTER PROGRAM

A series of actions or instructions that a computer can interpret and execute, referred to as *software* to differentiate them from *hardware,* the physical equipment used in data processing. These programming instructions cause the computer to perform arithmetic operations or comparisons or to input or output data in a desired sequence. Programs are often written as a series of cycles, which can be used in more than one program or at more than one point in the same program. Systems programs are those that control the operation of the computer. Chief among these is the operating system also called the control program, executive, or supervisor program, which schedules the execution of other programs, allocates system resources, and controls input and output operations. Processing programs are those whose execution is controlled by the operating system. Language translators decode source programs, written in a programming code, and create programs that are in machine language and can be understood by the computer. These include assemblers, which translate symbolic languages that have a one-to-one relationship with machine language; compilers, which translate a procedural language program into a machine language program to be executed at a later time; and interpreters, which translate source-language statements into object-language statements for immediate execution. Other processing programs are service or utility programs, which perform business functions such as payroll processing, accounts payable, and receivable posting, and simulation of environmental conditions. *See* Computer Programming, Hardware, Programming, Software.

COMPUTER PROGRAMMING

The process of developing and installing programs, or an inventory of commands, that control the operation of a computer, referred to in general as *software.* The programs that control the basic functions of the computer, such as language interpretation and input and output, are known as *operating systems.* These make it possible to undertake a wide variety of tasks, from accounting and bookkeeping to developing more efficient assembly-line operations. Computer programs are classified in terms of their programming languages.

Computer programming consists of the following phases: requirements definition, specifying the operations to be performed; design specification, directions for a step-by-step procedure to meet the above requirements; coding, transposing the design into an appropriate language; testing, verifying the correctness of the applications; and maintenance, a final, very lengthy stage in which enhancements and corrections are made. Current research has been focused on methods by which errors can be anticipated, detected, and eliminated. Computer programming is a complex, time-consuming operation, since the productivity of any program depends greatly on its reliability, accuracy, and the elimination of as many weaknesses as possible. Because high-tech maintenance is the most costly stage in programming, recent work has emphasized design, coding, and testing techniques that are able to accommodate changes in the original program. It has been pointed out by experts in this field that in the future more time will be allocated to requirements analysis and less to design, coding, testing, and maintenance, because these phases will be automated. *See* all other *Computer* references.

COMPUTER RUN

The actions and responses of a computer when running through and completing a program. *See* Computer.

COMPUTER SOFTWARE

The disks and programs that are inserted into or combined with the hardware of a computer in order to initiate an intended program and control the operation of the computer. The term can refer to the sum of all programs installed, or to a single program, in which data are stored as electrical impulses in the memory of a computer, in contrast to the hardware components. These electrical impulses are activated by the hardware as commands that guide or control the input and output for brief periods of time. Vast inventories of software programs are available to users of computers at all levels of capacity and sophistication. These are classified according to usage. A *compiler,* or *interpreter,* for example, is a software program whose purpose is to convert programs written in a high-level language into a low-level form that can be recognized by the circuits of the hardware, thus sidestepping the onerous job of communicating with a computer in its own binary language. An *operating system* is a software program that controls the computer function by arranging hardware functions, activating commands from the user, and, in the case of a time-sharing setup, allocating time and resources equitably. *Applications software* adapts the computer to the completion of specified tasks, such as revising a packaging procedure or realigning the components of a job-training program, and is customarily divided into two groups: *horizontal,* which spreads across many types of programs for many different applications and objectives, and *vertical,* which is tailored to narrow, specific assignments. Other familiar kinds of software relate to such activities as word processing, video games, desktop publishing, and financial analyses. *See* Hardware, Software, other *Computer* entries.

CON ARTIST

An individual who uses fraud and deception to achieve a nefarious goal or bilk others out of money, property, or valuables. *See* Better Business Bureau, Boiler Rooms, Ponzi Schemes.

CONCEALMENT

Relating to insurance, the withholding or hiding of facts in obtaining a policy or making a claim, to the detriment of the insurer. *See* Insurance.

CONCEPTUAL SKILL

The capacity of an individual to evaluate and understand the broad implications and potential of an organization's policies, concepts, and plans, especially in relation to the business affairs of the individual and his or her associates. *See* Personnel Administration.

CONCILIATION

In regard to labor relations, the process that attempts to resolve disputes through voluntary agreements and often compromises, in contrast to arbitration. *See* Labor/Management, Labor Unions.

CONCRETE PROPOSAL

A refined proposition that is revised from earlier drafts and presented as the final proposal from one party intent on doing business with another party. *See* Agreement, Proposal.

CONDEMNATION

The refusal by an authoritative group, such as a local government, to permit further use of a building or facilities because of hazardous conditions or unacceptable circumstances. *See* Real Estate, Regulations.

CONDENSED BALANCE SHEET

An abbreviated fiscal summary that contains only the highlights of an organization's finances. *See* Accounting, Bookkeeping.

CONDITIONAL CONTRACT

Also referred to as a *conditional agreement,* a formal compact in which the functions and benefits of the signatory parties depend upon the fulfillment of one or more special conditions. *See* Agreement, Contract.

CONDITIONAL VALUE

A value whose degree will be determined by a future situation or progression of events. *See* Assets, Assets Management.

CONFERENCE BOARD

An association of managers and business leaders, established to study and improve business policies and methods. *See* Associations.

CONFERENCE CALL

A telephone call, usually as a form of vocal business meeting, in which three or more people are hooked into the same telephone line and number and can talk concurrently. *See* Communications.

CONFIDENCE GAME

A fraudulent scheme to swindle people out of their money. *See* Better Business Bureau, Con Artist, Ponzi Schemes.

CONFIGURATION

A blueprint or graphic diagram to show layouts and relationships, such as the seating arrangement in a passenger jet or the work stations on an assembly line. Also, a grouping of interconnected machines that are programmed to function in a single system. *See* Blueprint, Production.

CONGLOMERATE

A corporation composed of subsidiary companies, often joined by mergers or acquisitions, some of which may be engaged in fields completely different from the original headquarters company. Of more recent prominence is the case of the company that is forced into becoming part of a conglomerate through a *hostile takeover,* despite the desires of is management to remain independent. *See* Hostile Takeover, Parent Company.

CONGRESSIONAL BUDGET OFFICE (CBO)

The agency that supports Congress in budget matters by providing research data, statistics, and evaluations of policies relating to fiscal and budgetary issues. *See* Budgets.

CONGRESSIONAL RECORD

The official publication of the United States Congress, which records daily proceedings and covers all legislation and debates of the House and Senate. The *Record,* which is available to the public, is not a word-for-word transcript of the proceedings, however, since members of Congress are free to edit or expand remarks they have made on the floor. *See* Legislation.

CONSERVATOR

An informed and experienced individual who is appointed by a court to liquidate a defunct business or oversee the affairs of incompetent managers.

CONSIGNEE

The receiver of a shipment of goods. *See* Consignment.

CONSIGNMENT

Merchandise or materials in shipment, the responsibility for which is still with the shipper until delivery and acknowledgment of acceptance by the recipient.

CONSOLIDATED FINANCIAL STATEMENT

A fiscal report that includes not only the corporation's official statement but those of subsidiaries and affiliates. *See* Annual Report.

CONSORTIUM

An alliance of organizations joined together because of mutual interests and in order to wield more clout as a group than as individual entities. *See* Associations.

CONSTITUTIONAL LAW

Federal laws that stem from, or relate to, the Constitution of the United States. *See* Business Law.

CONSTITUTIONAL RIGHT

Legal rights held by individuals under the Constitution of the United States, or, popularly, by any other major legal statutes or charters. *See* Civil Rights.

CONSULTANT

An independent specialist who provides expert evaluations and advice to clients under the terms of a long-range retainer or on an hourly or *per-diem* basis. Consultants are classified under two headings as either *specialists,* or *generalists.* The former would include professionals who are in such fields as banking, the law, accounting, advertising, medicine and health, or education. The latter might be people whose roots of expertise are more sociological or theoretical, such as members of community organizations, government leaders, the clergy, librarians, or even customers and clients. *See* Business Administration.

CONSUMER

In business, commerce, and industry, an individual usually recognized in classified groupings, who represents a major sales and marketing objective for a company. There are four categories by which consumers are classified:

1. *Demographic,* differentiated by age, gender, income, occupation, education, ethnic background, faith, health, and marital status.

2. *Sociological,* targeted according to their situations in regard to social class, reference group, lifestyle, status, and general role in the community.

3. *Geographical,* with the relationships determined by location, nature and size of their communities, adherence to local customs, seasonal activities, and their environment.

4. *Psychological,* with the focus on attitudes, beliefs, values, motivation, personality traits, and morals.

It is essential that a marketer know everything possible about consumer trends, tastes, preferences, purchasing potential, and susceptibility to advertising, promotion, and other media of communications. For this reason, the consumer is constantly and continuously the subject of business surveys, studies, and observations, both short-range and long-range alike. See other *consumer* entries.

CONSUMER CREDIT

That form of credit extended by a lender to a borrower for the purpose of financing expensive equipment, such as appliances or home improvements, and that is generally paid back in monthly installments over a period of one to two years. *See* Loans.

CONSUMER CREDIT PROTECTION ACT

Federal legislation passed to protect consumers from dangerous or faulty products, as well as overpricing, unfair competition, and unlawful credit terms. *See* Consumer Protection.

CONSUMER GOODS

Commonplace and familiar merchandise aimed at the consumer market for personal consumption by individuals and families. *See* other *Consumer* entries.

CONSUMER GOODS PRICING ACT

Preventive legislation to protect consumers from overpricing and to assure accurate and honest labeling of merchandise. *See* other *Consumer* entries.

CONSUMER INFORMATION CATALOG

A listing of more than 200 useful government publications, ranging from leaflets to full-length books, many of which are free or available at a low price. Published by the Consumer Information Center of the U.S. General Services Administration, the publications cover almost every subject that is of interest to the average consumer, including diet, health, benefits, insurance, financial planning, driving, drugs, education, and the care and handling of pets. To obtain the *Catalog,* send your name and address to: Consumer Information Catalog, Pueblo, CO 81009.

CONSUMER MARKET

The market composed of personal consumers, in contrast to markets associated with business and commercial products. *See* Marketing.

CONSUMER PRICE INDEX

A statistical reporting of periodic changes and fluctuations in the prices of merchandise and services purchased by families and single persons living alone who are wage earners.

CONSUMER PRODUCT SAFETY ACT

An act of Congress, initiated in 1972, which was written to protect the public against injury and other risks associated with products. Its purpose was also to develop uniform safety standards and to promote research and investigation into the causes and prevention of product-related injuries. *See* Consumer Protection.

CONSUMER PRODUCT SAFETY COMMISSION

A regulatory body that functions independently and whose purpose is to protect the public from damage, illness, and injury caused by products that are unsafe. CPSC promotes research and investigation regarding product-related injuries and death and formulates safety standards for products that could be potentially hazardous. *See* Consumer Protection.

CONSUMER PROTECTION

Individual and collective endeavors by government, business, and private groups to safeguard the interests of the consuming public. In recent times consumers' rights have been extended to such broad areas as product information and safety, satisfaction of grievances, advertising claims, and a voice in governmental decisions affecting the consumer. Early legislative action by the federal government included the Sherman Antitrust Act (1890), the Pure

Food and Drug Act (1906) and the creation of the Federal Trade Commission (1914), and the Food and Drug Administration (1931). The consumer movement made real inroads during the 1960s and 1970s when consumer activists succeeded in promoting laws that set safety standards for automobiles, children's clothing, toys, and a wide range of household products. The federal Truth in Lending Act was passed in the late 1960s to provide consumers with complete information on the real cost of credit. The United States Office of Consumer Affairs coordinates federal activities in this field, conducting investigations and surveys, acting on individual consumer complaints, and disseminating product information. The Consumer Product Safety Commission sets national safety standards and bans hazardous products. State and local governments also have become involved in consumer protection. The Consumer Federation of America, comprising about 220 organizations, is the largest consumer advocacy group in the United States Consumer protection on an international scale is coordinated by the International Organization of Consumers Unions. *See* Consumer Product Safety Commission, other *Consumer* entries.

CONTAINERIZATION

The transportation by rail, road, plane, or ship of goods that are sealed in large units or containers, sealed to protect the contents from theft or damage. *See* Shipping, Transportation.

CONTAINERIZED UNIT

See Containerization.

CONTEMPT

In legal matters and suits, the willful disobedience of an official court order or the commands of a judge. *See* Business Law.

CONTINGENCY

In legal, financial, and real estate dealings, a future situation or event that could become a reality, but is not predictable at the time a transaction is agreed upon. *See* Contingency Fund.

CONTINGENCY FUND

A sum of money set aside to cover a cost that is not actually foreseen but could be viable. *See* Contingency.

CONTINGENT ASSETS

Items that are on record but which may or may not become assets in a business. *See* Assets.

CONTINUING EDUCATION

Adult education, or any instruction that takes place after the conclusion of a person's formal education. *See* Career Education.

CONTINUOUS PRODUCTION

The kind of continuing manufacturing that generally yields only one product or related group of products and is seldom retooled or modified. *See* Manufacturing, Production.

CONTRACT

A legal agreement between parties engaged in a transaction of mutual interest, each of which has the authorization to sign the document and be responsible for the clauses therein. *See* Agreement, Business Law.

CONTRACT CARRIER

An independent shipper authorized to transport merchandise, materials, or other shipments on contract with customers. *See* Transportation.

CONTRACT OF ADHESION

A form of contract in which one party has no bargaining power. A common example is an insurance policy, which is standardized and does not provide any bargaining power for the insured. *See* Insurance.

CONTRACT OF SALE

An agreement that is legally binding between a purchaser and seller of property, written with the intention of conveying title after designated payments have been made and stipulated conditions have been met. *See* Contract, Sales.

CONTRACTUAL LIABILITY

The liability assumed by signatory parties for obligations specified in a contract. *See* Contract.

CONTROL CHART

In manufacturing and production, a chart that is used to indicate the system that has been devised to control the output, the speed, and the cost, among other things. *See* Industrial Management.

CONTROLLED CIRCULATION

That form of circulation desired and used by a publisher of a newspaper, magazine, or other periodical, who makes up an arbitrary list of recipients and distributes the publication directly to them. Controlled publications carry specialized news and advertisements for the most part, but do not solicit subscriptions or charge the recipients. *See* Advertising, Periodicals.

CONTROLLED CORPORATION

A company or other organization that is under the control of another organization, group, or individual.

CONTROLLED ECONOMY

An economy that is rigorously regulated and dominated by a government, as in the case of a dictatorship.

CONTROLLED INFLATION

The economic situation that exists in a nation when its authorities deliberately establish inflationary conditions in order to alleviate a recession. *See* Inflation, Recession.

CONTROLLER

See Comptroller.

CONTROLLING INTEREST

In finance, the position held by a shareholder or group of shareholders with sufficient stocks to control the issuing company. *See* Parent Company, Takeover.

CONVENIENCE GOODS

The kinds of merchandise that consumers purchase frequently, generally for household use, and to replace products that are regularly consumed. *See* Marketing.

CONVENTIONAL MORTGAGE

A mortgage that has not been issued under a government-insured plan. *See* Mortgage, Real Estate.

CONVERTIBLE

In foreign exchange, the kind of currency that can be readily converted into cash or the legal tender of another country. *See* Foreign Exchange.

CONVEYANCE

An instrument that is used to transfer from one party to another a title, as for a mortgage, deed, or bill of sale.

COOLING-OFF PERIOD

In labor/management relations, a legal provision that postpones a walkout or strike for a specific period in order to give the participating parties time to mediate their differences. *See* Labor/Management, Labor Unions.

COOPERATIVE

An association comprised of individuals or groups who have joined themselves together for the purpose of achieving mutual objectives, as in the case of a farm cooperative seeking to reduce restrictive legislation or seek better prices for goods and supplies. *See* Associations.

COOPERATIVE ADVERTISING

A type of advertising in which a wholesaler, retailer, or distributor (or combination thereof) pays a portion of the cost billed to the manufacturer of the products or supplies advertised. *See* Advertising, Marketing.

COOPERATIVE AGREEMENT

A joint agreement. *See* Agreement, Contract.

COOPERATIVE EDUCATION

An educational plan, generally at the college level, that permits students to work part time in jobs related to their field of studies, for which they receive appropriate course credits as well as modest wages. *See* Career Education, On-the-Job Training.

COOPERATIVE VENTURE

See Joint Venture.

CO-OPTATION

In management theory, the strategy used to influence opposing individuals and groups to drop their resistance and accept the principles and policies of management. *See* Business Administration.

CO PRODUCTION

Manufacturing or fabrication undertaken jointly by two or more principals, each of which may contribute different technologies or expertise or skills to the overall project. *See* Industrial Management, Production.

COPY

In advertising and publishing, the typescript or printed text for a passage, page, or complete publication.

COPYRIGHT

The legal right of ownership in any published or artistic creation, which is specified in a legal instrument and viable for a designated period of time. Copyrights can be applied to articles, books, musical scores, computer programs, and many other types of creative works of a kind not protected by a patent. *See* Patents, Trademarks.

COPYWRITER

The title given a writer in an advertising agency or company department whose assignment is to write the copy for printed advertisements, commercials, brochures, or other texts used in advertising, marketing, and promotion. *See* Advertising, Copy, Marketing.

CORPORATE ADVERTISING

Advertising whose purpose is not so much to sell products or services as to project the advertiser's philosophies or improve the corporate image. *See* Advertising, Corporate Image.

CORPORATE IMAGE

The conception and impression of a business organization that is uppermost in the mind of the public at large, and which may be positive or negative, favorable or disapproving. One of the major purposes of advertising and public relations firms, particularly the latter, is to improve and sustain a beneficial public image for corporate clients. *See* Corporate Advertising, Public Relations.

CORPORATE PLANNING

A staff function at the highest level, geared to generating both short- and long-range blueprints and strategies to upgrade operations, reduce costs, recruit necessary manpower, and otherwise enhance company growth and prosperity. *See* Business Administration.

CORPORATE STRATEGY

See Corporate Planning.

CORPORATION

A company or other coalition that has lawfully been granted a charter or commission by the government as a distinct and viable entity, havings its own rights and responsibilities in the conduct of business. Corporations are not limited to profit-making ventures, but also include many other disciplines, such as those that are educational, scientific, charitable, and religious. The corporation has a two-fold heritage: (1) the age-old tendency of people to join forces to strengthen the potential of a venture, and (2) the prototype of the chartered companies and the trading firms established in Western Europe in the late Middle Ages. As early as the beginning of the eighteenth century, British courts had established legal procedures for the formation of unchartered joint-stock companies that had all the characteristics of the modern corporate form described in a current management definition as "individuals joined in a voluntary association for commercial purposes, a group legally distinct from the personalities of the individual members, funds held jointly for common use, limited individual liability, a corporate legal personality extending beyond the life spans of individual members, ownership easily transferable from one individual to another in the form of shares in the company's capital or stock, and a specialized administrative structure." One of the essential advantages of investing in a corporation is that stockholders are not legally responsible for any debts or lawsuits faced by the company and stand to lose only all or part of their investment. Even the employees of the corporation cannot be held personally responsible for the derelictions by the corporation as a legal entity, though they could be held accountable for illegal acts perpetrated as individuals. Among the advantages held by large corporations over small ones or partnerships, for example, is the latitude they enjoy in being able to attract professional managers with substantial experience, sound education, and proven skills, which is why a majority of corporations are administered by hired professional managers who may have little ownership stake (other than stock options) in the corporate entity. The very size of many corporations, with thousands of employees and billions of dollars in assets, makes them subject to continuing controversy, especially since they have great impact on the structure of a nation's economy and often dominate major industries and can profoundly influence regional productive power. *See* Articles Of Incorporation, Multinational Corporation.

CORPORATION DE JURE

A corporation that was formed strictly according to law and has been authorized to do business as such. *See* Corporation.

COSIGNER

An individual who signs a document jointly with one or more other parties in a mutual venture and who usually shares in the obligations and stipulations set forth in the document. *See* Contract.

COST ACCOUNTING

A system of accounting that provides specific information on costs and expenditures, such as collections, disbursements, and indebtedness. *See* Accounting.

COST-BENEFIT ANALYSIS

A procedure for estimating the rates of return on investment purchases, especially those in the public interest, such as community parks, water-treatment systems, or sewers. *See* Public Works.

COST-EFFECTIVENESS

The degree to which the decision making and planning in an organization have resulted in favorable or unfavorable ratios of advantages to costs.

COST OF LIVING

Figures computed periodically to show the average costs, nationally and by region, of maintaining described living conditions. *See* Cost of Living Index.

COST OF LIVING INDEX

A tabulation in chart form, which is published periodically to show pertinent statistics about living costs, both nationally and regionally in the United States. *See* Cost Of Living, Price Indexes.

COST OVERRUN

Costs that are necessary, over and above budget, for manpower, materials, transportation, and anything else required to keep a project in operation. *See* Accounting.

COST PER THOUSAND (CPM)

An advertising term used in determining the cost of reaching 1,000 people with a printed advertisement, commercial, or other advertising medium. *See* Advertising.

COUNCIL ON ENVIRONMENTAL QUALITY

The federal agency that evaluates ecological matters and recommends to the President national policies to maintain or improve environmental quality in all of its ramifications. *See* Environment.

COUPON BONDS

See Municipal Bonds.

COUNTER TRADE

Trade, especially international, that is carried on with payments made entirely through the exchange of goods, rather than with monetary transactions. *See* Exports.

COURT OF APPEALS

The name for what was formerly referred to as the *circuit court of appeals.* This is an appellate court lower than the United States Supreme Court, which hears appeals from cases tried in federal district courts. In most cases, a decision by a court of appeals is final. *See* Business Law.

COVENANT

See Agreement, Contract.

CRAFT UNION

A union whose members are comprised of technically and technologically skilled workers, but not necessarily in the creative arts concept of "craft." *See* Labor/Management, Unions.

CREATIVE DIRECTOR

A manager in an advertising agency or corporate department who supervises the concept, planning, and production of copywriting, art, layout, music, and any other imaginative and original works to be used on behalf of the organization and its functions.

CREDIT ANALYSIS

A financial review of an intended borrower, whether an individual or a company, and the terms of the proposed loan, to determine the soundness of advancing the loan to the borrower and under the terms requested. *See* Loans.

CREDIT BUREAU

An agency established privately or publicly to evaluate holders of loans or other obligations and rate them according to their capacities to discharge indebtedness and to review their past fiscal history in doing so.

CREDIT INSTRUMENT

See Loan.

CREDIT INSURANCE

A policy that is underwritten to protect a lender, as in the case when a borrower dies, goes bankrupt, or persistently defaults on payments.

CREDIT LINE

The limit of credit advanced to the holder of a loan or personal credit card.

CREDIT RATING

A variable rating assigned to a company to reflect its proven ability and concurrence in meeting its financial obligations, based on its fiscal history, present financial stability, and future earnings projections.

CREDIT REPORT

A professional summary prepared by a credit bureau or similar agency for a client, to report on the financial health of a would-be borrower and the ability to meet the proposed obligation within a specified time frame.

CREEPING INFLATION

A gradual, marked increase in inflation from year to year, by as little as 3 percent annually.

CRISIS BARGAINING

In labor/management relations, an intensified style of bargaining that takes place when a walkout or threatened strike has become critically disruptive to both parties.

CRITICAL-PATH METHOD

A technique for controlling the functions, operations, and costs of a project by using graphics to chart the "paths" that various facets must follow if success is to be assured.

CROSSOVER ANALYSIS

The evaluation of alternate methods of production when an existing manufacturing begins to show signs of faltering or becoming too costly.

CRUNCH

In business, a slang term for a situation that is uptight or reaching crisis proportions.

CRYOGENICS

The field of study and performance that deals with the physics of extreme cold and its effect on products and materials.

CUMULATIVE DIVIDEND

Dividends of preferred stocks and other securities that, if not cashed in, accrue as obligations that must be paid before common stock dividends can be issued.

CURRENCY

Money in any form that is practical as a medium of exchange, such as paper money or coins, and that is in general circulation or readily available. Under the *international monetary system,* different national currencies may be exchanged for each other in world trade, following certain regulations and procedures. In foreign exchange, the price of local currency is determined by the relative supply and demand of the currencies in the foreign exchange market, and the *balance of payments* of the nations concerned. The balance of payments is a standard program that indicates the fiscal relationships between countries mutually engaged in trade and commerce. The demand for international exchange and foreign currency comes largely from exporters, importers, and firms engaged in worldwide travel and recreation. *See* Balance of Payments, Balance of Trade, Foreign Exchange, International Monetary System.

CURRENT ASSETS

Those assets that will be realized in the short term, generally within one year, and that include cash, receivables, liquid securities, acknowledged inventories on hand, and current prepayments.

CURRENT LIABILITY

A fiscal obligation or indebtedness that must be discharged within one year.

CURRENT RATIO

In corporate accounting, the measure of a company's liquidity, classified by dividing current assets by current liabilities.

CURRENT YIELD

In investing, the ratio of current income to purchase price of a security. *See* Investments, Securities.

CURRICULUM VITAE

A résumé or personal biography.

CUSTOMER-ORIENTED

Said of a company that sells products to consumers and has their interests in mind in the manner in which it does business with them.

CUSTOMER PROFILE

An evaluation of the nature, characteristics, and desires of a company's most likely customers, developed in order to meet market needs more successfully.

CUSTOMIZED PRODUCTION

The procedure used by a manufacturing company to evaluate its market and customers, individually and collectively, and develop plans for producing and delivering products to meet stringent specifications. This form of customization is prevalent, for example, in companies with government contracts for aircraft, naval vessels, and arms. *See* Production.

CUTBACK

A reduction in a manufacturing process or other function, or in the operating budget, generally because of rising costs or lessening product demand.

CYBERNETICS

A term, derived from a Greek word meaning "helmsman" and formerly used to describe an approach to the study of control and communication in animals, humans, machines, and companies. The concept stemmed from research on antiaircraft guns during World War II, applying the feeding back of operating data into a system from interactions with certain given situations. Later, the science of cybernetics was applied to the design and function of computers as they increased in use and sophistication. This field of study became widely known as *artificial intelligence* and was concerned with measuring the flow and accuracy of information and controlling errors in transmission. *See* Communications, Computers, Data Processing, Research and Development.

CYCLICAL UNEMPLOYMENT

Unemployment that occurs in cycles, for various reasons that may be seasonal in nature or caused by regular fluctuations in the income levels in the area of unemployment. *See* Unemployment.

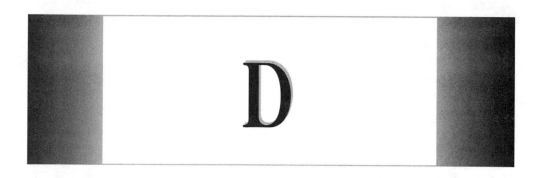

Data

The cumulative term for all facts, statistics, and pertinent information filed for immediate and extended use by organizations and individuals. There are two types of basic data resources: *primary data,* which include facts related to a subject field that are not available in standard sources of data, either within a company and industry or outside of them, and that require considerable time, work, and initiative to locate, and *secondary data,* which include information commonly available through conventional sources, such as the federal government, chambers of commerce, or commercial data services. Frequent business subjects are sales figures, market outlooks, inventory controls, training programs, payroll confirmations, insurance claims, medical records, and meteorological forecasts. *See* Data Processing.

Data Bank

A comprehensive collection of data in storage. *See* Data Processing.

Database

Specific collections, or bases, of data that can be applied to various operations in a business or industry. Electronic databases have been likened to entries in a telephone book or catalog, but that are far easier, quicker, and more comprehensive to use since they can produce multiple facts instantaneously, as well as search through whole collections of "catalogs" at the same time. There are two types of databases: *flat-file,* which store the data in the blanks—called *fields*—of one record; and *relational,* which store the small categories in different tables and are more feasible for undertaking sophisticated searches. *See* other *Data* entries.

Data Center

A data-processing facility provided for various users and usually computerized. *See* other *Data* entries.

DATA MANAGEMENT

The administration and management of data banks and other accumulations of facts, figures, and general data. *See* Business Administration, Data Processing.

DATA PROCESSING

A system, whether on computers, communications equipment, or other facilities for sorting data and inputting facts for designated purposes. Today, data processing and the storage and retrieval of vast amounts of information have been taken over almost entirely by computer systems, which process enormous compilations of information called *databases.* Government agencies such as the military, Social Security Administration, and the National Crime Information Center maintain databases, as do private and public industries and thousands of organizations of all kinds, large and small. Memory/data networks extend to a tertiary, or archival, level with capacity for trillions of bits of information, or hundreds of times more than can be contained in the world's most extensive encyclopedias. Yet even the tiniest details in these vast electronic storage bins can be called up to a computer screen in a fraction of a second. Digital computers process information in the form of binary codes, stored on disks, tapes, and drums, that utilize the property of magnetic material that allows particles to be oriented, or polarized, in one of two directions, corresponding to each of the values of binary code—zero or one. Strings of binary numbers, called *bytes,* are represented by arrays of magnetic particles. Individuals who use computers are likely to be most familiar with disks—rather than wotj tapes and drums—particularly the small, often flexible "floppy disks" that are easy to use and store—and that can hold several hundred thousand characters. Increasingly popular in data processing for the retrieval of information are *compact disks,* called *CDs,* which are round, metal-coated plastic laser discs on which digital information is stored in the form of pits and knobs. Information is retrieved from the disc by the reflection from the surface of a small laser beam as the disk rotates rapidly. Another form of disk, the *electronic disk,* has the advantage of not requiring any mechanical motion. Data processing of all kinds requires *software,* which is the term for the information and command units that instruct the computers and control their operation. *See* Byte, Compact Disk, Computers, Data Management, Hardware, Software.

DEAD LETTER

A letter or other dispatch that has been placed in the mail but is undeliverable, or is unnamable and cannot be returned to the sender.

DEAD TIME

Time periods when employees and others are unable to continue their appointed duties because of reasons beyond their control, generally break-downs of equipment, power shortages, or severe weather conditions.

DEALER IMPRINT

The name, address, logotype (logo), or other identification placed on materi-al conceived by an advertiser or marketer. *See* Logotype, Trademark.

DEBENTURE

A document describing the indebtedness of a company that is backed by cred-it rather than secured by any assets such as a mortgage or lien on property. *See* Loans.

DEBIT

The accounting term for negative entries in the financial records. *See* Asset, Bookkeeping.

DEBT

In financial dealings, a debt is defined as the obligation to pay a sum of money to a party known as a *creditor.* Usually a debt arises from a transaction in which one party, the debtor, receives something of value, such as goods, ser-vices, or money, from another in return for a promise to pay at a late date. Most debts include a promise to pay interest or some other premium at a specified rate. If debtors fail to meet their obligations, creditors may take legal action to force payment or seize property in lieu of payment. In one charac-teristic procedure, a judgment can be obtained against a debtor requiring that payment be made. If the debtor then fails to pay, laws provide that a law-enforcement agency may seize the debtor's property and dispose of enough of it to pay the sum owed, plus the legal costs incurred. *See* attachment, bank-ruptcy, national debt.

DEBT CAPACITY

The degree of financing a company can assume before the financing become prohibitively high. *See* Financing.

DEBT CAPITAL

In finance, funds borrowed to finance the operation of a business or industry. *See* Financing.

DEBTOR

An individual, group, or organization liable by contract or agreement to pay a claim for money that is owed. *See* Loan.

DEBT RATIO

Long-term debt as indicated by comparison with a debtor's capital, used as a measure of a company's financial leverage. *See* other *Debt* entries.

DECENTRALIZATION

A form of corporate operation in which decision making and authority are delegated to lower levels of management or spread geographically to other company locations, divisions, and departments. *See* Corporation.

DECISION MAKING

In management, the procedures and strategies for evaluating situations and options and selecting courses of action that will most likely lead to the objectives or outcomes desired. *See* Decision Theory.

DECISION THEORY

A research category relating to studies of how decisions are made, could be made, or should be made, in principle as well as in actual practice, recommending courses of action that might achieve designated objectives. The defined concept recognizes the fact that many different decision problems and options exist, those of individuals with single choices, for example, differing distinctly from those that involve groups of individuals with interests that may be in conflict. The concept further explores the difference between decisions made "under certainty," in which the outcomes are known, and those made "under uncertainty," in which the consequences are not known. In cases where probabilities can be speculated from past experience, the process is referred to as decision making "under risk." Decision theories take into account, too, that there are certain trade-offs, benefits and disadvantages alike. A common type of decision in this category is the one in which a marketing manager or buyer has to decide whether quality or low price is more important in the design of certain products for its areas of consumer distribution. *See* Decision Tree.

DECISION TREE

A graphic method of decision-making analysis that utilizes a treelike diagram to estimate values and compare the probabilities of outcomes in the variety of options depicted. *See* Decision Theory.

DECLARATION

In insurance dealings, that part of a policy that includes such basic information as the name and address of the insured, the type of property insured, the amount of coverage, valuations, and other supplemental data. In corporate finance, a formal document creating a liability to pay dividends. *See* Insurance.

DECLARATION OF TRUST

A formal agreement stating that property to which an individual or organization holds title in actuality belongs to another party, for whose benefit the title is maintained. *See* Property.

DECLARED VALUATION

The valuation placed on a shipment or stored goods placed in the hands of a carrier or storage facility. *See* Shipping, Transportation.

DEDUCTIBLE

Any value that can be used to lessen the amount of taxable property or income. In insurance, the amount a policyholder agees to assume, per claim or per accident, toward the total amount of an insured loss, thus reducing the rate of insurance. *See* Taxation.

DEED

An instrument establishing the legal ownership of real property, drawn up or presented at the time the property is transferred from one party to another. *See* Real Estate.

DEED OF TRUST

An instrument conveying to a trustee the title to property as security for the payment of a debt. *See* Trust, Trustee.

DEFALCATION

A type of embezzlement conventionally restricted to absconding with cash, rather than any other kinds of valuables. *See* Embezzlement, Fraud.

DEFAULT

The failure of a debtor to pay interest or principal on a debt when due, or to perform other conditions of an obligation. *See* Insolvency, Loan.

DEFEASIBLE

The term referring to anything that can be made void or annulled. *See* Contract.

DEFECTIVE

The classification for goods or merchandise that fail to meet the manufacturer's warranty or stated claims or expected standards for such merchandise. *See* Warranty.

DEFERRAL

Cash that has been collected before the revenue has been earned, or disbursed before an expense has been incurred. *See* Accounting, Bookkeeping.

DEFERRED ASSET

An asset that is purchased in advance of the actual utilization of its benefits and advantages. *See* Accounting, Bookkeeping.

DEFERRED COMPENSATION

The postponement of a distribution of a percentage of earnings until a later date, often as a sum dispensed at retirement.

DEFICIENCY JUDGMENT

The order by a court of law to a debtor to pay the balance owed on a loan if the proceeds from the sale of the collateral are not adequate enough to satisfy the loan agreement, in whole or in part. *See* Business Law.

DEFICIT

The amount by which the financial liabilities of a company exceed its reserves and assets. *See* Annual Report.

DEFICIT FINANCING

The established government procedure for deliberately budgeting expenditures in excess of expected, or actual, revenues. *See* Accounting.

DEFICIT SPENDING

The disbursement of public funds that are raised with loans rather than by taxation.

DEFLATION

In broad financial cycles, the period during which goods and services become lower in cost. *See* Inflation, Recession.

DEFLATIONARY GAP

The monetary amount by which demand falls short of full employment supply, thus deflating the value of the national output. *See* Gross National Product (GNP).

DEFRAUD

To use misrepresentation or deceit to cheat an individual or organization or deprive them of a right. *See* Embezzlement, Fraud.

DEFUNCT

Said of an organization that has gone bankrupt or otherwise ceased to function in a normal manner. *See* Bankruptcy.

DE JURE

A legal term of Latin origin, meaning "by right."

DELEGATION OF AUTHORITY

The practice in which managers give authority to individuals or groups under their jurisdiction to make decisions or take actions on their behalf. *See* Decentralization.

DELINQUENT

Said of a debt or interest that is due and has not been paid by an agreed-upon deadline. *See* Debt, Loan.

DELISTED

Said of a stock or other security that have been removed from the list of those being traded actively on a major stock exchange. *See* Investments, Securities, Stocks.

DEMAND CURVE

A chart or similar graphic representation to indicate quickly and visually the quantity of merchandise in demand in relation to price. *See* Supply and Demand.

DEMAND LOAN

A loan that must be repaid whenever the lender requests repayment in whole or in part, rather than at any designated date. *See* Banking, Loans.

DEMOGRAPHICS

Data that has been compiled and computed to present statistics about the makeup of population segments, specifically in regard to age, sex, education, location, income, ethical background, and religious faith. Demography is the scientific study of the size, distribution, and composition of human populations; demography is a branch of sociology that uses birth and death rates and related statistics to determine the characteristics of a population, discover patterns of change, and make predictions. A significant demographic tool is the life table, which converts numbers of deaths in a population to probabilities of dying and life expectancies. It is applicable to other types of conversions as well such as the probability that certain proportions of the population will become leaders or scientists, or that a machine has a life span related to the people who run it. Demography is used to ascertain relations among the components of a population, such as that between age groups. Age distribution has a direct bearing on the costs of schooling and of pensions, the demand for housing, and the need for many other durable and non durable commodities. For example, overall business promotions come sooner in a rapidly growing population than they do in a slowly growing one; demographic calculations can predict by how much. Demographic analysis shades off into various substantive fields of population study. Economists study the relation between demographic and economic variables; ecologists, the relation between demographic and environmental variables; sociologists, the relation between demographic and social variables. For example, under what circumstances does increase of income lower the birthrate? How much does environmental radioactivity increase cancer? Is the much higher early death rate for males due to more tension in their lives, some other difference in lifestyles, or simply to female constitutions that are biologically hardier? In every society where modernization has occurred, the birth as well as the death rate has fallen. Demographers are particularly concerned with the time lag between the fall in the death rate and the subsequent fall in the birth rate. It is important to know what social factors underlie the observed differences in fertility among the population in different income, educational, religious, and residential categories that might affect the transition from high to low rates. For these, and many other reasons, demographics are important in business fields such as marketing, where people and their habits can make a great deal of difference in such commonplace economic matters as distribution and sales. *See* Advertising, Distribution, Marketing.

DEMURRAGE

The charge made by a common carrier for loading, unloading, or storing goods for a longer period than originally specified. *See* Shipping, Transportation.

DEPARTMENTALIZATION

The manner in which a company or other organization is operationally divided. *See* Business Administration, Corporation, Decentralization.

DEPLETION

An accounting practice consisting of charges against earnings based on the amount of assets taken out of the total reserves in the period for which the accounting is made. *See* Accounting.

DEPLETION ALLOWANCE

A tax allowance for energy components, such as petroleum or coal, which reduces the value of the remaining assets in a mine, oil well, or gas well. *See* Energy.

DEPOSIT INSURANCE

A policy on deposits made to a financial institution to protect the depositor for any losses incurred, up to a specified amount, should the institution fail. *See* Banking, Insurance.

DEPOSITION

A statement that is made under oath and signed, for use in a trial or other legal function. *See* Business Law.

DEPRECIATION

The decrease in value or function of material things because of wear and tear, damage, obsolescence, or decline in price. *See* Accounting, Taxation.

DEPRESSION

The low phase in a business cycle, marked by a marketing slowdown, lower prices, and increased unemployment. *See* Inflation, Recession.

DEPTH INTERVIEW

In advertising and marketing, a method based on open-ended questions to obtain more comprehensive information from individuals interviewed about preferences in regard to products and services of an advertiser. *See* Advertising, Consumers.

DEREGULATION

The removal of rules, restrictions, and regulations, especially from government control, as in the case of prices, rents, or an industry. *See* Free Trade.

DESKTOP PUBLISHING

The use of a computer, with appropriate hardware and software, to prepare newsletters, brochures, and even books comparable to ones produced by conventional printing equipment. *See* Computers.

DEVALUATION

The lowering of the value of a nation's currency, especially in comparison with the currency of other nations with which it is engaged in habitual business and trade. Devaluation is commonly undertaken as a means of correcting a deficit in the balance of payments. Although devaluation occurs in terms of all currencies, it is best illustrated in relation to one other currency. For example, if the United States is losing money in its trade with France, it may decide to devalue the dollar by 10 percent. If one dollar had been worth 5.5 francs, a 10 percent devaluation would cause it to be worth only 5 francs. Such a move causes foreign products to become more costly for Americans and American products to become cheaper for foreigners. *See* Balance of Payments, Currency, Free Trade.

DEVELOPING NATION

A nation of lesser stature than the major countries, but one whose leaders and executives are beginning to use their resources and manpower to produce more, and better, goods and services. *See* Third World Countries.

DIAGONAL EXPANSION

Plans, operations, and procedures that make it possible for a manufacturer to create new, marketable products that can be produced with the same equipment and facilities that already exist. *See* Manufacturing, Production.

DIALECTIC CHANGE

A conceptual theory that recognizes that any changes introduced by management, however beneficial, will inevitably create situations out of which new problems will arise. *See* Business Administration.

DIFFERENTIAL COSTS

Those costs that reflect the difference between an actual situation and a proposed situation. *See* Accounting.

DIGITAL COMPUTER

The type of computer that processes data in the form of discrete (separate and unconnected) digits. If a machine must be worked by hand to initiate each arithmetical operation, it is usually called a calculator, whereas the term *computer* is reserved for equipment that can be programmed to perform various operations automatically. The distinction between calculator and computer is often a moot question, though, since recent progress in microelectronics has led to small, hand-held calculators that have programming capabilities. Characteristically, digital computers can perform ordinary mathematical functions, such as adding, subtracting, multiplying, and dividing. Yet such machines can be programmed to provide sophisticated and complex results within as many as twenty decimal places. It is also possible to introduce procedures that accelerate the built-in accuracy almost without limit by repeated operations. In principle, digital computers are able to calculate any mathematical problem for which procedures, or algorithms, are known and can do this to any required degree. *See* Computers, Data Processing.

DIMINISHING RETURNS

The theory that repeated use of identical techniques, such as advertising campaigns and marketing systems, will result in dwindling results. *See* Advertising, Marketing, Promotion.

DIRECT COSTS

Those costs and expenses that can be identified with specific operations or methods of doing business. *See* Production, Sales.

DIRECT FINANCING

Raising necessary capital without having to seek loans or underwriting. *See* Investments.

DIRECT MAIL

Mail addressed directly to prospective customers, clients, or supporters during marketing and advertising campaigns. *See* Advertising, Postal Service.

DIRECT SELLING

Selling products directly to consumers without relying on wholesalers or other middlemen. Also referred to as *direct marketing,* in the field of advertising and selling, the function is characterized by those situations in which purchasers place orders through the mail or some other nonstore channel, on the phone, or to a salesperson visiting the home. In recent years this type of mar-

keting has been highly successful as ordering techniques and distribution channels have improved and become more reliable, and as various advertising
media have been used to reach prospective consumers. Contributing to the
success of direct marketing have been such factors as *telemarketing,* the use
of sales forces trained in telephone selling, the increased availability of toll-free
telephone numbers for prospective purchasers, and TV shopping channels,
which promote products that viewers can order by phone. Most important has
been the creation of computer-generated mailings lists of potential customers,
pinpointed as to income, interests, occupation, past purchasing histories, or
any of a number of other earmarks that are used to define a market. *See*
Marketing, Merchandising, Telemarketing.

DIRECTOR

An individual elected by shareholders to serve on a board and help establish
company policies and procedures. The directors of a corporation elect the
chairperson, vice presidents, and other operating officers and decide if and
when stock dividends will be paid. *See* Business Administration, Corporation.

DISCLOSURE

The required explanation of a company's financial position and operations,
generally found in annual reports and other investment documents and used
to alert readers to any weaknesses or problems in the organization's structure.
See Annual Report.

DISCOUNT

In financial transactions, the amount of money by which a preferred stock or
bond or other instrument of value may sell below its par value. *See*
Investments.

DISCRIMINATION

The unfair, and generally unlawful, practice of treating individuals and groups
unequally because of race, creed, sex, or other personal characteristics.
Discrimination, in society, can be defined as the unequal treatment of equals.
Although the term refers mainly to minority groups, it occasionally refers to
majorities, as exemplified by racial discrimination in South Africa. There is a
distinction between discrimination and prejudice, the former expressed in
overt, concrete behavior, while the latter is depicted by attitude. It is usually
assumed that the person who discriminates does so because of prejudice, but
this need not be the case. For instance, supervisors may assign certain tasks
on the basis of company policies rather than on their personal attitudes.

Ethnic discrimination in America has been said to be closely related to historic patterns of immigration, associated more with timing than with prejudice. The earlier arrivals would typically be pushed upward onto a higher economic and social level by successive waves of newcomers. *See* Civil Rights.

DISK MEMORY

A form of random-access memory, in which data are stored magnetically on parallel computer disks. *See* Computers.

DISPOSABLE INCOME

That income which, for an individual or organization, is available after the payment of taxes. *See* Taxation.

DISTRIBUTION

In commerce, the process of moving merchandise from the producer to the consumer or retail or wholesale point of sale. In the economics sense, distribution refers fundamentally to the allocation of the Gross National Product to different groups, families, and individuals. The principles of distribution review the reasons why personal income differentials affect the manner in which the shares of national income going to the different segments of production are determined through the working of economic forces. The old, traditional theories of supply and demand in the marketplace have been greatly transformed and modified by new forces, such as the impact of more sophisticated managements, the power of organized labor, and invasive government intervention. The term distribution also refers to the channels through which goods move from the producer to the market. *See* Marketing, Supply and Demand.

DIVERSIFICATION

In industry, the steps taken to extend business operations into other fields, whether related or unrelated, in order to increase products, exploit more promising opportunities, or otherwise increase profitability and long-term potential. Diversification into new businesses, however, has been rated as one of the highest types of business risks, according to the National Business Information Center, which states that fewer than 20 percent of the businesses in America—particularly small businesses—have been successful when they tried to diversify. The chief reasons for failure are:

- poor selection of enterprises into which to diversify;
- lack of experience in, or knowledge about, the new field of business;
- allocating too much investment capital to an untried field of operations;

- overloading management with additional commitments and time-consuming problems;
- neglecting existing business in order to attend to the demands of the new business.

See Business Administration.

DIVESTITURE

The elimination by a company of a subsidiary, facility or other substantial property through a sale or spin-off. *See* Decentralization.

DIVIDENDS

The payments determined by the board of directors to be distributed to shareholders. On preferred shares, a dividend is generally a fixed amount, while on common shares, the amount varies with the fortunes of the company and the amount of cash on hand. *See* Investments.

DOLLAR COST AVERAGING

A system of purchasing securities at stated intervals with fixed dollar amounts. Under this plan, investors purchase by dollars' worth rather than by the number of shares. *See* Accounting, Investments.

DOOR-TO-DOOR SELLING

A form of direct marketing in which salespersons promote their products or services to prospective consumers in their homes or places of business. *See* Direct Marketing, Multilevel Marketing.

DOUBLE ENTRY

That form of bookkeeping in which each transaction is recorded by means of two or more entries that balance each other. *See* Accounting, Bookkeeping.

DOUBLE JEOPARDY

Being tried twice for the same offense, a circumstance that is prohibited under the Fifth Amendment to the Constitution of the United States and also by most state constitutions. This provision, however, is not always applicable, as in the case of trials that end in a hung jury or mistrial, for example, which are not considered to be trials in the legal sense and which may call for a defendant to be tried again. Also, the prohibition does not always preclude different jurisdictions from trying an individual for the same crime. The constraint against double jeopardy, though, does prevent accused persons from being retried for offenses of which they have been acquitted. *See* Business Law.

DOW JONES AVERAGE

A widely quoted stock average that is computed regularly, which includes industrial, transportation, and utility averages, and a combination of all three. *See* Investments, Securities, Stocks.

DOW THEORY

A market analysis based upon the performance of the Dow Jones stock price averages. The theory conjectures that the market is on an upward trend if the industrial or transportation average advances above a previous important high, accompanied by a similar advance in the other. A dip in both averages below a previous important low is regarded as a downward trend. *See* Investments, Securities, Stocks.

DRAFT

In banking, an instrument of credit drawn upon a bank and initiated by the person who is to receive the money. The drawer of the draft, which is also known as a *bill of exchange,* sends the document requiring payment to the drawee, who accepts it by writing his or her name across the face of the paper. Several types of drafts are in use, such as a *bank draft* which is a check drawn by one bank against funds deposited to its account in another bank, a sight draft, which is payable on demand, or a *time draft,* to be paid at some future date. *See* Banking, Bill of Exchange.

DROP SHIPMENT

The delivery of merchandise directly from a manufacturer to a retailer. *See* Distribution.

DUN & BRADSTREET REPORTS

A published source of credit information about corporations, which includes data about the nature of the business, management, credit history, any legal proceedings, current debts, and other germane statistics. *See* Corporations, Investments.

DURABLE GOODS

Substantial, usually costly, products and materials that can be expected to last and be functional over a long period of time, despite repeated use. *See* Merchandise, Nondurable Goods.

DURESS

A state of pressure, coercion, or intimidation under which some action is being taken. *See* Blackmail.

DYNAMIC ECONOMY

The description applied to a national or regional economy that is thriving and growing, usually with significant changes and that is classified either for short-range activity or long-range continuance. *See* Economics.

DYNAMIC PROGRAMMING

A procedure for the optimization of a multiple problem solution, in which a number of decisions are possible during each of the many stages of the process. Also called *linear programming. See* Computers, Data Processing, Programming.

Earned Income

The income received for goods or services already delivered and earned and for which no future liability will be incurred. *See* Accounting, Distribution.

Earning Power

The potential of employees in their jobs or future assignments to earn projected sums of money over periods of time. *See* Compensation.

Earnings per Share

The measure of a corporation's profit, as shown in terms of each share of common stock. *See* Annual Report.

Easement

The right of the owner of one parcel of property to use the land of another for a valid reason, such as access to part of his or her land, such as the right to cross another person's acreage to reach a main highway or to take water from a stream running through both properties. Although an easement may arise through custom, it is usually created by express agreement with a property owner. If a person has used a neighbor's road or driveway for a long period of time, a court may rule that an implied easement exists. Under ancient law, a landowner might even acquire an easement of light and air through "uninterrupted enjoyment" and could prevent an adjoining owner from erecting a building that impaired this easement, although this extreme has been rejected by American courts as tending to discourage the use of land in a crowded location. *See* Real Estate.

Econometrics

The study of economic measurements in order to explore economic theories and develop working hypotheses. A branch of economics that seeks to correlate the relationships between economic variables, merging economic theory with statistical methods. Examples of econometric analysis are patterns of the American economy created by the Federal Reserve Board and a number of business schools, designed to analyze economic fluctuations and predict variations in national income and employment. They are combinations of equations depicting relationships between prices, wages, output, employment, and capital investment in different sectors of the economy. Although such econometric models are tested against past experience, there is no assurance their predictions will be completely accurate in the future, unless they are on a small scale, such as one showing the relationship between construction starts and interest rates. The science of econometrics can also be used in the statistical analysis of demand, production, and supply of commodities, such as farm produce, or minerals and petroleum. *See* Economics.

Economic Analysis

The systematic method of choosing, among alternative approaches, how to employ scarce or uncommon resources and achieve given objectives in the most efficient and cost-effective manner. *See* Economics.

Economic Indicators

Classifications of data than can be used to analyze business cycles and forecast future operations. *See* Business Cycles.

Economic Opportunity Act

In the 1960s, the keystone of the administration's "war on poverty," which created the Job Corps and other work incentive programs.

Economic Planning

As a fundamental policy, this is the discipline guided by central government agencies in the economics field, in contrast to the guidance of economic forces by markets. Historically, this field of planning has been associated with economic control by a central government authority, such as those of ancient Egypt or Greece, or England in the Middle Ages when mercantilism and the acquisition of wealth led to state regulation of international commerce and the domestic economy. The development of economic planning systems, however, is a recent phenomenon, made possible by advances in science and technology, particularly data processing and computerization. An undesirable feature of economic planning is that is has been used to substitute for the free enterprise system of supply and demand by nations with state-dictated policies. This was the case with the five-year plans of the former Soviet Union, which set overall national economic policy and dictated prices and the production outputs of certain manufacturers. The contention of communists and socialists is that free capitalist markets result in both economic and political inequality. The socialist theory implies that it utilizes the productive forces of the economy, distributes goods to those most in need, and generates productivity through state power. Economic planning in non socialist countries employs an altogether different focus. Instead of centralized command structures, free enterprise relies on the marketplace, governed by individual self-interest, to prompt basic economic decisions. Regardless of political situations, economic planning exists in some form in every industrial society, the degree of domination determined by whether the government or market supply and demand triggers most of the decisive economic decisions. One effect of the decline of communism as a threat to the Western world has been to lessen the political significance of economic planning. Based on free trade, the world's overall economy tends to create a single world marketplace, an environment in which production programs move freely across national borders. During the past two decades, intense competition has taken place in the global economy and has changed the economic balance of power, giving those nations that were able to produce huge economic surpluses, like Japan and Germany, big leads in world industry. Indications are that this rise of the global economy may give new life to economic planning as nations seek to compete against one another. *See* Economics.

Economic Recovery Tax Act (ERTA)

The federal law that was part of the campaign to reduce the federal deficit and stimulate the national economy by decreasing income taxes.

Economics

The study of data and factors that affect the production, distribution, and consumption of wealth, locally, regionally, and worldwide, and the related study of resources that contribute to these factors and are catalysts in economic affairs. The basic goal of all economic activity has been stated as the aim "to achieve the highest level of present consumption of goods and services that is compatible with the supply of human and material resources available to produce them." The scarcity of personnel and materials, as evidenced by the existence of prices, imposes the necessity of making choices and allocating resources. Essentially, it is a matter of deciding the needs and priorities of consumer goods and services, such as housing, transportation, education, health, and sustenance, both for the present and the future, and pitting these needs against the production of capital goods, such as factories, highways, shipping docks, and airports. The selection process occurs both at the level of the household and at that of the business establishment, governed to a great extent by the laws of supply and demand. Since competitive performance in the business sector implies that firms direct their efforts toward maximizing profits, they must be responsive to the demands of the consumer sector, and they must combine their labor and material resources in such a way as to minimize production and distribution costs. This is the essence of efficient production. To the extent that it is accomplished, it will yield the largest possible output of goods and services with a minimum expenditure of resources. Research concerning the choices that households and business firms make is the concern of *microeconomic analysis,* the study of the behavior of individuals, organizations, and institutions in the economy. Such a study is only one part of economic analysis, however, the other being the study of the behavior of economic aggregates, or *macroeconomics.* This involves, among other endeavors, inquiries into economic performance, as measured in terms of production and income. One of the most familiar blueprints that gauge and display the economy's overall performance is Gross National Product (GNP), which depicts the market value of all goods and services produced during a given period, generally 12 months. The size of the GNP is dependent on aggregate effective demand—the consumption and investment demands of households and businesses. Macroeconomic aggregates are thus critically linked to the microeconomic decisions made in the household and business sectors of the economy. *See* Macroeconomics, Microeconomics.

ECONOMIC STATISTICS BUREAU

The agency assigned to maintaining data on economic matters and issue periodical statistical bulletins. *See* Economics, Statistics.

ECONOMIC ZONES

The concept for a much-disputed plan in the 1980s to create some 75 special zones to provide tax breaks and regulatory relief to companies operating within specified inner-city and depressed rural areas. The basic plan was to strengthen business investment by offering tax breaks to private companies, relief from government regulations, and the eventual upgrading of local government services. *See* Taxation.

EFFECTIVE CAPACITY

The capacity of a manufacturing or producing function under normal operational conditions. The capacity can be limited by numerous factors, or combinations thereof, such as material shortages, limited supplies of competent labor, or wear and tear on existing equipment. *See* Manufacturing, Production.

EFFICIENCY EXPERT

A consultant who is a specialist in operations research and related matters and can be engaged to advise an organization on ways to improve its efficiency and achieve its goals more handily by doing the right thing at the right time and in the right manner. *See* Consultant.

ELECTRONIC DATA PROCESSING

Commonly referred to as EDP, this is a process whereby electronic computers are utilized to compile information. *See* Data Processing.

ELECTRONIC MAIL

Popularly known as *E-mail,* this function is the transmission of messages from a computer to one or more other computers, but also refers to telex, electronic funds-transfer systems, computer conferencing, and other electronic programs. Users can send any type of message or material that can be prepared by computer, including graphic displays and typescript in a range of sizes and fonts. Such transmissions are received in computer "mailboxes" and can be held there indefinitely for the recipients. In business environments, such as offices, E-mail can also be used in a centralized system in which individual terminals are linked in a network to a large central computer, but can be classified as "private" or "confidential," like ordinary postal mail. *See* Computers, Voice Mail.

ELECTRONIC PUBLISHING

The application of computers and other data-processing equipment for the production of periodicals, books, and other printed matter. Although sometimes used to describe the application of computers to traditional print publishing, the term electronic publishing refers more precisely to the storage and retrieval of information through electronic communications media. It can employ a variety of formats and technologies, some already in widespread use by businesses and general consumers, and others still being developed. Two categories predominate in electronic publishing: those in which information is stored in a centralized source and delivered to users by a telecommunications system, and those in which the data is stored on a disk, the most common being the floppy disk, which has become a primary means of distributing software and storing data. Because their storage capacity is relatively limited, however, electronic publishers have generally limited their use to delivering updates and topical segments of a full information bank. Removable hard disks can be used for a larger, complete database. *See* Computers, Desktop Publishing.

ELECTRONICS

That branch of science that includes the study of electrons and other carriers of electric charges as they function in gases, in vacuums, and in semiconductors as *electric currents* following closed paths, referred to as *electric circuits*. Electronics originated in the early twentieth century with the development of electron tubes that could store and amplify electrical charges and signals. Today, semiconductors have largely replaced electron tubes, while electronic circuits have been made smaller, more intricate, and more efficient, making possible such state-of-the art consumer products as microwave ovens, computers, videotapes, and many kinds of recording and viewing equipment. *See* Communications, Computers, Data Processing.

E-MAIL

See Electronic Mail.

EMBARGO

An order by a government or persons in authority to halt the exports and/or imports of goods and commodities, either totally or in regard to certain specified foreign lands. *See* Foreign Trade, Free Trade.

EMBEZZLEMENT

The fraudulent appropriation of money, property, or other valuables, usually through secretive means. *See* Business Law, Fraud.

EMINENT DOMAIN

The rights of government bodies at any level to acquire private property at a reasonable price that is deemed necessary for public use, or to authorize the taking of property by private companies when so doing benefits the community or the public. The term used for the acquisition of property in this manner is *condemnation,* at which time the owner must receive just compensation for the property. One of the earliest, and most famous, exercises of the right of eminent domain in America occurred in 1896 when the United States Supreme Court upheld the federal government's right to acquire the battlefield grounds at Gettysburg for a national cemetery.

EMOLUMENT

Payment for work done, services provided, or goods delivered. *See* Compensation.

EMPIRICAL

Based on experience, rather than on knowledge.

EMPLOYEE ASSISTANCE PROGRAM (EAP)

A formal program by an employer to assist employees with personal problems of many kinds, both through internal counseling and through referrals to outside counseling resources. The objective of EAPs is to improve internal harmony and increase the productivity of individuals by solving distracting personal problems. *See* Personnel Administration.

EMPLOYEE BENEFITS

Benefits programs play a vital role in the lives of employees and their families and have a marked influence on the popularity of an organization as a workplace and most often on its financial success in the long run. Most businesses function in an environment where an educated workforce expects to find a comprehensive benefits program. The absence of such a program or the installation of an inadequate program can seriously hinder the ability of an organization to attract and retain good personnel. Financial investments in sound employee benefits programs can be costly but also can be money well spent.

Benefits programs can be segmented into four components:

1. Legally required benefits, which are mandated by federal, state, or local law, and that are comprised of plans already well established. They include Social Security, worker's compensation, and compensation for unemployment.

2. Health and welfare benefits, which are provided to work in conjunction with statutory benefits to protect employees from financial hazards caused by situations both on and off the job. Under these benefits, employees receive compensation and/or care for personal setbacks such as: illness and medication requirements; disability; whether temporary or permanent; the need for short-term or long-term medical care; the need for dental care and related plates, fittings, or accessories; problems with the eyes or eyesight; accidental death or dismemberment; legal threats and litigation; or similar problems with dependents.

3. Retirement plans that are instituted to help ensure that employees are able to maintain their standards of living after leaving their jobs. Retirement plans fall into two categories: (1) Well-defined contribution

plans that provide employees with an accumulated account balance at the time of retirement; (2) Pensions or similar plans that provide employees with periodic payments according to a long-range income schedule.

4. Prerequisites, commonly known as "perks," which consist of any additional benefits an employer designates, either to substitute for increased salaries or to attract certain types of people (such as salespersons) to the company. Common perks are automobiles, club memberships, travel, larger offices, restaurant privileges, or the right to attend out of-town conventions and training seminars.

Another increasingly popular employee benefit is the profit-sharing plan. This is defined by the Small Business Administration as "a contribution plan in which the sponsoring employer has agreed to contribute a discretionary or set amount to the plan. Any contributions made to the plan are generally allocated pro rata to each participant's plan account based on compensation. The sponsoring employer makes no promise as to the dollar amount a participant will receive at retirement." The amount of the income depends upon a number of factors, including the size of the employee's own contribution, the employer's share that is added, and the earnings on the accumulating sum during the participant's employment with the sponsoring company. It is important for the employer to make it clear to employee participants that they bear the risk of investment—as they would in purchasing stocks independently—and that there is absolutely no guarantee covering the end results. *See* Employees, Human Resources, Labor, Personnel Relations.

EMPLOYEE RELATIONS

That segment of personnel or human relations in a large organization that is devoted to maintaining sound relationships between management and employees, and making available facilities and specialists for solving the personal and professional problems of employees. *See* Personnel Administration.

EMPLOYEE RETIREMENT INCOME SECURITY ACT

Legislation enacted to protect personnel nearing, and reaching, retirement status and to inform employees of their rights and expectations upon retirement. *See* Personnel Administration.

EMPLOYEE TURNOVER

The nature and extent to which employees join or depart from an organization. A high turnover rate is normally an indication that company management and/or personnel policies need improvements. *See* Business Administration, Management, Personnel Administration.

EMPLOYER IDENTIFICATION NUMBER (ID)

A number assigned to companies by the government to provide identification when communicating with federal tax bureaus or other agencies. *See* Taxation.

EMPLOYMENT

Over and beyond its basic definition, employment is a measure of the human input in relation to the manufacturing or production operations. It is generally accepted that increasing employment in a country is a sign of an expanding economy, while declining employment warns of lagging growth or a trade decline. *See* Economics.

EMPLOYMENT AND TRAINING REPORTER

A weekly bulletin published by the Bureau of National Affairs to provide technical assistance concerning the best utilization of the nation's human resources, including where and how to apply for employment and training funds and how to develop successful programs. *See* Periodicals.

EMPOWERMENT

A personnel theory that holds that individual motivation is increased and improved when employees are given opportunities to become more involved in their work and the decisions and goals that pertain. *See* Human Resources.

ENCROACHMENT

The usurpation by one party of the rights, possessions, or property of another party, whether stealthfully or openly, but generally in a gradual manner. *See* Business Law.

ENCUMBRANCE

A lien or restriction against property, whether real or personal. *See* Real Estate, Taxation.

ENDORSEMENT

In finance, the use of a signature on a check or other monetary instrument, certifying receipt of the face amount. *See* Banks and Banking.

ENDOWMENT

A gift or bequest, generally large, to an organization, most commonly a college or other educational institution.

ENERGY DEMAND

The requirements of a nation, state, or region for sources and resources in the field of energy, such as coal, oil, gas, or water power. *See* Supply and Demand.

ENTERPRISE

In business rhetoric, a company, firm, or other commercial entity, whether private or public, for profit or nonprofit. *See* Corporation, Partnership.

ENTITLEMENT AUTHORITY

Legal authorization for the payment of benefits to any person or organization meeting the requirements established by law. Examples of entitlements are Medicare, Medicaid, and public welfare programs.

ENTREPRENEUR

An individual who organizes, creates, and manages a business venture as a personal undertaking (derived from the French, *entreprendre,* to undertake.) *See* Small Business.

ENVIRONMENT

The term used to pinpoint numerous kinds of external factors that affect a company's operations but are not always controllable. The major environments of significance to management are ecological, geographical, political, social, judicial, technological, and economic. A complete and total understanding of these environments is essential in the guidance of companies affected critically by one or more of them. Environment is defined in the dictionary as: "The circumstances or conditions that surround one; surroundings; the totality of circumstances surrounding an organism or a group of organisms, especially the combination of external physical conditions that affect and influence the growth, development, and survival of organisms; the complex of social and cultural conditions affecting the nature of an individual or a community; and an artistic or theatrical work that surrounds or involves the audience." In nature, the term broadly covers all the surroundings of an individual organism or a community of organisms, by which is meant all the nonliving and living materials that play any role in an organism's existence, from soil and air and heat and light to what the organism feeds on, as well as the organisms that may feed on it. In the case of human beings, cultural factors may also be included in the term. The environmental science of *ecology* relates to the study of the interactions of organisms with their environment. Because of the complexity of the subject matter, workers in this field call upon a wide range of disciplines in the physical and life sciences—for example, geology, meteorology, and microbiology, among many others. These separate disciplines themselves often incorporate areas of environmental specialization, as, for example, environmental geology, which deals with the effects of human actions on land forms. The word environment is in fact most commonly encountered in association with the adverse effects of human activities on their surroundings. *See* Ecology, Pollution.

ENVIRONMENTAL CONSERVANCY

An alliance of individuals and organizations whose mutual objectives are to preserve the environment, protect global ecology, and combat pollution of all kinds. *See* Environment.

ENVIRONMENTAL ECONOMICS

That area of environmental operations that relates to the social costs of pollution, the depletion of resources, and ecological degeneration. A basic issue in environmental economics is the evaluation of the costs of pollution in terms of illnesses or damage to materials, lost time on the job, and the formation of such undesirable conditions as soot, dust, and the generation of acid rain and global warming. On the other side of the picture, however, consideration must be given to the economic, social, and employment benefits of maintaining factories and other facilities that contribute to, say, air and water pollution, and the consequences weighed. Is the pollution in any given case strong enough to discontinue an operation that will cause a loss of jobs and eliminate products that are needed by the public? Since many plants that cause environmental problems have only limited motivation to eliminate functions that cause pollution—fines, for example—some legislators have proposed rigid taxes on certain kinds of factories and other pollution-producing facilities, the amounts to be equivalent to the costs of neutralizing the pollution in question. Although this step seems only logical, environmental economists point out that determining the size of the tax would be almost impossible without huge expenditures of money just to determine many of causes and effects. As a step in the right direction, the EPA has formulated what are referred to as *emissions trading programs,* whereby companies that reduce emissions below stated levels in some of their plants are given credits to permit trade-offs in the form of above-level emissions in other facilities. *See* Pollution and other *Environmental* entries.

ENVIRONMENTAL HEALTH

A growing field that, since the 1960s, has been bringing together a number of scientific disciplines whose combined objectives are to analyze and act upon the physiological impact of pollution and other ecological problems on human and animal health. Biologists, physicists, chemists, and engineers, for example, have been working together, using state-of-the art equipment and methods to prevent and alleviate environment-related health problems. Entire new health organizations have thus come into being in recent years, joining specialists in medicine, science, engineering, and environmental research, among others. Along with this development has come the emergence or enlargement of governmental regulatory bureaus, such as the Environmental Protection Agency (EPA), the Occupational Safety and Health Administration (OSHA), the Food and Drug Administration (FDA), and many federal and state and local public health services—all of which monitor environmentally related problems and take action to solve them. Among the basic concerns of those agencies and personnel in this field are:

- *Communicable diseases,* which require extensive research and development programs to combat, such as those that led to the identification of pathogenic organisms as the cause of disease, or the germ theory that led to the discovery that disease could be prevented by vaccination and controlled by interrupting the transmission of pathogenic organisms to humans.

- *Air pollution,* whose dangers were not fully realized until it was diagnosed as the cause of numerous respiratory ailments and even, in some cases, deadly smogs that sickened or killed hundreds and sometimes thousands of people in contaminated regions. Particularly affected were the very young and the aged, with no age group spared from lung damage and such illnesses as asthma, bronchitis, emphysema, and lung cancer. The villains in this category were discovered to be carbon monoxide, sulfur, and nitrous oxides, and various particulates, such as soot in the air, caused by emissions from fossil fuels, vehicle exhausts, manufacturing plant processing, and the incineration of refuse. This field of environmental study has also directed great attention to the vast problems caused by smoking, both by smokers and those who are secondary inhalers of smoke.

- *Water pollution,* which includes not only the contamination of water from obvious sources, such as sewage disposal, but the more devious problems that lead to mercury poisoning from eating fish, or the chlorination of drinking water that may eliminate bacterial contaminants, as planned, but also increases the toxicity of chemical contaminants. One of the sinister facts about water pollution is that health problems in individuals or among population groups may not come to light until many months, or even years, after exposure to contaminated water.

■ *Food and drug contamination,* which may originate not only with improperly preserved or stored products, but from components deliberately formulated in the manufacturing process, such as coloring, flavoring, texturizing, or chemicals used to enhance the appearance or blending of ingredients. Certain additives or processing formulas were also found to increase the threat of cancer in consumers who regularly imbibed certain types of foods or medications, or used cosmetics that contained carcinogens. Increasing problems led to an amendment of the Food, Drug and Cosmetic Act in 1958, which prohibited any additive to food if research proved that it caused cancer in laboratory animals.

■ *Contaminants,* particularly fertilizers, pesticides, and other chemicals that infiltrate plant and animal foods with chemicals or deposits that are harmful to users, or in a secondary way to nonusers who may come into contact with them, or with residues or dusts. Such contaminants are most prevalent in agriculture, in certain nutrients used for feed, or in the preparation of soil for crops, or the treatment of crops to kill blight-causing pests. Some contaminants, unfortunately, have such long-term effects that their dangers are not suspected until many months, even years, later when humans and animals suffer mysterious ailments. Similar problems exist in the medical field, as was true in one of the most celebrated cases, in the 1960s, when a prescribed drug was taken by expectant mothers and was later discovered to cause malformations in newborn infants.

■ *Radiation,* an undesirable byproduct of the nuclear age, caused by unprotected radiation that was discovered, tardily, to be the cause of cancer in animals and humans exposed to it. A prime example is that of nuclear power plants, where radioactive decay have caused cancer, leukemia, and other kinds of genetic damage. Even the disposal of radioactive wastes has become a cause for alarm and has motivated atmospheric radiation testing on an international scale.

■ *Work-related environmental hazards,* such as those associated with exposures to harsh chemicals, burning processing operations, or the inhalation of asbestos, silicon, and coal dust. Most occupational diseases fall into one of two categories: the short-term kind, which are identified quickly after problems have alerted the authorities to a dangerous situation, and those of long duration, when workers are exposed for many months before any problems are suspected. Working environments, as well as others, are also being studied more stringently to determine the effects of loud or continuing noises on people exposed to them. Noise has been identified as the culprit in many cases of permanent, or temporary, hearing loss, speech impairment, and sleep disorders.

ENVIRONMENTAL PROTECTION AGENCY (EPA)

An independent agency in the executive branch of the U.S. government, established in 1970 to combat all forms of pollution, whether air, water, earth, noise, or radiation, especially through research, the institution of national standards, and widespread monitoring programs. EPA publishes professional papers and educational statements, and coordinates environmental activities with states, municipalities, and citizen's groups. *See* Environmental Conservancy, Pollution.

EQUAL EMPLOYMENT

The fundamental rights of an individual to be equal to all others in the matter of finding and holding employment, without regard to race, color, religion, sex, age, or ethnic origin. *See* Equal Employment Opportunity Commission.

EQUAL EMPLOYMENT OPPORTUNITY COMMISSION (EEOC)

A body created under the Civil Rights Act whose mission is to end discrimination based on race, color, sex, religion, age, or ethical origin in all personnel matters, such as recruiting, evaluating, hiring, promoting, compensating, training, and firing. The EEOC maintains field offices in all states and encourages and assists voluntary action by employers, unions, and employment agencies in the matter of providing equal opportunities and discouraging discrimination. *See* Equal Rights, Equal Rights Amendment.

EQUAL PAY ACT

See Equal Rights.

EQUAL RIGHTS

See Civil Rights, Civil Rights Acts.

EQUAL RIGHTS AMENDMENT (ERA)

An amendment to the Constitution that was first introduced in Congress in 1923, approved by the House of Representatives in 1971 and by the Senate in 1972, but which fell short of ratification after an extension to 1982. The purpose of the ERA was to give women sex discrimination protection not afforded by the equal protection clause of the Fourteenth Amendment, but was opposed on the grounds that (1) inequality between men and women is biologically structured and cannot be changed; (2) that the amendment would have an adverse impact on such social institutions as marriage and the family; and (3) that the amendment was not necessary because women already have all the rights they need under the protection of the Fifth and Fourteenth Amendments. *See* Civil Rights, Civil Rights Acts.

EQUILIBRIUM

In economic matters, the factors and conditions that tend to maintain the state of the economy in proper balance. *See* Economics.

EQUITABLE CONVERSION

A procedure that makes it possible, lawfully and commercially, to convert real property into personal property. *See* Real Estate.

EQUITY

In finance, the capital furnished by the owners or stockholders of a business firm. It is distinguished from debt, or funds supplied by the firm's lenders and other creditors. On the firm's financial statements, equity is equal to its net worth. When the company's debts have been paid, the owners of equity are entitled to all the remaining earnings and property of the company. Equity owners take a greater risk than do other investors. If a company is successful, the owners will participate in its gains; if it suffers losses, they may lose their investment. Because they have first call upon a company's earnings and assets, creditors take less risk; their claims must be paid before stockholders may receive anything. A corporation's equity capital consists of all the funds paid into the corporation upon the issuance of shares of stock and the part of the company's net earnings that is retained in the business after dividends have been paid. *See* Accounting, Investments, Profits.

EQUITY CAPITAL

That portion of the capital of a business that is furnished by its shareholders.

EQUITY FINANCING

The sale of stock by a corporation. *See* Corporation.

ERGONOMICS

The specialized strategy for matching employees and machinery, tools, or other equipment to improve efficiency and increase production. Known popularly as the "science of work," ergonomics is a technological function that recognizes both the limitations and capabilities of humans in the application of designs for machinery and facilities of many kinds. This science evolved from earlier time-and-motion studies, and what was then called *human factors engineering,* in military installations and, later, in industry. The study of ergonomics has since found many applications in the design of consumer products and equipment, such as automobiles, computers, and power tools. It has also been a boon to the designers and manufacturers of equipment for the handicapped. *See* Industrial Design, Industrial Management, Personnel Administration.

ESCALATION CLAUSE

A specific monetary amount or proportion by which a stated contract price can be adjusted up or down if certain contingencies take place, such as price changes for raw materials, increased labor costs, or tax revisions. *See* Contingency, Contracts.

ESCAPE CLAUSE

A provision in a contract or other legal agreement that permits one or more parties to withdraw therefrom or to moderate commitments and responsibilities when changes or stipulated conditions exist. *See* Agreement, Contract.

ESCHEAT

The revoking of title and reversion of property to the government by failure of the party legally entitled to hold the property to lay claim to it.

ESCROW

The situation that exists when something of worth is held in trust by an individual not party to the matter until such time as clearly stated conditions are met. *See* Trust.

ESTATE

The title or right a party has been granted to property, as distinguished from the property itself. In traditional law, the word referred to property in land, but courts in the United States have ruled that the word estate covers everything a person owns, both real and personal. A common form of estate is the life estate, in which the possessor has an interest only in his or her lifetime. Afterwards, it passes to a designated person or reverts to the former owner or to his or her heirs. An estate may be held for the benefit of another party, as in the case of a *trust,* in which the *trustee* has legal title to the trust property, but the beneficiary of the trust has the equitable estate and is entitled to the exclusive benefit of the trust administered by the trustee. Another variation is the contingent estate, which is an interest that may or may not take effect in the future upon the occurrence of a certain event, such as the birth of an heir. An expectant estate is one not presently possessed by a person, but which may be possessed in the future. Similarly, a future estate is one that a person receives in the future, usually upon the death of the present owner. *See* Beneficiary, Estate Planning, Trust, Trustee.

ESTATE PLANNING

The legal and financial organization of an individual's affairs in such a way as to facilitate and expedite the passage of the assets in question to one or more beneficiaries with minimal taxes or legal entanglements. *See* Estate.

ESTIMATED INCOME

Income that is predicted to be available in the future over a designated period of time; data that help to improve the accuracy of budget planning proposals and projections. *See* Accounting.

ETHICS

In business and industry, the observance of principles that individuals and companies morally owe to the public and to all concerned directly or indirectly with the business and its operations. Today's concept of ethics is based on numerous previous philosophies going back to ancient times regarding studies and evaluations of human conduct in light of moral principles and the individual's standard of conduct in the matter of social obligations and responsibilities. Modern ethical theories are rooted in the perceptions of John Dewey, for whom morality was associated with personal experience, and of G. E. Moore, who conjectured an immediate awareness of what was morally right. *See* Business Ethics, Business Law, Morals.

ETHNIC CATEGORIES

Those classifications of individuals that relate to race, faith, national origins, and the like. *See* Civil Rights, Racial Discrimination.

EUROCURRENCY

Currency that is on deposit outside of its country of origin, for example, dollars on deposit at an offshore banking facility. Companies in international markets find that, in many instances, borrowing in Eurobanks can be handled more flexibly and at less cost. Such deposits are also known as *external currencies* or *international currencies. See* Currency, Foreign Trade.

EURODOLLARS

The name for U.S. currency on deposit in foreign banks, customarily in Europe. *See* Currency, Foreign Trade.

EUROPEAN COMMUNITY

The economic alliance, previously called the *European Economic Community,* which was founded in the late 1950s in order to encourage active trading and cooperation among EC's members. Popularly known as the *Common Market,* EC is an intergovernmental body of a dozen Western European nations, including Belgium, Denmark, France, Germany, Greece, Ireland, Italy, Luxembourg, the Netherlands, Portugal, Spain, and the United Kingdom, with its own substructures and decision-making provisions. The objective has been defined as the endeavor "to construct a united Europe through peaceful means and create conditions for economic growth, social cohesion among the European peoples, and for greater political integration and cooperation among governments." The member nations have established common policies relating to foreign trade, agriculture, fisheries, transportation, international financing and currency, energy, environmental protection, education, and research and development. The European Monetary System (EMS), established to create financial stability in Western Europe, maintains stable exchange rates among the member states. *See* Common Market, Foreign Trade.

EVALUATION TECHNIQUES

In most forms of research, the procedures and stratagems decided upon and used to assess the findings, prior to reaching a conclusion and reporting. *See* Research.

EXCESS CONTRIBUTIONS

Those contributions of a nonprofit or tax-exempt organization that are in excess of amounts allowed and therefore cannot be claimed as tax exemptions. *See* Exemptions, Nonprofit Organizations.

EXCHANGE RATES

The prices or rates at which the currency of one country can readily be converted into that of another country. Exchange rates play a critical part in the economy of countries that are engaged in worldwide business because even minor fluctuations, if unheeded, can have an enormous impact on profits and losses. *See* Central Banks, Gold Standard, International Monetary Fund, Money.

EXCISE TAX

A tax on the production, fabrication, manufacture, sale, or consumption of a commodity. Also referred to as a *license tax*.

EXCLUSIONARY CLAUSE

A mutually acceptable statement in a contract that limits the actions that one party can take if the other party fails to fulfill the provisions of the contract. *See* Contracts.

EXECUTIVE COMPENSATION

The total amount of money paid to an executive, including salary, bonuses, and other financial recompense, but excluding warrants or options to purchase the corporation's stock. *See* Compensation, Warrants.

EXECUTIVE ORDERS

A series of presidential executive orders in the 1960s, that prohibited employment discrimination because of age, race, color, religion, national origin, and other personal factors. *See* Civil Rights.

EXECUTOR

In the execution of a will, the party appointed to administer the affairs of the deceased. *See* Wills.

EXEMPT INCOME

See Exemption.

EXEMPTION

In taxation, a sum that, for one valid reason or another, is not taxable, such as the income required for the sole support of a dependent. *See* Taxation.

EXPECTANCY THEORY

In business planning, the concept that motivation is determined by two factors: that any actions taken will be followed by a predetermined outcome and that the results will be realized in terms of the attractiveness or offensiveness of that consequence. *See* Business Administration, Management.

EXPEDITE

In industrial terms, to facilitate and speed up manufacturing production and/or delivery of products and materials.

EXPERIMENTAL INVESTIGATION

An area of marketing research in which a number of options and variables are compared with the objective of determining the most effective method of selling and distributing merchandise or offering services. This form of research is conducted both in the laboratory and in the field. Sometimes referred to as exploratory research.

EXPERT WITNESS

In legal court proceedings, a witness who is either very knowledgeable or experienced in a stated subject field or one who, because of circumstances or chance, happened to witness a crime or some event connected with the crime. *See* Business Law.

EXPLOITATION

In the positive sense, taking advantage of a situation in which it is possible to capitalize on one's position, knowledge, or ownership of something valuable in order to realize personal gain. In the negative sense, taking unfair advantage of circumstances or events to make personal gains at the expense of others. *See* Marketing, Merchandising.

EXPORT-IMPORT BANK

Popularly known as Eximbank, this institution was originally formed by the Export-Import Bank Act of 1945 to compensate American exporters for subsidies granted to competitors by foreign governments. Eximbank is now considered to be the primary source of export credit for American companies. *See* Banks and Banking, Foreign Trade.

EXPORT MARKETING

Promoting and selling goods and services to foreign markets. *See* International Marketing.

EXPRESS WARRANTY

The legally binding statement made by a seller to a buyer that the products, goods, or services are as stated and described and that replacements or refunds will be made if the warranty is broken. *See* Guarantee, Warranty.

EXTENDED COVERAGE

When referring to business and industrial insurance policies, the coverage of risks over and beyond those commonly covered in policies of the type being underwritten. *See* Insurance.

EXTERNAL FINANCING

The procedure of approaching financial sources outside of the company to provide funds that internally might have been appropriated from profits or from the sale of capital assets. *See* Assets, Capital.

EXTRADITION

The surrender of an alleged lawbreaker by one political jurisdiction to another jurisdiction having authority to judge the charges and, if necessary, try the case. There are two kinds of extradition: *interstate,* the surrender of the accused party between states, under the federal and state statutes concerned, and *international,* under the judicial terms of the countries that are involved. Extradition is often denied by the country in which the person or persons charged may be temporarily residing—most countries, for example, generally will grant asylum to political offenders rather than surrender them, and extradition will usually be barred unless the same or a similar crime is deemed punishable in both of the nations involved. *See* Business Law, Political Asylum.

EXTRAORDINARY ITEMS

In accounting procedures, items in the records that are unusual in nature, as well as infrequent in occurrence, and hence are presented net of tax income effect separately in income statements. *See* Accounting, Bookkeeping.

EXTRATERRITORIALITY

In international law, the principle that permits foreign citizens or international organizations to be excused from certain laws or legislation of a host nation. For example, diplomatic missions and embassies are exempt in foreign countries on the grounds that they are part of the territory of, and under the jurisdiction of, their own governments. The kinds of individuals who benefit from extra territoriality are heads of state and their representatives who frequently travel abroad, members of armed forces assigned to foreign duty, government ships in foreign waters, and United Nations personnel. *See* Diplomatic Relations, International Law.

EXTRINSIC MOTIVATION

Personal incentives on the job that are not part of the work itself or any enjoyment deriving from the assignment. A person who works for monetary rewards, for example, is extrinsically motivated. *See* Compensation.

Fabrication

In manufacturing and construction, the term used to describe components and parts that are produced and reassembled for quicker and easier installation at job sites. *See* Manufacturing, Production.

Face Value

The declared value on the face of paper currency, a check, treasury bill, certificate, or other instrument of worth. *See* Currency.

Facsimile (FAX)

A machine capable of instantly transmitting and receiving copies of printed or pictorial matter over telephone lines. Although considered a recent invention, FAX transmissions in various forms have been in use since the early 1900s and leaped into prominence with the development of sophisticated scanning techniques in computer and communications equipment and the establishment of standards that made it possible for facsimile machines to communicate with each other over telephone lines. Transmission is made possible when a document is fed into the machine, scanned by mirror/lens devices or diodes, and then translated by a receiving machine into patterns of gray and black on white spaces. The resultant image is then printed out on heat-sensitive paper, using procedures similar to those for copying machines. *See* Communications, Digital, Modem.

Factor

Administratively, an individual or firm financing and coordinating transactions of business.

Factoring

The sale of a producer's accounts receivable to an agent, or factor, which undertakes to collect them; this procedure is common in the manufacture and marketing of textiles, furniture, and hardware. Factoring concerns differ from other commercial or financial companies in that they have little capability for resolving credit problems. *See* Marketing.

FACTORY STRUCTURE

This term refers to a system that is the most sophisticated in the chain of manufacturing and production, the others (in order of advancement) being: the cottage industry, which is mainly family oriented; the crafts, in which artisans, working independently or in small shops, create specialized products; and the letting-out operation, in which materials, and sometimes equipment, are loaned to workers and specialists who are charged with processing and producing them according to exact specifications. The factory structure differs from the other forms of industrial organization in the following ways, among others: It brings workers together in a plant wholly or largely assigned to the manufacturing process; it requires collaboration and coordination in the work force; and it utilizes power-driven equipment that is too heavy or extensive for transportation to outside installations and locales. The factory structure harks back to the Industrial Revolution of the eighteenth century, first in the United Kingdom, then continental Europe, and ultimately the Americas, and had become predominant throughout all industry in the United States in the decade following the Civil War. Over and beyond its industrial and economic force, the factory structure has been pinpointed as one of the major influences in the social and political structures of the civilized world as well. It was responsible, for example, with the rise of the capitalistic system, for the gradual decline in the ranks of the artisan and craftsman, the emergence of a rapidly escalating labor force, the urbanization of America, and the proliferation of new types of mass-produced products available to millions upon millions of consumers. *See* Manufacturing, Production.

FAIR LABOR STANDARDS ACT

The federal law that regulates the amounts and types of wages paid to employees by companies that are engaged in interstate commerce. *See* Labor/Management.

FAIR MARKET PRICE

The price a willing purchaser would pay and a willing seller world accept in an open and unrestricted market. *See* Competition.

FAIR TRADE ACTS

Regulations passed by various states and other government bodies with the intention of forcing wholesalers, retailers, and other sellers to maintain designated prices on select merchandise. *See* Competition, Retailing, Wholesaling.

FAIR TRADE AGREEMENT

An agreement mutually acceptable to manufacturers and their customers or distributors, setting minimum resale prices on the trademarked merchandise of the manufacturer. *See* Competition.

FAMILY CORPORATION

A corporation whose stock is held, for the most part, by members of one family or another such closely knit group. *See* Corporations.

FEASIBILITY STUDY

A formal evaluation of a designated project, to establish its validity and practicality in order to make decisions whether to proceed, scrap the undertaking entirely, or revise it. *See* Research and Development.

FEATHERBEDDING

The practice by labor unions of employing a larger-than-necessary work force than is considered essential by management for the assignment at hand. An example is the custom of the imposition of rules whereby employers are forced to hire duplications of workers or unnecessarily lengthen the period of time in which work is performed. A classic case was the insistence of unions that firemen continue to ride diesel locomotives, which had no fires to tend. Some union officials, while admitting questionable practices, defend them as the only way to protect their members when jobs are threatened by technological advances too quickly and too extensively. *See* Labor/Management, Labor Unions.

FEDERAL ADVISORY COUNCIL

A commission of the Federal Reserve system that was established to advise its board of governors on major developments and operations in momentary and fiscal matters. *See* Federal Reserve System.

FEDERAL AVIATION ADMINISTRATION (FAA)

As an arm of the U.S. Department of Transportation, this agency is responsible for regulating commercial air transportation, mainly by mandating safety standards for aircraft and medical standards for personnel, maintaining communications and control equipment at airports, testing navigation equipment and aircraft, providing technical services, assisting in the planning of new or remodeled airports, and investigating plane accidents. *See* Transportation.

FEDERAL COMMUNICATIONS COMMISSION (FCC)

The federal body authorized to regulate all interstate and foreign communications systems that originate in the United States. As an independent U.S. government agency, it also grants licenses to radio and television broadcasters, assigns frequencies, and monitors broadcasts to make sure its regulations are followed. The FCC maintains three basic arms: The Mass Media Bureau, which regulates radio and television broadcasting; The Common Carrier Bureau, which regulates public services such as telephone, telegraph, and satellite communications; and the The Private Radio Bureau, which regulates police, taxicab, and other vehicular radios, as well as citizens band radio. The FCC's Mass Media Bureau has also been instrumental in such matters as expediting the development of FM and color-television broadcasting, monitoring TV advertising, and enforcing the equal-time provision to ensure equitable noncommercial broadcast time to political candidates. *See* Broadcasting, Communications, Media.

FEDERAL DEPOSIT INSURANCE CORPORATION (FDIC)

The agency of the United States government that insures bank deposits and pursues measures to uphold the solvency of the nation's banks and protect depositors. All national banks are required to belong, and most state banks are voluntary members. An example of the potency of the FDIC was the case in 1989 when the Resolution Trust Corporation and the Savings Association Insurance Fund were formed under the FDIC to try to rescue shaky savings associations, which reached a total of nearly 500 insolvent thrift institutions in just the following year. *See* Banks and Banking.

FEDERAL HOME LOAN MORTGAGE CORPORATION

An institution formed by the government to help maintain the availability of mortgage credit for residential buyers and to develop an active nationwide secondary market in conventional mortgages. *See* Mortgages.

FEDERAL HOUSING ADMINISTRATION (FHA)

The branch of the government charged with improving housing standards and conditions, providing adequate systems of mortgage insurance, and circulating information to the public about housing needs and potentials. FHA was founded in the mid-1930s as an agency to insure mortgages and thus provide banks and other lending institutions with a guarantee that their housing loans would be adequately secured. Equally important, FHA injected a stimulus in the housing industry at a time when almost no new homes were being built. In 1965, the FHA was incorporated into the new Department of Housing and Urban Development (HUD) to continue its goals as a mortgage guarantor and to widen its areas of responsibility, particularly in regard to multifamily dwellings and public housing. *See* Mortgage Insurance, Mortgages.

FEDERAL LAND BANKS

A farmer-owned system of banks supported by land bank associations through which borrowers can apply for mortgages and other financial assistance, particularly in regard to farmlands, rural real estate, ranches, and the like. *See* Banks and Banking.

FEDERAL RESERVE BANKS

A dozen regional reserve banks created by the Federal Reserve System and operating under its authority. Nicknamed the *Fed,* this is the central bank of the United States, with two main functions: (1) to hold deposits of the commercial banks and operate a nationwide check-clearing system; and to (2) serve as the basic controller of credit in the American economy, in effect determining the size of the money supply and the ease or difficulty of borrowing. The Federal Reserve is divided into 12 privately controlled banks located in Atlanta, Boston, Chicago, Cleveland, Dallas, Kansas City, Minneapolis, New York City, Philadelphia, Richmond, St. Louis, and San Francisco, each responsible for a specified district. The governors of the Federal Reserve Board and the presidents of the 12 Federal Reserve banks control the issuance of currency, determine monetary policies, oversee banks that are members of the Federal Reserve System, and regulate the functions of bank-holding companies. The Federal Reserve also serves as the government's official buyer and seller of foreign currencies, holds gold deposited in the United States by other countries, and handles purchases and sales of U.S. government securities on behalf of foreign governments. Almost half of all the commercial banks in the United States belong to the Federal Reserve. *See* Banks and Banking.

FEDERAL RESERVE SYSTEM

The system established by the government of the United States to establish a network of banks in key locations and oversee banking practices throughout the country. *See* Federal Reserve Banks.

FEDERAL TRADE COMMISSION (FTC)

The agency established to promote free and fair competition in the marketplace and the enforcement of antitrust laws and other legislation affecting the free enterprise system. The FTC takes action against monopolies, restraints on trade, and unfair trade practices by issuing advices for businesses to comply with voluntarily and by taking legal action in cases where legal violations are flagrant. Legislation monitored by the FTC includes the the Federal Trade Commission Act, anti-trust acts, the Fair Packaging and Labeling Act, the Truth in Lending Act, and the Fair Credit Reporting Act. *See* Competition, Free Enterprise.

FEEDBACK

In personnel parlance, the degree to which the assignments of a job result in the compilation of information that can help employees to evaluate their performance at work. In technology, feedback refers to a system, process, or machine in which part of the output is fed back to the input in order to regulate the operation. When feedback reinforces the trend of any system, it is said to be *positive*. When it opposes the trend of the system, it is called *negative* and is usually employed to help stabilize operations. *See* Personnel Administration.

FEE SIMPLE

The outright ownership of real estate and other property without restrictions or encumbrances. *See* Real Estate.

FIBER OPTICS

The channeled transmission of light along glass fibers as thin as spider webs, in a manner that prevents the light from escaping through a process of internal reflection. This technology has its greatest commercial impact in the field of telecommunications, where optical fibers make it possible to transmit audio, video, and data information as coded light pulses. This use of light has a number of advantages over other methods of transmission, including vastly increased communications-carrying capacity, fewer transmission failures, lower cost of basic materials, smaller cable size, and strong immunity from interference. Other applications include the simple transmission of light in tight spaces—as in intricate internal surgical operations— image guiding for remote viewing, and sensory perception in the measurement of various properties of materials, structures, or living things. *See* Communications, Telecommunications.

FIDELITY BOND

In insurance, a category of coverage designed to reimburse employers for losses caused by the dishonest acts of employees. *See* Insurance.

FIDUCIARY

An individual or institution charged with the custody of securities or other instruments of value. A fiduciary is also described as one who administers the affairs of another party in confidence. *See* Trust, Trustee.

FIELD SURVEY

A sampling by a marketing group of opinions and data on location, at the premises of customers, consumers, and others pertinent to the interests of the marketer. *See* Marketing, Research.

FIFTEENTH AMENDMENT

Ratified in 1870, this amendment prohibits federal or state governments from infringing on a citizen's right to vote "on account of race, color, or previous condition of servitude." Although it gave the federal government power to legislate qualifications for voting, a right formerly left to the states, it had little impact until after World War II, particularly with the passage of the Civil Rights Act of 1957 and the Voting Rights Act of 1965, which were designed to eliminate discrimination in voting and increase voter registration among minorities. *See* Civil Rights, Discrimination.

FIFTH AMENDMENT

A provision of the Bill of Rights intended to protect persons accused of crimes and prohibit the deprivation of life, liberty, or property without due process of law. This amendment was responsible for the origins of the phrase "take the fifth," referring to its specification that individuals have the right to refuse to answer questions in court proceedings on the grounds of possible self-incrimination. *See* Business Law.

FILTERING

The procedure when using a communications network of screening information and submitting only those facts selected. *See* Communications.

FINANCE

As seen from the corporate viewpoint, the planning and acquisition of funds and the management of these funds for various operations. There are three main areas of financing: (1) Short term, meaning for a year or less, for which sources are trade credit, commercial bank loans, and commercial paper. Trade credit is a short-term debt that results from credit sales, an important source of funds for many firms. Commercial bank loans are another source, particularly for firms that need to finance seasonal increases in inventories. Larger companies often obtain short-term funds by selling commercial paper, unsecured promissory notes, usually issued in large denominations, with interest rates that are competitive with those of other short-term loans. (2) Intermediate term, for periods of one to five years, often in the form of term loans from commercial banks and life-insurance companies and covered by a contract in which the borrower agrees to repay the principal and interest over the relevant period, usually in installments. (3) Long term, for which permanent funds are obtained by selling securities, either equity or stock, or bonds. The management of funds is a demanding and critical obligation of any business administration, since a company must allocate its available funds among various uses on the basis of financial plans. Such plans assume that the funds spent will produce sufficient profits in order to pay the interest on debt capital and to earn a satisfactory income to the owners on their equity capital. Another management responsibility is the strict supervision of a company's surplus funds, commonly invested in commercial paper or short-term notes that pay interest. Purposeful evaluation and planning are necessary to assure that all funds are protected and will be available when and where they are needed. *See* Bonds, Equity, Financial Accounting, Financial Planner, Securities.

FINANCIAL ACCOUNTING

That aspect of accounting that focuses particularly on corporations large and small that rely on periodic reviews and statements in order to protect capital, solicit investors, and comply with government regulations at all levels. The accountant's principal duty is to compile figures that relate to such financial matters as profits, losses, costs, tax liabilities, and other debts, and to present them to the firm's management in a form that is consistent and readily understood. For companies that offer securities for sale to the public, accountants also prepare regular reports to outsiders who are concerned with the company's financial health: investors, brokers, creditors, and the like. At the end of each fiscal year, the published annual report of a corporation must include the judgment of an outside independent accountant, called an *auditor*, as to its accuracy. These reports, the major communication a company has with stockholders, are prepared in accordance with rules known as Generally Accepted Accounting Principles and focus on a *balance sheet* comparing the company's assets and liabilities. Assets include cash, accounts receivable, the cash value of inventories, and the worth of property, plant, and equipment.

Liabilities include company debts, the amount of stock held by investors, and the amount of retained earnings, or assets, that are invested back into the company, rather than disbursed in the form of dividends.

Although some balance-sheet items, such as cash, are easily measured for reporting, the value of others, such as plant and equipment, must be estimated. Plant and equipment are usually represented by figures that are reduced by a certain proportion each year. The percentage of depreciation varies according to the depreciation method used, but almost every item of plant and equipment is subject to depreciation, which is listed by accountants as an expense. Inventory valuation is also subject to a variety of accounting methods, since many inventory items cannot be specifically costed. The statement of changes in financial position shows the sources and applications of working capital and indicates whether the company generated sufficient cash to fund operations, or whether borrowing was necessary. The income statement shows the results of a company's operations over time, as well as for the current period. Income is the difference between revenues and expenses. Accountants usually report revenues at the time when they are earned, and expenses only when they are incurred, rather than when they are paid out. The practice of relating current expense with current revenues earned is called *accrual accounting* and is fundamental to almost all accounting systems. The simpler cash method, which records revenues when cash for sales is received and expenses when cash is disbursed, rarely presents a true picture of an organization. The statement of *retained earnings* and *stockholder's equity* demonstrates for investors what has happened with their ownership in the company, how earnings and new stock issuance have increased its worth, and what dividends were paid. Each of these reports will contain figures for previous quarters and years, as well as for the current period, providing a way of comparing present and past company performance. *See* Accounting, Assets, Auditing, Liabilities, Stockholder's Equity, Retained Earnings.

FINANCIAL PLANNER

A professional who is engaged in providing personal counseling to individuals or commercial counseling to businesses in matters relating to investments, budgets, retirement, banking, and other monetary planning. Financial planners assist clients by evaluating their financial history, reviewing the available options, preparing financial plans, identifying problem areas, and advising them about other sources of financial assistance to solve any current or future needs. *See* other *Financial* entries.

FINANCIAL POSITION

The status and monetary health of an organization, as described in a formal document, combining the assets and liabilities of its balance sheets. *See* Accounting.

FINANCIAL RISK

When referring to corporations, the risk of either insolvency or undesirable fluctuations in earnings because of excessive costs, interest payments, and increasing competition, among other things. *See* Risk.

FINANCIAL STATEMENT

Any supporting statement in accounting procedures that provides data about a company's financial condition, including balance sheets, income reports, or summary of funds. The basic statements used to document the financial status of a company are the *income and expense statement* and the *balance sheet,* which are prepared periodically. Before preparing the financial statements, a trial balance is made to be certain that the debits equal credits. If a particular trial balance shows that certain items are losing value as a result of age and use, then this loss, called *depreciation,* must be calculated and recorded prior to preparing the statements. Depreciation lessens the value of the asset and increases the firm's expenses, therefore a depreciation entry must be made in the general journal and then posted. Another expense that must be recorded before financial statements are prepared is the value of the office supplies that have been used, as well as insurance, interest, and any other prepaid expense. Other entries of record include bad debts, unpaid taxes, salary payments that are overdue or not yet recorded, inventory losses, and damages. The income-and-expense statement reports any change in the owners' equity as a result of current operations and shows the net income the company has earned in the interval since financial statements were last prepared. *See* Accounting, Annual Report, Balance Sheet.

FINDER

An individual who usually is not in the employ of a company, but who seeks out clients or customers voluntarily, in return for a stated fee, a commission, or some other form of compensation. *See* Broker.

FIRM COMMITMENT

The agreement by one party in a contract to honor certain obligations, whether monetary or otherwise, in a particular way and on a specified date. *See* Agreement, Contract, Warranty.

FIRST AMENDMENT

This initial provision of the Bill of Rights prohibits Congress from passing legislation that restricts freedom of religion, speech, or the press, or the right to assemble peaceably and to petition the government for redress of grievances. *See* Civil Rights.

FISCAL PERIOD

A period of time used by companies as their accounting and reporting cycles. Many corporations use a *fiscal year,* ending, say, in the spring, rather than a calendar period ending in December. *See* Accounting, Annual Report.

FISCAL POLICIES

Policies established by the federal government with respect to such economic matters as spending, debt management, or taxes, with the intention of upgrading the country's economic goals, particularly with respect to the gross national product, employment, pricing stability, and monetary equilibrium. A related subject is *monetary policy,* which monitors government spending and those factors that relate to employment and unemployment, as well as inflation, in the economy. *See* Financial Accounting.

FIXED ASSETS

Capital assets. *See* Capital.

FIXED CHARGES

Also called *fixed costs,* those expenses that remain stable in a production operation and do not vary with the size or extent of the manufacturing processes. *See* Production.

FLAT RATE

A special rate charged for a job or service in lieu of the cost that would be charged on an hourly or per-unit basis. *See* Package Rate.

FLEXIBLE MANUFACTURING SYSTEM (FMS)

A production system that is completely automated, can function with very little attention by personnel, and can be calibrated to revise, increase, or decrease the operations being performed. The components of an FMS network include such things as computers, robots, calibrating instruments, and remote controls. *See* Manufacturing, Production.

FLOWCHART

A diagram, chart, or other graphic presentation that shows the course and nature of an activity in relation to other activities in a company program. Flowcharts may show things that are tangible, such as a fabricating and assembly line or that are abstract, such as profits and losses or positive and negative reactions to an advertising campaign. *See* Graphics, Manufacturing.

FOCUS GROUP

A conference of people, from a few to ten or more, who are interviewed by a moderator, sometimes called a *facilitator,* who not only asks questions, but motivates individual and group discussions on a selected subject. Such groups are useful in marketing research, for example, and might be in session to discuss the merits and drawbacks of a new consumer product that is being tested and that the participants have sampled. *See* Marketing, Research.

FOOD AND DRUG ADMINISTRATION (FDA)

The government agency charged with authority over the safety and purity of foods, drugs, and related merchandise, such as cosmetics, dental cleaning products, or the containers used for such products, and the operation of the National Center for Toxicological Research. The FDA is associated with such legislation as the Pure Food and Drug Act, the Food, Drug, and Cosmetic Act, and the Orphan Drug Act. *See* Consumer Safety, Product Safety.

FORCED SALE

Any sale of real estate, property, merchandise, or equipment that is made under a court order or other mandate. *See* Business Law.

FORD FOUNDATION

A private foundation established by Henry Ford and his family, which today has assets of some $6 billion and that helps to support philanthropic programs in six fields: education and culture, government and public policy, human rights, international affairs, rural poverty , and urban poverty. Two out of every three grants are domestic and the rest are international. *See* Foundations, Grants.

FORECASTING

In financial planning, a realistic evaluation of long-range profits and losses, as based on records from the past, present statistics, and future predictions. *See* Financial Planning.

FORECLOSURE

The legal term for the action taken by a lender under the terms of a mortgage or deed or other obligation, in which property is expropriated for the purpose of selling it and applying the proceeds of the sale to payment of the defaulted debt. *See* Deed, Mortgage.

FOREIGN EXCHANGE

A transaction in which the currency of one country is exchanged for that of another at a predetermined rate, the values of which are determined by a number of factors, including the balance of payments of the nations involved and the relative supply and demand of the currencies in the foreign exchange market. *See* Balance Of Payments, Currency, International Monetary System. *See also* the back-of-the-book Supplement, "Foreign Currencies" on page 446.

FORFEITURE

See Default.

FORMAT

The graphic arrangement of information in a predetermined manner so that the specifics can be quickly and easily interpolated at a later date. *See* Charts, Graphics.

FORMULA TRANSLATION (FORTRAN)

A form of computer language applied in technological areas, particularly mathematical, engineering, and scientific problem solving. Developed as a medium for simplifying scientific programming, FORTRAN was one of the first computer languages to be machine-independent and requires very little data-processing time. Hence, it is particularly useful in undertaking lengthy scientific computations. *See* Computers, Data Processing.

FOUNDATIONS

Institutions, usually private, that distribute private wealth for the public good by offering grants to other nonprofit organizations and individuals engaged in social, educational, charitable, or religious activities. The basic foundations are: *independent,* relying on financial support from a single source, such as an individual or family; *operational,* which make few grants but implement plans and programs administered by their own staffs; *communal,* which derive funds from many donors, usually make grants locally, and are governed by boards whose members are from the immediate community; *corporate,* which are funded by profit-making companies but are independent; and *federal,* which make grants in science, the arts, and humanities from appropriations that are approved by Congress. *See* Nonprofit, Philanthropies.

FOURTH AMENDMENT

The measure, which originated with the Bill of Rights, that guarantees freedom from unreasonable search and seizure and certain other prearrest activities by law enforcement officials, without "probable cause" or a valid search warrant. In recognition of the arrival of the electronic age, the Supreme Court broadened the prohibition against wiretapping, which is now illegal without a valid warrant. *See* Bill of Rights.

FOURTH ESTATE

The phrase used to describe the press, the journalistic profession, or its members. It originated when the noted Scottish historian and essayist Thomas Carlyle wrote that the reporters' gallery in the English Parliament had been called "a Fourth Estate more important by far than the other three estates of Parliament: the peers, bishops, and commons." *See* Journalism.

FRANCHISE

A business enterprise that is established under the authority and jurisdiction of a parent company, known as a *franchiser,* and subject to the latter's operational policies, procedures, and stipulations. The concept of franchising dates back to mediaeval times when Lords of the land granted the right to one of their knights to govern part of their domain. Markets and fairs were also conducted under franchise, as were certain other commercial activities. Today the terms of a franchise contract may include such items as rates and services to be provided by the grantee, payments to the grantor, and provisions for termination of the franchise. Municipalities grant franchises to public utility companies giving them monopolies in electrical, gas, or telephone services but reserving the right to regulate them. Common forms of business in which franchises thrive are retail operations, hotels and motels, fast food chains, printing, photocopying, mailing services, automobile dealerships, and greeting card shops. The franchiser furnishes the franchisee with its name and trademark, architectural design, and operating procedures. Approximately one out of every three dollars in the retail field goes to a franchise operation. *See* Entrepreneur, Franchisee, Small Business.

FRANCHISEE

The individual(s) or firm that consents to operate a franchise from a parent company, under a license with exclusive rights to sell products or perform services within a designated geographical territory. *See* Franchise.

FREEDOM OF INFORMATION ACT

Legislation requiring that the records of U.S. government agencies be made available to the public, generally within a period of two weeks, to the individual or organization requesting it. Agencies can actually be sued for withholding data without cause. There are a number of exemptions, however, including information related to national security, trade secrets, investigatory files, and classified data. The Freedom of Information Act was later supplemented by the Privacy Act of 1974, which requires federal agencies to provide individuals with any information in their files relating to them and to correct erroneous entries. *See* Communications, Civil Rights.

FREE ENTERPRISE

See Capitalism.

FREE MARKET

A market that merchandise moves into and out of with few, if any, restrictions, unhampered by tariffs, duties, taxes, or other trade barriers. *See* Common Market.

FREE ON BOARD

A delivery contract that places the full responsibility with the seller of materials and merchandise until they have been safely and securely placed aboard a ship. *See* Shipping.

FREE PORT

An area at a seaport, airport, or other transportation terminal that has been designated for the sale and/or handling of duty-free merchandise. Sometimes referred to as a *foreign trade zone* or *free zone.*

FREE TRADE

Trade between nations that is conducted without tariffs, customs duties, or other internation restrictions, a concept that originated as a reaction against mercantilism in the eighteenth century. Economists of the day asserted that international trade would flourish under a *laissez-faire* policy in which nations could focus on exporting goods that they were most efficient at producing and importing goods that they were less competent in manufacturing. All nations, they claimed, would benefit by this policy if there were no barriers to the exchange of goods. In modern times, the trend toward free trade was reflected in the Bretton Woods Conference, GATT, the European Community, and plans for a greater North American free trade zone. *See* Bretton Woods, European Community, GATT, Laissez-faire, Mercantilism, Protectionism.

Fringe Benefits

In personnel and human relations terminology, nonwage benefits that are granted to employees, whether full or part time. Such benefits include sick leave, insurance, pensions, paid vacations, holidays, uniforms, and the use of recreational or sports facilities. *See* Compensation, Personnel Administration.

Front-end Funding

In commercial real estate, funds that are required to start a development, usually made available to the developer as a capital contribution to the project. *See* Real Estate.

Frozen Assets

Those assets and capital resources of an individual or business that are not available, whether by decree or situation, or that cannot be sold or otherwise disposed of without serious loss. *See* Accounting, Assets.

Full Disclosure

In fiscal affairs, the revelation of all of the facts about a subject that are needed by prospective investors. Such disclosure is necessary and mandatory, for example, in the sale of securities to the public by an offering corporation. *See* Corporations, Financial Accounting, Securities.

Futures

In the investment field, contracts to purchase or sell commodities or securities of specified quality and quantity at a specified price, on a specified future date. Such transactions are normally enacted on a major stock exchange and are highly speculative in nature. No money changes hands between the buyer and seller when a trade is made, but both must post collateral, known as *margin,* to show good faith. Futures are vital to the economy, since they permit parties to shift financial risks to others more capable of bearing them. This market is administered by commodity-futures exchanges, originally established in the Midwest for agricultural commodities, such as grains and meats, but now greatly broadened to include financial instruments, such as currencies and government obligations. In the United States the Commodity Futures Trading Commission regulates all futures trading. *See* Commodities. Futures Market, Hedging, Margin, Speculation.

FUTURES MARKET

A stock market established specifically for trading in futures contracts. *See* Commodities, Futures.

G

GALLAGHER'S PRINCIPALS

A list of precepts for business enterprises, which include the following, among others:

- Formulate clear written objectives.
- Place experts in charge of departments and divisions.
- Avoid spreading management too thin.
- Eliminate nepotism and favoritism.
- Delegate decision making to the lowest reasonable level.
- Centralize control, but decentralize decision making.
- Provide for unity of command.
- Formulate clear job and assignment descriptions.
- State company policies clearly and keep them updated.
- Establish personal employee goals, as well as management's.
- Provide logically for the succession of management.

See Business Administration, Management.

GALLOPING INFLATION

The rapid and unlimited, and often uncontrolled, rise in prices, with consequent increases in the cost of living. *See* Inflation.

GAME THEORY

An operations research technique dealing with competitive situations where two or more participants pursue conflicting objectives. The theory attempts to propose optimal strategies for the participants. *See* Management.

GANT CHART

A technique in chart form, to help make decisions about general management, company planning, financial control, and other professional matters. The chart displays time requirements and goals and events in a series of bars. *See* Business Administration, Management.

GARNISHMENT

The legalized process by which an individual's salary or other periodic income is seized by a debtor for payment of a debt. *See* Debt.

GENERAL ACCOUNTING OFFICE (GAO)

An independent and nonpolitical government agency that audits and reviews federal monetary transactions, investigates the expenditures and appropriations of federal offices, determines whether expenditures conform to law, and settles claims made against the country by individuals, organizations, or governments. Under the leadership of the comptroller general, the GAO's responsibilities have also been broadened to include the analysis of program management and policy decisions by the executive branch in fields ranging from defense to welfare. *See* Government.

GENERAL AGREEMENT FOR TARIFFS AND TRADE (GATT)

An international treaty that has established a code of conduct for international trade, based on the principles that trade should be conducted equitably, that duties should be reduced through multilateral negotiations, and that member countries should confer regularly to surmount trade problems. GATT, administered by a secretariat in Switzerland, maintains an International Trade Center, which is operated jointly with the United Nations Conference on Trade and Development as a facility to help developing nations to improve their export trade. *See* Exports, Free Trade, Imports, International Trade.

GENERAL PARTNERSHIP

A form of partnership in which the individual partners assume responsibility for the liabilities of the firm up to the full extent of their personal assets. *See* Partnerships.

GENERAL SERVICES ADMINISTRATION (GSA)

Through 11 regional offices, the GSA serves as the government's procurement agency in four service areas: information resources management, federal supply, public buildings, and federal property resources. Among its chief functions are the construction and maintenance of federal buildings, the dispersion of supplies and services to federal agencies, the operation of information centers, the disposal of government-owned property, the stockpiling of critical materials, and the administration of transportation and travel services. *See* Government.

GENTLEMAN'S AGREEMENT

An unwritten, unsigned, and unsecured understanding on the part of two or more individuals that they will honor certain commitments to each other and perform certain prescribed duties. *See* Agreement.

GEOGRAPHICAL DIFFERENTIAL

The variation in salary scales and wage rates for identical duties performed in different regions of the country. *See* Compensation.

GEOTHERMAL ENERGY

The heat energy that occurs naturally within the Earth, where the molten interior contains vast quantities of thermal power that remains fairly constant, provided in part by the decay of radioactive material. Geothermal energy is virtually an inexhaustible source of energy, which has been tapped for centuries but has only recently been utilized on any substantial scale. Examples of such energy are molten magma existing only a few miles below the surface, hot springs, running streams of nearly boiling water, and fissures that exude clouds of steam. One of the greatest evidences of geothermal availability is in Iceland, where more than 60 percent of the nation's heat supply comes from these underground resources. Although the industrial use of geothermal energy has largely been limited to operations requiring heat below 400°F., there is great potential for this natural resource in the generation of electric power. Geothermal power plants exist not only in the United States, but in China, Indonesia, Italy, Japan, Kenya, Mexico, New Zealand, the Philippines, and the Soviet Union. The largest plant in the world is near San Francisco, where since 1960 steam has been used to produce power with a generating capacity of more than 2,000 megawatts. *See* Energy.

GIFT TAX

Any tax imposed on individuals or organizations at the transfer of property from one living person to another. *See* Taxation.

GILT-EDGED

A synonym for *blue chip* when applied to stocks and other securities of companies with top financial ratings. *See* Investments.

GINNIE MAES

The popular name for a certain type of mortgage insured by the Government National Mortgage Association ("Ginnie Mae"). A number of individual mortgages with similar characteristics are pooled and sold to investors. *See* Mortgage.

GOAL SETTING

The function, almost universal in American companies, large and small, of establishing criteria for identifying feasible objectives, both for short-range and long-range operations. The communication of the objectives and the means of attaining them is referred to as *goal orientation*. Goal setting should relate directly to the descriptions and specifications presented by management in its initial *business plan* and should include references to all areas of operations that have been developed during a specified period of activity, generally one year. *See* Business Plans.

GOING CONCERN

An active business or organization.

GOING PUBLIC

The situation that exists when shares of stock of a company become publicly available on a major exchange, after having been held by relatively few shareholders. *See* Investments.

GOLD STANDARD

The international custom among nations of using gold held in their treasuries as a financial standard with which to back their printed and minted currency. The gold standard prevailed largely since 1870, when the English pound dominated international trade. By the end of World War I, however, the United States was the only Western country where paper money was still convertible into gold coins, and by the end of World War II, American dollars had almost entirely replaced gold in international transactions. *See* Foreign Currency, International Monetary Fund.

GOODS AND SERVICES

See Merchandise.

GOVERNMENT

Defined as "the legal and political institutions that regulate the relationships among members of a society internally and nurture relationships with similar societies externally, governments have broad authorities, as determined by their individual and separate citizens' organizations." The powers of a government vary widely, depending upon the degrees to which it is limited and restrained and the nature of the human resources that are contained within its jurisdictions. Within the national government entity lie many different levels of government, such as provinces, states, counties, cities, towns, villages, and boroughs. At the national level, there are the following principal forms of government:

Monarchy. This was the most common form of government from ancient times until the beginning of the twentieth century, denoting rule by a hereditary king or queen, and occurring in any one of three stages: absolute monarchy; limited monarchy, in which the most powerful members of the nobility had their say in governmental affairs; and constitutional monarchy, in which the monarchs are symbolic, rather than being actual rulers, as is the case in the United Kingdom, Sweden, and Spain.

Constitutional Government. This is the form common to most governments today, by which constitutions provide a legal blueprint that stipulates the manner in which power is to be exercised and controlled. In democratic countries, the constitution can be modified at any time by popular vote, either directly or through a system of elected representatives. Even though some one-party nations, such as those in the Communist bloc, have constitutions, political power lies in the hands of the leaders of the party.

Democracy. In a true democracy, the constitution is an honest guarantee that its provisions will be followed and enforced and that citizens will be free to make revisions only through due legal and political processes. Democratic governments follow several formats, most commonly those that are either *parliamentary,* as in Canada and Australia, or *presidential,* as in the United States. In the former, political power is concentrated in the parliament or the legislature, whose members include a prime minister or premier. In the latter, the voters elect a chief executive who has powers independent of the legislature, but whose actions are defined by the constitution.

Dictatorship. Largely an outgrowth of the twentieth century, this form of government is concentrated almost solely in the hands of one person, generally a military leader, and his immediate gang, backed by no formal or valid rule of law. The principal objective of a dictator is to corner control of all governmental functions and, in so doing, the whole nation and its population. The most extreme form of dictatorship is referred to as *totalitarian,* epitomized by the governments of Nazi Germany, present-day China, and Cuba, in which even the beliefs and ideologies of the people are under the thumb of the dictator.

Confederation. This is the weakest form of national government, since the member states in a confederation retain their sovereignty, delegating to the central government only those powers that are essential to its subsistence. The individual and separate states make their own laws, collect their own taxes, and otherwise exert certain powers, while the central government serves largely as a coordinating body to protect the interests of the states. Examples of flourishing confederations, in whole or in part, are the British Commonwealth of Nations, the European Community, and the Commonwealth of Independent Nations established among the former Soviet republics.

Systems of *international government* are also offshoots of the confederation principle, but with very little governing power. Examples are the League of Nations, which existed from 1919 until World War II, and the United Nations, with its many internal, specialized organizations that coordinate operations in such diverse areas as agriculture, civil aviation, health, labor, nuclear energy, and monetary matters. *See* International Relations. *See also* back-of-the-book supplement "Government Systems," on page 452.

GOVERNMENT BONDS

The class of bonds issued as obligations of the government of the United States and rated worldwide as the highest grade issues on the market. *See* Bonds, Investments.

GOVERNMENT PRINTING OFFICE

In the United States, the GPO was established by Congress to print and distribute federal government publications that now include the *Congressional Record* and almost 30,000 government agency publications. Lists of GPO publications are available from the Superintendent of Documents, Government Printing Office, Washington, DC 20242.

GRACE PERIOD

An extension of time past a specified due date for the payment of a debt or the completion of an obligation. *See* Loans.

GRANDFATHER CLAUSE

A condition in a contract, agreement, ordinance, or legal instrument of any kind that translates existing rights in terms of previous privileges that were granted in the past (hence to one's grandparents or ancestors). *See* Grandfather Lease.

GRANDFATHER LEASE

A lease specified in the Economic Recovery Tax Act of 1981 concerning property placed in service prior to the Act.

GRAPH

A chart used to help visualize statistics and other written data, often using vertical or horizontal bars. *See* Chart.

GRAPHIC ARTS

The field of creative endeavor that utilizes symbols and pictorial effects, and oftentimes printing, to present visual displays on any of a variety of media. Also, the industry itself. *See* Visualization.

GRETHAM'S LAW

A theory holding that when an item has a use as both a commodity and money, it will be utilized where its value is greater. The disappearance of silver certificates is an example of this concept. *See* Commodities, Currency.

GRIEVANCE

A formal protest filed with an employer by an employee, group of employees, or labor union stating complaints of bias or a breach of a collective agreement. *See* Labor/Management, Labor Union.

GROSS INCOME

The accumulation of income and revenues prior to reductions for expenses, taxes, and other deductible items. *See* Accounting, Annual Reports.

GROSS NATIONAL PRODUCT (GNP)

The accumulated total current market value in dollars of all final goods and services produced in the American economy in a given period. Although GNP is traditionally quoted in annual terms, data are compiled and released quarterly. GNP consists of the following bases: personal consumption expenditures, gross private domestic investment, government spending, and net exports—exports minus imports. *See* Production.

GROSS PROFIT

The excess of prices paid for merchandise and/or services before taxes and expense deductions are made for the costs of operations. *See* Accounting, Profit.

GROUP INSURANCE

An insurance plan under which a number of persons and their dependents are insured through a single policy that is issued to their employer or to an association, confederation, or club to which they belong. *See* Insurance.

GROWTH STOCK

Shares of securities in a well-rated corporation that have excellent prospects for future increases in value and price. *See* Investments, Stock.

GUARANTEED ANNUAL WAGE

A labor contract specifying that an employer is committed to paying employees certain wages or other compensation each year, regardless of the need for the employees in question or the degree of production accomplished. *See* Compensation.

GUARANTEES

In the language of Washington, that type of federal credit aid in which the government pledges financial liability for loans made by private, state, or local government institutions.

Habeus Corpus

A legal document requiring the presence of an individual in a courtroom or other place of law, often used to bring before a judge a prisoner in order to determine the legality of his imprisonment. Developed from principles of due process in English common law, habeas corpus had a long history in America as one of the most important protections of personal freedom before it was guaranteed in the Constitution: "The Privilege of the Writ of Habeas Corpus shall not be suspended unless when in Cases of Rebellion or Invasion the public Safety may require it." Under certain circumstances, this writ can be invoked by individuals or organizations when it is deemed that a person has been deprived of a due process of law or some other constitutional right. *See* Business Law.

Handbill

An advertising publication, usually a single sheet, promoting a product or service, and distributed by hand. *See* Advertising.

Hard Cash

Coins, as distinguished from paper money. *See* Hard Currency.

Hard Currency

Any form of cash, whether coin or paper. The term also refers to currency that is widely accepted in world markets, as opposed to soft currency, which is seldom acceptable outside the country of origin. *See* Currency, Hard Cash.

Hard Goods

Products that are substantial, durable, and usually on the expensive side. *See* Merchandise.

HARDWARE

In computer language, the mechanical and electronic processing equipment, as distinguished from the programming or software. Characteristically, hardware consists of the central processing unit (or CPU), the main storage facility, the keyboard, the monitor (or CRT), one or more storage drives, and *peripherals,* auxiliary equipment such as printers, modems, and CDROM (Compact Disk, Read-Only Memory) players. *See* CDROM, Peripherals, Software.

HARVESTING

A form of marketing strategy in which a company sharply cuts back all current expenses and outlays in order to improve its profit picture. Harvesting has the disadvantage, however, of sometimes reducing sales because of the expense limitations and thus stifling business. *See* Marketing.

HEAD HUNTER

Slang term for an individual in an executive search firm whose job is to find managers and other top-ranking professionals for clients. *See* Consulting, Personnel Administration.

HEAD START

A federally financed education program in the United States that serves the developmental needs of some 600,000 disabled youngsters and children from low-income families, it offers a wide range of services to enhance their intellectual development, self-esteem, and physical and mental health, as well as advisory services to the parents of the young participants.

HEAD TAX

A tax that is levied equally and equitably on individuals. *See* Taxation.

HEALTH AND HUMAN SERVICES DEPARTMENT

Formerly the U.S. Department of Health, Education, and Welfare, HHS came into being in 1979 as part of legislation establishing a separate Department of Education. The department's earlier history included a number of historic operations, including the production and distribution of the newly discovered Salk polio vaccine, the distribution of Social Security benefits to retirees, innovative programs to combat air pollution, the establishment of national health statistics, research into chromic diseases, the coordination of federal programs for the aging, implementation of new Civil Rights acts, the introduction of new Medicare and Medicaid programs, establishment of a center for disease control, the enforcement of child support, and nutrition programs for the elderly. *See* Government.

HEALTH INSURANCE

This form of insurance includes all kinds that relate to financial loss from illness or injury, including the expenses of hospitalization, surgery, and other medical services and any documented loss of income while a person is ill. Among the prevalent forms of health insurance are the government-supported Medicare and Medicaid programs and commercial policies offered by nation, privately operated, nonprofit plans, such as Blue Cross and Blue Shield and the fixed prepayment services of health organizations, all of which cover normal and emergency hospital expenses, surgery within certain limitations, and regular medical expenses for doctors and treatment inside or outside hospitals. Many of the illness-related problems are concerned with a fourth category, major medical expenses, and the need for insurance to cover catastrophic charges for intricate operations, high-priced prescriptions, and lengthy hospitalization.

During this century, and until recently, provisions for health care have become the responsibilities of almost every major nation except the United States, usually in the form of state-run insurance systems financed by taxes on both labor and management. Traditionally, Americans have rejected the concept of health-related interference by the government, and it was not until the inability of millions of citizens to pay for even minimal levels of care that the government was forced to intervene. "Today," says a current report on the situation, "the American medical-care system is a complex mix of public and private payments, is enormously costly, and is characterized by an inefficient distribution of resources and serious inequities of access." Under these circumstances, most people rely on private commercial insurance, which, even so, covers far less than half of the medical costs. The area of greatest government involvement has been Medicare, which covers some 35 million people over the age of 65, or who are totally disabled, and Medicaid, which covers about 25 million people who are medically indigent.

The major public agencies involved with health care are: The Department of Health and Human Services, which is responsible for administering federal health-care activities; the Public Health Service, which deals with health matters across state boundaries, the Centers for Disease Control, which investigate epidemics and new forms of disease; the National Institutes of Health, which conducts research; the Food and Drug Administration, which establishes standards and regulations; and the Department of Health and

Human Services, which is charged with controlling and licensing medications. *See* Health Maintenance Organizations and entries covering the organizations mentioned above.

HEALTH MAINTENANCE ORGANIZATIONS (HMOS)

Since prototype organizations traditionally operated on a budget that was the sum total of their patients' fees and could not afford to prescribe too-lengthy hospital stays or unnecessary surgery, legislation was passed in the 1970s to encourage the formation of HMOs, in the hope that they would prove an effective means of holding costs down. By the late 1980s, 650 HMOs had enrolled 30 million people, using a patient control system of "managed care," in which insurance companies had to approve nonemergency services, hospitalization, or tests: and the patient had to provide a doctor or hospital under contract with the insurer to charge agreed-upon fees. Despite these ongoing programs and positive outlooks, escalating medical-care costs continue to trouble the HMO concept and generate many internal and external controversies and dissenting viewpoints. *See* Health Insurance, Insurance, Personnel Administration.

HEAVY INDUSTRY

Any industry-producing machinery, metal products, or other products of a "heavy" or substantial nature. *See* Production.

HEDGE

To buy or sell commodities in the futures market in such a way as to prevent loss caused by price fluctuations. One method, for example, is to buy futures contracts at the *current* price, a strategy that works when price increases are anticipated. *See* Arbitrage, Commodities, Futures.

HEURISTIC

In management, a form of problem solving in which the results are determined by the independent determinations of a manager and rule of thumb and intuition, rather than by optimization. *See* Business Administration, Management, Optimization.

HIDDEN ASSETS

Those assets and resources of a company that are not readily apparent and identifiable on the organization's financial balance sheets or similar records. *See* Accounting, Assets.

HIDDEN CLAUSE

Referring to contracts, agreements, and bills of sale, any not readily notice-able provision stipulating requirements and conditions that may be against a buyer's or contractor's interests. *See* Contracts.

HIDDEN OFFER

A strategy used by advertisers whereby a special offer may be buried in the text of an advertisement or other promotional copy to determine whether the reader has thoroughly studied the message. *See* Advertising, Promotion.

HIGH TECHNOLOGY

The phrase applied to new and rapidly expanding technologies such as those involved in electronics, microelectronics, computers and other data-process-ing equipment, communications, genetic engineering, and laser optics. *See* Technology.

HOLDBACK

In a contract or settlement, that portion of an agreed-upon payment that is not payable until certain stipulations have been fulfilled. *See* Agreement, Contract.

HOLDING COMPANY

A firm whose primary function is the ownership of shares in other compa-nies. Through the purchase of even small amounts of other businesses—as little as 10 percent—holding companies can often gain effective control over the companies in which they invest, especially if stock ownership in them is widely distributed. A holding company is fundamentally a commercial enter-prise that owns a controlling interest in the stock of another commercial enterprise, but which also provides a convenient way for a company to diver-sify its activities, even when legal restrictions prevent the company from entering directly into another industry. In such an arrangement, each sub-sidiary firm retains its own identity and its own assets and liabilities. *See* Investments.

HOLD IN TRUST

To formulate a legal agreement whereby a property is held by a third party, or trustee, for the benefit of another party. The trustee is given specific instructions regarding the management and control of the trust. *See* Trust.

HOMESTEAD LAW

Historically, a federal law granting homestead lands, in designated parcels or tracts, to persons who agree to settle and improve them. Although rare today, homesteading in various forms is still practiced in many regions in the United States and abroad. The Homestead Act of 1862 (finally repealed in 1977) granted 160 acres of public land in the West as a homestead to "any person who is the head of a family, or who has arrived at the age of twenty-one years, and is a citizen of the United States, or who shall have filed his declaration of intention to become such." The homesteader had merely to pay a small filing fee, live on the property for five years, and make improvements in order to hold title to the land. *See* Business Law.

HONORARIUM

A moderate payment made to recompense or honor a person who has agreed to make a speech, offer a public service, or otherwise perform a duty for which custom or protocol implies that no price be set.

HORIZONTAL EXPANSION

The creation of additional facilities, with the necessary equipment and personnel, to permit a firm to expand its business in the same field in which it is currently operating. *See also* Vertical Expansion.

HORIZONTAL MERGER

The merger and alliance of two organizations engaged in the same field of business and with similar commercial interests and objectives. *See* Joint Venture, Merger, Vertical Merger.

HORIZONTAL PRICE FIXING

An agreement, often illegal or unethical, in which competitors at similar levels of sales and distribution set prices.

HOUSE ADVERTISING AGENCY

An agency that is either an arm of a parent company or has only one client. *See* Advertising.

HOUSE BRAND

The brand named and used by a wholesaler with its own name, but purchased unlabeled from another supplier. Most supermarkets, for example, have their own line of labels on goods they purchase wholesale and sell retail, but do not produce.

HOUSE OF REPRESENTATIVES OF THE UNITED STATES

The larger of the two chambers of Congress, whose members serve two-year terms and whose entire membership stands for reelection every second year. To serve in the House, a person must be at least 25 years old, an American citizen for at least seven years, and a resident of the state in which he or she is chosen. Representation is apportioned for each state on the basis of population, which, of course, can change from one election period to another. In addition to the representatives, the House includes a resident commissioner from Puerto Rico, and delegates from the District of Columbia, Guam, and the Virgin Islands, all of whom are nonvoting, but who may participate in speaking and debates. The presiding officer of the House, traditionally the leader of the majority party, is the Speaker, who is elected at the beginning of each two-year term of Congress by the membership of the House.

HOUSE ORGAN

Any publication of and by a business concern or other organization that contains articles of narrow interest to employees and customers. *See* Periodicals.

HUMAN FACTORS ENGINEERING

A field of technology that designs machines, plans operations, and nurtures environments to match human skills, capabilities, and limitations, drawing heavily on the life and physical sciences, but with strong ties to the engineering professions. This science owes its origins to World War II, when it was developed and applied to such military functions and equipment as bomb sighting, marksmanship, pilot control, underwater demolition, and other operations requiring better coordination between man and machine. Although the immediate postwar period saw the applications continuing in military operations, human factors engineering began to be applied to the design of civilian products such as automobiles, communications equipment, computers, and appliances. Certain elements of this science have also been instrumental in lessening the monotony of production and assembly-line operations, combating on-the-job fatigue, honing inspection procedures, providing job-enrichment programs, and solving certain kinds of pollution problems. *See* Ergonomics.

HUMAN-ORIENTED LANGUAGE

A category of computer programming language that is more similar to human language than that of an electronic communicator. *See* Computers, Programming.

HUMAN RELATIONS

The area of activity, formerly referred to as *personnel,* in an organization that is involved with people and management requirements and problems in dealing with employees. *See* Personnel Administration.

HUMAN RESOURCES

Those resources in an organization that consist of people, rather than facilities or equipment. Reports and records in this field usually categorize such resources in terms of skills and proficiencies, experience, and availability, as well as the relationships between an organization and its employees. Among new developments in the human resources field is *human factors engineering,* a branch of technology that helps design machines, operations, and environments to match human abilities and limitations. While training programs are employed to adapt people to machines or work functions, the purpose of human factors engineering, also called *ergonomics,* is to design machines to meet the capacities of people. Although this field of engineering was born during World War II and applied largely to military machines, it was readily transferable to applications in the production of communications equipment, vehicles, planes, and computers. It was a natural for solving problems of fatigue and monotony on the assembly line. Specialists in human resources coordinate their efforts with those of the design engineers by providing data about commonplace problems such as accidents, errors, production damage and waste, and employee complaints, all of which are then incorporated into design solutions.

A major component of human resources is *human resources planning,* a responsibility of top management, to help orchestrate such functions as the recruitment of employees, placing people in the right positions, anticipating employment problems, considering personnel solutions, motivating employees, and reducing the turnover rate. HP, as it is popularly referred to, is composed of the following sequential steps:

1. *The inventory,* an appraisal of current employees, noting their specific job titles, salaries, qualifications, and relative experience, and recognizing which individuals have matured with the job and which have remained on plateaus.

2. *The profile of growth,* pinpointing the changes in growth and development throughout the company that have taken place in the past, seem to be taking place today, and will probably take place in the future.

3. *Matching people with actions,* outlining on paper which individuals have been associated with which fields of growth, and which are likely to be coordinated with future patterns of change.

4. *Turnover,* charting the rate at which employee turnover has affected business in the past, and anticipating the kinds of turnover for the future, as well as plotting a plan of action for lessening the rate of personnel depletion.

5. *Orientation,* establishing a curriculum for education and training, whether for new employees, for individuals moving from one position to another, or for updated familiarization with new tools, equipment, or procedures.

6. *Salary administration,* developing a workable *pay administration plan* (PAP), whose objective is to make employees aware of where they stand in the matter of wages, salaries, bonuses, and benefits, with projections into the future for all major forms of recompense that might alert personnel to long-term opportunities and their likelihood of raises and promotions.

Successful human resources planning is essential for implementing the kind of employee growth plan that will keep people on the job, motivate them, and stabilize the business. *See* Ergonomics, Human Factors Engineering, Personnel Administration.

HUMAN RIGHTS

Those privileges and entitlements that citizens of a country enjoy as protection against bias or restrictions that are prohibited by law, convention, or custom. Among the historic rights abuses are kidnapping, torture, detention, slavery, involuntary servitude, discrimination on racial, ethnic, religious, or sexual grounds, and denial of the rights to due process of law, free expression, free movement, and peaceable assembly. Despite steady gains on behalf of human rights, there is no country in the world that does not have its share of violations of person. Though the most widely recognized transgressions are forms of torture, such as beatings, burnings, rape, and bloodshed, the less obvious are complex patterns of mistreatment such as depriving victims of sleep, water, and food, rendering partial asphyxiation, exposure to extremes of heat and cold, refusing medical attention in cases of severe injury, wounds, or illness, and immersion in water to the point of near-drowning. Yet, even in the so-called "civilized" societies, such as the United States, human rights violations are commonplace in the form of bias and prejudice and the acts and actions taken against people because of gender, race, age, politics, faith, financial standing, ethnic background, or other personal characteristics. *See* Civil Rights, Free Enterprise, Minorities.

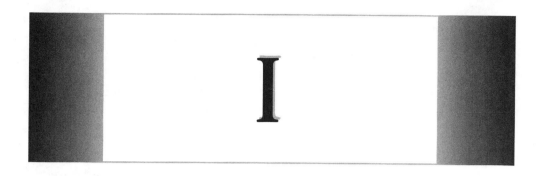

IDEAL CAPACITY

The maximum number of products, materials, goods, or other units that could be manufactured in a given production system, over a stipulated period, with no allowance for unexpected personnel layoffs, stoppages, down time, or other interruptions in a plant. *See* Manufacturing, Production.

IDENTIFIER

An emblem, symbol, code, or other graphic device used to identify or name a body of information, as in data processing or computer programming. *See* Code, Programming, Software.

IDEOLOGY

Any expressed structure of convictions intended to bring about changes that would make the world, or a part of it, a better place, whether for personal, political, economic, or ecological reasons. The formal concept of *ideology* originated in Europe during the eighteenth century by a group of philosophers unhappy with the contemporary state of affairs and seeking to find guidance in emerging sciences, coupled with human understanding and intellect. The current concept of ideology is that of "systematic sets of principles that link perceptions of the world to explicit moral values" and that are composed of three elements: content, function, and reasoning. Historically, some of the most pronounced examples of ideology are conservatism, liberalism, social-ism, communism, and fascism. These ideologies have all followed a typical course of action: communicating a point of view, establishing a connection platform for those espousing a related cause, providing ammunition against those opposed to the cause, and mobilizing human efforts on behalf of the ideology being expounded. *See* Human Resources, Motivation.

IDLE TIME

Down time.

IMAGE

The public's perception of an organization and its reputation and financial standing, particularly as that impression is enhanced through advertising, public relations, publicity, and other communications. *See* Industrial Relations, Public Affairs, Public Relations.

IMAGE BUILDING

A specific objective of public relations and other communications departments to improve an organization's image in the eyes of employees, customers, suppliers, and the general public. *See* Public Relations.

IMPLEMENTATION

The action of phasing a project into operation, usually under the supervision of a project manager whose goal is not only to meet the specifications of the enterprise but to stay on schedule and within the budget. *See* Management.

IMPLIED CONTRACT

A contract in which the parties concerned communicate situations by their actions rather than by written or spoken rhetoric. *See* Contract.

IMPLIED WARRANTY

A representation, not in writing, but often legally binding, that particular conditions exist. *See* Warranty.

IMPORT DUTY

Any tax or levy on goods or materials that are imported from another country. *See* Duty, Import Quota.

IMPORT QUOTA

The authorized maximum on the quantity or value of merchandise that may be imported into a given location over a specified period of time.

IMPOST

A form of tax that is commonly used to describe import and export duties. *See* Foreign Trade, Taxation.

IMPREST SYSTEM

A structure established to handle disbursements by entrusting a set sum of cash to an individual or firm.

IMPULSE BUYING

The immediate and unintended purchase of merchandise by consumers at the point of sale. *See* Marketing.

IMPUTED VALUE

The description of value of products, materials, securities, or other items of worth when no cash payment is declared, in order to establish that value.

IN ARREARS

Said of a bill, interest, or other obligation that has not been paid in a specified amount by a deadline date. *See* Loans.

IN BOND

Said of merchandise shipped by a manufacturer to a retailer or wholesaler several months before a customary selling season and warehoused until actual sales begin. *See* Inventory, Wholesaling.

INCENTIVE PLAN

A blueprint for inducing employees to work or produce above a certain level by offering certain benefits or other compensation when they exceed the level specified. When the benefit is monetary, this is known as *incentive pay*. *See* Motivation.

INCOME DISTRIBUTION

The manner in which personal income is segmented and distributed throughout the many socioeconomic levels in any given geographical or political entity. *See* Economics.

INCOME FUND

A mutual fund whose purpose is more to produce income periodically than to grow in value over a period of time. *See* Mutual Fund.

INCOME PROPERTY

Land, residences, facilities or other real property—generally commercial, industrial, or residential—that is owned or purchased as a means of generating financial returns through leasing, renting, or periodic use. *See* Real Estate.

INCOME STATEMENTS

Records and summaries of the revenues and expenses of a business enterprise, defined for specified accounting periods and sometimes projected into the future. *See* Accounting.

INCONVERTIBLE MONEY

Currency that is irredeemable and cannot be converted into the standard. A prime example is United States money, which is not redeemable in gold. *See* Gold Standard.

INCORPORATION

The legal procedure of bringing a corporation of any size, type, or worth into being as an independent entity, described as "an artificial being, invisible, intangible, existing only in contemplation of the law." The organization thus legalized, rather than its owners as individuals, owns cash and other monetary valuables, as well as property in many senses of the word, and—apart from the managers and employees within its structure—can sue, be sued, enter into legal and commercial negotiations of all kinds, and can fail and go bankrupt in its own name. *See* Business Law, Corporation.

INCORPOREAL PROPERTY

Personal property that is intangible or abstract.

INCREASING-COST INDUSTRY

An industry whose manufacturing expenses and costs of raw materials increase gradually or abruptly as new companies enter its field of operations. *See* Manufacturing, Production.

INCREASING RETURNS

A condition that exists in which manufacturing production becomes increased and more efficient, even though there has been no change in the various factors that customarily affect production, such as labor, management, capital, or space. *See* Manufacturing, Production.

INCREMENTAL COST

In manufacturing, the added expenses that are incurred in the processes of completing an assembly, adding the finishing touches, or advancing to a higher degree of production. *See* Manufacturing.

INCURRED LOSSES

Financial losses of all kinds that occur within a fixed time period, normally 12 months. *See* Accounting, Annual Report.

INDEMNITY BOND

A bond that protects the holder against any losses that result from the failure of the principal to fulfill stated obligations. Also referred to as an indemnity agreement. *See* Agreement, Contract.

INDEPENDENT CONTRACTOR

An individual or firm agreeing to perform specific services for another party and, though responsible for the outcome, not subject to direction and guidance by the hiring party. *See* Contracting.

INDEX OF LEADING ECONOMIC INDICATORS

A series of financial indicators that tend to predict changes in economic activity. The series is the prime barometer of the government for forecasting business trends, since each of the series has a tendency to change before the economy takes a major turn upward or downward—hence the term, "leading indicators." The series, published monthly by the Department of Commerce, is a composite of 12 and covers such subjects as the average workweek of manufacturing workers, unemployment insurance, the performance of vendors, changes in liquid assets, fluctuations in the prices of crude materials, contracts for plants and equipment, stock prices, and building permits. *See* Economics.

INDICATOR

A formalized system or chart used to demonstrate significant changes taking place as various factors that are pertinent change in magnitude, nature, or direction. *See* Economic Indicator.

INDIRECT COST

An expense that cannot be associated with the factors and circumstances identified with a business function or operation or pinpointed on a cost-control graph. *See* Accounting, Bookkeeping.

INDIVIDUAL RETIREMENT ACCOUNTS (IRAs)

Personal pension plans that are commonly made available to individuals who are not covered on the job by any defined group or joint pension plan.

Participation, however, can also be elected by individuals who are enrolled in corporate pension programs. *See* Personnel Administration.

INDIVISIBLE CONTRACT

In legal matters, an agreement that stands complete and that may not be separated into parts, and under which all portions must be fulfilled in order to comply with the contract. *See* Contracts.

INDUCED INVESTMENT

The additional capital required by a manufacturer to purchase more property, plant facilities, or machinery in order to meet the increased spending by consumers for the kinds of products and materials being produced. *See* Manufacturing, Production.

INDUCTIVE METHOD

In management and research, that form of reasoning that approaches a problem from the viewpoint of its particulars and arrives at generalizations, emphasizing data gathered from empirical sources. *See* Management.

INDUSTRIAL CONCENTRATION

The situation that exists when a large proportion of an industry's products and sales are related to only a few manufacturers. *See* Distribution, Marketing.

INDUSTRIAL ENGINEERING

Engineering designs, applications, and installations of integrated systems and their relationship to equipment, machinery, materials, and workers. As a branch of both engineering and industrial management, this field is primarily concerned with the analysis of the processes of production and the design of methods for making them more efficient. Experts in this field are concerned with the following activities, among others: designing production facilities, setting labor standards, planning time and motion studies, setting wage scales based on levels of skill, and initiating quality-control procedures. *See* Human Factors Engineering.

INDUSTRIAL ESPIONAGE

The practice of obtaining confidential business or technological information through covert means, a custom that has long existed but is a growing concern in industry wherever competition or sensitive conditions exist, as in the case of defense contracts or the manufacture of state-of-the art computers and programs. Although industrial espionage is most pronounced in industry, where it costs American firms more than $22 billion each year, scientific and technological espionage flourishes on an international scope as well. Outright theft and bribery are not always necessary in industrial espionage, however, for a great deal of supposedly confidential data can be gleaned from products and materials themselves, simply by purchasing them and breaking their components and compositions down in the laboratory. Experts hope that international accords like the General Agreement on Tariffs and Trade (GATT) and the licensing of scientific and technological research will diminish industrial espionage and the stealing of trade secrets and patents. *See* Blackmail, General Agreement on Tariffs and Trade (GATT).

INDUSTRIAL MANAGEMENT

That form of business management directly concerned with the administration of manufacturing and production facilities, including responsibilities for related functions such as industrial relations, distribution, marketing, and research. Historically, the concept of industrial management is said to go back to the heydays of the Greeks, Romans, Egyptians, Chinese, and even the Incas, who could not have constructed such elaborate and often gigantic works as those depicted in the history books without it. Industrial management as modern executives know it, however, was a byproduct of the industrial revolution, coming into its own in the late eighteenth and early nineteenth centuries, when administrative responsibilities became more structured and the forerunners of manufacturing research, such as time-and-motion studies, were seen in early prototypes. There was even some evidence of assembly-line production, which would not really flourish for an entire century, with the technological innovations of Henry Ford prior to World War I. During this stage, management was also beginning to rely on mathematical models for reducing costs and streamlining inventories. This evolved later into linear programming, vastly enhanced by early data-processing capabilities and, of course, the modern computer.

INDUSTRIAL PSYCHOLOGY

The branch of human relations and psychology directly concerned with the behavior and motivation of workers, individually and as groups. Its major functions include: personnel selection, on-the-job training, general orientation, the enhancement of the work environment, lifting employee morale, motivation, and the improvement of both individual and group productivity. *See* Employee Relations, Ergonomics, Personnel Management.

INDUSTRIAL RELATIONS

In management and human resources, the study and application of methods to improve relationships between employers and employees in industrial companies and plants. The following functions are all considered to be basic components of an industrial relations operation: recruiting new employees, classifying jobs and assignments, training and orientation, negotiating with labor unions, monitoring government regulations that affect the work force, providing work incentives, measuring the quality or work, and maintaining regular and continuing communications with all employees. Industrial psychology has come into its own as more and more surveys and studies have documented the fact that employees who obtain satisfaction from their jobs are more motivated and productive. *See* Employee Relations, Public Relations.

INDUSTRIAL REVOLUTION

The historical upheaval that started in the late eighteenth century at a time when rapid advancements were being made in manufacturing, largely as a result of new forms of machinery and the advent of steam power. *See* Manufacturing.

INDUSTRIAL STANDARDIZATION

A system of applying a formulated plan of action to enhance the production methods of a manufacturing company in achieving its production objectives. *See* Manufacturing, Production.

INFLATION

The procedure in which the level of prices increases at a substantial rate over a period of time, thus requiring more money each year to buy a given amount of goods and services. The term varies greatly from one country to another and is considered to be the rate that makes a formidable difference in the economy of the nation concerned. Whereas an inflation rate of 4 percent in the United States may be cause for alarm, some foreign countries expect the rate to be ten times that, or more, before perceiving that there is a grave economic problem. From a monetary viewpoint, inflation is the result of an excessive growth rate of money, based on the theory that rising prices are similar to the falling value of money—the more money there is, relative to the goods and services to be bought, the less valuable is each dollar. A period of increasing prices occurs when the quantity of money grows faster than real demand for it, measured in terms of the goods and services the money buys.

Thus, an inflation requires either a rapid growth in the money supply or a persistently falling real demand for money. *See* Economics, Recession.

INFLATION ACCOUNTING

A form of accounting directed at evaluating the impact of inflation on corporate assets, deficits, and profits. *See* Accounting.

INFLATIONARY SPIRAL

An imaginary spiral, often translated in graphic terms, demonstrating how employees demand greater compensation in times of rising prices, which in turn increases industrial and commercial costs, forcing marketers and manufacturers to demand still higher prices for merchandise. *See* Economics.

INFORMATION RETRIEVAL

The application of various systems and procedures to recover specific information from data banks and other types of statistical storage. *See* Data Processing.

INFRASTRUCTURE

The fundamental composition of a country's economy, including major areas of operation such as communications, transportation, and other public services regularly relied on for broad economic well being. *See* Economics.

INFRINGEMENT OF COPYRIGHT

Reproducing printed material, computer programs, musical arrangements, or other creative productions without the express consent of the copyright holder or agent, and usually without any form of remuneration. Other types of infringements relate to trademarks, logotypes, slogans, or patents. *See* Copyright.

INQUIRY TESTING

A strategy for testing advertising campaigns by computing the numbers of inquiries received from readers, listeners, or viewers. *See* Advertising.

INSIDER

A term, now often having negative meaning, relating to an executive or other individual having access to confidential information about a company, stocks, or future planning. *See* Investments.

INSOLVENCY

The inability of an organization or individual to meet obligations when they become due, in whole or in part. *See* Arrears, Bankruptcy.

INSTALLMENT BUYING

A retailing, merchandising plan for purchasing goods or services with little or no payment down, but with partial payments and usually interest at regular intervals. *See* Merchandising, Selling.

INSTANT VESTING

A privilege held by employees that grants them the right to change jobs and/or employers within a given occupational field without losing pension and retirement rights. *See* Human Resources.

INSTITUTIONAL ADVERTISING

That form of advertising that seeks to enhance favorable opinions of advertisers rather than motivate consumers to purchase any of the company's products or services. *See* Advertising.

INSTRUMENT

In business, law, and finance, a document or certificate that has meaning and/or value in transactions. *See* Contract, Deed.

INSURANCE

Any system in a very wide variety of types and options that indemnifies or protects an individual or organization against loss. Insurance agencies and companies function on the basis of accumulating funds from multitudes of policy holders over long periods of time and investing them so that they will pay not only for individual losses, but to maintain the company, provide widespread employment, and make a profit. The insurance industry utilizes a system of *reinsurance,* whereby many companies pool their funds in order to meet the enormous obligations incurred in times of major disasters, such as floods, hurricanes, or earthquakes. *See* Risk Management, Risks.

INSURGENT

When used in business or commercial applications, a member of a group rebelling against an organization, its managers, or its policies.
Intangible asset. Any advantage that is beneficial to an organization, but has no monetary value or substance. Examples are goodwill, trademarks, logotypes (logos), and positive public relations. *See* Assets.

INTANGIBLE REWARDS

Rewards or compensation that are not material and have no monetary value, such as honors or letters of appreciation. *See* Compensation.

INTEGRATED CIRCUIT

An assemblage of interconnected electrode components contained within the top layer of a tiny semiconductor chip, usually made of silicon, which is one of the few elements that can be made to act as a semiconductor—that is, conducting and not conducting at will in order to function as desired. Such circuits are commonly used in computers and other high-tech electronic equipment. *See* Chip, Semiconductor.

INTEGRATED COMMERCIALS

Radio and television commercials that are blended into the editorial or entertainment segments of the program rather than being aired separately. *See* Advertising, Broadcasting.

INTEGRATED SOFTWARE

In computerization, this form of programming comprises two or more modules that perform together, combining such functions as word processing, database management, spreadsheets, elecommunications, and graphics. *See* Computers, Software.

INTEGRATOR

A manager or foreperson who is empowered to coordinate the efforts of individuals, teams, and departments whose assignments overlap. *See* Management, Personnel Administration.

INTELLECTUAL PROPERTY

A comprehensive expression referring to values that are non-material in nature, such as copyrights, royalties, patents, trademarks, slogans, industrial designs, and legal rights to artistic works and presentations. *See* Copyright, Patents.

INTERACTION

In data processing, the science of programming computers to follow certain commands, either independently or upon designated signals, in collaboration with other computers or data-processing equipment. *See* Computers, Data Processing.

INTERACTION ANALYSIS

A technique designed to observe groups working on problem solving, in order to develop profiles of human relationships that can be measured and utilized. *See* Human Relations.

INTERCORPORATE STOCKHOLDING

An unethical, if not illegal, practice in which one company purchases the stocks of competitors deliberately in order to interfere with their operation.

INTERDICTION

In international law, the prohibition of traffic and commerce between one country and enumerated other companies or foreign ports. *See* Foreign Trade.

INTEREST

A sum of money paid at regular intervals for the use of another amount of money, called the principal. Banks and other financial institutions pay interest to savers for the use of money deposited in savings accounts, while borrowers pay interest for the use of money loaned to them. Interest, sometimes referred to as a *finance charge* or *terms,* is usually stated as an annual percentage of the principal involved. Interest is calculated in two different ways: as simple interest and as compound interest. Simple interest means that the interest payment for the year is the principal amount multiplied by the interest rate; for example, the interest on $1,000 is $60 if the interest rate is 6 percent. Most borrowing, lending, and saving, however, uses compound interest. When compound interest is computed, the basic one-year period is divided into smaller periods, and the interest earned in each shorter period is added to the principal amount. Since the principal amount becomes larger throughout the year, the total amount of interest paid for the entire year is larger under compound interest than it would be if calculated by a simple interest rate. *See* Banking, Finance, Loans.

INTEREST GROUP

In personnel training and motivation, an assemblage of employees who will be working together in orientation sessions, or interacting in some other manner, but with the same goals and objectives. The concept of the group is that it can accomplish more with members working jointly than its individuals could on their own. *See* Personnel Administration.

INTERGOVERNMENTAL REVENUE

Money, grants, or other forms of revenue received by a government or agency from another government or agency, often for services rendered or the payment of taxes. *See* Taxation.

INTERIM FINANCING

Lending, commonly on a short-term basis, to finance a project from the time it was authorized or commenced until a more permanent form of lending has been instituted. *See* Financing.

INTERMARKETING

The practice of assigning sales personnel so that individuals are able to serve two or more related departments, rather than being limited to one. *See* Sales, Marketing, Merchandising.

INTERMEDIATE GOODS

Materials that are essential to the production of other materials, goods, or products. *See* Manufacturing, Production.

INTERNAL AUDIT

The audit of a company's finances and operations that is conducted by an employee of the organization itself, known as an *internal auditor. See* Auditing.

INTERNAL CONTROL

Plans of action and supervision by management to make certain that operations and procedures are carried out as conceived and stipulated. *See* Business Management.

INTERNAL FINANCING

Meeting certain expenses for new projects or other financial needs through existing monetary resources, such as profit reserves or the sale of property or equipment. *See* Financing.

INTERNAL MEMORY

The components of a computer or other electronic data processing mechanism that has the capabilities for retaining information that can be produced on command. *See* Computer, Data Processing.

INTERNAL REVENUE SERVICE (IRS)

Although this federal tax collection agency was formed during the Civil War period, it did not exist at all as we know it today until its format and functions were specified in the Sixteenth Amendment to the Constitution in 1913. As a division of the Treasury, the IRS administers all internal revenue laws and regulations except those relating to alcohol, tobacco, explosives, and firearms, and is most noted for collecting individual and organizational income taxes, Social Security taxes, and estate, excise, and gift taxes. The IRS structure incorporates seven regions, each headed by a regional commissioner, and 64 districts under the jurisdiction of district directors. The national headquarters in Washington, DC, issues tax policies and supervises the field organizations. *See* Taxation.

INTERNATIONAL BANK FOR RECONSTRUCTION AND DEVELOPMENT

An institution that was established to aid Third World countries and other undeveloped regions by encouraging reconstruction endeavors and providing loans for economic development. *See* Free Trade, Third World Countries.

INTERNATIONAL DATE LINE

On maps and charts, an imaginary line that runs approximately along the 180th degree meridian in the Pacific Ocean, to mark an 1884 international agreement whereby the earth day is considered to begin immediately west of the line and to end immediately east of it. Since the times zones on each side of this date line are 24 hours apart, those who cross the line from west to east repeat one day, while those traveling the reverse course *omit* one. However, in the few places where the 180-degree meridian crosses land, the international date line deviates so as not to bisect any populated region or political entity.

INTERNATIONAL DEVELOPMENT ASSOCIATION

Created in the early 1960s, this institution is an affiliated arm of the International Bank for Reconstruction and Development, which is commonly known as the World Bank, to which IDA members must belong. The basic purpose of the Association is to extend credit to Third World nations for economic development and foreign trade on terms that are more lenient and compliant than those of the World Bank. For example, developing nations that borrow money through IDA have up to 50 years to make repayments, have no interest, and pay a service charge of only 1 percent. IDA borrowers may repay their loans over a period of up to 50 years, with a service charge of less than 1 percent instead of interest. *See* Free Trade, International Bank for Reconstruction and Development, World Bank.

INTERNATIONAL FINANCE CORPORATION

This specialized affiliate of the United Nations works closely with the World Bank to provide funds for private enterprise in Third World nations. The IFC invests in business enterprises when private capital is not sufficiently available, acts as a clearinghouse to bring together investment opportunities, and often provides management and administrative capabilities for underdeveloped nations. *See* World Bank.

INTERNATIONAL MONETARY FUND (IMF)

An establishment to make provisions for nations to obtain foreign exchange to meet temporary needs in their balance of international payments. Through IMF, such nations can avoid international trade barriers and the depreciation of their currencies. *See* Foreign Exchange.

INTERNATIONAL MONETARY MARKET (IMM)

A prime market for foreign currency that is a division of the Chicago Mercantile Exchange. It is engaged also in trading futures in U.S. Treasury bills, certificates of deposit, and Eurodollar deposits. *See* Foreign Exchange.

INTERNATIONAL MONETARY SYSTEM

A complex network whereby different national currencies may be exchanged for each other in world trade, following certain regulations and procedures, and dependent upon a number of factors, including the balance of trade and the supply and demand of the currencies in question. *See* Balance Of Trade, Foreign Exchange, Foreign Trade.

INTERNATIONAL PRESS INSTITUTE

As a confederation of publishers, editors, and radio and television broadcasters, the IPI was founded to safeguard global freedom of the press and to promote responsible journalism in all media. Founded in 1951 and headquartered in Switzerland, the organization has some 2,000 members in more than 60 countries. *See* International Relations, Press.

INTERNET

In the field of computers and data processing, an electronic network of networks, in which literally millions of computers are hooked together around the world. Computer owners and users who have modems and other equipment to communicate with others so equipped can use an *internet provider,* an organization that, like international telecommunication services, can place them in the network. *See* Communications, Computers, Telecommunications.

INTERNET PROVIDER

See Internet.

INTERPOLATE

In accounting, to estimate a single value somewhere between two known values by proportioning them and using any other available data. *See* Accounting, Bookkeeping.

INTERSTATE CARRIER

Any transportation facility organized as a common carrier and whose business extends beyond the boundaries of a single state. *See* Intrastate Carrier.

INTERSTATE COMMERCE

Commercial activities that extend across state lines. *See* Intrastate Commerce.

INTERSTATE COMMERCE ACT

A federal law established to regulate commerce between the states and especially the transportation of merchandise, materials, and passengers by bus, train, plane, or other carriers with interstate terminals. *See* Interstate Commerce Commission.

INTERSTATE COMMERCE COMMISSION (ICC)

This agency, whose duties are defined by the Interstate Commerce Act, regulates surface transportation among the states by trains, trucks, buses, water carriers, and companies that carry freight or parcels. Headed by five commissioners, the ICC is chiefly involved with these modes of transportation, and focuses on hearings and other proceedings concerning freight or operating rights. *See* Interstate Commerce Act.

IN TRANSIT

The state in which items being shipped are in when they have left the premises of the consignor and are en route to their destination. *See* Shipping.

INTRASTATE CARRIER

A common carrier whose operations are confined to business entirely within a single state. *See* Interstate Carrier.

INTRASTATE COMMERCE

Commercial activities that are confined to a single state. *See* Interstate Commerce.

INTRINSIC VALUE

The valuation placed on an article, or any object of worth, that represents the material value of the item itself, apart from any other relative value or added worth it may have in use.

INTROJECTION

In field research, a lack of objectivity displayed largely in the tendency of interviewers to evaluate what they learn from interviewees in their own personal terms, whether negatively, positively, or neutrally. *See* Advertising Research.

INTUITIVE PRICING

In marketing, the practice of establishing prices and other monetary values on the intuition of a responsible party. *See* Marketing.

INVENTORY

The sum total of all products or materials of a certain category or belonging to a specific organization that are available for sale or use. There are three standard classifications of inventory in a business: raw materials, work-in-progress, and finished goods. The last-mentioned refers to the sum of goods that are in storage, in transit, or already out on consignment. Inventory is customarily reported on the balance sheet as an asset, as long as it is free and clear. *See* Inventory Control, Inventory Management.

INVENTORY CERTIFICATE

A document obtained by a sales or marketing firm or department by an independent auditor, which certifies the basis of evaluation and ownership of goods in an inventory. *See* Inventory Control.

INVENTORY CONTROL

A procedure used by sellers and warehousers to control merchandise in stock by physical methods and acceptable accounting systems. *Emergency inventory control* is a form of control used to regulate inventories in times of crisis—during wartime, for example, to prevent hoarding and make certain that materials and goods are put to the best possible use. *See* Inventory Management.

INVENTORY MANAGEMENT

Inventory is one of the more tangible aspects of business, visualized most often as raw materials, parts and products on the shelves, goods being processed, boxes and other containers, and stocks of just about anything necessary to conduct business. Such objects, whether on the company's premises or on display at retail outlets, represent a large percentage of the business investment total and must be properly managed in order to maximize profits. Many businesses—especially small to medium-sized enterprises—fail primarily because they cannot absorb the kinds of losses that arise from the inept management of their inventories. An experienced inventory executive advises managers under his or her jurisdiction:

- Refrain from keeping inventories on the high side for no reason.
- Keep stocks trim without sacrificing service.
- Maintain a wide assortment of stock, but don't spread the margins too thin on rapidly moving items.
- Forecast the need for seasonal items coming up.
- Increase inventory turnover with promotions to move slow items.
- Obtain lower prices by making volume purchases, but not so much as to cause a warehouse glut.
- Study buying trends and don't get caught with obsolete items.

Successful inventory management involves the simultaneous function of balancing the costs of inventory with the benefits of inventory. Many managers fail to understand fully the true costs of carrying a large inventory. This expenditure includes not only the direct cost of storage but related insurance, taxes, and supervisory personnel. Overlooked too often is the fact that inventories tie up funds that might be used for other productive purposes, such as the modernization of processing machinery, better transportation facilities, or improved customer service.

Other subjects related to inventory management include:

ABC Method. This system of inventory control focuses on the major elements of an organization's inventory and establishes priorities so that products and materials in demand are readily available. It also takes into account the time required to manufacture or process units in an inventory.

Just-in Time Method. An approach whose goal is to eliminate inventories rather than optimize them. The inventory of raw materials and work in progress is limited to what is needed for a single day. This goal is achieved by reducing setup times and lead times so that small lots may be ordered. Suppliers may have to make deliveries more often—even several times a day—and sometimes move their facilities closer to the plant to support this plan.

Material Requirements Planning. An information system in which sales are converted directly into loads on the facility by sub-unit and time period. Materials are scheduled more closely, thereby reducing inventories and resulting in delivery times that are shorter and more predictable.

Turnover Rate. A measure of managerial skill and performance that provides a guideline for managers to follow. The guideline varies widely in regard to the type of business and how the ratio is tabulated (whether on sales or cost of goods sold, for example). The variation can be seen dramatically in the case of one producer's paper board containers, whose turnover rate ranged from five to more than twenty.

See Accounting, Automatic Data Processing, Record Keeping, Seasonal Fluctuations, Turnover.

INVENTORY TURNOVER

In accounting, the rate at which the average amount of inventory on hand is sold within a specified period of time. *See* Inventory Management.

INVERSE DEMAND

A condition under which prices and volumes may vary at the same time, resulting in more sales at higher prices than at lower prices. *See* Distribution, Marketing.

INVESTED CAPITAL

See Investment.

INVESTMENT

Investments are central to any definition of economics, entities that occur when savings or profits are transformed into financially productive capacities, such as securities, real estate, factories, equipment, and public works. Some business economists prefer to use the term capital formation rather than investment. In their relationship to savings, investments function under the theory that the level of voluntary saving tends to adjust itself to the level of capital formation that producers are prepared to make. When people attempt to save more than business wants to invest, national income shrinks, but when business wants to invest more than can be financed out of current savings, the increased investment raises income. Thus, investment as an economic activity tends to be cyclical. See Economics, Investment Banking, Securities. *See* also the back-of-the-book supplement, "Investment Terms and Phrases," on page 458.

INVESTMENT BANKER

A banking specialist who serves as a middle agent between the purchasing public and corporations issuing new stocks and other securities. *See* Investment Banking.

INVESTMENT BANKING

The distribution of new issues of stocks, bonds, and other financial instruments to the investing public. Investment banking firms serve as intermediaries between the issuer of the security and the investors who may be individuals or institutions such as mutual and pension fund establishments or insurance companies. In practice, investment bankers purchase large blocks of securities from the issuer and sell them in split quantities to the public and may sometimes form a syndicate to market a large issue. Through underwriting, the banks establish potential markets and sell securities at an agreed-upon price, losing money if they are unable to find buyers at the offering price. Investment banking enables the capital market system to function smoothly by providing prompt investment opportunities. *See* Banking, Investment, Underwriting.

INVESTMENT COUNSELOR

A trained and experienced financial expert whose profession is to advise clients on investments and/or manage the purchase and sale of investments. *See* Investments.

INVESTMENT TAX CREDIT (ITC)

A motivational form of discount granted by the federal government to firms that purchase equipment and supplies for the improvement of business. *See* Investments.

INVESTMENT TRUST

A fiduciary primarily concerned with making investments that distributes the income and profits therefrom in accordance with strict rules and covenants agreed upon by the directors of the trust. *See* Investments.

INVESTOR

In the financial world, an individual, group, or organization purchasing stocks, bonds, or other securities and fiscal instruments with the objective of securing regular dividends, making short- or long-term profits, or achieving an expected rate of capital appreciation. *See* Investment.

INVITATION TO BID

Any communication, such as an advertisement or direct-mail letter, issued by an individual, group, or organization seeking to contact appropriate parties to bid on a proposed project. *See* Contracting.

INVOLUNTARY BANKRUPTCY

That form of bankruptcy that is made mandatory by the petition of one or more creditors. Also known as *forced bankruptcy*.

INVOLUNTARY LIEN

A lien on goods, equipment, or property that is brought about without the consent of the owner. *See* Lien.

IRREVOCABLE LETTER OF CREDIT

A letter of credit that cannot be nullified until after a declared date without the consent of the individual or firm in whose name it is drawn. *See* Letter of Credit.

IRREVOCABLE TRUST

That form of trust that cannot be amended, canceled, or modified by the party making the trust. *See* Trust.

ITEMIZED DEDUCTIONS

Those expenses, contributions, losses, or other reductions in profit or earnings that fall within the category of sums that can be deducted from taxable income. *See* Income Tax.

ITERATION

In business management and professional consulting, the term for any procedure whereby the repetition of a sequence of consistent steps or stages results in the improvement of a function, operation, or production process. *See* Management, Production.

JOB ACTION

A protest or demonstration by employees and/or labor representatives that falls short of an actual strike. *See* Labor/Management.

JOB ANALYSIS

A methodical study and evaluation of the specific duties and responsibilities inherent in a job or assignment, as well as the nature and degree of salary, wages, benefits, or other recompense. Proper job analysis leads to job enrichment programs and procedures. *See* Job Enrichment, Personnel Administration.

JOBBER

In marketing and sales, a middle person who purchases commodities or goods from producers, wholesalers, or importers and markets them to retailers. *See* Distribution, Retailing.

JOB CORPS

A federal agency, established by the Economic Opportunity Act of 1964 to provide vocational training, job searches, remedial education, health care, and counseling to disadvantaged youth. Modeled after the Civilian Conservation Corps of the 1930s, the Job Corps was organized to help combat unemployment among young people from 16 to 21 years of age. *See* Economic Opportunity Act, Training.

JOB-COST SYSTEM

In accounting, a procedure for determining the actual costs of individual products and materials, as determined by the manpower hours and production processes necessary to produce them and ready them for market. *See* Accounting.

JOB DESCRIPTION
See Job Analysis.

JOB ENRICHMENT
Also referred to as *job enlargement,* a plan of action for increasing the scope and significance and responsibilities of a job, position, or assignment to improve an employee's morale and satisfaction with his or her work. An example of job enrichment can be seen in the case of an electrician assigned to the office of a corporate headquarters, who not only installs and improves the building's electrical systems, but is further assigned the responsibility of inspecting and approving the electrical systems in some of the company's out-lying facilities. *See* Job Analysis, Personnel Administration.

JOB LOT
A sundry collection of products or parts of various types, sizes, colors, and other characteristics bought at a bargain price, usually on a "no guarantee" basis. *See* Marketing, Purchasing.

JOB PROCESS SYSTEM
Sometimes referred to as *intermittent production,* this is a method of man-ufacturing or fabrication in job shops that is fashioned to produce small orders of atypical products, which may vary from job to job in regard to size, shape, materials, colors, and other specifications. Job process systems are applied to the kinds of products that are tailor-made, personalized, or varied according to seasonal requirements, for example, but have enough similarity in general so they can be produced in modest quantities at reasonable price, and within practical time deadlines. *See* Manufacturing, Production.

JOB ROTATION
A formalized educational process by which employees, especially in manage-ment training, are transferred periodically through a series of different posi-tions in order to acquire experience and more extensive knowledge for future use on the job. *See* Personnel Administration, Training.

JOB TICKET
In printing and publication, a card with directions for processing an assign-ment through the various stages, each of which is checked off as it is com-pleted, with any related notations.

Joint Account

Any type of financial account, but most commonly associated by bank checking and savings accounts, that is drawn up by two or more persons, groups, or organizations. *See* Banking.

Joint Agreement

In labor, a contract between labor and management when more than one union or employer is involved. *See* Labor Relations.

Joint and Several

The legal term that applies in which parties may be sued alone or together in a lawsuit, each one bearing responsibility for the other(s).

Joint Contract

An agreement involving two or more individuals or organizations, each of whom assumes designated responsibilities to the other(s) as joint obligators to the contract and the other signer(s). *See* Contract.

Joint Ownership

The ownership of or interest in property, facilities, or other entities of substantial worth by two or more parties. *See* Real Estate.

Joint Production Costs

In manufacturing, those costs of producing products or materials that are fabricated in a single (joint) operation and that cannot be identified with individual units on the production line until later in the manufacturing sequence. *See* Manufacturing, Production.

Joint-stock Company

A class of partnership having many of the attributes of a corporation, including the issuance of securities whose shares may be transferred from one owner to another and whose management is centralized in a board of directors elected by the shareholders. This type of corporation, however, has become less popular as state statutes have made it easier to form other kinds of corporations. A J/S company differs from a corporation in that the former's shareholders can be personally liable for the company's debts, similar to the partners in a partnership. *See* Corporation.

JOINT TENANCY

The rights to a property title or real estate held by two or more parties with equal rights to possession and use. It is distinguished from other types of mutual ownership in that each tenant owns the undivided whole, while the co-ownership contains a right of survivorship, meaning that, upon the death of one joint tenant, his or her interest passes to the remaining joint tenant(s), rather than to heirs. *See* Real Estate.

JOINT VENTURE

A commercial or business enterprise entered into by two or more parties who share the responsibilities and benefits to the degree specified in their agreement and that cannot be terminated until enumerated conditions have been met to the satisfaction of all concerned. *See* Entrepreneur.

JOURNAL ENTRY

A written registering of a business transaction, focusing on the monetary amounts, if any, dates, locales, and the impact on the business. *See* Bookkeeping.

JOURNALISM

The profession of mass-media activities that relate to the compilation and publication or broadcasting of news-related material for both general and specialized divisions of the public at large, but not including advertising, merchandising, or public relations stories. Two types of media play key roles in journalism: the print media (newspapers and magazines) and the broadcast, or electronic, media (radio and television). As a business, journalism, referred to as the *fourth estate,* is rated as one of the top industries in the United States, at the forefront of communications technology and calling upon specialists such as journalists, reporters, staff writers, editors, columnists, editorial writers, cartoonists, feature writers, photographers, correspondents, production managers, commentators, news directors, newscasters, and producers. As one journalist editorialized, "Journalism, an activity that is vital to society, particularly to industrialized, democratic societies, has been called a cement for society, providing the population with information for the effective management of social institutions. It contributes to public opinion, disseminates news and opinion, entertains, monitors government, probes social institutions, and provides raw grist for the mills of debate and discussion." *See* Advertising, Communication, Media, Public Relations.

JOURNALIZE

To record entries regarding business transactions, generally using the double-entry method. *See* Double Entry.

JUDGMENT

A legal award or decision that substantiates a claim and states the circumstances of its enforcement, whether for the payment of money, the restitution of something of worth, or the performance of other obligations by the party whom the judgment is against. The decision results in the naming of both a *judgment creditor* and a *judgment debtor.* A judgment is a court decision, customarily based on conclusions derived from evidence presented at a trial, settling finally and authoritatively the issues in dispute. Judgments can be appealed to higher courts and may be set aside by them. *See* Business Law.

JUDICIAL REVIEW

The power of courts to decide the validity of acts of the legislative and executive branches of the government. The courts can decide that a legislative act is unconstitutional and nullify it, as well as overrule any decisions of the executive and administrative agencies if they are not deemed to conform to the law or the Constitution. Subsequently, states adopt the same view, and their superior courts commonly nullify acts of legislatures that conflict with the state constitutions. Constitutions adopted by other countries, such as Germany, Italy, India, and Pakistan, often provide for some form of judicial review. Great Britain does not recognize judicial review; the final authority in British law is Parliament. The Court tends to observe the principle that any censure of the validity of a statute must overcome a presumption of its constitutionality, and it also states that it will not question the wisdom of particular legislative and executive actions and will avoid political issues. *See* Business Law, Legislation.

JUDICIAL SALE

Any sale of property, goods, or other valuables that is conducted by the order of and under the jurisdiction of a court of law. *See* Business Law.

JUDICIARY SYSTEM

See Legislation.

JUNK BONDS

Certificates that have low credit ratings and may even be in default, are high risks, and sell at substantial discounts. *See* Bonds, Investments.

JUNKET

A trip that is taken presumably for business reasons, but that also includes pleasurable or recreational activities and that is paid for by the employer of the person(s) making the journey. *See* Compensation.

JURISDICTION

The legal power of a court or other authority to hear a case and determine the course of action. A court may act in disputes only within its jurisdiction and generally cannot profess authority, say, over a defendant who resides outside of its area of jurisdiction. In addition to geographical limitations, there are also restrictions on the kinds of disputes that courts may hear, regardless of whether they feel that injustices have occurred; not every court may grant a divorce, for example. Disputes are presented to the appropriate courts by attorneys, who must determine first that there actually is a valid dispute and not simply a misunderstanding that can be settled out of court. If any party in a court case is dissatisfied with the outcome, there is still access to a higher court, which will then review the lower court's decision. In such cases, courts known as *appellate courts* determine whether the case has been handled properly or whether errors in the proceedings justify a retrial or other form of legal action. *See* Business Law, Legislation.

JURISPRUDENCE

The profession and practice of law. *See* Business Law.

JUSTICE DEPARTMENT (U.S.)

The legal agency of the federal government, headed by the attorney general of the United States, charged with the enforcement of federal laws, the representation of the government in pertinent legal matters, and the provider of legal counseling to the President and the heads of the executive departments. The Justice Department includes the Federal Bureau of Investigation (FBI), the Federal Bureau of Prisons, the Board of Parole, the Immigration and Naturalization Service, the Board of Immigration Appeals, the Drug Enforcement Administration, the Law Enforcement Assistance Administration, and six divisions. *See* Government.

JUSTICE OF THE PEACE

A public official with limited judicial power, who is usually elected, but in some states appointed, and who has been granted the authority to try minor criminal cases and civil cases involving only small amounts of money. A justice's other duties might include issuing arrest and search warrants, holding preliminary hearings in certain types of criminal cases, holding inquests, and performing marriage ceremonies. Historically, the position originated in England in the Middle Ages, as an agent of the king, charged with maintaining the peace in each borough. *See* Business Law, Courts.

JUSTIFIED PRICE

A price that is considered fair in the eyes of informed buyers and sellers of merchandise, goods, and services. *See* Merchandising.

JUSTINIAN CODE

An ancient sixth-century Roman code from the *Corpus Juris Civilis* ("Body of Civil Law"), created during the reign of Emperor Justinian as a compilation of laws that had accumulated over a period of one thousand years. The Code was influential in the development of European law hundreds of years later, and its impact is still felt in legal matters today. *See* Business Law, Jurisprudence.

JUST-IN-TIME (JIT)

A practical strategy that was developed in Japan in the mid-1970s and that focuses on the elimination of waste in manufacturing and the continuing upgrading of production processes. The theory is based on timing manufacturing procedures at all levels so that materials and supplies are replenished precisely when they are needed and neither early enough to have to be stored or late enough to interrupt the smooth flow of the production line. *See* Production, Production Management.

K

Kanban

In management, a procedure that authorizes supplies and materials for use only when and if there is a need for them and that utilizes tabulator cards to approve the supply, withdrawal, and processing of materials in a manufacturing configuration. *See* Just-in-time (JIT).

Kapital, Das

A politico-economic study authored by Karl Marx, which served as the basic theory of socialism and communism and claimed that all history is determined by man's relationship to material wealth and that governments represent only the interests of the ruling class. Marx prophesied that capitalism would result in a concentration of wealth in the hands of a few and that this situation would end with a revolution that would first establish socialism and then communism. Marx's critics asserted that he failed to take into account capitalism's ability to regulate itself and to foster a more even distribution of wealth. *See* Capitalism, Economics.

Keelage

A form of charter paid by shipping, transportation, and handling companies in a port for the use of facilities in, or adjacent to, a harbor. *See* Shipping, Transportation.

Keogh Plan

A pension program designed for the private sector and established by law that permits self-employed individuals to establish their own retirement and pension programs. *See* Retirement Planning.

Keyboard

The common term for a computer keyboard that is used to feed commands and information into a computer, consisting of an arrangement of keys that can be manually depressed and that electronically activate the input or output of information. The most common type of keyboard closely resembles that of an electric typewriter, with keys for letters, numbers, and punctuation, as well as for others that activate the computer's various functions. *See* Computers, Data Processing, Hardware.

KEYED ADVERTISING

Advertising, whether print, broadcast, or other, that is keyed in such a way that replies from consumers identify the medium and location in which they received the advertiser's message. *See* Advertising, Merchandising.

KEY-EXECUTIVE OPTION

A privileged alternative extended to managers and other key executives whereby they can purchase stock in the company from a block of securities set aside for the purpose through a vote by the stockholders. *See* Compensation, Securities.

KEY INDUSTRY

Any industry that is of major importance to a nation, state, county, or other geographic entity because of its positive impact on employment, public affairs, and the economy in general. *See* Industry.

KEY-MAN INSURANCE

Life, accident, and health insurance policies that are taken out in the name of top—or "key"—managers and supervisors, with the objective of protecting the interests of the company (which is usually the purchaser of such policies) in the event that the policy-holder dies, is incapacitated, or otherwise is unable to execute normal duties. *See* Insurance.

KEYNESIAN ECONOMICS

The economic theory propounded by the noted British economist John Maynard Keyes in the 1930s and since modified, which takes the stand that government involvement in the economy is the most forceful, reliable, and intelligent way to moderate excessive and undesirable fluctuations in the business cycle. Keynes, one of the most influential economists in the twentieth century, was an exceptional individual, who was not only an economist, but a high government official, editor of an academic journal, a superb business-man, author of numerous books, a brilliant teacher at Cambridge University, a college bursar, a collector of rare books, an economic seer, and a patron of the arts. One of his central theories was that times exist in a market economy when the total demand of consumers and investors are insufficient to purchase all the goods the society has produced, that business managers, finding they cannot sell all they have on hand, would cut back on production and employment, and that a depression would result. He also insisted that one solution during periods of high unemployment was for the government to increase the money supply, thus lowering interest rates and encouraging investment. But he also advocated a fiscal policy of deficit spending on public works and other projects and the maintenance during depressions of an unbalanced budget to increase the aggregate demand for goods and services. Although Keynes's opinions about the economy were unconventional and controversial, his views became widely accepted among economists in England and the United States. *See* Economics, also Fiscal Policies, the term for the government's strategy to tax and redistribute wealth through federal expenditures.

KEY PERSONNEL

Those individuals in an organization, whether commercial or nonprofit, who are responsible for the management of important operations or whose professional accomplishments are such that they cannot easily be duplicated by substitute executives. *See* Business Management.

KEYSTONE PRICING

A questionable merchandising practice in which the marked price of a product is deliberately made to look higher than the selling price in order that buyers feel they are getting a bargain. *See* Merchandising.

KEY WORD

A reference to whatever single word in a title, slogan, missive, or other heading most aptly pinpoints the contents of the text that follows. *See* Communications.

KICKBACK

An illegal form of extortion in which monetary demands lead to payments to managers or employees that are detrimental to the economic health of an organization. *See* Business Law, Extortion.

KINETIC ENERGY

The energy of motion in which solid objects and fluids alike possess energy simply because of their motion. Mathematically, the kinetic energy of a moving object is expressed as half the product of the object's mass and the square of its speed. Kinetic energy is only one of several types of energy that are important in the study of physics, and engineers seek efficient ways to convert one to the other. *See* Energy.

KITING

The practice of issuing checks in excess of the signer's bank balance with the expectation of making deposits in time to cover the checks. Also, the criminal act of altering a check so that the cashier receives a higher amount than was intended by the issuer. *See* Banks and Banking, Business Law.

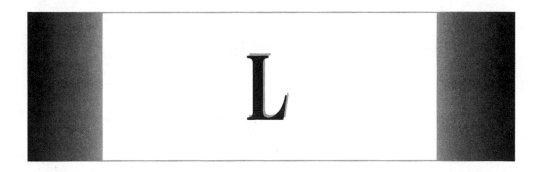

L

LABOR AGREEMENT

A contract between an employer and a union that protects employees by specifying in detail the conditions of their employment. *See* Labor Management Relations Act, Labor Unions.

LABOR DEPARTMENT

The federal agency that was established "to foster, promote, and develop the welfare of the wage earners of the United States, to improve their working conditions, and to advance their opportunities for profitable employment." The department administers some 140 laws governing wages, working conditions, discrimination, and employment, publishes statistical data, maintains public employment agencies, supervises labor training programs and emergency job programs, sets labor standards, assists veterans in readjusting from military to civilian occupations, and supervises labor-management relations in the federal government. Among the department's affiliates are the Employment Standards Administration, which administers the minimum-wage and hour laws and various other laws involving worker compensation, the Occupational Safety and Health Administration, which enforces safety and health standards in industry, and the Bureau of Labor Statistics, which compiles the Consumer Price Index and publishes information on employment and earnings. *See* Bureau of Labor Statistics, Consumer Price Index, Labor Force, Labor\Management, Occupational Safety and Health Administration.

LABOR FORCE

The phrase referring to all individuals and groups who either hold existing jobs or are available for work, which is used statistically, especially by the Bureau of Labor Statistics, to indicate the status of employment in a nation, state, or other political entity. In the United States, the total work force under this category, including both civilian and military employment, is about 130 million individuals, which figure includes a dramatic increase in the number of females

199

and certain minority groups. *See* Bureau of Labor Statistics, Labor Force, Labor Department.

LABOR INTENSIVE

Said of any situation in which an excessive application of manpower has been applied in order to complete a job more quickly, or to increase output or earnings. *See* Business Administration, Underemployment.

LABOR MANAGEMENT RELATIONS ACT

Better known as the Taft-Hartley Act, this legislation was enacted to limit some of the more aggressive activities of labor unions in the United States, amending an earlier act that had delineated the rights of unions to organize and to bargain with management. Among the revisions was the forbidding of unions to force employees to become members, the banning of closed shops, and the restricting of certain types of boycotts. The act also authorized the President of the United States to impose delays on any strike or lockout that might threaten the national health or safety, required unions to furnish specific data about their finances, permitted employers to replace striking workers, and imposed restrictions on union contributions to political campaigns. *See* Labor/Management, Labor Unions, Strikes.

LABOR MOBILITY

The ease with which workers in an organization can be shifted from one job to another, or one type of work to another, without excessive training or delay.

LABOR POOL

A predetermined source of workers, whether already on site or available on call, from which workers can quickly be recruited. *See* Labor Force.

LABOR RELATIONS

That area of communications and public relations that deals with the relationships between employers and employees and whose primary objective is to maintain both cordiality and respect between the two groups. *See* Employee Relations.

LABOR UNION

A confederation of workers whose purpose is to bargain with management in matters relating to wages, other forms of compensation, hours, working conditions, and related situations. In the United States, between 16 and 19 percent of all of the people employed or unemployed belong to unions or similar employee associations, a considerably smaller portion than in many other countries, particularly those of Europe. However, the number of employees affected by union activity is much greater, since union-activated programs and achievements greatly affect the lives and jobs of nonunion workers as well. Unions are basically involved with four functions: recruiting new members, negotiating with management, planning strikes and work stoppages when necessary, and working to achieve legislation favorable to their membership. In regard to the last-mentioned function, unions are often the major influence in effecting changes in government policies and practices, largely because of their lobbying strength and their many effective efforts to convince legislators at all levels to bring about changes—political, economic, and social alike. *See* all other *Labor* entries.

LAISSEZ FAIRE

From the French "let be," the word used for an economic doctrine of noninterference. *See* Free Enterprise.

LAND GRANT

The contribution of public land by a government or one of its agencies to be utilized for the public good, most often for parks, recreational use, historic sites, and education. In regard to the last-mentioned category, land-grant colleges have benefited particularly, since these institutions of higher learning were either founded or expanded because of the assistance of federal lands granted to the states specifically for the enhancement of education in the United States, in such fields as agriculture, science, industry, and teaching. *See* Environment, Homesteading.

LANGUAGE

In technical, business, and commercial applications, the use of characters, ciphers, and symbols to communicate quickly and graphically, as in computerized systems. *See* Major Section on Communications.

LAPPING

The illegal practice of concealing shortages of materials or supplies by using a series of entries that on paper postpone the receipt of an asset from one accounting stage to the next. *See* Accounting.

LASER TECHNOLOGY

The application of that type of light known as the LASER, the acronym for "light amplification by stimulated emission of radiation," which moves in the form of varying waves at high velocity to produce different colors and frequencies. Similar to radio waves, laser beams can transmit information, in this case encoded in the beam as variations in the frequency or shape of the light wave, and with much greater capacity. Besides velocity and volume, another advantage of the laser beam is that it can produce light that is not only essentially in a single frequency but also harmonious with the light waves all moving along together in unison.

LATENT DEFECTS

Imperfections and flaws in products or materials that are not visible to the touch or to the naked eye. *See* Ultrasonics, X-ray.

LATIN AMERICAN FREE TRADE ASSOCIATION

As a confederation founded to liberalize trade among its member countries, LAFTA has been active in Argentina, Bolivia, Brazil, Colombia, Ecuador, Mexico, Paraguay, Peru, Uruguay, and Venezuela, but has been impeded by internal dissensions and the high costs of operating. costs, economic nationalism, and the efforts of member countries to protect sheltered markets. *See* Free Trade, International Trade.

LAWS THAT AFFECT BUSINESS

The following laws and federal regulations are those that are most common in business and industry, listed alphabetically and not in any order of priority:

- Age Discrimination in Employment Act
- Civil Right Act
- Clayton Act
- Consumer Credit Protection Act
- Consumer Products Safety Act
- Employee Retirement Income Security Act
- Equal Credit Opportunity Act
- Equal Employment Opportunity Act
- Equal Pay Regulations
- Fair Credit Billing Act
- Fair Credit Reporting Regulations
- Fair Debt Collection Regulations
- Fair Labor Standards Act
- Fair Packaging and Labeling Act

- Federal Trade Commission Act
- Federal Wages and Hours Regulations
- Federal Warranty Regulations
- Fibrous Materials Regulations
- Flammable Fabrics Regulations
- Food, Drug, and Cosmetic Act
- Hazardous Substances Regulations
- National Labor Relations Regulations
- Natural Materials Regulations
- Occupational Safety and Health Act
- Pure Food and Drug Act
- Robinson-Patman Act
- Sherman Antitrust Act
- Social Security Regulations
- Wheeler-Lea Act

See also Business Law.

LEADERSHIP

Defined as "the personal capacity to guide and influence others, whether for better or worse, good or evil, but with definite goals and purposes in mind." In business and industry, the qualities of leadership include, among other attributes, the ability and motivation to think like a manager, respect people, venerate time, develop a professional style, know the capabilities of employees, perfect insight, communicate often and well, and act at all times as a leader. See Management.

LEADERSHIP TRAINING

Individual and inclusive programs of management training established to upgrade the skills and perceptiveness of participants through seminars, conferences, workshops, and other curricula, generally under the active supervision of managers of the type the sponsors hope the students will emulate. See Leadership.

LEAD TIME

In production, the length of time that exists between startups and the completion of finished products on the manufacturing line. See Production Management.

LEAGUE OF WOMEN VOTERS

An organization that was established to provide objective information about political candidates and issues and motivate citizens to orient themselves about the options, come to reasonable decisions, and vote in all elections, national, state, or local. Although the League was originally limited to women when it was founded in 1920, and placed more emphasis on problems and issues affecting women, it later extended its membership to males. Today, it conducts studies, distributes information on candidates and issues, runs voter-registration drives, takes stands on pending legislation, and sponsors political debates. *See* Civil Rights, Minorities.

LEASE-BACK

An agreement that is reached in order for the owner of property or a facility to sell it to another party on condition that the original owner can lease it back for a stipulated period of time at a predetermined rent. *See* Real Estate.

LEAVE OF ABSENCE

An extended period of time off from work, usually without loss of seniority and sometimes with whole or partial pay, with the expectation of returning to the job. One of the most common examples is the leave of absence granted to a pregnant woman just before her child is born, and extending for two or three months, with pay. *See* Compensation, Employee Relations.

LEDGER

In accounting, a book of accounts known as a *general ledger,* which has separate pages for each account. If a large portion of an organization's business involves cash transactions, a separate cash journal can be used instead of the general journal for all those transactions affecting the cash account. All entries not affecting cash are made in the general journal. Periodically, entries are recorded, or *posted,* in the ledger accounts. As each journal entry is recorded on the planned side of its account, a mark is placed in the post column of the journal to show that it has been recorded in the ledger. The date used in the ledger is the date on which it was first entered in the journal. The post column in the account is designed to show which page this entry was posted to in the ledger. If a cash journal is used, the monthly cash totals, rather than each entry, can be posted to the cash account. *See* Accounting.

LEGAL ENTITY

Any organization, such as a partnership, that has the capability and authority to enter into contracts and discharge debts and other obligations. *See* Business Law.

LEGAL LIST

An inventory of investments licensed by state governments in which certain institutions, such as banks, fiduciaries, and insurance companies are permitted to invest.

LEGAL MONOPOLY

An organization that is privately owned, but which is granted an exclusive right by the government to operate in a designated market as a monopoly, under strict regulation and pricing. *See* Cartel.

LEGISLATURE

A decision-making body of a government, whether national, state, or local, engaged in making laws and existing today in all Western countries and throughout the world. Most legislators are elected by public vote, although legislatures may also contain some members who are appointed or who are entitled to membership as replacements for individuals who have died, retired, or have been judged to be incompetent. Legislatures vary greatly in their influence on laws and governmental affairs. Those in authoritarian governments, such as dictatorships, serve in name only and have little impact on the state of their nations, while those in democracies are full-fledged lawmaking bodies. Others, like the British House of Commons, are influential, but tend to follow the lead of the ruling party. Although the American public tends to think of legislatures as being *bicameral*—that is, having two houses, such as the House and the Senate—about two thirds of the world's federal legislatures are *unicameral* and have only one house. Bicameral legislatures are characteristic of democratic systems of government, where one chamber represents the people and the other represents the states or provinces. The United States and some other democracies favor the *congressional system,* in which the principle of the separation of powers mandates that members of the legislature are elected separately from the chief executive and thus are independent. By contrast, the *parliamentary system* dictates that the political leader (comparable to the president) be a member of the legislature and the head of the party then in power. A typical legislature in a free country, regardless of its underlying structure and method of formation, executes four major functions: the recruitment of leaders; the management of conflicts among diverse social, economic, or political groups; the linkage of government bodies and officials with the citizenry; and the passage of laws. *See* Government.

LENDING INSTITUTION

A bank, finance company, small loan service, or other organization that is licensed or chartered to lend money, within certain interest scales, and that profits from the advancement of funds to individuals, firms, and other parties. *See* Banking, Loans.

LETTER OF ATTORNEY

More commonly referred to as a *power of attorney,* which see.

LETTER OF CREDIT

An empowered document issued by one bank on behalf of a buyer for use with another bank or financial institution, thus giving the buyer the privilege and backing of the issuing bank. Commercial letters of credit are commonly used by importers and exporters as a convenient method of underwriting the purchase of merchandise. A familiar form of letter of credit is the traveler's check. *See* Banking.

LETTER STOCK

A form of security that is unregistered on any exchange and is customarily issued by a new firm to skirt the expense of formal underwriting.

LEVELING

In the personnel field, a procedure in time-and-motion studies that is utilized as a means of measuring and evaluating the efficiency and output of employees tested. *See* Personnel Administration.

LEVERAGE

That portion of the costs that represent a risk to a firm when it borrows money and reinvests it or uses it to produce a return exceeding the expense of borrowing. The term *financial leverage* is used as a measure of financial risk. *See* Finance.

LEVERAGED BUYOUT

A situation that occurs when a company or other entity borrows money in order to buy another company. The acquiring company commonly uses the assets of the company acquired as collateral for the transaction. *See* Finance.

LIABILITY

The amount that an organization owes to another firm, group, individual, or any other party to which it is indebted. Any amount that is not owed and is free of debt is called the owner's *equity*. Since everything that is owned is either owed or is free of debt, assets equal liabilities plus equity, a situation referred to as the *accounting equation*. Assets, liabilities, and equity are entered separately in a company's books and are known as an account. An account has two positions, for debits and credits respectively. All assets are increased on the debit side of the account, and any decrease in value is shown on the credit side. Liabilities and equity, the other half of the equation, are increased and decreased in the opposite manner. Liabilities and equity are increased on the credit side and decreased on the debit side. The owners' equity can be increased either by investing more money in the firm or by earning a profit, and is decreased by the withdrawal of funds from the business, as well as by business losses. Withdrawals and expenses incurred without receiving an asset are increased on the debit side, for each additional expense or withdrawal takes from the owners' equity. *See* Bookkeeping.

LIABILITY LEDGER

A record maintained by a bank or other financial institution to show all outstanding loans made to borrowers. *See* Liability.

LIBERALISM

A brand of political philosophy, which originated in Europe just before the French Revolution and that stressed the needs and advantages of personal, individual freedom. In many countries, it was highly controversial, if not damned, because it favored emancipation from conventional and traditional restraints and was strongly against monarchies and many of the stricter church denominations. By the early twentieth century, liberalism in the United States began to be associated with the concept that government should play a larger role in the economy and be concerned about the well being of the country's citizens, even to the extreme of being labeled a "welfare state."

Those who were known as liberals were at the forefront of movements that felt capitalism had become too unregulated and that the government should take action to correct some of the evils that had resulted. The liberal movement was thus the catalyst in the formation of such institutions as Social Security, minimum-wage programs, public education, environmental agencies, and antitrust legislation. An extreme form of liberalism was socialism, although it did not go so far as to include communism or Marxism. *See* Socialism.

LIBERALIZATION

In personnel relations, the increase of privileges or rights and benefits granted to individual employees or employees as a group. *See* Personnel Administration.

LIBERTARIAN PARTY

A political party in America, founded in 1971, that emphasizes individual liberties and expounds the belief that the power of government should be sharply curtailed, even to the extent of repealing laws that limit personal freedom, such as gambling, prostitution, and free sex. Libertarians also support a free market economy, without government intervention, a neutral foreign policy, and the withdrawal of the United States from the United Nations. *See* Liberalism.

LIBRARY OF CONGRESS

Established in 1800, this national library was originally intended to provide books for the use of the Congress, and not for the general public. Since then, however, LOC, though supported largely by funds authorized by Congress, has become the nation's official and universal library, serving all branches and affiliates of the government, as well as the public at large. For more than a century, it has also administered the American copyright system. In addition, it publishes the National Union Catalog, an aggregate record of the books housed in some 2,500 libraries in the United States and Canada, maintains a Congressional Research Service, prints and distributes cataloging data for subscriber libraries and constantly updates a numerical system it created for subject classification. The library's own collections include some 15 million books and 40 million manuscripts, as well as countless accumulations of maps, music, art, photographs, motion pictures, videotapes, periodicals, and other materials. *See* Congress, Government.

LICENSING AGREEMENT

A contract permitting one party to assume one or more operations of another party, such as manufacturing, selling, or servicing, in consideration for monetary remuneration or other benefits, as specified. *See* Contract.

LIEN

An attachment by one party to the property of another party, which will result in penalties to the owner, or possibly the loss of the property, if certain stipulations are not met before a deadline date. *See* Attachment.

LIEN AFFIDAVIT

A legal document attesting to the fact that there are no liens against a particular property, or listing and describing them if such do exist. *See* Lien.

LIFE ESTATE

The condition that exists when an individual is given a freehold interest in land, but which is limited to the lifespan of the individual. The person holding a life estate is referred to as a life tenant.

LIMITED ACCESS

Said of land or other property that is difficult to reach for natural reasons or which has purposely been made more inaccessible. *See* Real Estate.

LIMITED LIABILITY

Limited responsibility for debts and other obligations, a condition that applies particularly to a corporation, whose officers and employees have little or no liability for any financial burdens of the company and its operations. *See* Limited Partnership.

LIMITED PARTNERSHIP

A business partnership in which the liabilities and obligations of one or more of the partners is limited to a specified amount. *See* Partnership.

LINEAR PROGRAMMING

In manufacturing, a stratagem for portraying the methods by which parts and/or materials should be combined to eliminate waste, improve performance, expedite assembly, and eventually result in greater profits. *See* Production Management.

LINE BALANCING

In manufacturing and production, a system for assigning duties to individual work stations, the objective being to limit the number of stations and to reduce the time during which stations, individually and collectively, are idle. *See* Manufacturing, Production.

LINE OF CREDIT

An agreement with a customer by a bank or other financial institution that extends a limited amount of credit as a loan, but on which the customer pays interest only on the borrowed portion. *See* Banking, Credit.

LINE OF DISCOUNT

In marketing, the maximum credit that a lending institution will extend to a merchant on the basis of his or her accounts payable, which the customer discounts with the lender. *See* Banking.

LIQUID ASSETS

Any assets that can quickly be converted into cash. *See* Assets.

LIQUIDATION

The process of turning assets into cash, or the equivalent. Also, the act of closing out a business, particularly when it becomes bankrupt and goes into receivership. *See* Liquidation Value.

LIQUIDATION VALUE

The worth of a company or property that is being forced into a sale, generally the amount that would realistically be realized if the entity in question were to be sold and all costs and obligations were deducted from the sum received. *See* Liquidation.

LIST

In advertising and merchandising, a specialized directory of potential purchasers that is carefully selected on the basis of purchasing habits, income, location, age, sex, and other factors. *See* List Broker.

LIST BROKER

An agent engaged in compiling, updating, and leasing lists of prospective purchasers to clients who are selling products or services by direct mail. *See* List.

LIST PRICE

The designated price, usually published or posted at the point of sale, which is used as a criterion, but may be reduced during a sale or in the case of volume purchases or special discounts. *See* Merchandising.

LOAD FUNDS

Mutual funds that are sold by sales representatives who receive commissions based on the price and quantity. *See* No-load Funds.

LOADING

The practice of increasing an installment payment price to include finance charges, administrative costs, and sales commissions—sometimes in an unethical manner that leads purchasers to think they are buying merchandise at a lower cost than is the case. In the selling of securities, such as mutual funds, this is often referred to as a *loading charge.*

LOBBYIST

An individual whose job or assignment it is to influence the general public or the government to take beneficial action on behalf of a client's interests, or at least to hold a positive opinion of the subject matter being lobbied. The term originated with the frequenting of the lobbies of government buildings in the early nineteenth century by individuals intent on bending the ears of influential legislators about matters with which they were concerned. Today, Washington has become infiltrated by organizations promoting just about every kind of cause imaginable, whose members are intent upon influencing the nation's decision makers by direct contact, as well as through all of the major advertising and promotional media. Despite periodic complaints and controversies, not to mention occasional charges of bribery, lobbyists are recognized as being essential to the course of government and oftentimes providers of valuable and practical information that busy legislators do not have the time to compile. Lobbying is protected by the Constitution, particularly the First Amendment, and is monitored by the Federal Regulation of Lobbying Act, which, among other things prohibits lobbying by high public officials until at least one year after they have left office. *See* Government, Press, Public Relations.

LOCAL BRAND

A brand of merchandise that bears the imprint of a wholesaler or other regional marketer and is sold only throughout a limited geographical area. *See* Merchandising, Trademark.

LOCKOUT

The closing of a place of business by an employer as a means of preventing employees from working, and thus pressuring a union into settling a labor dispute in management's favor. *See* Labor/Management, Strike.

LOGO

The popular name for *logotype,* a distinctive trade mark or symbol used by marketers and advertisers to distinguish themselves. *See* Trademark.

LOGO

An instructional computer language created in the 1970s by the Massachusetts Institute of Technology to help young pupils to distinguish letters, words, and sounds, as well as colors, shapes, and directions. Through the manipulation of symbols on the scanning screen, children learn how to use computers to solve problems, get answers, experiment with designs, or devise plans. *See* Computers.

LONG POSITION

In the investment field, the term used to describe securities that are being held by the purchaser with the expectation that the value and price of shares will rise considerably and result in a substantial profit.

LONG-RANGE PLANNING

That form of corporate or organizational planning that evaluates present and past operations and projects them into the near and distant future, generally for periods of more than one year.

LONG-TERM ASSETS

Capital investments, fixed assets, and other resources of worth that have continuing value and are not designated as current assets.

LONG-TERM CONTRACT

In labor relations, any contract or agreement between unions and management that is negotiated for a period of more than one year.

LONG-TERM DEBTS

Loans and other financial obligations that do not become due until one year or more after the signing of the contract. Also referred to as a *long-term liability.*

LOOP

Instructions or directions on a sequential computer program or other data-processing setup where the final entry triggers the system to repeat itself. *See* Loop Modification.

LOOP MODIFICATION

The revision of data or sequences in a loop by means of instruction to the automated system. *See* Loop.

LOSS LEADER

In merchandising, a product that is advertised and promoted at a bargain price, which will lose money on the sale of that product but attract prospective customers to other—usually higher-priced—merchandise.

LOT

A group or pack of products or materials of a similar or related nature that are bought or sold in a single transaction.

LUMP-SUM SETTLEMENT

An amount of money or other liquid assets that is offered and accepted to discharge a claim or obligation, most commonly for an insurance policy or lawsuit. *See* Business Law, Insurance.

LUXURY MARKET

A reference to those consumers who have the wherewithal and inclinations to purchase high-priced, or luxury, products and services. *See* Consumers, Marketing, Retailing.

LUXURY TAX

Any tax imposed on merchandise, materials, property, or amenities not considered essential for ordinary living. *See* Taxation.

Machine Code

In manufacturing and production, a code or automated order that a machine is programmed to recognize and act upon. *See* Manufacturing, Production.

Machine Rating

In production and manufacturing, a measure of a machine's capacities, capabilities, and proficiency, in terms of safety, efficiency, durability, energy requirements, output, control, and operational costs. *See* Manufacturing.

Macroeconomics

The branch of economics that deals with aggregates and composites of related data, such as the Gross National Product (GNP). *See* Microeconomics.

Macro Environment

The broad aspects of the "environment" in which an industry, business, or other organization functions, including not only the natural environment and the ecology of the region, but the political, ethnic, commercial, and even spiritual climate that may affect management, employees, and day-to-day operations. *See* Environment.

Magnetic Tape Memory

A data/memory system programmed for the sequential provision of information that is stored on a magnetic tape. *See* Data Processing.

Mailing

A bundle of letters, literature, or other printed matter that is mailed at one time, and usually at a lower postal rate than individual mailings. An item in a mailing is referred to as a *mailing piece. See* Advertising.

MAIL-ORDER ADVERTISING

That form of advertising that relates to the sale and purchase of items by mail, commonly promoted by mailed catalogs and brochures, but also announced in newspapers, magazines, and in commercials during radio and television broadcasts. *See* Advertising.

MAIL-ORDER BUSINESS

Firms that do business in this merchandising and marketing category are fundamentally retail distributors that solicit their orders primarily through the mails, although they may also attract prospective customers through print advertisements, paid commercials on radio and television, and by distributing catalogs and brochures. The mail-order business was launched in the late nineteenth century by such giants as Montgomery Ward and Sears, Roebuck and Co., which were aimed largely at rural consumers, and not until the 1970s did this form of business start to escalate into its present-day strength in the merchandising field. *See* Direct Selling, Marketing, Merchandising, Retailing.

MAIN FRAME

The basic structure of a computer, which houses or is joined to the other components of the installation, and the memory necessary to process information. *See* Computer.

MAJORITY STOCKHOLDERS

Those owners of securities in a corporation who jointly own more than 50 percent of the voting stock and therefore have a controlling interest. *See* Securities, Stocks.

MAJOR MEDICAL INSURANCE

Policies That Are Designed and written to cover predominant and costly medical expenses, including operations, hospitalization, and long-term care (but generally not nursing homes and similar institutions), and that customarily have a deductible amount that is assumed by the policyholder before any insurance is payable. *See* Health Insurance.

MAKEUP TERM

An undesirable period of time that must be utilized in a production or manufacturing operation to complete reruns to compensate for equipment failures or human errors in a previous run. *See* Production.

MALICIOUS PROSECUTION

Lawsuits or other legal proceedings that are motivated in bad faith as a form of harassment and without reasonable grounds or the expectation that the actions will be successful. *See* Business Law.

MALPRACTICE PROTECTION

Basically, a form of insurance that protects policy holders, who are usually, but not necessarily, in one of the medical professions, from claims against them for real or supposed negligence in the performance of their duties. *See* Business Law.

MALTHUSIAN LAW

A population theory that espouses the belief that the world's population increases faster than the available food supply and that, hence, starvation will always be with us. *See* Population.

MANAGEMENT

Defined in its briefest form as "the art and science of getting things done through other people," management is a highly complex function that requires individuals to take charge in five crucial areas:

1. *Planning.* The mental action of visualizing today what is necessary, expedient, and promising for tomorrow, including the genesis of ideas and the conception of events that will make goals and objectives possible, realistic, and favorable. Successful managers emphasize that a good plan will serve a company well, even if executed poorly, but the absence of plans—both long-range and short-range—will breed breed economic disaster.

2. *Organization.* Essentially, this action consists of allocating assignments to individuals and groups, matching tasks with skills, facilities, and tools, and establishing goals and timetables in order to expedite the goals and objectives elucidated during the planning stage. The elements of organization are employees, departments or divisions, time, function, products or services, customers or clients, economics, and administration.

3. *Staffing.* This area of performance includes evaluating area demographics, assessing company needs and requirements, recruiting, interviewing, testing, screening, hiring, orienting, training, and maintaining a loyal and dedicated work force. Managers with proven credentials in this field of activity know, too, that it is one of the most sensitive areas of

management and administration, requiring charisma in dealing with people, judgment in evaluating character, and tact in relationships with labor unions and community officials.

4. *Leading and motivating.* The ability to lead and induce others to follow is a skill that is both inborn and acquired, best achieved by those managers who are strongly motivated and who, in turn, are able to earn personal respect and motivate others by instilling in them the conviction that they can achieve their own individual goals and realize their dreams through their jobs and in the organization in which they work. There are almost as many styles of leadership as there are leaders, the most common general classifications being autocratic, democratic, charismatic, exemplary, militaristic, and low-key. No single style can said to be "best," since the results depend greatly on the nature of the business, the location, the disposition of the employees, and the kind of leadership needed to get the job done.

5. *Exercising control.* Many managers have proven to be highly effective in meeting the mandates of the first four functions, above, but have tripped on this final basic requirement, keeping the troops on course in the manner intended. Positive control demands four management accomplishments: setting standards of performance, measuring performance against the standards, taking immediate corrective action when standards are not met, and providing ongoing incentives and rewards for achievement. Control is characterized by both *productivity* and *quality,* tempered by a realistic adherence to schedules and time frames.

Since the beginning of the 1980s, management in business and industry has tended to move away from the traditional corporate administrative structure and delegate more planning and authority to line managers and others who supervise operations at either lower or broader levels. In many instances, managerial decision making at the top level has actually depended to a great extent on the counsel and decisions of managers down the line who are specialists or have acknowledged expertise in certain fields. *See* Business Administration.

MANAGEMENT PITFALLS

The business-rating firm of Dun & Bradstreet conducted a nationwide study and compiled a list of nine major pitfalls that often prove to be the undoing of managers, particularly those who are owners or heads of small- to medium-sized businesses:

- Lack of experience, especially well-balanced experience.
- Inadequate financing, both for starting a venture and for maintaining the organization through early stages of growth.
- Selecting the wrong location, for either the headquarters, key branches and divisions, or both.
- Mismanaging inventory, either by having too little to meet consumer demand or too much and thus becoming burdened with excessive handling, warehousing, and carrying costs.
- Investing too heavily in capital equipment, particularly when much of it lies idle and when it has been purchased with borrowed funds.
- Extending too much credit to customers, both by sacrificing the company's cash flow and by risking an above-average number of payment delinquencies.
- Overpaying top managers to the extent that illogical monetary cutbacks have to be instituted in functions that can ill afford them.
- Attempting to expand the business, unreasonably or without prudent plans for the anticipated growth.
- Having the wrong attitude, generally by expecting too much too soon or by shifting the blame for setbacks on others who are not at fault.

MANAGEMENT ACCOUNTING

A procedure for furnishing managers and other key personnel in an organization with financial information that can be utilized in the planning and administration of the organization at all levels of operation. *See* Accounting.

MANAGEMENT ADVISORY SERVICES (MAS)

Services that are executed by professional accountants to aid the management of an organization by assisting in such services as budgeting, computer usage, controls, personnel handling, and general decision making. MAS demands that certain standards be maintained and procedures followed to keep the work of the accountants independent and their recommendations objective, as advocated in a reference manual published by the American Institute of Certified Public Accountants. *See* Accounting.

MANAGEMENT AUDIT

An evaluation of the ability of management to conduct operational activities, make decisions, and control risks and negative influences. *See* Operational Audit.

MANAGEMENT BY OBJECTIVES

The theory that managers, supervisors, and those who report to them can take concerted action to establish mutual objectives within certain areas of operation and over specified time frames. *See* Business Administration.

MANAGEMENT CONSULTANT

A professional who, personally or as a staff member of a firm, provides expert consultation to clients on ways to improve management practices and functions. *See* Consultant.

MANAGEMENT DEVELOPMENT

An individual-growth curriculum of leadership training for top-level and middle-level managers to upgrade their skills, improve their capabilities, and put their incentives and motivations to work in a more positive manner. Also known as *management training.*

MANAGEMENT GAMES

Educational exercises sponsored by management seminars and business schools to provide graphic insights into better management and leadership in the business world. Such games are forms of simulation, using mathematical models and data and motivating participants to make decisions at various stages. While "games" may connote activities that are more pleasurable than educational, these programs have earned great credit for improving an individual's ability to make decisions, forcing players to apply principles they have learned in management classes, developing the ability to recognize needs for more data, stressing the value of good communication, pinpointing the relationships between different departments and divisions in a corporation, and improving the ability to function more cooperatively and effectively in group situations. *See* Game Theory, Management, Training.

MANAGEMENT INFORMATION SYSTEMS (MIS)

A system that has been computerized and programmed to supply management with sufficient data to make beneficial decisions and, further, to communicate useful information to customers, distributors, and suppliers to expedite and coordinate joint actions and operations. *See* Business Administration.

MANAGEMENT SCIENCE

The application of the theory that certain kinds of managerial decision problems in business and government can be solved by a structured approach that employs algebraic equations, calculus, and probability hypotheses. The procedure relies on the creation of representative models of management situations to be analyzed, such as expediting warehousing facilities and flow, determining optimum manufacturing goals, establishing new product lines, streamlining service programs, computing transportation shortcuts, or reassigning personnel to upgrade performance levels. Such models may be abstract mathematical formulations of the problem, as in the case of a petroleum refinery manager seeking to blend crude oils more effectively for use in fuel for a new type of high-performance marine engine. This type of model making is known as *linear programming*. Other techniques include inventory models used to recommend production sequences and limits and simulation models that can test the performances of complex interactive systems, such as the reorganization of an urban vehicle traffic pattern that involves great changes in flow, grid-lock problems, and a complex arrangement of stop lights, signs, and intersections. Management science had its origins in the military use of decision models for operational research during World War II that were first copied in the United States as a means of correcting production-line problems as the nation began retooling for peacetime manufacturing. Research managers had discovered that the wartime decision models allowed better scheduling and sequencing of production procedures, as well as more efficient management of entire projects. The application of models for projects in marketing, pricing, advertising, and finance soon followed, and by the 1990s, when corporate administrations began to move away from the highly centralized, top-down approach to leadership, many programs in the field of management science were turned over to line managers and department heads for application to specific, localized problems. *See* Business Administration, Management, Operations Research.

MANAGERIAL ACCOUNTING

The administrative procedure whereby management in an organization is provided with accurate data to evaluate costs, practice budgetary planning, review profits and losses, and evaluate employee and executive performance. This field of activity is the bailiwick of the managerial, or cost, accountant, whose responsibility is fundamentally to determine the cost of manufacturing specific products or providing a well defined service. The managerial accounting procedure requires complex estimates of overhead, variable costs, and unit costs for related services such as research or product testing. With computerized bookkeeping, costs can be monitored daily and data can be reported almost instantly after being collected. Such monetary statements help management to determine whether it might be more profitable to make or to buy a part, to invest in new machinery or refurbish existing equipment, or to hire more employees or use robotics and maintain a spare staff. As consultants to departments and divisions, managerial accountants can assist decision-making processes by preparing budgets based on realistic estimates of what can be accomplished. Comparing actual performance with expressed goals is another function of managerial accounting and is useful in evaluating the performance of individual company units and supervisors. *See* Accounting.

MANAGERIAL GRID

A graphic formula for measuring the leadership style, experience, and potential of administrators in terms of the extent of their consideration of people, assignments, production, and other determinants. *See* Business Administration.

MANDATE

A command, directive, or authorization, as in a case where a government regulation *mandates* that a company follow certain legal procedures or rules of conduct.

MANPOWER

See Personnel.

MANUAL SKILL

The ability of workers to use their hands and bodily motions efficiently in the operation of tools, instruments, and equipment. *See* Human Factors Engineering.

MANUFACTURERS' AGENT

A specialist who represents one or more manufacturers, arranging sales of the clients' products and materials to wholesale and retail purchasers on a commission basis. Also known as a *manufacturing broker.*

MANUFACTURING

The process by which raw materials or components are fabricated and assembled into finished products, a modern-day phenomenon that evolved from a relatively simple system of hand-tool production carried on locally by individual workers into the complex factory operation, with its huge, highly mechanized labor force. Throughout the Colonial period in America, goods produced for local consumption were largely of household or workshop manufacture. Particularly in rural areas, the spinning and weaving of woolens was common in most households, as was the making of homespun garments and shoes. Consumer demands in the larger towns were usually supplied by imports or by skilled craftsmen working in small shops. By the end of the eighteenth century, the forces of change were already apparent as America focused more on the development of domestic sources of commodities and then to the exploration of the sales potential of regions beyond the Atlantic seaboard. A century later, large population segments had reached the Pacific coast and the most promising regions in the interior. The growth of the population and its westward movement opened up economic opportunities for the eastern states, and against this background, manufacturing began to expand and acquire some of its later characteristics, influenced also by the industrial revolution taking place in Europe. Manufacturing techniques developed by the British during this period, notably the factory system and the use of fossil fuel for energy, were welcomed in the United States, which had a scarcity of labor. By the end of the eighteenth century, faced with a scarcity of accumulated funds, entrepreneurs adopted the *corporation* as a device for acquiring necessary capital. The proliferation of skilled labor increased the adaptability of new machines, while higher wages attracted the workers to operate them. Major developments in the nineteenth century were continuous-process manufacture, in which materials moved smoothly through successive processing stages, the use of interchangeable parts, impressive advances in improving the speed and accuracy of machines, and the expanding machine-tool industry, which by mid-century was prepared to supply standardized machines or to build special equipment for customers.

From the turn of the century in 1900 until the end of World War I, the American economy assumed most of its modern characteristics, evolving from an agricultural to an industrial economy and reflecting the influence on manufacturing of the following improvements in technology: the introduction of more productive methods of using energy, an improved process of producing iron and steel that increased the quality of materials used both in the construction of machinery and the fabrication of consumer goods, the further growth and complexity of the machine tool industry, and the large-scale mass-production technology of Henry Ford, who by 1914 had combined inter-changeable-parts and continuous-flow manufacture to establish the assembly line. These revolutionary innovations were characterized by the proliferation of mechanized industries, which by World War I were turning out huge quantities of consumer products ranging from foods and beverages to ready-made clothing, hardware, toys, office equipment, and appliances. Despite enormous economic and population fluctuations, accentuated by the Depression, political upheavals, and World War II, manufacturing grew impressively. By the end of the 1970s, the manufacturing labor force of 20 million was more than double its counterpart of 1920, while industrial output expanded nearly six fold. Significant industrial innovations sparked this growth, most notably: an escalating electric-power industry that gave birth to multitudes of electrically operated products, including office machines, broadcasting equipment, power tools, and kitchen appliances; the internal-combustion engine, using gasoline, gas, or diesel fuel, and designed for increasing numbers of uses; developments in the fields of chemistry and chemical engineering in the creation of synthetics in almost every field from tires and fertilizer to dyes, explosives, and fabrics; and the conception of the new field of microelectronics. The postwar period in the United States also saw a dramatic shift of resources to the service sectors of the economy, such as transportation, home decorating, business consulting, and communications. Despite this drain of manpower from the manufacturing sector, which escalated the difficulties of modernizing, and despite inroads of foreign products—particularly from Japan and Germany—manufacturing in the United States continued its favorable ascent. The upward swing was strongly buoyed by a new force on the industrial horizon. Beginning in the 1980s, forward-looking manufacturers began assessing the potential of computer-aided design, popularly known as CAD, and computer-aided manufacturing (CAM) to create dramatically new factory systems. Whereas computers had previously been used for routine tasks, such as monitoring the flow of materials or controlling robots, the advancing technologies began playing a role in such complex functions as the computer design of product parts and a control system known as Computer Integrated Manufacturing (CIM). As one industrial computer expert stated, "On its simplest level, computer design produces parts that are cheaper and easier to assemble. Connected with automated machine tools, however, computers can aid in the manufacture of higher-quality, longer-lived parts that often can be robotically assembled. As machinery is automated, flexibility in manufacturing increases, allowing for a wide variety of products to be made and changeovers to take place within a short time, without the retooling that was once necessary. Smaller manufacturing units prove more efficient than the cavernous factory spaces of the past. The installation of CIM systems is costly, but manufacturers find that they pay for themselves quickly, while labor costs plummet." *See* Production.

MANUFACTURING ENGINEERING

A professional operations field that fits into the manufacturing sequence between product design and full-scale production. It encompasses *process engineering,* which develops the logical sequence of manufacturing operations for each product or part; *tool engineering,* the adaptation of existing tools and the creation of new ones for the particular job(s) on hand and scheduled; *materials handling,* the physical movement of materials and parts from one part of a plant or assembly line to another; *plant engineering,* the designing of plant layouts to locate tools, equipment, personnel, and supplies so they can be processed in the most efficient and economical manner; and *standards and methods,* a quality-control function that assures that each product or component complies with the exact specifications and that working methods and practices support the specified procedures. *See* Manufacturing Production, and other *Production* entries.

MARGIN

In the investment field, that portion of the cost of a stock or other security that is paid by the purchaser, who then submits the security to the broker as collateral for the balance. *See* Securities.

MARGINAL LAND

The designation applied to acreage that will probably repay the cost of products grown on it or resources taken from it, but will not yield further revenue. *See* Real Estate.

MARGINAL PRODUCER

A manufacturer or fabricator who is barely able to meet the cost of operations after selling the goods produced, with little profit. *See* Manufacturing.

MARITIME LAW

Any law or legal restriction or mandate that pertains to seagoing operations or functions directly related to shipping and the sea. Concerned primarily with oceangoing commerce and based on long-standing historical traditions, maritime law tends to have global uniformity, even though other areas of jurisprudence may be greatly different between nations. *See* Shipping, Transportation.

MARKET

In sales and distribution, any group of people representing potential buyers for a product or service, usually classified according to age, sex, income, and other demographic factors. Other pertinent definitions are: a public gathering held for buying and selling merchandise; a place where goods are offered for sale; a store or shop that sells a particular type of merchandise, such as a meat market; the business of buying and selling a specified commodity; a market price; a geographic region considered as a place for sales; a subdivision of a population considered as buyers; and an exchange for buying and selling stocks or commodities. *See* Advertising, Demography, Marketing, Selling.

MARKET ANALYSIS

A function of market research that measures the size, extent, durability, growth, and other factors in one or more markets. *See* Marketing, Market Research, Sales.

MARKET AREA

The geographic, physical, or population boundaries of a sales market. *See* Marketing.

MARKET AUDIT

A research project or program in which the marketing structure and potential of a company are studied and evaluated. *See* Audit.

MARKET DEMAND

The volume of sales of items in a singular market, particularly measured in purchases by consumers, rather than wholesalers or other middle persons. *See* Marketing, Merchandising.

MARKETING

The economic system by which goods and materials are sold and purchased and services are promoted. The process ranges from simple acts of buying and selling to highly sophisticated programs whereby goods are moved from suppliers to consumers. Simple marketing activities began with the development of local trade, even barter, with goods being transported by individuals, caravans, or ships. Village markets, seasonal fairs, and peddlers were all involved in primitive marketing activities, followed by the birth of the general store and much later by supermarkets, chain stores, and the like. As a result of many diverse factors, modern marketing has evolved into a complex and sophisticated field with many interactions in related fields, such as sales, advertising, merchandising, promotion, publicity, retailing, wholesaling, discounting, transportation, distribution, and consumer research. Since the downline objective of marketing is to acquire, retain, and satisfy customers, marketers begin by identifying the market for their product, then tailor their efforts to meet the needs and desires of customers within that market. Prospects range from individuals to wholesale and retail chains, other companies, warehouses, and any organization, large or small, that might be interested in merchandise and services offered. Marketing is a substantial investment, since its costs average at least half of the total expenditure of producing consumer goods, covering a broad spectrum of activities, including product design, market research, consumer testing, distribution, credit plans, and warranties. There is no limit to the types of organizations that require sound marketing techniques—even governments, nonprofit institutions, colleges, and political parties, to name a few.

Marketing in the United States has been greatly complicated by exterior forces over which marketers have little control, such as federal, state, and local government regulations, consumer movements on behalf of product safety, truth-in-advertising campaigns, unpredicted changes in taxation, and the increasing inroads of foreign marketers. At the same time, with the growth of multinational corporations, marketing has greatly expanded its range and scope, so that today for many companies, the whole world is their marketplace. It is not at all rare to see a major manufacturer introducing a product line simultaneously in a dozen or more countries, with advertising campaigns in as many different languages. Managers of such global marketing activities must, of course, take into account the multitudes of international differences in customs, business practices, protocol, and even the sensitivity of certain words, expressions, and viewpoints. *See* Advertising, Distribution, Merchandising, Promotion.

KEY MARKETING MISTAKES

According to the Marketing Practices Division of the Federal Trade Commission, the most common blunders made by marketers included the following:

- Ignoring the needs and tastes of customers in the expectation that they will be the same as those of the marketing managers.

- Misjudging the actual numbers of potential customers or patrons.
- Failing to conduct interviews or make studies to determine consumer preferences, either for new products or for modifications of existing ones.
- Miscalculating the size and nature of the competition.
- Resting on results when sales are satisfactory, rather than developing follow-up strategies.
- Overlooking market trends that warn of steady reductions in the demand for certain products or product groups.
- Failing to grasp the implications of new product spin-offs from existing products and materials that have established brand identities and loyal purchasers.
- Cutting back on market-research funds and projects when business seems to be moving favorably.

MARKET OUTLOOK

A forecast of the volume of sales to expect on any specified market, sometimes with variations to project sales expectations following a variety of advertising, marketing, and sales campaigns. *See* Advertising, Marketing, and Selling.

MARKET PENETRATION

The degree to which a company is able to infiltrate a specific market, judged also in terms of the share of the market held by a company in terms of product types and volumes. *See* Market Share.

MARKET RESEARCH

The application of known factors and statistics to the development of short- and long-range planning to forecast the future potential of a market if certain strategies and plans are followed. This form of research also pays close attention to known, as well as inferred, data about consumer buying habits and the continuing state of the economy. *See* Advertising, Marketing.

MARKET SHARE

The percentage of sales of a marketer in any designated market(s), as well as the share of a company's products in its field of distribution. *See* Market Penetration.

MARKET STRATEGY

The individual and collective tactics used, or to be used, in developing plans for increased sales and distribution in a market or a selection of markets. Such planning may often be limited geographically or demographically to study a more concentrated measure of projected activity. *See* Marketing, Market Penetration, Market Share.

MARKET VALUE

Also referred to as the *prevailing price.*

MARKUP

That proportion of the basic price of merchandise that is added to the cost to determine the selling price. *See* Sales.

MASS COMMUNICATION

The distribution, whether vocally or in print, of a profusion of messages that are the same or similar to large segments of the population, locally, regionally, or nationally. *See* Communication.

MASS MARKETING

The application of numerous kinds of techniques by a producer, marketer, or advertiser to sell massive volumes of products to large volumes of people. *See* Marketing.

MASS MEDIUM

Any advertising medium, such as newspapers, magazines, and television, that reaches large segments of the population. Mass media are the instruments by which mass communication takes place today, falling into four major categories: *print,* including magazines, books, newspapers, and other periodicals; *broadcasting,* including radio, television, and telecommunications; *motion pictures;* and *recordings,* such as cassettes, videotapes, and records. Mass production and *ever-evolving* communications technology assure rapid delivery from source to audience, keep the costs low, and tend to reach increasingly large segments of the population, even in remote regions. The drawbacks are that mass media are on a one-way street; readers, viewers, and listeners seldom have opportunities to make media contacts and get responses; and the frequency of communication is so great that the recipients have minimal times in which to absorb information before being inundated with continuing exposure to new facts and figures. Yet advertising and marketing studies have shown that the impact of mass media—even for fleeting messages—can be great.

The impact of television in the 1950s was the first indication that enormous technological advances were on their way in this field of communication, which has since made instantaneous global communication a reality and, through computers, has tremendously magnified the capabilities of all media to communicate in infinite detail. Among the mass-media innovations have been cable TV, home videocassette recorders, compact discs, laser transmissions, and fiber optics, to name just a few. *See* Advertising, Communications, Media.

Mass Production

The manufacturing and distribution of goods in quantity through the use of automation, high-speed machinery, assembly lines, specialized workers, and moving belts. *See* Manufacturing, Production.

Mass Transit

Extensive transportation facilities, most often in large cities, to move great numbers of commuters short distances by rail, bus, ferry, or other common carrier. *See* Transportation.

Master Schedule

In production and fabricating control, a timetable established for the scheduling of products and their components in such a way as to expedite all related processes, limit costs, and minimize down time. *See* Production.

Masthead

The name of a periodical or other publication in the form and font of its own special design, displayed on the front cover or first page.

Materials Costs

Those expenditures that cover raw materials only and not affiliated costs such as finishing, labor, transportation, wear and tear of equipment, and the leasing of facilities.

Materials Handling

The scientific application of methods, equipment, manpower, and transportation whose purpose is to expedite, improve, and economize the production, storage, handling, and moving of products and materials. Also known as *materials management.*

Matrix Organization

A personnel program in which the members of a defined organization exercise a dual allegiance to their department or division and to their task at hand. *See* Personnel Administration.

MATURE ECONOMY

The financial environment that exists in a country or region when there is a declining rate of population growth and a drop in the percentage of income available for new developments and capital investment. *See* Economics.

MATURITY

The date on which a bond or other financial obligation becomes due for payment and the transaction expires. *See* Bonds.

MEASUREMENT MERCHANDISE

In the field of shipping and hauling, the type of goods and materials whose freight charge is measured by their cubic footage rather than by weight. *See* Shipping, Transportation.

MEASURE OF VALUE

A standardization formula that identifies the results and accomplishments or failures of a given production operation, using monetary units as common denominators in comparing different examples with a norm. *See* Production.

MECHANIZATION

The use of machines or devices to assist or replace human operation and control. *See* Automation.

MEDIA

Collectively, the vehicles of communication used especially for advertising, including among other entities newspapers, magazines, other kinds of periodicals, radio, television, and billboards. *See* Advertising, Advertising Agencies, Communications, Marketing.

MEDIA INDUSTRY

The communications industry that reaches readers, viewers, and other communicants through its production of books, newspapers, magazines, broadcasts, mailing pieces, and various other information channels. *See* Advertising, Media.

MEDIAN

Used in statistical studies to pinpoint the midpoint between minimum and maximum extremities, whether relating to the population, money matters, employment, or other data being researched and defined. *See* Research.

MEDIATION

The steps taken to reconcile differences and reach agreements and understanding during labor disputes and dissensions between unions and management. *See* Labor/Management, Labor Unions.

MEDIATOR

The individual or team acting, with hoped-for objectivity, as a third party in attempts to resolve differences between two other parties, most commonly managers and union representatives. *See* Labor/Management, Labor Unions.

MEDIUM

Singular for *media,* which see.

MEDIUM OF EXCHANGE

Currency or any other commodity of value that is widely recognized and used in the buying and selling of goods and services and the discharge of debts and diverse obligations. *See* Currency.

MEGALOPOLIS

An urban conglomerate of two or more large cities that are not separated substantially by open spaces and rural zones.

MEMBER FIRM

In the world of finance, a brokerage firm that is organized as a corporation, and whose director is a member of a stock exchange, as well as a holder of voting stock in the corporation. *See* Broker, Stock Market.

MEMORY

The component of a computer or other data-processing mechanism into which units of information can be deposited, stored, and retrieved instantly at any given time. *See* Computers, Data Processing.

MERCANTILE

Engaged in commerce or trade.

MERCHANDISE

Products, goods, materials, crafts, or other articles that are finished, held temporarily in inventory, and bought and sold, particularly at wholesale and retail levels, by consumers. *See* Retailing.

MERCHANDISE MANAGER

The individual in a retail establishment who is charged with the planning, supervising, purchasing, selling, and storing of all the inventory items that make up the business of the establishment. *See* Marketing, Retailing.

MERCHANDISING

The combination of all the functions, operations, and activities associated with the distribution, advertising, promotion, and marketing of a product or commodity. *See* Distribution, Marketing, Selling.

MERCHANT WHOLESALER

An individual or firm engaged in the acquisition of merchandise and its resale to retailers or other organizations stimulating sales to consumers. *See* Distribution, Wholesaling.

MERIT RAISE

An individual salary or wage increase that is based on improved performance on the job or in recognition of some other superior performance or service to the employer. *See* Compensation.

MICROCOMPUTERS

Miniature computers that are basically comprised of a central processing unit, a computer memory, timing circuits, and input/output controls. Although microcomputers have many business and scientific applications, they are best known to consumers as home or desk-top or lap-top computers. From slow, small-capacity instruments, later microcomputers were developed that could perform millions of operations per second and hold a half million bytes of memory—more than the enormous main-frame computers of just a few years earlier. *See* Bytes, Computers, Fiber Optics, Telecommunication.

MICROECONOMICS

The branch of economics that concerns itself with studies of individual employees or single products or groups of merchandise. *See* Economics, Macroeconomics.

MICROELECTRONICS

A field of electronics characterized by both individual electronic components and complete electronic circuits, as exemplified in the *integrated circuit,* which consists of an electronic circuit fabricated by a complex series of production steps on or in a tiny semiconductor chip. Since the individual components are so compact and interconnecting wires and shields eliminated, microelectronic units can be installed in very small spaces and yet have the capabilities of earlier, and much larger, devices. *See* Chip, Integrated Circuit.

MICROMOTION STUDY

See Time and Motion Study.

MICROPROCESSOR

A minute electronic chip that contains multitudes of components required for computative processing. *See* Chip.

MICROSECOND

One millionth of a second, a measurement used to describe computer responses, for example, that occur almost instantly. *See* Computers.

MIDDLE MANAGEMENT

The level of administrators and managers reporting directly to top management in a corporation or other large organization and responsible for carrying out the directives of the administration and the board of directors. *See* Business Administration, Management.

MILITARY/INDUSTRY COMPLEX

The collaborative operational programs established in the joint ventures of civilian corporations and the military in the production of weapons, equipment, and defense materials. *See* Production.

MINERAL RIGHTS

The prerogatives given to a company to extract petroleum, coal, or minerals from specified tracts of land that it owns or leases, usually limited to some extent by environmental restrictions and constraints. *See* Energy, Environment.

MINIMUM SUBSCRIPTION

That section of a business plan or prospectus that states the minimum financing required by the prospective company in order for it to become an operational entity. *See* Corporation.

MINIMUM WAGE

A legal prescription that mandates the lowest hourly wage that must be paid to workers, whether full time, part time, or temporary. *See* Labor Unions.

MINORITY INTEREST

The interest of common shareholders whose stock holdings in a corporation are not sufficient for them to control the corporation or consolidate their interests with a group to gain such control. *See* Stockholders.

MINUTES

The accounts that are recorded and transcribed in a company's books during its regular prescribed business meetings.

MISBRANDING

Labeling products or materials in such a way as to overvalue items in the eyes of consumers or to infer that the qualities of the items are greater than they actually are. Also known as *mislabeling. See* Misrepresentation.

MISMANAGEMENT

Inferior or weak management of an organization as a result of bad judgment, lack of knowledge, disinterest, or any other reason. *See* Management, Managers.

MISREPRESENTATION

In business, presenting misinformation, deliberately or through ignorance, in such a way as to make claims about a company or situation that will lead to false conclusions. *See* Misbranding.

MISSION STATEMENT

A formal statement of the basic objectives and purposes of an organization, usually contained in no more than a few sentences. It is aimed at orienting all members of an organization—particularly those who are managers or supervisors—about business philosophies, policies, and targets. Every organization, large or small, needs a mission statement and many require pronouncements of this kind for each major unit within the organization.

A typical mission statement addresses itself to six significant topics:

1. The reasons why the organization exists.
2. Products and/or services offered.
3. Customers or clientele served.
4. Nature of the business and geographic territory or regions in which it functions.
5. Areas of specialization.

6. Expansion or changes anticipated.

Example of a brief Mission Statement:

The Pinetree Production Corporation is dedicated to the manufacture and distribution of high-tech parts and products for biomedical research. The goal is not only to supply such units, largely to private firms engaged in biomedical research, but to provide prompt and reliable service when customers need adjustments, repairs, or counsel. The company's operations are—and will be in the future—limited to Southern New England. Growth will come through the addition of products and components to the PPC line, rather than through expansion into new geographical territories.

See Forecasting, Goals, Objectives, Planning.

MIXED ECONOMY

A national commercial economy that fits neither the free enterprise nor the social category, but is a combination of each. *See* Free Enterprise, Socialism.

MIXED PROPERTY

Land or other property having the characteristics of both personal and real property. *See* Real Estate.

MODE

In statistics, the most frequently occurring datum in a group of data being studied or presented. *See* Data Processing.

MODEM

In the field of computers, a device used to transmit data electronically, generally as a voice or audio signal on a telephone line. A modem affixed to a computer performs a conversion of data and transmits them to another modem, which permits the computer to use the information transmitted. A *fax* modem makes it possible for a computer to transmit and receive printed data from a fax (facsimile) machine. *See* Computers, Facsimile, Hardware.

MODULE

A particular segment of data in a statistical evaluation. Also, in data processing, individual components or accessories that can be plugged in quickly and easily. *See* Data Processing.

MODUS OPERANDI

Latin for "mode of operation."

MONETARY POLICY

The strategy pursued by a government at any level that is intended to control credit and the supply of money in the economy of the geographical area that the government represents. *See* International Trade.

MONETARY RESERVES

The amount of the precious metals, such as gold and silver, held by a government's treasury to support the issuance of paper money, coins, and other currency in circulation. *See* Gold Standard.

MONETARY STANDARD

The underlying principle that determines the amount of money that a government can legitimately issue. *See* Currency, Gold Standard.

MONEY

An abstract unit of accounting by which the value of goods, services, and obligations can be measured and that historically has included such a wide range of objects and materials as gold, silver, shells, ivory, tobacco, furs, and even dried fish. Money does not, however, depend on its value as a commodity, as in the case of paper currency, which has little intrinsic worth, but is backed by some commodity of real value into which it could be converted on demand. By contrast, *fiat money* is currency made legal tender by the decree of a government, but with no backing. The American monetary system was based on both gold and silver during the nineteenth century, but was backed by a single gold standard in the early twentieth century. The Gold Reserve Act of 1934, and later legislation, reduced the dollar's dependence on gold, and in 1971 the United States abandoned gold convertibility altogether. Most U.S. currency in circulation today consists of Federal Reserve notes, but currency and coin are less widely used as a means of payment than checks, which represent about 90 percent of all payments. In the United States the money supply, or total amount of money in the economy, is measured in different ways and is influenced by the actions of the Federal Reserve System. *See* Banks And Banking, Currency, Financial Accounting.

MONEY BROKER

An agent or middle person who deals in foreign exchange, generally in a private business as a dealer. *See* Money.

MONEY LAUNDERING

Processing illegal funds in a variety of secretive ways so that they, and any profits derived from them, cannot be traced by the authorities. *See* Banks And Banking, Fraud, Offshore Banking.

MONEY MARKET

The financial market that trades in high-grade, short-term open-market assets such as commercial paper, U. S. Treasury bills, and banker's acceptances. *See* Banks and Banking, Investments.

MONEY MARKET FUNDS

Investment vehicles that are short-term and relevant mainly to individuals. *See* Money Market.

MONEY SUPPLY

The total amount of currency that is circulating in a nation or other geo-graphic and political entity at any defined period of time. *See* Currency, Money.

MONITOR

Any person or machine whose function is to observe, report on, and perhaps record information on a changing situation, operation, or continuing event.

MONOLITHIC

Derived from *monolith,* the name for a giant block of stone carved in ancient times, the term now connotes a business situation in which a large corpora-tion is centrally controlled, or even denominated by an individual or small group of individuals. *See* Corporation.

MONOPOLISTIC COMPETITION

A degree of competition that is small, mainly in an industry or business where few firms produce or sell products and services that are much different from those of competitors. *See* Monopoly.

MONOPOLY

In commercial trading, the nearly complete control of a commodity, products, labor supply, components, or services in a given market. *See* Cartel.

MONTE CARLO SIMULATIONS

In marketing research, a trial-and-error technique and random sampling, used most frequently when more scientific investigations and analyses are too costly, time-consuming, or error-prone to be feasible. *See* Marketing Research.

MOONLIGHTING

Slang expression for the act of holding more than one job and working during off hours.

MOOT POINT

A point made about an issue that is debatable because the issue has already been decided or has been rated too ambiguous for any coherent decision. *See* Business Law.

MORATORIUM

The suspension of action or discussion or legal rights for a period of time agreed upon by all concerned.

MOST-FAVORED-NATION PROVISION

The proviso in a covenant or contract that guarantees equal treatment and empathy to each party in the agreement. *See* Foreign Trade, Free Trade.

MOTION STUDY

A study of the movements made by an individual performing a repetitive task in order to evaluate the actions and results and determine ways to accomplish the same processing objectives more efficiently and economically. *See* Time And Motion Studies.

MOTIVATION

In the narrow category of industrial human relations, the incentives and stimuli that are needed to activate positive and useful responses in employees, both as individuals and as teams. *See* Personnel Management.

MULTICORPORATION

A large industrial complex under a single management, but with many branches, some or all of which may or may not be in the same industry or classification of business. *See* Corporation.

MULTILATERAL

In a business or political contract or concordance, the mutual agreements made by more than two parties to the transaction. *See* Agreement, Contract.

MULTILEVEL MARKETING

Also referred to as *direct sales,* this form of marketing refers to the sale of retail products directly to customers, without distribution to stores and other retail outlets, through a network of distributors who recruit and train subsidiary distributors. Among major companies engaged in this field of selling are Amway, Shaklee, and Mary Kay, which have created huge sales forces that function in this multilevel pattern. *See* Direct Sales, Marketing.

MULTINATIONAL

Said of companies and industries that conduct operations, market products, or have substantial financial interests in more than one country. *See* International Trade.

MULTIPLE ACCESS

Access to an operational system in such a way that output and input can be readily controlled from a central station or from a number of terminals at any time. *See* Random Access.

MULTIPLE BRANDS

The use of more than one brand name on essentially the same product in order to open up new markets or increase the number of purchases in an existing market. In some instances, a national trade mark will be used for a product, such as mayonnaise, and the brand name for a supermarket chain will be used on the very same product for sale in the supermarket's outlets. *See* Merchandising, Trademark.

MULTIPLE LISTING

In real estate sales, commercial and residential alike, a listing of properties that is distributed to all members of a real estate association so that each office has an opportunity to sell the properties so listed. *See* Real Estate.

MULTIPLE MANAGEMENT

That form of management in a corporation or other large concern in which the administration is the function and responsibility not only of top managers, but of designated middle managers and sometimes teams of employees who are assigned specific areas of supervision. *See* Business Management.

MULTIPLE SALES PROJECTION

A merchandising strategy whose objective is to sell several related products to customers, rather than just one item at a time. *See* Merchandising.

MULTIPLE WRAPPING

Packaging several related products in the same package or joined together so that more than one item will automatically be sold at the same time. The retail practice is to advertise the package as a bargain or "special" because items contained therein are individually discounted. *See* Merchandising, Sales.

MULTIPROCESSING

Installing a computer or data operation system that contains more than one operational unit. *See* Data Processing.

MULTIPROGRAMMING

Running a computer system with two or more programs that can function individually or jointly at the same time. *See* Programming.

MUNICIPAL GOVERNMENT

The term for that form of government that administers urban and suburban communities that are not managed directly by metropolitan or regional governments, but that are concerned with a broad scope of economic, welfare, political, environmental, esthetic, and infrastructural functions and operations. In recent times, municipal governments have been going through extensive changes, forced into recognizing declining federal support and the need to turn to semi-private partnerships to promote economic growth. As a result, successful municipalities are managed like commercial corporations, combining public and private funds to construct schools and public buildings, plan cultural facilities, and maintain roads and other transportation works. To do so, they also have to promote economic growth through tax abatements, municipal bond issues, and private subsidies. *See* Government, Municipal Bonds.

MUNICIPALS

The popular name for municipal bonds and other securities issued by city, county, state, and local governments, or by a public authority or nonprofit corporation. Such bonds commonly take 10 to 40 years to maturity and are wholly or partially exempt from federal income taxation. *See* Bonds, Securities.

MURPHY'S LAW

A humorous name for the widespread theory in the business and political world that "If something can go wrong, sooner or later it will." A corollary of

Murphy's law is that "everything that is promised for immediate delivery will take much longer than planned."

MUTUAL CORPORATION

An organization that does not underwrite or issue common stock, but whose profits are distributed among owner-customers in proportion to their participation in the company's operations or business activities. *See* Corporation.

MUTUAL FUND

A fund established by a form that is authorized to invest shareholder's money in the securities of selected corporations, governments, and other issuing organizations. Many mutual funds are categorized so that they offer investors opportunities in limited fields of choice, for example, by industry, geographical location, or price. *See* Securities.

MUTUAL SAVINGS BANK

An institution that is owned, not privately or corporately, but by the depositors themselves, with no capital stock, and generally managed by an elected board of trustees. Dividends from the bank's investments are distributed to depositors after deductions for expenses. *See* Banking.

NANOSECOND

One billionth of a second, used in communicating the tremendously high speeds of state-of-the art computers and components. *See* Microsecond.

NARROW MARKET

The situation that occurs when the demand for a security is so restricted that small changes in supply and demand will trigger major—sometimes drastic—fluctuations in the market price. *See* Securities.

NASDAQ (NATIONAL ASSOCIATION OF SECURITIES DEALERS AUTOMATED QUOTATIONS)

A basic market for over-the-counter trading. Prices of stocks traded on NAS-DAQ are quoted simultaneously on the New York Stock Exchange and eleven regional exchanges, providing the best possible prices uniformly. The program provides comprehensive data about each stock listed, including dividends, daily volume, high and low prices, changes from the previous day, and the stock's history. NASDAQ maintains minimum listing requirements for the approximately 4,500 stocks it covers. *See* Investments, Securities, Stock Market, Stocks.

NATIONAL ADVERTISING

Any form of advertising that covers the entire country, rather than regions or urban areas alone. *See* Advertising.

NATIONAL ARCHIVES AND RECORDS ADMINISTRATION

Known as the *National Archives,* this independent agency of the federal executive branch was formed in the 1930s, but not officially incorporated into the government until 1985. NARA administers the Presidential Library System and other historical records, presents informational programs for the public, and maintains a museum in the nation's Capitol, which houses such priceless documents as the original Declaration of Independence, the U.S. Constitution, and the Bill of Rights. *See* Government, Research.

NATIONAL ASSOCIATION OF MANUFACTURERS (NAM)

A volunteer organization formed a century ago to promote foreign trade, plan the Panama Canal, and rehabilitate the merchant marine, the NAM represents groups of business and industrial firms joined together to foster their trade, business, and financial interests to encourage greater communication among manufacturers and to promote the advantages of a free-enterprise economy. The association also studies such related matters as industrial financing, patents, trademarks, tariffs, transportation, taxation, conservation, and personnel administration. *See* Industry, Manufacturing.

NATIONAL ASSOCIATION OF SECURITIES DEALERS (NASD)

The professional association of dealers in stocks, bonds, financial instruments, and other securities. *See* Finance, Securities, Stock Market.

NATIONAL BANK

A financial institution whose charter is granted by the federal government, and that becomes then a member of the Federal Reserve System and of the Federal Deposit Insurance Corporation (FDIC). *See* Banks and Banking, Federal Deposit Insurance Corporation, Federal Reserve System.

NATIONAL BRAND

Any brand, but particularly for consumer products and goods, that is advertised, promoted, and distributed widely across the entire country. *See* Distribution, Trademark.

NATIONAL BUREAU OF STANDARDS AND TECHNOLOGY

Functioning as an agency of the Department of Commerce, the Bureau provides the basis for American measurement standards works to assure accurate measurement data throughout the government, as well as in scientific, industrial, and commercial disciplines. Other activities involve manufacturing technology, energy conservation, environmental research, fire prevention, and consumer safety. The Bureau also maintains the National Measurement Laboratory, National Engineering Laboratory, and Institute for Computer Sciences and Technology. *See* Weights and Measures.

NATIONAL DEBT

The total debt owed by a nation, usually computed in terms of money and not other unfulfilled obligations. In the United States, the national debt was relatively small until World War II, during which it grew from about $43 billion to $260 billion in 1945, and has continued to grow since, reaching an estimated $4 trillion by the early 1990s. *See* Debt, Government.

NATIONAL EDUCATION ASSOCIATION (NEA)

Originally termed the National Teachers' Association, NEA is a professional federation of educators, administrators, and others concerned with American education, from kindergarten through college. NEA is committed to the following basic programs, among others: supporting public education, fostering human and civil rights, encouraging professional excellence, bringing leadership to the solution of social problems, supplying an independent teaching organization, improving the working environment of teachers, and providing economic security for educators. *See* Career Education, Education.

NATIONAL FEDERATION OF INDEPENDENT BUSINESS (NFIB)

The nation's largest advocacy organization representing small and independent business owners, with a membership of more than 600,000 business owners, ranging in interests from high-tech manufacturing to farming, retailing, transportation, crafts, and personal service. *See* Small Business.

THE NATIONAL INSTITUTE OF EDUCATION (NIE)

A federal agency committed to the support of scientific educational research and the teaching of basic skills, the improvement of the quality of education in America, the distribution of information about educational procedures, improving the cost-effectiveness of educational institutions, upgrading training for careers, and assisting students from backgrounds that limit their educational opportunities. *See* Career Education, Education, National Education Association.

NATIONAL INSTITUTES OF HEALTH (NIH)

As a component of the Public Health Service and a division of the Department of Health and Human Services, these institutes conduct biomedical research into the causes, prevention, and cure of diseases, encourage research training, and foster the development of research resources. The various institutes cover these specialized areas of medicine and health, among others: aging; allergies; arthritis and musculoskeletal ailments; cancer; dental disorders; eye problems; diabetes; digestive ailments; infectious diseases; kidney diseases; heart, lung, and blood disorders; skin diseases; strokes; and neurological and communicative disorders. *See* Government, Health Insurance.

NATIONALIZATION

The term, usually disparaging, associated with the takeover of a company or other business, previously privately owned and operated, by the government. Nationalization is a commercial blight most often associated with dictatorships. *See* Authoritarianism, Dictatorship.

NATIONAL LABOR RELATIONS ACT (NLRA)

Enacted in the mid-1930s, and popularly known as the Wagner Act, this legislation was aimed at encouraging and monitoring collective bargaining between labor and management to correct "the inequality of bargaining power" between employers and employees. The act specified certain unfair labor practices, including discrimination against employees because of union activity, and established guidelines for selecting and recognizing appropriate unions by employers. Administration of the act was entrusted to the National Labor Relations Board. *See* Labor/Management, Labor Unions, National Labor Relations Board.

NATIONAL LABOR RELATIONS BOARD (NLRB)

A federal agency that was founded in the 1930s for the purpose of resolving labor/management disputes. *See* Labor/Management, National Labor Relations Act.

NATIONAL ORGANIZATION FOR WOMEN (NOW)

Claiming the largest membership of any female civil rights organization in the world, with some 275,000 members, NOW focuses on achieving, in its own words, "full equality for women in truly equal partnership with men." It strongly supports the Equal Rights Amendment to the Constitution and has made great strides toward eliminating prejudice and discrimination against women by using communications, education, voting privileges, litigation, and in some cases boycotting to achieve its goals. *See* Associations, Civil Rights.

NATIONAL SCIENCE FOUNDATION

As an independent federal agency, headed by the National Science Board, the Foundation initiates and supports research in the United States in the scientific disciplines through grants and the support of universities and independent research organizations and promotes science education and the public distribution of information about scientific curricula. Among its recent projects have been an Antarctic petroleum research project, the Ocean Drilling Program, and scientific ventures by many national centers, such as the Kitt Peak National Observatory, the National Astronomy and Ionosphere Center, the National Center for Atmospheric Research, the National Radio Astronomy Observatory, and the Sacramento Peak Observatory. The foundation also promotes programs in science education, fosters improved dissemination of scientific information, surveys levels of resources available to science, and takes part in international programs. *See* Education, Science.

NATIONAL SMALL BUSINESS UNITED (NSBU)

A private, nonprofit association representing more than 60,000 small business owners throughout the United States, from virtually all service and industrial sectors. Placing a major emphasis on small-business advocacy, NSBU takes a bipartisan approach in working with members of Congress and other government officials, striving to improve the national economic climate for the survival, growth, and economic health of small business. *See* Small Business.

NATIONAL TECHNICAL INFORMATION SERVICE

As a unit of the U.S. Department of Commerce, this agency is responsible for producing and distributing unclassified research reports from material compiled by technological organizations, both domestic and foreign. These reports are available as hard copy and microfilm, along with abstracts and indexes as electronic databases and in other subscription formats. *See* Science, Technology.

NATURAL DISASTER

Also referred to as "an act of God" and frequently applicable in insurance claims when businesses have been heavily damaged during earthquakes, floods, hurricanes, and the like. *See* Casualty.

NATURAL RESOURCES

Those riches that are supplied by nature, such as petroleum, coal, minerals, timber, gems, and precious metals. *See* Primary Coverage Of Resources, Pages.

NAVIGABLE

Said of any waterways, such as rivers, streams, or canals, and portions of large bodies of water, such as lakes, bays, and sounds, that continuously provide sufficient depth for vessels and are not prone to underwater obstacles or severe currents. *See* Shipping, Transportation.

NEGATIVE ASSURANCE

In accounting, the practice of evaluating financial statements and reporting that nothing came to the attention of the reviewing accountant(s) that suggested anything detrimental in the corporate records. Negative assurance is commonly requested by investment bankers evaluating an equity or debt issue to indicate that the auditors found no suspicion that the financial statements reflected anything but the truth. *See* Accounting.

NEGLIGENCE

In legal matters, the failure to exercise due and reasonable care to prevent property damage or bodily harm, thus contributing to the cause or unfortunate results of an accident. *See* Business Law.

NEGOTIABLE

Capable of having its ownership transferred without signature, as exemplified by currency, negotiable bonds, and bearer checks. *See* Negotiable Instrument.

NEGOTIABLE INSTRUMENT

A widely recognized commercial paper that meets approved legal and financial standards and can be transferred from one party to another by endorsement, such as a check, bank draft, money order, bearer bonds, traveler's check, certificate of deposit, or promissory note, payable on demand or at a future date to the order of a named person, or payee, or to the bearer. Most negotiable instruments are transferable from one party to another by endorsement. *See* Banks and Banking, Commercial Paper.

NEGOTIATED PRICE

Any price obtained by a purchaser who has managed to convince a seller to accept a price lower than originally quoted. *See* Distribution, Sales, Supply and Demand.

NEGOTIATIONS

In business, the dealings between two parties, such as management and a union or a realtor and a property buyer, to come to a mutual agreement. *See* Agreement, Contract.

NEPOTISM

The practice of hiring relatives as employees in the same organization without regard to protestations by others that better skilled and more qualified employees can be found outside the family circle. *See* Personnel Administration.

NET

That which remains after expenses, taxes, and other costs have been deducted from the gross in a financial accounting. *See* Gross, Gross Income.

NET ASSET VALUE

In corporate finance, the accumulated value of all assets, often depicted in relation to the value at the time of purchase, as well as at the close of the previous year's books. *See* Assets.

NET CHANGE

The change that takes place in the price of a stock or other security between the closing price on one day and the closing price on the following day of trade. *See* Investments, Securities.

NET EARNINGS

The final figure representing the gross earnings of a company minus deductions, operating costs, taxes, and any other expenses, and before the payment of any dividends. *See* Accounting, Bookkeeping.

NET INCOME

See Net.

NET LOSS

The situation that exists when expenses, taxes, and other losses during a designated period exceed the revenues and gains during the same time frame. *See* Annual Report.

NET NATIONAL PRODUCT (NNP)

The gross national product (GNP) after deductions for capital expenditures. *See* Gross National Product GNP).

NET PRICE

The retailer's cost price, which represents the price a purchaser must pay the seller for merchandise. *See* Merchandising, Sales.

NET PROFIT

See Profit.

NETWORK

Any interconnected group in a related field of activity, such as a system of information gathering or research, a chain of retail outlets, or radio and television stations that broadcast the same commercials simultaneously at a reduced per-station rate. *See* Broadcasting, Media.

NET WORTH

The worth of an individual or organization in terms of the excess of total assets over liabilities. It is often used as a guideline for lenders to assess the risk rate of a prospective borrower. *See* Capital, Equity.

NEW DEAL

Historically and politically, the popular designation for White House policies during the administration of President Franklin Delano Roosevelt. *See* Government, Social Security.

NEW ISSUE

In financial trading, a stock, bond, or other security that is being issued for the first time. *See* Corporations.

NEW PRODUCT DEVELOPMENT

The steps and procedures taken to introduce a new product to a market, including sampling, testing, individual market research, and related advertising and promotional campaigns. *See* Marketing, Merchandising.

NEWSLETTER

A small publication that is compiled, edited, and distributed periodically and that contains condensed news items, generally about an organization or other limited subject. *See* Media, Periodicals.

NEW YORK STOCK EXCHANGE (NYSE)

An association of members who execute securities transactions, mainly on the floor of the Exchange, and whose activities are monitored by specialists who are responsible for maintaining an orderly market for the trading of stocks and bonds. The term is also popularly used to denote the Exchange building, located in lower Manhattan in New York City. *See* Broker, Investments, Securities, Stock Exchange, Stocks.

NEW YORK STOCK EXCHANGE COMMON STOCK INDEX

See Securities, Stock Exchange, Stock Index.

NICHE MARKETING

A sales and marketing strategy used by relatively small companies intent on exploiting segments of the market that are of little interest to their larger competitors. *See* Distribution, Marketing, Supply and Demand.

NIELSEN RATING

In advertising research, one of the earliest methods of ranking broadcasting stations and networks in terms of the number of households tuned in to each station at a given time or for a specific program. *See* Advertising Research.

NINETEENTH AMENDMENT

This amendment to the Constitution was enacted in 1920 to provide men and women with equal voting rights, stating that the right of citizens to vote "shall not be denied or abridged by the United States or by any State on account of sex." Although this equality was implied in the Fourteenth Amendment in 1868, few states really recognized women's suffrage, and it took half a century for the women's rights movement, often militant, to achieve this goal. *See* Civil Rights, Women's Rights.

NO-FAULT INSURANCE

A form of insurance, most commonly issued to automobile drivers, that specifies that, regardless of who is to blame for an accident, claims payments are made by the insurance company to its own policyholder. Such coverage eliminates the need for extensive, often costly, studies to place the blame, but also usually limits the amount of damages that an accident victim may be paid. One of the most significant aspects of no-fault insurance is that automotive insurance becomes mandatory for all drivers, who must carry liability insurance for themselves and the passengers in their car. *See* Insurance, Liability.

NO-LOAD FUNDS

Mutual funds that are sold without benefit of a salesperson. *See* Broker, Load Funds, Securities.

NOMENCLATURE

In retailing, the procedure for assigning group identification to different categories of products, such as detergents, personal care, produce, or baking goods. *See* Retailing, Trademark.

Nominal Group Technique

A plan of business evaluation in which no more than a dozen authorities meet to discuss a project and forecast strategies for its implementation. *See* Business Administration.

Nominal Partners

Individuals who, for reasons of prestige or influence, lend their names to a business enterprise or nonprofit institution, but are not active participants in the functions and operations. *See* Partnerships.

Nominal Price

The price quoted for a commodity or futures contract during a period in which no actual trading is taking place. *See* Commodities, Futures.

Nonassignable

A business pact whose rights and stipulations cannot legally be transferred from the assigned individual or group of individuals to another party. *See* Agreement, Contract.

Nondegradable Materials

Substances that are potential pollutants and are not biodegradable, or easily absorbed back into the earth without damage to the environment. *See* Ecology, Environment, Pollution.

Nondurable Goods

Merchandise that has only a brief lifespan when in use. *See* Merchandising, Retailing.

Nonperformance

In marketing and sales, the failure of a contractor to supply goods or services that stand up to the claims in an agreement. *See* Guarantee, Warranty.

Nonprofit Organization

Any organization or association established in the interests of the public good, whether social, religious, educational, health-oriented, or philanthropic, that has been legally approved to function without profit. *See* Nonprofit, Organization.

Nonrecurring Costs

Monetary charges, expenses, or unexpected losses that are not likely to occur again in the course of normal business functions. *See* Accounting, Bookkeeping.

NONRENEWABLE RESOURCES

Natural resources that are consumed in the process of acquisition, production, and use and are not renewable, such as petroleum, coal, and metals. *See* Renewable Resources.

NORM

In industry, a condition or situation that represents normalcy and can be used in operational studies as a key point on which to judge cost factors and the efficiency of various related functions. *See* Business Administration, Production.

NORMATIVE ECONOMICS

The study of economics in which outcomes and conclusions depend upon the value judgments of the participating economists, as well as upon available statistical data. *See* Economics.

NO-STRIKE OPTION

The clause in a management/labor contract that prohibits a strike during the life of the contract. *See* Labor Union, Management/Labor, Strikes.

NOTARIZE

To acknowledge a signature on a legal document by the countersigning of an attorney or notary public. *See* Business Law, Notary Public.

NOTARY PUBLIC

An individual authorized by a state to administer oaths when necessary, certify documents, such as deeds, contracts, and identification papers, and take official affidavits and depositions. To qualify for the appointment, an individual must be of legal age, a resident of the state or county in which the position will be recognized, and of good moral character. *See* Business Law, Notarize.

NOTE

In finance, an instrument, such as a promissory note, that recognizes the existence of a particular commercial debt. Also referred to as a *note payable* or *note receivable*. *See* Promissory Note.

NOT FOR PROFIT

See Nonprofit Organization.

NOTICE OF DEFAULT

A document submitted to a borrower to report that a loan, or the payment on a loan, is delinquent and that certain steps will be taken to penalize the borrower or demand full and immediate repayment. *See* Loans.

NOVATION

A mutual agreement to replace an existing legal document with a new, or revised version. *See* Business Law.

NUISANCE

In legal terms, any bizarre or continuing conduct that creates an annoyance, inconvenience, embarrassment, or actual damage to an individual or property. *See* Business Law.

NUISANCE TAX

An unpopular excise tax, generally small but aggravating, that must be paid by consumers. *See* Excise Tax.

NULLIFICATION

The cancellation, in whole or in part, of a contract, covenant, or other instrument that has been legally binding. *See* Agreement, Contract.

NUMBERED ACCOUNT

In banking, an account that is identified only by a number, or combination of numbers and code letters, with the name of the depositor a secret. *See* Swiss Bank Accounts.

NUMERAIRE

A French term in international finance, this refers to the currency that is selected by a given firm as a reference against which all other currency cash flows can be computed. *See* International Currency.

NUMERICAL CONTROL

A system of programming, as for computers, in which coded numbers that are electronically or magnetically stored control the functions and output of an installation. *See* Computers, Programming.

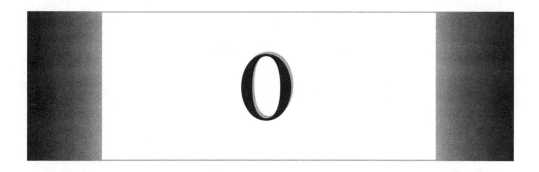

OBJECTIVE VALUE

The purchase price a product or service can command in relation to the price of other, similar purchases available. *See* Pricing.

OBSERVATIONAL RESEARCH

Also referred to as *observational methods,* this is a research technique used in marketing whereby researchers use their powers of observation and compile a record of what they *see,* rather than using the standard procedure of interviewing consumers. Although there are limitations, in that researchers cannot record personal feelings, desires, or opinions, this technique has certain advantages in many cases. For example, it is useful in the marketing of toys for very young children because researchers can use one-way mirrors to observe children playing with a variety of toys and compare product appeal in a significant manner. *See* Research and Development.

OBSERVED DEPRECIATION

A technique used on the production line to determine the extent of individual and collective depreciation of equipment through the physical inspection of operating units and parts. The amount of accrued depreciation is conventionally reported in terms of devaluation, expressed as a percentage of the original cost and the replacement cost. *See* Durable Goods, Obsolescence, Planned Obsolescence.

OBSOLESCENCE

The state of being out of date or unequal to current demands, said of almost any form of mechanical equipment or durable goods. *See* Durable Goods Planned Obsolescence.

OCCUPATIONAL ANALYSIS

A study of related jobs and duties to determine better ways of grouping them under a more integrated classification. *See* Ergonomics, Personnel Administration.

OCCUPATIONAL DISEASE

A condition, negative and often pathological, resulting from certain forms of employment or on-the-job conditions. When the problem relates to accidents and injuries, rather than illness, it is referred to as an *occupational hazard*. *See* Health Insurance, Personnel Administration.

OCCUPATIONAL SAFETY AND HEALTH ADMINISTRATION (OSHA)

A federal agency, established by the Occupational Safety and Health Act of 1970 and addressed to all employers whose businesses affect interstate commerce, "to assure so far as possible every working man and woman in the nation safe and healthful working conditions." OSHA cooperates with the National Institute of Occupational Safety and Health to undertake research to establish basic safety standards and assigns inspectors to make inspections of workplaces to see that standards are maintained. OSHA safety regulations include standards relating to worker exposure to acrylonitrile, cotton dust, asbestos, noise, toxic chemicals, lead, and pesticides. *See* Government, Health Insurance, Product Safety.

ODD LOT

In the securities field, an amount of stock that is less than the established units of trading, from one to 99 for most issues, and whose price is geared to the auction market. In marketing and merchandising, small lots of products and goods that are generally sold by the bundle, rather than by individual units. *See* Investments, Securities.

OFF-BALANCE SHEET

A financial record of a company that is not used in formal accounting procedures, such as periodic statements, but that has an impact on the operations of a company. A pending litigation might be cited on an off-balance sheet, which would alert reviewers to the possibilities of a future financial impact. *See* Accounting.

OFFSHORE BANKING

Banking and investment facilities that are located on islands offshore, such as the Cayman Islands, or in remote regions where supervision by government authorities is often weak or erratic. *See* Banking, International Trade.

OMBUDSMAN

A specialist assigned to duties on behalf of consumers or employees of an organization to investigate complaints in an objective manner. Ombudsmen also function as investigators of public protests against government policies and actions. *See* Employee Relations, Public Relations.

ON CONSIGNMENT

Describing merchandise that has been turned over by the owner to another party with the expectation that it will be sold. Although the phrase was originally used in a broad, commercial sense, recent years have seen a flurry of small businesses that are basically second-hand shops receiving items from private, would-be sellers "on consignment." *See* Entrepreneurs, Merchandising.

ON DEMAND

The term for a loan or other obligation that must be paid by the borrower, usually immediately and in full, upon demand by the lender. *See* Loans.

ONE-STOP BANKING

Services offered to consumers so they can complete a range of common monetary transactions at a single bank. *See* Banks and Banking.

ONLINE

The communications setup that exists when computers and other electronic devices are under the supervision and control of a central processing unit, which makes it possible for users to access thousands, even millions, of sources of data and communication. Commercial online services, such as CompuServe and America Online, provide such sources in every field and subject area conceivable. *See* Computers, Internet.

ONLINE COMPUTER

A computer designed to respond to new data and tasks at a rate determined by their arrival at the computer input terminals generally by having the input fed directly into the computer under the control of a central processing unit. Such systems are usually provided with programs that contain priority allocation means so that the computer can process several projects at the same time, without necessarily completing each immediately, storing the partial results in memory, and handling each task by priority. This sequential system is referred to as *on line time sharing. See* Time Sharing.

ONLINE SYSTEM

In computing, a structure in which the accessories and peripheral equipment are not controlled by a central processing unit but require human supervision. *See* Computers, Data Processing.

ON-THE-JOB TRAINING

The educational procedure used by an employer whereby workers are instructed and tested while they are engaged in their regular duties or in some other productive assignment at the same time they are learning. *See* Education, Training.

OPEN ACCOUNT

The term for a financial account that extends credit, unsecured, for a specified period of time and with predetermined limits. *See* Loans.

OPEN-DOOR POLICY

An international entitlement in which the citizens of foreign countries receive the same treatment in the host country as the domestic citizens. This policy can also apply to the transportation, purchase, and sale of foreign goods and merchandise. *See* Foreign Trade, International Relations.

OPEN-END AGREEMENT

In personnel management, a settlement between the employer and an injured employee in a worker's compensation case in which the latter is paid for work-related disability costs us long as the employee is unable to work. *See* Personnel Administration.

OPEN-END MORTGAGE

That type of mortgage in which the borrower (mortgagee) is permitted to reborrow money paid on the principal, up to the original amount. *See* Mortgage, Real Estate.

OPEN-END QUESTION

The type of question posed during market research interviews that does not require a single answer, but leaves respondents free to answer in their own words and provide as many relevant opinions as they desire. *See* Advertising, Market Research.

OPEN LETTER

A communication that may be addressed to an individual, but which is produced in quantity and mailed to a selected list of recipients in the hope of influencing them to share the writer's opinion or take a suggested form of action. Many such letters are published in newspapers and other periodicals in the form of an advertisement. *See* Advertising, Publicity.

OPEN LISTING

See Real Estate.

OPEN SHOP

A labor/management arrangement that gives workers the right to decide whether they want to join a union. *See* Labor/Management, Unions.

OPERATING COMPANY

A company that is actively engaged in the operation of a business, in contrast to a holding company. *See* Holding Company.

OPERATING CYCLE

The complete sequence of functions, as well as the time period necessary, to take raw materials and fashion them into finished products. *See* Manufacturing, Production.

OPERATING LEVERAGE

In selling and distribution, a situation that exists in a company whose sales costs are largely stable and constant, to the point where even slight increases above the break-even point result in large profits, while slight decreases can cause significant monetary losses. Such leverage is regarded as an *operating risk*. *See* Operating Losses, Operation.

OPERATING LOSSES

Those losses, usually anticipated and accounted for, that are incurred during the conventional operation of a business. *See* Accounting, Annual Report.

OPERATING STATEMENT

See Income Statement.

OPERATION

In its broadest terminology, the combination of all procedures, processes, and functions necessary to the gainful and favorable day-to-day life of an organization. *See* Corporation, Operations Research.

OPERATIONS RESEARCH

The scheduling and application of technological methods, instruments, and checks and balances to a company's operations, individually and collectively, to determine ways to correct problems, improve productivity, and lower costs. Having originated during World War II as a method of analyzing air-defense strategy, logistical problems, and other military functions, operations research is now a recognized management tool for inventory control, production planning, transportation scheduling, product distribution, marketing, and many other functions. In the course of studying common operations problems, researchers construct mathematical models and computer simulations, detailing circumstances and objectives to help managers evaluate situations and make decisions. The art of successful operations research depends heavily on the researcher's ability to formulate problems and construct and test models. *See* Game Theory, Linear Programming, Research and Development.

OPINION LEADERS

Recognized experts in their fields who can predict trends that have, or will have, an impact on a company's future—such as the acceptability potential for a new line of products or an intended expansion of services. *See* Consultants.

OPINION POLLS

In advertising and marketing, these are studies and surveys to determine what substantial numbers of people think and feel about various current subjects, products, or situations, in order to assist management in coming to decisions and making strategic plans. Typical opinion polls are those conducted by the Harris Poll and the Gallup Poll, the Survey Research Center at the University of Michigan, and the National Opinion Research Center at the University of Chicago. Sampling strategies have been scientifically developed over the years to improve the efficiency of opinion polling and to reduce errors by taking into account deviations related to the nature of populations being studied, such as age, sex, race, and socioeconomic status. Statistical denominators have been perfected so that no matter how large the population being studied, the size of the sample is the factor that determines the range of error in a probability sample. Samples of as few as 1,500 or 2,000 people, for example, can assure no larger a margin of error than plus or minus 3 percent, while larger samples yield only slightly smaller differentials. *See* Advertising Research.

OPTICAL COMPUTING

A scientific system of computing that utilizes tiny blips of light, called *photons,* to process data, instead of electronic switches or other devices, thus eliminating wiring and making it possible to have an almost unlimited number of controls and activators. In addition, photons have the advantage of functioning much faster than electrons and can pass through each other without causing internal distractions. As a result, optical computers are thousands of times faster than their electronic counterparts. *See* Computers, Fiber Optics.

OPTICAL READER

An instrument capable of interpreting type, symbols, and even handwriting and feeding them into a computer programming system. Also referred to as an *optical scanner.*

OPTIMIZATION

A strategy for evaluating the most desirable operating conditions based on certain selective criteria, and generally analyzed through computer programming. *See* Data Processing.

OPTIMIZATION MODELS

Quantitative models that attempt to provide an optimal solution to a problem regarding the proper allocation and utilization of resources—materials and manpower alike. *See* Resources.

OPTIMUM

In a production or manufacturing cycle, that combination of factors and mechanization and instrumentation that results in the most effective and efficient operational program. *See* Optimum Capacity, Production.

OPTIMUM CAPACITY

The quality and quantity of a running output that results in the minimum cost per product or unit produced. *See* Production.

OPTION

In the investment field, the privilege of exercising a right to purchase or sell designated securities in the future at the price stipulated when the purchase was transacted. *See* Investments, Securities.

ORAL HISTORY

In publishing, that form of text that is compiled through personal interviews with people who have either taken part in historical events or are familiar with those events through associations with people who are, or were, knowledgeable about them. Although often considered a modern form of reporting and writing, particularly by such well known authors as historian Allan Nevins and Studs Terkel, the technique can be traced back to ancient Greek historians, including Herodotus and Thucydides, who personally interviewed survivors of some of the battles they described. Modern oral history owes its development in large part to research projects undertaken by Columbia University, starting in the mid-1940s.

ORDINARY INCOME

For personal income tax reporting and returns, the income that does not qualify as capital gains. *See* Capital Gains, Income Tax.

ORGANIZATION

The combination of facilities, personnel, property, policies, patterns, and capabilities, among other factors, that result in a functioning enterprise, whether private or public, revenue-seeking or nonprofit. *See* Corporation.

ORGANIZATIONAL CHART

A visualization in graphic form of a company or other organization, broken down by divisions, departments, and functional units and displaying the relationships between these units, the flow of communications, allocated responsibilities, and the chain of command. (See chart on page 263.) *See* Business Administration, Business Management.

ORGANIZATIONAL CLIMATE

The nature of the environment in which an organization functions, including the locale, available personnel, political structure, governmental restrictions, labor unions, transportation composition, financial accessibility, and other considerations that affect the organization's operations and stature. *See* Environment.

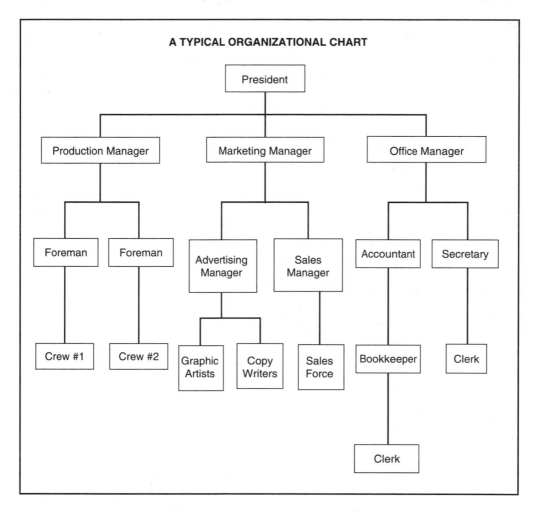

A TYPICAL ORGANIZATIONAL CHART

ORGANIZATION OF AMERICAN STATES (OAS)

An association of countries in the Western Hemisphere concerned with the maintenance of peace, economic cooperation, the settlement of disputes, and other political matters within the inter-American system. More than 30 nations are traditionally members of the OAS, including Antigua and Barbuda, Argentina, Bahamas, Barbados, Bolivia, Brazil, Chile, Colombia, Costa Rica, Cuba, Dominica, the Dominican Republic, Ecuador, El Salvador, Grenada, Guatemala, Haiti, Honduras, Jamaica, Mexico, Nicaragua, Panama, Paraguay,

Peru, St. Kitts-Nevis, Saint Lucia, Saint Vincent and the Grenadines, Suriname, Trinidad and Tobago, the United States, Uruguay, and Venezuela. The OAS originated at the First International Conference of American States (1889–1890), when an International Union of American Republics was formed, which later (1910) became the Pan-American Union. The OAS is composed of the General Assembly, the Permanent Council, the Inter-American Economic and Social Council, and the Inter-American Council for Education, Science, and Culture. *See* International Affairs.

ORGANIZATION FOR ECONOMIC COOPERATION AND DEVELOPMENT (OECD)

An international assemblage established in Paris at the beginning of the 1960s to help, through forums and mutual cooperation, to stimulate world-wide economic development. The OECD accepted a role as the catalyst in the development of a global environment that would be conducive to the economic growth of the world's developing countries. *See* Third World Nations.

ORGANIZATION OF PETROLEUM EXPORTING COUNTRIES (OPEC)

Universally recognized as "the most important international commodity group in the world," OPEC wields a significant impact on the global price of oil, strongly influences the balance of payments of nations, and is the accepted model for a successful international cartel. *See* Exports, Foreign Trade, Imports.

ORGANIZED LABOR

See Labor Unions.

ORIENTATION

The application of education and communication in either a broad or limited manner to train employees and other personnel, or in many instances to cope with pressing problems and work situations. *See* Education, Training.

OUTDOOR AVERTISING

The use of billboards, posters, aircraft signs, and other means of getting across messages out of doors. *See* Advertising, Media.

OUTLET STORE

A retail outlet, usually positioned near a manufacturer, that sells the company's products directly to consumers, customarily at a discount. *See* Discounts, Retailing.

OUTMODED

See Obsolescence.

OUT-OF-POCKET EXPENSE

An expense that is paid for by an employee or other individual working on behalf of a company and for which reimbursement will be asked at a later date. *See* Compensation.

OUT OF STOCK

Merchandise that has been temporarily discontinued by a supplier, or is unavailable in a store when requested by customers. *See* Distribution.

OUT-OF-WORK BENEFITS

Payments and other benefits that are furnished by a union to its members who are unemployed. *See* Labor Relations.

OUTPUT

In computer language, the information provided by any data-processing and programming system and displayed on a screen or printed out. *See* Computers, Data Processing.

OUTSOURCING

The industrial term for the practice, now widely employed, of purchasing parts from a variety of outside suppliers. Many manufacturers have discovered that it is cheaper and more feasible for them to buy, rather than make, certain kinds of parts that are either specialized, require unique skills, or fluctuate widely in demand. By purchasing components from the outside when, and as, they need them, producers avoid storage problems, the risk of being out of stock, or the problems of searching for skilled, often temporary, labor. *See* Production.

OVERALL MARKET CAPACITY

In marketing and merchandising, the volume of products or materials that can be absorbed in a given market without regard to prices or competition. *See* Marketing, Merchandising.

OVERCAPITALIZED

The situation that exists when there is a high capital investment but sales and distribution efforts are unsatisfactory. The term can also be applied to a manufacturing system whose installation and operating expenses do not justify the low rate of production. *See* Capital, Production.

OVERFLOW

The proportions of a manufacturing output that exceed the storage capacities that were estimated. *See* Inventory.

OVERHEAD

Expenses that are incurred in the operation of a business that cannot be listed in the books as costs for identifiable services or individual units of production. *See* Accounting, Bookkeeping.

OVERPRODUCTION PRINCIPLE

The hypothesis that manufacturers are forced into providing excessive amounts of production-line expansion whenever consumer demands increase. *See* Supply and Demand.

OVERRIDES

Commissions paid to salespersons and merchandising executives that are added to their salaries. *See* Salesmanship.

OVERRUN

In advertising, the number of pieces of advertising literature that are produced in addition to the originally intended amount. *See* Advertising.

OVERSELLING

Promising to deliver more products, goods, or services than can realistically be supplied. *See* Inventory.

OVER-THE-COUNTER (OTC)

Said of the sale of an unlisted security. *See* Investments, Securities.

OWNER'S EQUITY

That which results when liabilities and losses are deducted from assets. Also, the basic value in a company, or share of its stock, apportioned to the owner(s). *See* Assets, Equity.

PACE SETTERS

Selected employees who have been identified by management as being experienced, skilled, knowledgeable, and motivated, and can thus be assigned as leaders for fellow employees in their departments or divisions, or on corporate operating teams. *See* Business Management.

PACKAGE ADVERTISING

A plan in which advertisers are given discounts when they purchase a group of time slots in broadcasting or pages in periodicals. *See* Advertising, Broadcasting.

PACKAGE ENGINEERING

The scientific designing of packages and containers that can serve their function properly, yet be low in cost, lightweight, easily assembled, and environmentally acceptable. Also referred to as *package designing.*

PAPER MONEY

Any currency printed on paper, which is essentially of no material value, but whose real worth is determined by the gold or silver bullion held in its support in government vaults. When there is no backup bullion, the issuing government is said to be on the *paper standard. See* Currency, Gold Standard.

PAPER PROFITS

Those profits that look impressive on paper, but are unrealized. *See* Assets, Profits.

PAPER TITLE

A title to property, or anything else of value, that is proclaimed on a document that appears to impart proof of ownership, but that may not convey a proper title at all. *See* Property, Real Estate.

PAR

The situation that exists when the monetary value of an instrument or certificate is equal to that expressed on its face without consideration of any discount or premium. *See* Banks, and Banking.

PARALLEL PROCESSING

A data processing technique in which many operations can be executed simultaneously, rather than in sequential order, by using a network of interconnected microprocessors, from just a few to many thousands. The idea for this kind of computer processing came from studies of the human brain and its interconnected system of neurons that made intricate thought processes possible; and such systems are sensitive enough to adapt to voice recognition controls and commands. *See* Computers, Microprocessors, Programming.

PARAMETER

Data that are usually variable, but that are given a constant value in order to evaluate a business venture or situation and expedite the decision-making process. *See* Management.

PARENT CORPORATION

A company that owns two or more sub-companies or affiliates and manages and controls them. *See* Affiliate, Corporation.

PARITY

In economics, a term used to refer to the measurement of two types of equivalencies, as in a case where the level of current government subsidies are granted in terms of the equivalent purchasing power of a period in the past. Another common definition of *parity,* also known as *par value,* refers to the value of one country's currency expressed in the equivalent value of another country's currency. *See* Currency, Exchange Rate, Foreign Exchange, Subsidy.

PARITY POLICY

The active principle that functions on the doctrine that the degree of responsibility and authority that rests with individual employees should be equal to that of the employer. *See* Employee Relationships.

PAROCHIAL

In marketing, the arrangement of sales territories and regions so that they are limited in extent. *See* Distribution, Sales.

PARTIAL MONOPOLY

A situation in which, while there is no deliberate monopoly in a sales region, there are so few competitors that a virtual monopoly exists. *See* Monopoly.

PARTNERSHIP

A business that is run by two or more principals, who serve as partners, and whose objective is to make a profit. A legal contract entered into by two or more persons in which each agrees to furnish a part of the capital and labor for a business enterprise, and by which each shares a fixed proportion of profits and losses. A relationship between individuals or groups that is characterized by mutual cooperation and responsibility, as for the achievement of a specified goal. *See* Limited Partnership.

PAR VALUE

The face value of a security or certificate. *See* Par.

PASS TITLE

To take the necessary legal, administrative, and financial steps to transfer the title of a business enterprise to another party. *See* Title.

PASSWORD

Also referred to as a *code,* this is a word, string of characters, number, or similar selection that must be activated before a computer, a program, or both can start functioning. Passwords were devised as a means of protecting classified information and/or preventing undesirable operators from using computers and programs. *See* Computers, Data Processing, Programming.

PATENT

The exclusive right, protected by government decree, granted to an inventor or group to enjoy any profits or benefits derived from an invention, and proscribing anyone from infringing the patent by making, using, or selling something patented without the consent of the patentee. That person is then liable for damages and possible lawsuits and may be enjoined from using the patent. Patent law is highly complex, since the rights and restrictions vary, sometimes greatly, from one country to another. In the United States, only certain classes of inventions are patentable, including machines or machinery, manufactured articles, the compositions of matter, production processes, creative designs, computer software programs, genetically engineered organisms, and specially bred botanical plants. Inventions are not considered patentable if they can be easily created by persons with practical skills in the field in question, or if they were already known or used previously by people other than the inventor, or if they were in public use more than one year before application for a patent. Patent applications require comprehensive information, exacting details, specifications, sketches, if applicable, and descriptions of the invention and its applications and uses. Patent rights may be transferred to others by written agreement, as well as by licensing, but are generally valid only in the country of origin or within certain geographical and political limits. *See* Copyright, Patent Pending, Trademark.

PATENT PENDING

A temporary right granted by the patent office while a search is undertaken to ensure the patentability of an invention. *See* Patent.

PATERNALISM

The provision of benefits, social welfare programs, or other special treatment by a government on behalf of its citizens or by a company on behalf of its employees. *See* Employee Relations.

PATRONAGE

A retail sales term to refer to the body of consumers comprising a store's customers. *See* Consumers, Retailing.

PAYBACK PERIOD

The time period necessary for the cash input from an investment or undertaking to equal its initial cost. *See* Investments.

PAYMENT IN KIND

Any payment that is made, not in terms of money, but as an offer of goods or services. *See* Barter.

PEAK CAPACITY

In manufacturing and fabricating, the absolute capacity of production machinery, assembly lines, and operating personnel, without regard for cost, overall efficiency, quality, or wear and tear on equipment. *See* Manufacturing, Production.

PEAK SEASON

That period in the calendar year during which a product, material, or service is in greatest demand, calculated in regard to the actual duration of the demand in terms of days, weeks, months, or seasons. *See* Consumer Demand.

PEGGING

The manipulation of the prices of merchandise and services so they remain within very narrow confines and have little or no fluctuations. *See* Merchandising.

PEG POINT

An arbitrary wage rate for a specific job position that then becomes the base from which other related wage scales are calculated. *See* Compensation, Labor/Management.

PENALTY CLAUSE

A statement in a contract that is mutually acceptable to all parties in the contract and that requires fines or prepayments if certain stipulations are not met. *See* Agreement, Contract.

PENETRATION PRICING

An artificial establishment of uneconomically low prices in order to introduce products more quickly to a new market. *See* Pricing, Retailing.

PENNY STOCK

A low-priced issue, selling usually at a dollar or less per share and considered highly speculative. Such stocks have a reputation for being promoted, often fraudulently, in boiler-room operations. The term is used disparagingly, although some penny stocks, issued for fledgling companies, have developed into investment-caliber issues. *See* Boiler Rooms, Investments, Stocks.

PENSION

Periodic payments to employees who retire because of age or disability. In the nineteenth century, France and Great Britain provided government pensions to civil servants. In the United States, government pensions have been given to all war veterans since the Revolution and to federal employees since 1920. Today private pension plans, organized by municipalities, labor unions, corporations, professional associations, and others supplement Social Security, which was instituted in 1935. The federal Pension Benefit Guaranty Corporation insures the pension plans of participating American companies. *See* Compensation, Social Security.

PER CAPITA TAX

A tax to be paid by each individual, which is arrived at by dividing the total tax sum by the number of people being taxed. *See* Taxation.

PERCEPTUAL THEORY

In the classical approach, a theory in which the first step was to divide sensory experience into modalities such as vision, touch, and smell, and to subdivide the modalities into elementary sensations from which all more complex perceptual experiences—such as those of objects and events—were presumed to be constructed. Sensations were to be explained in terms of their physiological bases and the physical energies to which the receptors are specially adapted were to respond. *See* Psychology, Research.

PERFORMANCE EVALUATION

The formal review of an employee's performance on the job, to determine the quality and effectiveness of his or her work. *See* Ergonomics, Personnel Administration.

PERFORMANCE REPORT

A summary that compares actual results and costs with those anticipated in a stated budget. *See* Accounting, Budgets.

PERIOD CHARGES

Costs that are entered in the books as those relating to a specified period of time in which they are incurred, rather than being related to an inventory. *See* Bookkeeping, Inventory.

PERIPHERALS

In computer installations, the term is used to refer to any components of equipment that are separate from the central processing unit, especially those such as printers, CD-ROM players, and modems, which are part of the outside communications system. *See* Computers, Data Processing.

PERISHABLE GOODS

Any products or materials that are subject to deterioration or decay unless they are refrigerated or given other special storage. *See* Durable Goods, Merchandising.

PERKS

Popular name for *prerequisites,* fringe benefits that are drawing cards in attracting employees to jobs or in giving extra status to an executive position. *See* Compensation, Employee Relations.

Permit Postage

Postage on an envelope or package that is imprinted by machine, rather than by using a stamp, and that records the amount of charge and the permit holder's number. *See* Postal, Post Office.

Perpetual Inventory

A stock-control system in which orders, sales, and receipts are tabulated as they occur and as the inventory is computed. *See* Inventory.

Personal Computers

A rapidly growing array of small and moderately priced computers that are largely used at home for personal use or for the conducting of a small business. Many such computers are now used by employees while at home or in transit to handle business homework or catch up on office-related assignments. *See* Computers, Data Processing, Hardware, Integrated Circuits.

Personal Finance Company

A credit service that lends small sums of money to consumers for personal needs, usually at higher interest rates than banks. *See* Banking, Loans.

Personal Property

That classification of property that is owned by individuals, families, or other small groups of people, particularly items such as securities, furniture, jewelry, clothing, cameras, and sporting goods, in contrast to real property, which includes land, minerals, trees, crops, and buildings. Personal property can, however, include minerals taken from the ground, felled trees, and lumber. *See* Assets, Property.

Personnel

See Employees.

Personnel Administration

The management of full-time employees and all other personnel whose work and services are relevant to the operations and functions of an organization, including recruitment, screening, hiring, recompensating, orientation, training, assigning, and discharging. The Small Business Administration (SBA) compiled a list of activities and programs that should be kept foremost in mind by personnel managers, of which the following (not necessarily in order of priority) are examples:

- Never assume that new, or recently reassigned, employees will have a clear understanding of their responsibilities, and make these duties clear at the outset.

- Review organizational charts frequently and discuss them regularly at management meetings, to determine ways of improving both efficiency and employee morale.

- Keep tabs on key employees who are approaching retirement age, seem restless, or are logical targets for recruitment by competitors, and determine who their logical successors might be.

- Be prompt in remedying any employee-related situation that involves conflicts of interest, dissensions, or confusions about overlapping duties and responsibilities.

- Hold regular reviews of duties and responsibilities with middle managers, supervisors, fore persons, and others regarding the personnel under their jurisdiction.

- Line up and maintain good contacts with all resources for recruiting personnel, including employment agencies, educational institutions, and the media.

- Provide adequate transportation, or data about transportation for employees, including car pools and special rates and accommodations for mass transit.

- Communicate regularly with employees through all practical media, internal and external.

- Provide orientation programs for new employees and special sessions for all personnel whenever there are significant changes in the company or its management.

- Provide awards, honors, and other recognition programs for employee achievement and make public announcements where appropriate.

- Offer bonuses and other monetary incentives for employees who have completed long service or have achieved meaningful goals.

- Place employee morale high on your list of priorities.

- Arrange meaningful social events and sports programs for employees, particularly in cases where getting to know one another can be helpful to corporate unity and attitude.

- Work to enhance and improve the company image but always credit employees with changes for the better.

- In addition to giving minorities chances above and beyond the laws and regulations, make it a point to hire more people who are handicapped, yet able to function well when placed in the right jobs.

- Be forthright when talking confidentially with employees about job-related or personal problems, but be tactful and sympathetic at the same time.

- Before facing a difficult confrontation with an employee, do your homework, list the facts, and make sure of your position and of company policies.

- Create an open dialogue and respect opinions that differ from yours.

- Encourage managers at all levels to communicate better and more frequently with their subordinates about departmental goals and aspirations.

- Do everything possible to make employees feel that they are part of the team and that what benefits the company will in turn benefit them.

An editorial in *Personnel Journal* stated that many business experts consider *people* to be a company's vital and indispensable resource, not only because labor is the single greatest financial outlay to which most organizations are committed, but because those companies with the best documented records of success are more often than not ones in which the employees have a personal stake and make valuable contributions. *See* Employee Relations, Human Relations Department, Management.

Personnel Department

See Human Relations Department.

Personnel Management

See Personnel Administration.

Personnel Relations

See Employee Relations.

Peter Principle

A tongue-in-cheek theory that, in a hierarchy, every employee tends to move toward his or her level of incompetence.

Phillips Curve

A curvilinear statistical image displaying the relationship between unemployment and inflation. *See* Inflation, Unemployment.

PHYSICAL DISTRIBUTION

The movement of products and merchandise from a manufacturer or supplier to wholesale and retail outlets and the consumer. *See* Distribution.

PHYSICAL INVENTORY

A count of merchandise observed in an inventory by actual identification, rather than by records. *See* Inventory.

PIE CHART

Any chart that is circular, or pie-shaped, and divided into sectors to compare proportionate shares of the whole. *See* Graphics.

PILOT PLANT

A manufacturing facility in which experimental production runs can be made on a new product or revised production system in order to test methods, time periods, and costs, or to eliminate bugs. *See* Ergonomics, Human Factors Engineering, Production, Production Engineering.

PLACEMENT

In personnel management, the scientific positioning of employees in the jobs and assignments for which they are best suited, often using appropriate tests and studies. *See* Human Relations, Personnel.

PLANNED ECONOMY

An economic system in which a government or ruling body influences decisions on what to produce, when, how, and in what amounts. *See* Economics, Gross National Product (GNP).

PLANNED OBSOLESCENCE

The deliberate designing and manufacturing of products that will have a shorter-than-necessary life, in order to promote and sell successor products of a similar kind at a later date. *See* Obsolescence.

PLENARY SESSION

Said of a conference or meeting that all of the expected delegates actually attend.

PLOW BACK

To reinvest in a business or investment plan for the future, generally by setting aside portions of profits and earnings for that purpose, rather than by issuing dividends. *See* Dividends, Investment.

PLUTOCRACY

That form of government that is controlled by the wealthy, often in a manner detrimental to the interests of the middle and lower economic classes; government by the wealthy. From the Greek ploutokratia : ploutos, wealth + -kratia, -cracy. *See* Autocracy, Government.

POINT FOUR PROGRAM

An American foreign-aid and technical-assistance program approved by Congress in 1950, to improve living standards by helping people in underdeveloped countries acquire industrial and agricultural equipment and skills, and also with the intention of erecting a barrier in the West against Communism. The prototype of later developmental programs, it was funded by a number of American agencies, as well as by the United Nations. *See* Foreign Trade, Third World nations.

POINT-OF-PURCHASE (POP) ADVERTISING

Advertising that consists largely of signs, posters, and other graphic displays right at the point where sales of the advertised product are being made. *See* Advertising, Retailing.

POLICY EVALUATION

The study of the value and impact of a policy to determine its feasibility from a social and behavioral viewpoint. *See* Management.

POLITICAL ACTION COMMITTEE

Popularly known as PACs, these committees are generally founded and supported by private groups to back candidates for public office. After increasing in number dramatically during the 1980s, they fell into disfavor in the early 1990s because of public clamor against special-interest groups, at which time many political candidates openly refused to accept financial contributions. *See* Government.

POLITICAL SCIENCE

The discipline that studies the composition and actions of governments and the private and public forces that influence them, with special focus on three fields: domestic politics, international politics, and comparative politics, or the in-depth study of the similarities and differences among certain selected countries or governments. A related area of study is *political philosophy,* the analysis of the principles and ideals to which governments have been expected to conform, historically, as well as in different cultures. *See* Government.

POLLUTION

In environmental terminology, pollution is defined as "any discharge of material or energy into water, land, or air that causes or may cause acute or chronic detriment to the earth's ecological balance, or that lowers the quality of life." Pollution, formerly a local problem in most areas, has gradually spread—largely because of industrialization and the escalation of large numbers of motorized vehicles and the explosion of the human population—until it has become a national and even a global dilemma. Coupled with this growth has been the enormous increase in waste by-products, including the discharge of untreated wastes into waterways, the spewing of particulates and gases into the atmosphere, the escalation of disposable products, and the use of new and often untested chemicals. The major categories of environmental pollution are:

Water Pollution. The discharge of biological, chemical, or physical debris into fresh and ocean waters to a degree that degrades the quality of the water and negatively affects the organisms living in those waters. Population growths in urban areas have contributed directly to the increase in the discharge of untreated, or poorly treated sewage in almost every major city of the world, where treatment facilities have not kept pace with the increased need. In addition, many nutrients such as nitrogen and phosphorus can accelerate the aging process of freshwater lakes, leading to an overgrowth of aquatic vegetation and the eventual extinction of the lake itself.

Thermal Pollution. The discharge of waste heat from power plants and factories, caused by energy dissipation, into cooling water and thence into nearby waterways, causing ecologic imbalance and environmental problems.

Land Pollution. The deterioration of land surfaces through a number of causes, including deforestation, agricultural misuse, mineral exploitation, the dumping of industrial waste, and the illegal disposal of garbage and residential wastes. Another culprit is soil erosion, stripping of the land and the removal of rich topsoils through poor farming practices and the overcutting of timber or the stripping of surface minerals.

Pesticide Pollution. The unrestricted application of harsh chemicals that are nondegradable and become accumulated within the bodies of consuming organisms, which, ironically, they were supposed to protect from the ravages of insects and other pests.

Radiation Pollution. Resulting from the detonation of nuclear devices and the release of energy from nuclear-powered generating plants, as well as from certain kinds of mining operations and experimental energy projects.

Noise Pollution. The cumulative effect of hundreds of sound-producing sources, such as motor vehicles of all kinds, supersonic jets, loud stereo systems, blaring radios, and construction projects—particularly in dense population areas.

Air Pollution. The accumulation of substances in the atmosphere are concentrated enough to endanger human health or produce other negative assaults, not only on people and animals, but on physical materials, such as homes, public buildings, vehicles, and clothing. Among the major sources of air pollution are power generation, the burning of solid wastes, factory emissions, and all forms of transportation, which emit such noxious substances as carbon monoxide, hydrocarbons, nitrogen oxides, particulates, and sulfur dioxide.

Even humans alone cause certain degrees of pollution, which, on a global scale, can have an injurious effect on the environment if not controlled or neutralized. *See* Ecology, Environment.

POLLUTION CONTROL

The planned management of undesirable discharges and wastes in order to minimize the effects of all forms of pollutants on people and on the environment, mainly by. reducing factory operations when conditions are poor, perfecting pollution-control devices wherever serious problems exist, neutralizing industrial emissions, supervising the collection and disposal of all forms of waste, conducting environmental research programs, conserving energy, reducing traffic, improving production efficiency, and enforcing environmental regulations. *See* Environment, Pollution.

PONZI SCHEME

A pyramid investment fraud, named after one of the most famous perpetrators of this con game, whereby those who invest early increase their profits, but a huge percentage of those who follow lose their shirts. *See* Better Business Bureau, Con Artist, Fraud, Pyramid.

POPULATION DYNAMICS

A research discipline whose objective is to study changes in population densities and interpret them in terms of related biological forces, to evaluate associated ecological patterns and to seek solutions to problems of human economy, such as biological conservation, pest control, and the administration of wildlife. For purposes of study and planning, a "population" can be composed of humans, animals, birds, insects, or any combinations of living organisms, but preferably within a well-defined geographical region where the interaction of beings within one population group, or within several such groups, can be observed and measured by census. In many instances, projections are made not only from sightings of population members, but from examinations of various items of evidence, such as habitations, tracks, wastes, and vocalizations. *See* Demographics, Population Control, Population Studies.

POPULATION STUDIES

Research in the form of surveys and interviews, as well as reviews of previous data, to determine facts about population characteristics and future expectations of change. *See* Census, Research, Surveys.

PORTAL-TO-PORTAL EXPENSE

A payment made to an individual not only for work and services performed, but for the time spent in transportation to and from the job. *See* Compensation.

PORT AUTHORITY

An official body, usually established by an urban government, to supervise port-related functions, such as ship traffic, docking, loading and unloading, manpower requirements, passenger traffic, tariffs, and nearby shore transportation. *See* Port of Entry, Shipping.

PORTFOLIO

A selection of investment securities held by an institution or individual and managed either by the owner or by an outside adviser. A typical portfolio contains a mixture of preferred stocks, bonds, and common stocks that are, in toto, well balanced. *See* Broker, Financial Planning, Investments, Securities.

PORT OF ENTRY

A seaport, rail terminal, or airport that has international traffic, and where customs duties are collected. *See* Port Authority, Shipping.

POSTAL SERVICES

Those services, whether public or private, with responsibilities for the collection and distribution of mail, funded through the sale of postage stamps or through itemized payments at the time of service. In most countries, the postal service is operated by the government, as it was in the United States until the Postal Service was established under the Postal Reorganization Act of 1970, as an independent, nonprofit corporation.

POTENTIAL DEMAND

In marketing, the demand for products, materials, and services that can be anticipated at a near or distant future time period, particularly in order to plan schedules that both meet the increased demand and command a favorable price. *See* Consumer Demand, Retailing, Supply and Demand.

POWER OF ATTORNEY

In law, a formal, signed document that empowers one person to act legally on behalf of another. *See* Business Law.

PRACTICAL CAPACITY

In industrial production, the optimum level at which a combination of fabricating operations and assembly lines can operate both efficiently and economically. *See* Production.

PRECIOUS METALS

Gold and silver, selected because they are internationally recognized as government commodities for the support of paper currency and coinage. *See* Currency, Gold Standard.

PRECLUSIVE BUYING

The deliberate purchase of merchandise to prevent someone else—perhaps a competitor—from obtaining it. *See* Competition.

PREDATORY PRICE SLASHING

The offering of products and services below cost as a means of driving a competitor out of business or an exclusive market. *See* Competition.

PREEMPTIVE RIGHT

In the purchase of securities, as well as certain scarce products and materials, the right to be among the first to be permitted to make a purchase. *See* Investments, Securities.

PREFABRICATED

Any unit that will be joined with other units, such as components of a house, and that is fashioned in advance prior to delivery and installation at the site. *See* Housing, Construction.

PREFERRED POSITION

In advertising, a location in a magazine, newspaper, or other periodical that commands a premium insertion price because it is more likely to be seen and acted upon favorably by readers. *See* Advertising, Media.

PREFERRED STOCKS

Securities that are redeemable in a liquidation situation prior to the repayment of any common stock dividends. *See* Common Stock, Dividends, Investments.

PREMIUM REMUNERATION

A wage or salary whose rate is higher than normal because of on-the-job performances overtime, on holidays, on weekends, or during days off. *See* Compensation.

PREPACKAGING

The packaging or containerizing of produce or other fresh foods by the distributor prior to shipment and delivery. *See* Distribution.

PREROGATIVES

The options, rights, and privileges held by an individual that others do not have. *See* Agreement, Business Law, Contract.

PRESCRIPTION

In real estate, entitlement to a property, or the rights to title, based on uninterrupted possession or use. *See* Real Estate.

PRESUMPTIVE TITLE

A nonexistent title that is assumed to be held by a party seemingly in possession of property, whereas in reality no such title is valid. *See* Real Estate, Title.

PRICE CONTROL

The governmental regulation of prices for goods and services, which is intended to prevent exorbitant costs or to maintain a stable economy during crisis periods, as in the case of a war or natural disaster. *See* Regulations.

PRICE DISCRIMINATION

Charging different prices to various categories of buyers for the same quality and quantity of merchandise. *See* Merchandising.

PRICE FIXING

The practice, usually illegal, of establishing set prices in collusion with other companies in the same business. *See* Business Law.

PRICE INDEX

A financial device that graphically shows the percentage changes in the price of goods in selected categories by using a base number value, often 100.

PRICE LEADER

See Loss Leader.

PRICE SUPPORTS

Subsidies offered by the government to farmers, producers, or distributors in accordance with regulatory procedures to prevent market prices from dropping below specified minimum levels. *See* Commodities, Subsidies.

PRIMARY DATA

In market research, facts collected by researchers from original, not secondary, sources. *See* Market Research.

PRIME COSTS

The direct costs of materials, labor, and transportation incurred by manufacturers before other costs, such as taxes or surcharges are added on. *See* Manufacturing.

PRIME RATE

The interest rate charge at any specified time by banks to their preferential borrowers; also the lowest rate of interest available to borrowers. *See* Banks and Banking, Interest.

PRIME TIME

Those time slots in broadcasting that are considered advantageous from the standpoint of audience size and potential. Arbitrarily, prime time is considered the three-hour period in the evening from 8:00 to 11:00, Eastern Standard Time. *See* Advertising, Broadcasting, Media.

PRIVATE ENTERPRISE

A business venture that is owned and managed by individuals or a group whose objective is to make profits. Business activities unregulated by state ownership or control; a privately owned business enterprise, especially one operating under a system of free enterprise or laissez-faire capitalism. *See* Entrepreneur, Small Business.

PRIVATE SECTOR

The area of business and industrial operations that consist of organizations that are not under direct government control, except for normal regulations and limitations. *See* Privatization.

PRIVATIZATION

In business and economics, the reduction in government ownership or control of companies and production facilities, which, at the national level, is referred to as *denationalization.* The term is a product of the 1970s in the United States, coined to describe a number of government enterprises that were being sold off to buyers for private ownership. The term is also used popularly for certain kinds of services that are still under government control but are contracted out to nongovernment service companies, such as transportation, printing, or maintenance. *See* Government.

PROBABILITY

In advertising research, the likelihood that certain events will occur or certain situations will hold true, based on past history and experience. *See* Advertising, Media, Research.

PROBLEM SOLVING

In business and industry, measures that can be taken either routinely or through special actions to come to grips with internal and external problems, especially when the objective is clear but the means to the end are not. Problem solving involves the following basic steps, in sequence: (1) recognizing that a problem exists; (2) identifying the problem; (3) isolating the problem as to persons, places, and things involved; (4) pinpointing options and alternatives; (5) running test problems or reviewing comparable problems that have been solved in the past; (6) compiling opinions both from those close to the problem and from experts; and, finally, (7) deciding what steps should be taken to correct the problem. One more step is important, following the above sequence of actions: verifying the fact that the solution is, indeed, feasible. *See* Business Administration, Leadership, Research.

PROCEDURE

Taking a series of calculated, identifiable steps in a repetitive commercial operation, such as production, marketing, or employee management. *See* major section on *procedures,* page 413.

PROCESS CONTROL

The expression applied to certain techniques for regulating variables present in industrial operations, such as temperature, pressures, and flow rates of liquids. The more widespread and complex manufacturing processes came to be, the more it was necessary to institute this type of control. The chemical industry offers many such examples in the processing and production of synthetics of all kinds, where temperatures and pressures are exceedingly critical if quality is to be assured and hazards avoided. Early controls were accomplished manually at first through the use of common instruments and to a degree successful or not, depending upon the experience and orientation of the controller. Later, automatic systems—sufficient for their day—were developed that could measure, evaluate, and adjust without direct human intervention.

Essentially, process control involves only three distinct functions: (1) *measurement,* which is accomplished by converting information about a variable into a signal proportional to this value to be used for feedback: (2) *evaluation,* a function performed by electronic or pneumatic instruments called controllers, which compare the variable to a desired value, and trigger warning signals if an error is detected. (3) *adjustment,* in which the feedback signal determined by the evaluation is used to affect the process itself. The combined triumvirate of the elements—measurement, evaluation, and adjustment—constitutes a *process-control loop,* where "loop" refers to the cycle of feedback of adjustments to the process following measurements. Industrial applications contain many variables and thus require numerous loops. Oftentimes, loop variables interact with one another so that adjustments for one of them will affect others along the line. The microprocessor process-control system, which has come into widespread use, is the aggregate of all these loops and can control from one or two to hundreds of variables. It is also possible, in very complex control structures, to interconnect individual process-control systems. *See* computer-aided design (CAD), computer-aided manufacturing (CAM), controls, data processing.

Process Intervention

Taking predictable steps to moderate the attitudes and perspectives of employees to assure a better attainment of enumerated objectives. *See* Employee Relations.

Processor

In computer language, this is the *chip,* which handles all of a machine's calculations and that can function at extraordinary speeds. As a general rule, the higher the speed of the processor, the faster the computer runs, a condition that might not be of great importance to the average user, but that is vital in large commercial installations that have to process endless, heavy loads of data. *See* Chip.

Procurement

The acquisition of goods and materials necessary for manufacturing and processing operations. *See* Purchasing.

PRODUCER

A manufacturer, fabricator, or constructor. In broadcasting and the entertainment field, the individual charged with the responsibilities of putting together a creative production. *See* Advertising, Broadcasting.

PRODUCT DEVELOPMENT

The scientific procedures and research necessary to generate new or improved goods and ready them for market. *See* Marketing.

PRODUCT DIFFERENTIATION

A merchandising plan for producing and selling lines of similar products with only slight variations, the objective being to obtain larger shares of the markets. *See* Marketing, Merchandising.

PRODUCTION

Also referred to as *production engineering,* this field of operations covers the planning and control of the physical and mechanical means of changing the shape, condition, and relationships of materials in order to produce products that have significantly greater utility and value than the combined raw materials. As technology and the state of the art advances and industries become more sophisticated, the engineering of products and goods requires extremes of both breadth and specialization. For this basic reason, production in any company and any industry is initiated as a complex planning activity, incorporating such relevant subject components as product design, personnel skills, manufacturing capabilities, handling, transportation, distribution, and consumer demand. Products for which there is a growing market, for example, would not be commercially feasible for a company if they required production machinery that was way out of line in cost, was too difficult to ship, or required on-line skills that the company neither had nor could afford.

The purpose of production engineering and planning has been defined as being "to refine and adjust the design of the product to the problems involved in its proposed manufacture. Conversely, it should solve certain problems, mainly functional and mechanical, such as those involved in workmanship, processing, operational sequence, tools, dies, and special equipment required to manufacture the product or commodity efficiently, profitably, and according to the technical specifications." One of the major responsibilities of production managers is to determine whether (1) to manufacture a product in toto or contract with another producer to do so, (2) let out contracts for some of the parts of a product and make the rest and handle the assembly, or (3) obtain all of the parts from an outside producer and be involved just with assembly. The decision rests on many factors, including the overall utilization of company facilities, the capabilities of existing personnel, the economics of each alternative, competition, supply and demand, and company policy and objectives in the matter of expansions and/or diversification. Since the entire future of a company may rest on its production policies and decisions, great care goes into the selection of manpower and equipment. According to the American Society of Mechanical Engineers (ASME), prime consideration must be given to the following factors, among others:

- Demand for the product, whether short or long term.
- Permanency of the product, whether it will virtually remain the same over the next few years or require radical changes to avoid technological obsolescence.
- Competitive advantages gained by choice of product design or production equipment.
- Integration with other products, materials, and services offered by the company.
- Suitability of present manpower and equipment in regard to the end product.
- Effect on quality of the product.
- Cost of operating and maintaining the production equipment.
- Source and availability of capital for each option.

In most industrial companies, production is the basic function of the manufacturing division, with its own management answering to the corporate administration and having the responsibility of performing such divisional functions as setting goals, confirming budgets, training employees, and coordinating with other divisions and departments, such as personnel, warehousing, transportation, marketing, and sales. Production management requires a comprehensive understanding of both the intention and purpose of product design and its relationship to other products manufactured—or to be manufactured—by the company. Engineers and planners take into consideration such factors as performance, appearance, safety, durability, maintenance, repairability, and other functional conditions, and are charged with the responsibility of testing preliminary models and prototypes. *See* Manufacturing, Process Control, other *Production* entries.

Production Control

The supervision and management of manufacturing operations in such a way as to maintain efficiency, minimize waste, and produce a maximum number of goods and materials economically. *See* Production.

Production Department

In manufacturing, the unit charged with the responsibility of meeting production needs and outputs. *See* Manufacturing.

In advertising, the department or unit of an agency whose job it is to produce advertisements and other printed matter, or to produce commercials and shows for broadcasting. *See* Advertising.

Production Efficiency

The state that is reached in a manufacturing or production operation beyond which there is no probability of increasing the yield more quickly, effectively, or at lower cost. The measure of this state of the art is called *productivity*. *See* Manufacturing, Production.

Productivity

In manufacturing and processing, defined as "the output of any aspect of production per unit of input, the measure of the output of a worker, machine, or an entire national economy in the creation of goods and services." A strong national productivity exists under conditions when the output level is high in proportion to the input. *See* Economics, Gross National Product (GNP), Production.

Product Liability

In legal and insurance terminology, any form of liability associated with damages caused by faulty or inferior products. *See* Business Law.

Product Line

An assemblage or related products or units that are generally promoted and often sold in combination. *See* Retailing.

Product Manager

In marketing, the executive in charge of one or more products whose duties are to promote and distribute them and often to participate in their creation and development. *See* Distribution, Marketing.

PRODUCT OBSOLESCENCE

See Obsolescence.

PRODUCT SAFETY COMMISSION

Established in the early 1970s, this federal agency sets national safety standards and bans hazardous products. State and local governments also have become involved in consumer protection. The Consumer Federation of America, comprising about 220 organizations, is the largest consumer advocacy group in America. Consumer protection on an international scale is coordinated by the International Organization of Consumers Unions. *See* Consumers Federation of America.

PROFESSION

A recognized occupation that can be claimed by an individual only after he or she has received proper education and training and received a degree or certification attesting to that fact. Familiar examples of *professionals* are attorneys, engineers, and Certified Public Accountants (CPAs). *See* Business Administration, Human Resources.

PROFILE EVALUATION

The appraisal of individuals on the job to determine the qualifications, experience, and orientation necessary for high performance and thus to create a *profile* and pattern to follow in employee management. *See* Personnel Administration.

PROFIT

The excess of revenues over costs, also referred to in corporations as *net earnings* or *income,* and computed before taxes and dividends are disbursed. Corporations traditionally release only a predetermined percentage of the profits as dividends to shareholders, retaining the balance to meet financial contingencies, finance capital improvements, and expand their facilities and services. Profit has been defined as the single greatest force motivating management and shareholders to make innovations and take risks with the company's capital. *See* Annual Reports, Finance.

PROFIT AND LOSS STATEMENT

A required financial statement by an organization to show clearly its proceeds and losses over a stated period of time. *See* Accounting, Annual Reports.

PROFIT MARGIN

See Finance.

PROFIT SHARING

An employee benefit established so that those in the plan can share in the earnings of a corporation, either on a current or a future basis. *See* Compensation.

PROGRAM

Any sequence of actions and instruction necessary to the effective performance of a planned function. In computer operation, a plan for preparing a computer to store and release information of a type specified. *See* Computers, Programming.

PROGRAMMED LEARNING

In the field of data processing and electronics, this educational field refers to procedures that enhance self-instruction by means of computers and their related instruction programs, which are attuned to the demographics of the users as well as to subjects and scope of coverage. An important phase of programming is testing, to assure that an instructional program will enable students of a certain age, background, and ability to achieve intended learning objectives. The function involving the perfecting of such materials, which was first initiated in the 1950s for industrial and military training, has been called *programming,* but also *instructional systems development.* The key to the system is the relegation of what are often complex and comprehensive curricula into component parts, to simplify the learning procedures during each program. As a result, these programs, which can cover almost any imaginable topic, tend to be *linear* or *branching* in composition, that is, requiring students to master each segment before proceeding on to the next in sequence. *See* Computers, Education, Programming, Training.

PROGRAMMER

A specialist who plans, creates, and utilizes programs. *See* Computers, Programming.

PROGRAMMING

In data processing, the act of providing solutions to specified problems by formulating a program that will activate a computer and render solutions. In broadcasting, selecting the time slots and sequences in which commercials and programs will be aired. Programming in the data-processing sense involves language, syntax, grammar, and symbols or words by means of which instructions are given to a computer. Because computers work with binary numbers, the most primitive means of instructing the computer is through machine language. This is usually an octal, decimal, or hexadecimal representation of the binary codes for operations such as "add," "subtract," and "compare." Because it is difficult to write programs in machine language without error, many languages have been designed to make programming easier and faster. The earliest of these, called symbolic languages or assembly languages, are written using simple mnemonics such as "A" for add or "M" for multiply, which are then translated into a machine language by a computer program called an assembler. An extension of such a language is the macro instruction, a mnemonic such as "read," for which the assembler substitutes a series of simpler mnemonics to save the programmer time. The next advance was the algorithmic, or procedural, language, which is designed for solving a particular type of problem and, unlike machine or symbolic languages, varies very little among computers. All algorithmic and procedural languages must be translated into machine code by a computer program called a compiler or interpreter. *See* Advertising, Broadcasting, Computers, Data Processing, Production.

PROMOTER

An individual who undertakes to organize individuals and activities to publicize and carry out a plan of action on behalf of a business venture, public event, or cause. *See* Promotion, Publicity.

PROMOTION

In the presentation of products and services—as well as in any other facet of business and industry—promotion has been called the fuel that lights the fire under advertising, marketing, merchandising, public relations, and other vehicles of communication, whether paid for or complimentary. Promotion essentially is threefold: to create public awareness of a business and its products and services, to stimulate a consumer desire for those services, and to attract customers to places or into positions where they can readily obtain what the company has to offer. A promotion for *promotion* itself has been labeled *AIDA*, in which the first "A" stands for "Attention getting," while "I" is "Interest awakening," and "D" is "Desire stimulation," and the second "A" represents "Action getting." Promotion, in the above sense, requires that promoters make themselves totally knowledgeable about what prospective customers and clients read, listen to, view, attend, travel by, and experience in their day-to-day lives, and then target the ones they want to reach with their promotional message. When experienced promoters lack this kind of knowledge, or any fraction of it, they do their homework, conduct studies, schedule interviews, and work around the clock until they have the subject in hand and are ready to *promote.* They are well aware that their efforts must be well rounded, that the facts must be honed to a sharp edge, and that they must be on target. *See* Advertising, Marketing, Merchandising, Publicity, Public Relations.

PROOFREADING

In common usage, but especially in the field of publishing, the formalized scrutiny of texts—whether handwritten, typed, or printed—before they are prepared for publication or distribution. In the business world, proofreading is essential in the preliminary review of texts that contain detailed data, statistics, and financial records, such as a company's prospectus, annual report, or legal documents. In the publishing professions, proofreading is conventionally an editorial function performed after texts have been set in type, at which time the type proofs are compared with the original manuscripts and corrected or revised as needed. Most publishers retain skilled and experienced proofreaders for this purpose—individuals who are trained to spot errors quickly and efficiently, as well as editors who have been assigned to improve an author's work or make other kinds of revisions. Proofreading is often a separate function from *copy editing,* which is an examination of a manuscript just before it is submitted to a typesetter, with the specific objective of correcting spelling, grammar, and punctuation. Both proofreaders and copy editors use a standard set of symbols.

PROPERTY

See Real Estate.

PROPOSAL

In business, a document or presentation that suggests a plan of action and the necessary investment, personnel, and equipment to achieve a stated goal.

PROSPECTUS

A detailed document issued by a corporation or brokerage house to describe a security or other investment opportunity. To be valid, a prospectus must follow the very rigid stipulations of the Securities and Exchange Commission (SEC) and other regulatory bodies. *See* Securities and Exchange Commission.

PROTECTIONISM

In foreign trade, the favoring of high tariffs and other import constraints so that domestic products and goods can be sold more competitively against foreign ones. Just the reverse of *free trade,* protectionism is characterized by taxes on imports, tariffs, duties, and other restrictions that discriminate against foreign products. On the positive side, protectionism is justified on the grounds that it can generate tax income, improve a country's economic self-sufficiency, offset the competitive privileges of foreign manufacturers, and enhance the working conditions of labor and management in the region that is being protected. One of the earliest forms of protectionism was the *mercantilism* movement in Europe during the eighteenth century, at the time of the *Industrial Revolution.* Mercantilism was more or less followed in the United States and had been since the first days of independence. American trade expansion policies, countering the country's historic protectionism, really began during the Depression of the 1930s, when an economic revolution was needed, and culminated in the establishment of the General Agreement on Tariffs and Trade (GATT) in the mid-1990s. Currently, protectionism is on the decline in most western nations, although certain restrictions are often imposed, by their very nature, such as stringent product safety regulations, which can outlaw some foreign products, or efforts to strengthen designated national industries that have suffered severe unemployment or economic failures. *See* Foreign Trade, General Agreement on Tariffs and Trade (GATT), Mercantilism.

PROTOTYPE

A preliminary model of a machine or device that can be operated and studied and, if necessary, improved upon before it is produced in quantity for commercial sale. *See* Manufacturing, Production.

PROXY

An individual in a corporation with authority to vote in the place of another person. Also, the instrument representing a single vote. *See* Proxy Dispute.

PROXY DISPUTE

A battle between two or more rival parties in a corporation, in which each tries to gain control of enough proxies to gain control of stock. *See* Proxy.

PSYCHOMETRICS

The field of research that studies mental testing, often used in testing employees regarding their psychological capabilities in a specified field of work. *See* Employee Relations.

PUBLIC CORPORATION

A company, usually a member of a stock exchange, whose shares of stock are open to purchase by the public. *See* Corporation.

PUBLIC DOMAIN

The state or circumstance reserved for creative works, such as books and music, that are no longer, or never have been, protected by copyright. The term is also used for unprotected patents and government-owned property and land that is open to the public, most of which is in the western states. *See* Copyright, Patent.

PUBLIC INTEREST

The term used to describe neighborhood volunteer programs or any endeavors that are undertaken, usually without pay or other recompense, to improve the community. *See* Volunteerism.

PUBLIC OPINION

The term used for that area of opinion that is based on the feelings, sentiments, and convictions of individuals and groups, but not necessarily based on verifiable facts or findings. The results of *public opinion polls,* for example, can include statements and assertions that are based on hearsay and preference, rather than on scientific fact. In addition, the word *public* may refer to a national or statewide assembly of individuals or to a very limited selection of people who share certain characteristics or outlooks. Public opinion may also be at the mercy of the authority compiling the information, as in the case of a dictatorship in which such views are mandated and censored in order to serve the needs and notions of the ruling party. Public opinion may also depend upon the interpretations of those who are citing the opinions, as in the case of controversial issues such as abortion, handguns, pollution, or political party affiliation. *See* Advertising, Public Relations.

PUBLIC RELATIONS

The field of business communications whose activities and policies are employed to create public interest in a person, idea, product, institution, or business establishment. P.R., as it is commonly known, is practiced by independent firms, divisions of advertising agencies, or departments of large corporations, in each case serving particular interests by presenting them to the public in the most favorable light. Toward this end, many research techniques and communications media are used. Public relations differs from propaganda, which is generally government supported, international in scope, and political in nature. One of the earliest forms of public relations, and still widely practiced, is publicity, whose principal instrument is the press release. Public relations is a general term describing a wide variety of techniques used by corporations, government agencies, charitable foundations, and trade groups to present themselves in a favorable light to the general public and to specific audiences such as stockholders, the financial community, employees, customers, and legislators. P.R. programs often include assisting in the delineation of policies and practices that must be communicated to the public, after being reviewed by a public relations practitioner in order to assess their possible impact on public interests and opinions. Prepared texts follow editorial formats, since, unlike advertising, the aim is to place messages within the editorial context of newspapers, magazines, broadcasting programs, and other media. The public relations function is to inform rather than compel and to do so in such a way that the integrity and independence of the media are not compromised.

Public relations is a relatively new industry, having reached an acceptable state in communications after World War I when industries and "Big Business" began to be on the receiving end of newspaper accounts that sharply criticized the corporate world for its overemphasis on making money and its disregard for the welfare of employees. Once the profession became established, its practitioners began experimenting with ways to take valid editorial stands and help to shape public opinion on major political and social issues. The timing was excellent, since the burgeoning press was constantly in need of material to fill its pages and broadcast time, and well-written press releases, devoid of promotional gaff and outrageous claims, were achieving a reputation for acceptability. Another aspect of P.R. that editors and broadcast programmers came to appreciate was its facility for providing experts who could make public appearances, provide sound research, or serve as specialists—without expecting any form of remuneration. The depth and volume of acceptable subject matter, including visual materials and recordings as well, proved to be a boon to small-town newspapers, trade publications, local broadcast stations, and other media whose owners and managers operated on very limited budgets. *See* Promotion.

PUBLIC SECTOR

The area of the economy that consists of government-owned property, organizations, and enterprises, in contrast to those that are privately owned. *See* Private Sector.

PUBLIC-SERVICE ADVERTISING

Any form of advertisement that promotes institutions, events, activities, or people in the interest of the public good or community betterment. *See* Advertising, Public Relations.

PUBLIC UTILITY

Any of several types of business that are vital to the public welfare and hence are controlled or regulated or owned in whole or in part by government bodies and sometimes referred to as *natural monopolies*. Among the most familiar are electric power and gas companies, railroads, telephone companies, and waterworks, all of which are characterized by the necessity of maintaining a uniform, if not singular, scope of business operations. Cities, for example, generally own and operate their own water and sewer services and frequently their own mass transit systems. *See* Government, Utilities.

PURCHASE ALLOWANCE

In sales and distribution, the lowering of the price of goods or products when the merchandise does not meet the quality or condition specified on an invoice or purchasing order. *See* Retailing, Sales, Supply and Demand.

PURCHASING AGENT

A sales representative who works independently for clients as an agent in the purchase of merchandise or property, and who is often more qualified than internal staff members in locating and judging the value of the items sought for purchase. *See* Sales, Wholesaling.

PURE-MARKET ECONOMY

The economic climate that exists when there is open competition, and prices are determined by the unhindered interactions of supply and demand. *See* Economics.

PURPOSIVE SAMPLING

In advertising and marketing research, selecting a relatively small number of average individuals to represent a large population of consumers, for product testing. *See* Advertising.

PUTS AND CALLS

In stock-market terminology, options that grant the right to buy and sell designated amounts of securities at a specified price and time.

PYRAMID BUSINESS

See Multilevel Marketing.

PYRAMIDS

Schemes, often questionable, in which people are recruited by other people to invest in an organization or selling plan in such a way that those who are in at the beginning will profit, sometimes heavily, while those who join later lose all or part of their investments. *See* Better Business Bureau, Con Artist, Ponzi Scheme.

QUADRANT

In manufacturing, a machine part or other mechanical device that is shaped like a quarter circle. Also, an early instrument for measuring altitude of celestial bodies, consisting of a 90° graduated arc with a movable radius for measuring angles. *See* Manufacturing, Production.

QUADRAPHONIC SOUND

Popularly known as *quad,* a system of sound recording in which the acoustical quality of the sound is enhanced and is more authentic than stereophonic recording and, of course, of much finer verity than single-channel sound. Quadraphonic sound utilizes four separate inputs, fed through separate amplifier and loudspeaker channels to achieve its caliber of reproduction. *See* Stereophonic Sound.

QUALIFICATION

A quality, an ability, or an accomplishment that makes a person suitable for a particular position or task. A condition or circumstance that must be met or complied with. *See* Qualified.

QUALIFIED

Having the appropriate qualifications for an office, a position, or a task. Also, limited, restricted, or modified. *See* Human Resources.

QUALIFIED ACCEPTANCE

The acceptance by one party of a proposal or other presentation by another party, but with certain reservations or questions. *See* Agreement, Contract.

QUALITATIVE ANALYSIS

The evaluation of factors that are difficult to measure in terms of money, such as the effect of company operations on morale, relationships with suppliers and dealers, the impact on prospective customers, and the long-term bearing on profits and losses. *See* Quantitative Analysis.

QUALITY CONTROL

A system for ensuring the maintenance of proper standards in manufactured goods, especially by periodic random inspection of the product. *See* Industrial Management, Manufacturing, Production.

QUALITY MARKET

In sales and merchandising, a market made up of consumers who rank quality more important than quantity or price. *See* Promotion, Retailing.

QUALITY OF EARNINGS

The nature of earnings in terms of their quality, durability, and derivation, and the impact they will have on the future earning power of a company, as revealed in its net-income listings. The quality of earnings is favorable when they accurately reflect the economic reality of a company's transactions, the degree of risk minimized by sound financial policies, and the predictability of factors that may affect future growth. The quality of earnings is unfavorable when accounting changes are inconsistent with reality, when there is evident manipulation of figures and statistics, and when a company is vulnerable to seasonal or other periodic fluctuations. *See* Accounting, Annual Reports, Earnings, Qualitative Analysis.

QUANTITATIVE ANALYSIS

The evaluation of factors relating to the quantity of goods manufactured and distributed and their effect on the market. *See* Consumers, Marketing, Qualitative Analysis.

QUANTITY DISCOUNT

A per-unit reduction in price granted to customers who purchase products and commodities in quantity or in bulk. *See* Retailing, Wholesaling.

QUANTUM

The amount of energy regarded as a unit, a term often used to modify another noun, such as "quantum advances in technology."

QUANTUM JUMP

In physics, an abrupt change from one energy level to another, especially such a change in the orbit of an electron with the loss or gain of a quantum of energy. Also referred to as a *quantum leap*.

QUANTUM THEORY

A modern physical theory that holds that energy and some other physical properties often exist in tiny, discrete amounts. The older theories of classical physics assumed that these properties could vary continuously. Quantum theory and the theory of relativity together form the theoretical basis of modern physics. *See* Energy.

QUARTERLY REPORT

An interim financial report for a corporation that is released every three months and that includes information about income, cash flow, liabilities, and other pertinent financial data. *See* Accounting, Annual Reports.

QUESTIONABLE

In business ethics, the modifier used to imply that a certain policy or practice may not be morally right, is problematic, and might, in fact, be unlawful. *See* Ethics.

QUESTIONNAIRE

A printed form containing a set of questions, especially one addressed to a demographically significant number of subjects as a way of gathering information for a survey. *See* Demographics.

QUEUE TIME

Based on the word *queue*, waiting line, the term is used in industry to designate the amount of time wasted between operating functions. An example would be a ten-minute wait for each product at the end of an assembly line before it could be boxed and readied for transportation. There are two categories of queue time: single phase and multiple phase. The former relates to jobs lining up for a single procedure, such as packing a crate. The latter involves a sequence of waiting periods, such as sorting items, wrapping them individually, and then placing them in a crate. If separate workers are engaged in the project, or if the job requires transferal from one location to another, the result could be a queue-time buildup. Related to this subject is what is known as *queuing theory*, a discipline that studies the behavior of queues as they relate to business and economic problems, such as waiting in line for service in a bank, using inordinate amounts of time in office and medical waiting rooms, or become delayed in traffic. Such studies weigh the economic difference between living with queue times or hiring extra help to eliminate them, and try to anticipate the queuing problems so that reasonable decisions can be made about practical solutions. *See* Business Administration, Ergonomics, Management.

QUICK ASSETS

The assets of a company that are readily convertible into cash. *See* Assets, Cash Flow, Profits.

QUICK RATIO

The proportionate ratio between the quick assets of a company and its current liabilities, a figure that provides an immediate indication of the company's ability to meet its financial obligations. *See* Quick Assets.

QUIT-CLAIM DEED

An instrument drawn up so that a holder of real estate can convey title to another party, yet without making any claim that the property is free of encumbrances. *See* Deed, Real Estate.

QUORUM

The number of individuals, proportionately speaking, who must be present at a meeting in order to transact business or make decisions legally. *See* Business Administration, Business Law.

QUOTA

In sales, the assigned minimum number of sales or orders that must be achieved if a specific marketing objective is to be met. In international trade, a quota is a form of trade restriction, which countries might place on imports or exports of specified goods. Quotas differ from tariffs in that the latter involve additional costs but do not necessarily limit the amounts of goods that may be imported. Developing nations often impose quotas to protect fledgling industries, while industrial nations frequently impose export quotas in order to conserve raw materials that are in short supply, or to maintain higher price levels. *See* Exports, Free Trade, Imports, Tariffs.

QUOTATIONS

In the investment field, the publishing or disclosure of the current prices of securities or commodities, or other financial instruments, for the orientation of prospective buyers and sellers. Also referred to as *quotes*. *See* Investments.

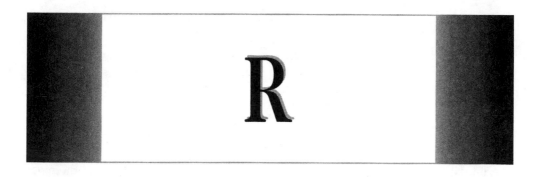

Rack Goods

Merchandise that is generally low in quality and price and is displayed on racks in retail outlets for self-service and quick sales. *See* Bargains, Retailing.

Radial Transfer

In data processing, the conveyance of information between the internal memory of a computer and the peripheral equipment appended to it. *See* Computer, Data Processing.

Raider

An investor who purchases a majority stake in a corporation through aggressive means with the expectation of taking control of the stock and the company. *See* Business Management, Corporations, Takeover.

Raised Check

A bank check on which the digits have been fraudulently tampered with to change the amount to a higher figure. *See* Banks and Banking.

Rally

Said of stock prices when they recover from a decline. *See* Bull Market, Investments, Stocks.

Random Access Memory

Popularly referred to as RAM, a computer capability that permits the operator to extract data from its storage disks without having to search through the stored information to obtain the desired facts. Random access is like the short-term memory of a computer—the bigger the RAM, the more programs a computer can handle at the same time. Also called *multiple access*. *See* Computers.

RANDOM SAMPLING

In consumer research, the style of sampling in which the factors are entered according to chance. *See* Advertising.

RATE CARD

In advertising, a card supplied by the various media to agencies and advertisers to inform them of the rates charged for print ads, commercials, and other media. Rate cards generally contain other pertinent data about the audiences, such as demographics or pass-along readership. *See* Advertising, Cost-Per-Thousand, Media.

RATE OF EXCHANGE

See Currency Exchange.

RATE OF INTEREST

See Interest Rate.

RATE OF RETURN

The income for a specified investment period divided by the asset value at the beginning of the period in question. *See* Asset Value.

RAW DATA

Information that has been assembled, as for a survey or research study, but that has not yet been evaluated and applied to a situation that is being assessed. *See* Research.

RAW MATERIALS

Those ingredients accumulated for the manufacturing or assemblage of products, but not yet utilized. Common examples are metals, timber, and oils. *See* Manufacturing, Production, Resources.

REACH

In advertising, the extent to which a selected medium influences an audience of readers or viewers and can also be passed along to other potential consumers. *See* Advertising, Media.

READERSHIP

The total number of individuals who read a newspaper, magazine, or other periodical, a figure determined by multiplying the circulation by the average number of people who read an issue. *See* Media, Periodicals.

REAL ESTATE INVESTMENT TRUST (REIT)

A firm specializing in real estate and mortgages and that functions much like a closed-end mutual fund, investing the money of shareholders in diversified real estate or mortgage portfolios instead of in stocks or bonds. REITs trade shares on the major stock exchanges, as well as over the counter, and by law must distribute 95 percent of their net earnings to shareholders. There are three types of REITs: those that invest in income-producing properties, those that lend funds to developers and builders, and those that do both. *See* Mortgages, Open End, Real Estate.

REAL INCOME

The total purchasing power of the income-producer, which may range from individuals to nations. *See* Income, Profits.

REALIZE

To sell or exchange merchandise or services and convert them into cash or other liquid assets. *See* Assets, Profits.

REAL PROPERTY

Raw land, developed land, buildings, improvements to land or facilities, and other property that may be classified as real, in comparison with personal property. *See* Real Estate.

RECAPITALIZATION

Modifying the capital structure and value of a corporation by increasing or decreasing its capital stock. *See* Capital.

RECEIVABLES

Popular term for *accounts receivable,* which can be recorded in statements as cash and which are payable on demand. *See* Cash Flow.

RECESSION

In the financial business cycle, a period that is short of a depression, but is marked by higher unemployment, lower consumer prices, and a decline in capital investments, savings, and inventories. In economic terms, a recession is defined as "two consecutive quarters of shrinking gross national product (GNP)," a situation that is most likely to occur near the end of an industrial cycle when inventories pile up and consumer spending wavers. Recessions are generally regarded as worrisome, since they have in past history been followed by depressions. However, government intervention, based on long, comprehensive economic studies, has lessened the likelihood of these events, and financial disasters have been prevented through such measures as the creation of jobs through the increase of spending and the increased supply of money in circulation. Experience has proved that when employment expands consumer spending increases and the economy recovers. *See* Depression, Economics, Gross National Product (GNP).

RECIPROCAL TRADE AGREEMENTS

Mutual agreements between two or more nations to adjust tariffs, duties, and customs restrictions in order to increase international trade and improve border-to-border relationships. *See* Foreign Trade.

RECLAMATION

Land-management planning and operations to reclaim land that is economically unproductive, to enhance the environment, and to salvage raw materials that are going to waste. *See* Environment, and Management.

RECONCILIATION STATEMENT

A financial statement the details a company reconciliation, the determination of the items necessary to bring the balances of two or more related accounts into agreement. *See* Accounting, Bookkeeping.

RECRUITMENT

The function of seeking, interviewing, classifying, and hiring personnel, either through internal efforts or in conjunction with an outside recruitment agency. Employees have been described as the mother lode that determines whether a company is hitting pay dirt or just barely remaining solvent, depending to a large degree on whether management is aggressive when it comes to recruiting personnel or simply sees this activity as some kind of seasonal chore. It has been well documented that recruiting people with sound educational backgrounds, pertinent experience, and sharp mental capacities can energize a company's progress in every field of its endeavors, from research, sales, and marketing to production, transportation, finance, and management. Speaking characteristically, one company president commented that personnel directors should "recruit the person, not the position," meaning that people who are motivated and respected and who have an interest in the business are more valuable in the long run than those who claim to be experts. *See* Human Resources, Personnel Management.

Redeployment

The shifting and reassigning, and usually retraining, of employees to utilize their skills and experience better, often when changes in operations have resulted from such factors as technological advances, the acquisition by another company, the opening of new departments, or changes in corporate policies and planning. *See* Management.

Red Herring

Slang term for something that is used to divert attention from the real issue at hand.

Reengineering

A business buzzword, more properly known as *business process engineering*, used by corporate managers and defined as "the fundamental rethinking and radical redesign of the business process to achieve dramatic improvement in critical measures of performance." *See* Business Administration, Operations Research.

Referendum

The term applied when a public issue is referred to registered voters, or others who qualify, to reach a decision by consensus, whether as a step in the passage of a specific constitutional amendment or simply to indicate where the populace stands, pro or con. There are two kinds of action: direct, in which proposed legislation is placed on a ballot for voter approval, and indirect, in which a proposal is first sent to the state legislature, at which time it may be either enacted or placed in referendum. Although some states make regular use of the referendum principle, this alternative has many political critics who assert that voters simply do not turn out in sufficient numbers, that the subjects are often too specialized or complex for public understanding, or that the outcomes are often swayed by lobbyists and other political power groups. *See* Political Issues, Voting.

Registered Bond

A bond issued in the name of the owner and entered in the books of the issuing organization. *See* Bond.

Registered Trademark

A trademark that has been officially filed with the United States Patent Office, giving the owner an exclusive use of the trademark. *See* Patents, Trademark, U.S. Patent Office.

REGISTRAR

The executive charged with the corporate records listing the names and addresses of the company' shareholders and bond holders. *See* Corporation, Management.

REGISTRATION STATEMENT

A certificate issued prior to the public offering of securities that details the financial facts about the corporation, its history, background, and biographies of the company's administrators. *See* Corporation.

REGULAR DIVIDEND

See Common Dividend.

REGULATION A

A Securities and Exchange (SEC) mandate that permits small corporations to mount a stock issue of up to $5 million. *See* Corporation.

REGULATION T

A regulation imposed by the Federal Reserve Board that establishes the maximum amount of credit that may be granted by stock brokers for the purchase of buying securities. *See* Regulation U.

REGULATION U

A regulation imposed by the Federal Reserve Board governing the amount of credit that can be advanced by a bank to its customers for the purpose of buying securities. *See* Regulation T.

REINVESTMENTS

Investments that have been purchased in a continuing series by using the proceeds from dividends already owned by the investor. *See* Dividends, Investments, Portfolio.

RELATIONSHIP MARKETING

A style of marketing in which there is a congenial interaction between suppliers, distributors, retailers, and consumers, which thus makes it possible for marketers to build trusting, long-term relationships with each party in the selling chain and to be able to count on excellent service and cooperation. *See* Marketing, Public Relations, Selling.

RELIABILITY ENGINEERING

Designing, planning, and manufacturing in such a way as to ensure the reliability of products or components. *See* Manufacturing, Production, Quality Control.

REMOTE ACCESS

In data processing, the ability to communicate with a computer facility by one or more stations that are distant from the main frame. *See* Computer, Main Frame.

RENAISSANCE

Since the term, which means *rebirth* in French, described a period in Europe from the fourteenth to the late sixteenth centuries, when there was a marked revival of interest in classical antiquity, the word today connotes great cultural achievement. Hence, in the business world, a "Renaissance man" or "Renaissance woman" is recognized as a person of culture and intellect, well educated, and with skills in several fields of endeavor. *See* Entrepreneur.

RENEWABLE RESOURCES

Natural resources, such as timber, that can be renewed in such a way as to continue productivity in the future. *See* Nonrenewable Resources.

REORGANIZATION

In management administration and planning, the alteration of a company's composition and capitalization and usually its executive and personnel structure, to meet changing needs, such as those triggered by acquisition by, or merger with, another company. *See* Business Administration, Management.

REORIENTATION

The structured process of training employees for growth by making sure they keep up with the times and thus providing them with practical, relevant, and readily accessible instruction covering changing needs and objectives within the company and new developments in the industry(ies) with which the company is associated. *See* Orientation, Training.

REPATRIATION

When used in international fiscal affairs, the transfer of capital from a foreign bank or financial institution back to a domestic account. *See* International Banking.

REPEAT DEMAND

A situation much desired by marketers in which advertising and promotion result in the continuing demand for frequently purchased expendable products. *See* Marketing, Repeat Time, Supply and Demand.

REPEAT TIME

The number of times the average consumer purchases a given product within a stated period of time. *See* Repeat Demand.

REPLACEMENT COST

In today's market economy, the increased cost of purchasing new equipment, tools, or machinery to replace obsolete or damaged units, regardless of the age or original installation dates. *See* Obsolescence.

REPLICATION

Compiling data for a study, survey, or legal investigation by repeating one or more methods by which information is gathered and research resources mined. *See* Research.

REPRODUCTION

In information processing, any duplicating, photocopying, or printing system that makes facsimiles from originals. *See* Photocopying, Printing.

REPROGRAPHICS

The combined techniques, conversions, and implements used in the multiple reproduction of documents. *See* Printing.

REPUBLIC

That form of national government in which authority rests in the hands of citizens who have the privilege of electing officials, including the head of state, who hold office for limited periods of time, or until reelected. Contrary to popular belief, a republic is not necessarily a democracy, since the degree of power in the hands of the chief executive may depend strongly upon such variable factors as the freedom and universality of the vote, the degree of suffrage, the strength of the common vote, and the reality of the electoral options. *See* Government.

REPURCHASING AGREEMENT

A compact in which the seller agrees to buy back equipment or facilities from the purchaser when the latter has no further use for what has been bought. *See* Purchasing.

RESEARCH AND DEVELOPMENT

Popularly known as *R&D,* this aspect of scientific investigation and planning is often a substantial component of a company's makeup, particularly in those fields where a competitive edge depends upon new breakthroughs or innovative improvements to existing products and services. R&D is essential in every industry that has a stake in technological development and scientific know-how. It has been estimated that there are some 8,000 government, university, independent, nonprofit, and commercial research centers of standing in almost 150 nations around the globe and as many as 13,000 nonprofit research and development companies in the United States and Canada alone. One of the most vital fields of research is directed at the evolution, planning, design, and manufacture of products, parts, and related materials and accessories. Production engineering, for example, is almost totally devoted to the physical and mechanical means of developing products that will meet market demands, satisfy purchasers and users, and turn a substantial profit for the manufacturer, with a minimum of delay and the replacement or repair of defective merchandise. Like all forms of research, this field of investigation, experimentation, and study depends upon a very close working knowledge of new technologies and state-of-the-art techniques. In the pharmaceutical industry, research is directed not only at the materials, equipment, and tools for the processing of medical and health products, but at the components that must be examined, blended, and analyzed in laboratory programs that may take many months, even years, of endless testing. In the food and beverage industry, a large proportion of research is likely to be not only in culinary laboratories but in the field, inquiring into the needs and preferences of consumers. And in the service industries, the thrust of research may be almost entirely in the field, tracking down statistics and records to determine what kinds of services are in demand, where, and during what chronological periods or seasons of the year.

In recent years, strong focus in industry has been on *operations research,* particularly in the field in which researchers approach problems and proposed projects by constructing models of facilities and systems for advance study. Such models, which constitute the heart of operations research, might be expressed in mathematical equations, computer simulations, or composites thereof, but without having to create expensive physical and material prototypes. In each case, objectives must be considered and stated carefully in order to achieve the intended research responses, and this preliminary planning stage has been recognized as perhaps the most important phase of this type of research and development. Researchers in this field often apply the *game theory* technique, which, as the name implies, pits several "opponents" against one another in simulation, the objective being to study the advantages and drawbacks of various competitive approaches. The game theory could be used, for example, to help a manufacturer of consumer products to determine which channels of distribution used by competing marketers would sell the most merchandise for profit in a given period of time, or in the long run.

Technological developments, the enormous spread of computers, and the increasing importance of commercial innovation have played strong roles in bringing research and development from its rather limited base in industry to a position of great prominence, sometimes referred to as "today's Industrial Revolution." Companies in the science-intensive industries can no longer remain competitive without maintaining R&D laboratories, some of them employing more workers than almost any other corporate departments. In addition, there has been a rapid escalation of private research firms, government-sponsored R&D agencies, and industry-oriented units in the science departments of major universities and academic research institutes.

Another essential area of business research, particularly for applications in advertising, marketing, public relations, and other communications, focuses strongly on *demographics,* the in-depth study of people and populations. This field of study looks at the population from the standpoint of age, race, gender, marital and family status, income, ethnic background, religious faith, employment, nationality, and other personal characteristics, and attempts to associate these data with economic factors such as consumer needs and demands, buying habits, discretionary spending, brand loyalty, and the like. Related to this is *personnel research,* which studies people and the work environment, with a view to improving on-the-job conditions and attracting a higher caliber of employee. Such research studies situations and circumstances relating to offices, work posts, job-associated equipment, eating facilities, restrooms, recreational facilities, medical and health programs, first-aid stations, parking and transportation, communications, and other factors, even including the beauties (or lack of same) of the surroundings.

Today, there is almost no aspect of business and industry—regardless of size or breadth—that does not have a substantial percentage of its economic commitment and funding associated with research and development. *See* Advertising, Demographics, Game Theory, Production Engineering, State of the Art, Technology.

RESEARCH VALIDITY

Internal and external yardsticks used to evaluate business and industrial research projects, particularly to determine whether small samplings covered in the procedures can be projected to viable larger groups and even generalized to a total population. *See* Research and Development.

Resolution

An expression, in documental or vocal form, of the determination of an individual or group of individuals to achieve an end, as set forth in its wording.

Response Time

In data processing, the time lag that occurs between giving a command to a computer and the information output that follows. *See* Data Processing.

Responsibility Accounting

A financial accounting procedure that appoints an individual or team of individuals to be responsible for overseeing, evaluating, and reporting on stated areas of a company's operations. *See* Accounting.

Restraining Order

A court directive that in effect freezes the actions in progress in a lawsuit or legal proceeding until all the parties involved can be communicated with and made aware of the procedures underway. *See* Business Law.

Restraint of Trade

Any action or deed deemed by the government or other authority to be wrongly interfering with the rights of others, as in the case of refusing to sell products competitively in the open market. *See* Competition.

Restrictions

Those clauses in a contract or agreement that limit the rights and benefits of one or more of the signatories, or that confine the geographical area in which the stipulations are viable. *See* Business Law, Contracts.

Restrictive Covenants

Mutually understood and expressed agreements that restrict or limit the use of property, as in the case of public areas defined by the members of a private landowners association in a residential development. *See* Real Estate.

Résumé

A personal biography that is typed or printed and that outlines an individual's history, education, job experiences, qualifications, and aspirations in seeking employment. *See* Personnel Administration.

RETAILER

A merchant or dealer who generally orders and receives merchandise from a wholesaler and, in turn, sells directly to consumers. *See* Retailing.

RETAILING

The promoting and selling of merchandise directly to customers, augmented by advertising, store promotions, and personal contacts in the community where the retailer's outlet is located. Retailing is the selling of finished goods and services to the consumer for personal or family consumption. It includes store retailing, such as department stores, nonstore retailing, such as direct selling and mail order, or service retailing, such as dry cleaning. One out of every six employed persons in the United States works in retailing, including franchising. The most familiar types of retail businesses are department stores, which command large sales volumes by providing a wide variety of merchandise and by offering extensive customer service; supermarkets, the kinds of large, self-service food stores that have replaced the old corner grocery; chain stores, which function as groups of stores with similar attributes and common ownership; independents, or voluntary chains that operate cooperatively; wholesale warehouses, which are really "bargain basements" on a large scale and are often located in a warehouse-style building; and consumer cooperatives, which are retail stores owned by consumers to take advantage of their collective buying power. Major retailing operations are found in the complexes of shopping centers and malls, with their clusters of complementary stores. Originally developed for the suburbs, they are now becoming prevalent also in the hearts of major urban areas. Shopping centers emerged as an important retail development after World War II, with the growth of the suburbs, increased use of the automobile, and traffic congestion in downtown areas. One of the fastest-growing retail operations in America is the mail-order business, whose owners inundate the mails with millions of catalogs, many of them fancy and expensive. They originated in the late nineteenth century, with companies such as Sears Roebuck and Ward's, and later L. L. Bean, but saw very little growth until the 1970s and 1980s. *See* Franchising, Merchandising, Retailer.

RETAIL INVENTORY METHOD

In accounting, a system used by merchants to determine the valuation of ending inventory, by which a cost-to-retail ratio is applied to the final inventory reported at selling price. Also referred to as *inventory valuation*.

RETAINED EARNINGS

The accrued profits of a corporation after deductions for stock dividends, taxes, expenses, loan obligations, and other financial debits. *See* Earnings, Profit and Loss.

RETAINER

A fee that is paid in advance by an individual or company to an outside specialist or professional, such as an attorney, engineer, or architect, to secure the right to services that will be rendered and accounted for at a later date. *See* Business Law.

RETIREMENT FUNDS

Sums set aside by a company, under strict regulations, to apportion to employees when they retire, either in lump sums or continuing monthly pension payments. *See* Retirement Income, Retirement Plans.

RETIREMENT INCOME

The income regularly received by retirees, from retirement funds, and/or other investment plans established specifically for retirement purposes. *See* Retirement Funds, Retirement Plans.

RETIREMENT PLANS

Plans formulated by the personnel administration department of a company, following authorized guidelines, so that employees will be granted pensions or annuities when they retire, based on salary, length of service, and other considerations.

RETROACTIVE

A stipulation that affects earlier transactions and is updated to the present. A common example is *retroactive pay,* which is a delayed wage bonus for work completed by employees for a time when they were being paid less for similar job performances. *See* Compensation.

RETURN ON EQUITY

The net income after debt service, declared as a percentage of the owner's equity. *See* Equity.

RETURN ON INVESTMENT

The sum of the interest plus repayment of principle and the per-annum yield generated by an investment or commercial venture. Also known as *yield on investment. See* Yield.

REVALUATION

Relating to national currency, the restoration of the value of a depreciated currency to its original worth. *See* Currency, Gold Standard.

REVENUE EXPENDITURE

An expense that occurs in a period of less than 12 months and is, therefore, immediately expensed on the account books. An example is a necessary repair to a capital asset, such as heavy production equipment. *See* Capital Expenditure.

REVENUE SHARING

A plan whereby the federal government shares a proportion of tax revenues with state and local governments, based on the proposition that the federal government is a more effective tax collector, but that local governments should have the empowerment to allocate tax money for community needs. Revenue sharing in this manner has also been cited as a means of curtailing the growth of the Washington bureaucracy and of shifting monetary programs to the localities where they belong. *See* Government, Taxation.

REVERSE TAKEOVER

Said of the situation that applies when ownership of a larger company is assumed by a smaller company. *See* Takeover.

REVOLVING CREDIT

A financing plan that permits a participant to charge purchases against an account periodically, as long as the balance does not exceed a predetermined limit. Also referred to as a *revolving loan.*

REWARD STRATEGY

The business practice of offering rewards and benefits, over and beyond wages, salaries, and other monetary compensation, to recruit and hold desirable personnel. Two types of rewards are particularly applicable: *extrinsic,* which cover the physical and environmental surroundings that make the workplace a pleasant and congenial site for employees, such as cheerful offices, comfortable seating, and ready access to good cafeterias and off-duty lounges; and *intrinsic,* which cover personal satisfactions that go with the job, such as decisio making, encouragement to make productive suggestions, and leeway to exercise personal judgment in the performance of assigned tasks. *See* Compensation, Personnel Administration.

RIGGED MARKETING

The practice, sometimes unethical, when sales and purchases are distorted in such a way as to falsify normal and expected supply-and-demand prices. *See* Marketing, Supply and Demand.

RIGHT OF RESCISSION

The prerogative of a purchaser or borrower to cancel a sale or contract under certain circumstances within a short period of time without penalty and with full restitution of any payments made. *See* Contracts.

RIGHT OF SURVIVORSHIP

The right that determines that a joint owner and holder of a title assumes full ownership upon the decease of the other party. *See* Business Law.

RIGHT-TO-WORK LAWS

Legislation, generally at the state level, that prohibits labor/management agreements requiring workers to join a union in order to obtain or hold employment. These laws restrict what are known as the *closed shop* or *union shop,* in which employers hire only union members, or those who agree to join a union within a certain period of time after being hired. *See* Labor/ Management, Unions.

RIPARIAN RIGHTS

The property rights of owners of land bordering on lakes, streams, rivers, tide-waters, or other bodies of water. *See* Water Rights.

RISK

A prominent economist once asserted that a synonym for "business" was "risk" and that no individual could start a company and no company could have its existence without essentially being a gamble. By the time a company has reached the growth stage and has emerged from its formative period, it is likely to be—statistically at least—at great risk. The gamble becomes even more one sided when management interprets growth as an invitation to venture even farther and involve the business in new ventures—and an increasing minefield of new and different risks. As a result, new business enterprises stand only about a 50/50 chance of surviving for five years before going bankrupt, and of the half that do endure, only one third are able to show any significant growth for the next five years. *See* Risk Management.

RISK ANALYSIS

A technique used in evaluating situations and circumstances of a widespread nature that introduces options and probabilities in order to help foresee risks involved with the possible decisions that can be arrived at. See Risk Management.

RISK MANAGEMENT

That facet of management responsible for overseeing and administering programs whose objective is to preserve the assets and earning power of a business and guard the company against the risks of accidental losses. Almost every organization, from the smallest to the largest, operates in an environment where there is a certain degree of risk. Risks range from problems that may cause financial downfalls or trigger costly lawsuits and malpractice charges to environmental disasters (such as earthquakes, windstorms and floods) the deaths or disabilities of indispensable personnel, or the failure to keep up with changing consumer demands. For these reasons, and many others, risk management is a critical function of almost every business operation.

"Is your business a risky business?" asks the headline in a leaflet published by the Office of Business Development. "You bet! Every business is. Just think for a minute about the hundreds of things that most business owners worry about. A few are predictable or, at the very least, are items that you can plan for and perhaps even control to a certain extent, such as: expected sales volumes, salary costs, taxes, overhead expenses, equipment and supply costs, the prices you charge customers. Others are unpredictable, such as..."

Among the most common risks listed are the following:

- *Aggressive competition.* Successful risk managers evaluate not only the existing competition, but the possibility of other competitors invading their areas of operation and taking business away.

- *Consumer fickleness.* Many retailers rely too heavily on consumer loyalty or the superiority of their products and fail to communicate with existing customers and prospects or keep an eye on buying trends.

- *Criminal activity.* Risk management must be heavily centered on methods to avoid or minimize such crimes as robbery, hijacking, vandalism, shoplifting, petty larceny, fraud, forgery, embezzlement, employee theft, or the unauthorized use of credit cards. Risk managers can expect outside assistance from security firms, the police department, experienced insurance agents, and local crime-watch groups.

■ *Financial flaws.* Obtaining enough money to finance a venture is only the first risk. Keeping the cash flowing, generating profits, staying solvent, and avoiding bankruptcy are never-ending efforts on the part of top managers. Experienced risk managers, while aware that the organization's monetary specialists are mainly responsible for the company's financial health, constantly monitor financial matters because they can look at them objectively and perhaps spot weaknesses from a broader point of view.

■ *Labor disputes.* Consultants familiar with union and labor controversies are emphatic in stating that the companies with fewer labor problems are the ones whose managers keep the closest tabs on employee grievances, establish labor/management committees to investigate and minimize problems, and take action promptly. Risk management must include plans for anticipating and dealing with problems before they get out of hand.

■ *Seasonal vacillations.* For merchants who have not properly foreseen changes in traffic patterns and consumer demand from month to month, it comes as a shock when sales suddenly slack off. Even more traumatic are those occasions when retailers are deluged with would-be buyers at certain times of the year but have run out of stock. A function of risk management in a retail organization is to keep abreast of seasonal, and other, buying trends.

■ *Underinsurance.* With insurance rates soaring, it is tempting to the financial management of a company to look for "bargain" policies, cut corners, or hope they can be lucky and avoid certain casualty risks. But this is a very poor area of business in which to economize, what with natural disasters, liability claims, equal employment opportunity grievances, claims resulting from workers' accidents and illnesses, and similar legal and casualty assaults on business that have become commonplace. Sound risk management is critically needed in this area. *See* Employee Compensation, Insurance, Liability, Management, Natural Disasters.

ROBERT'S RULES OF ORDER

An accepted set of guidelines for governing public meetings, first developed many years ago as a method for conducting debate in different kinds of organizations without having to devise new rules or adapt existing parliamentary rules. Robotics. The industrial installation and application of robots and other automatic—often computerized—devices for the performance of routine tasks. With the advent of robotic equipment that is more sophisticated in recent years, with vastly improved systems of memory, dexterity, and control, the kinds of usages possible have escalated dramatically. The type of robot referred to in robotics installations has been defined as "a completely self-controlled mechanism consisting of electronic, electrical, or mechanical units, and programmed to function as a specialized, controllable substitute for a human worker." The word *robot* is, in fact, the Czech translation for *worker* and was based on a 1920s story in that language about a mechanical man. The whole science of robotics has broadened from the industrial field into many other areas of human endeavor. *See* Ergonomics, Human Resources, Manufacturing, Production.

ROCKEFELLER FOUNDATION

A private, nonprofit foundation founded in 1913 by John D. Rockefeller, whose stated goal is "to promote the well-being of mankind throughout the world." The foundation makes grants to individuals, supports many institutions, and operates its own worldwide philanthropical programs, which include support to projects involving equal opportunity, international relations, population studies, medicine and health, agricultural science, the arts, and the humanities. *See* Foundations, Philanthropy.

ROLE DISCERNMENT

In personnel administration, the development of attitudes and opinions regarding the performance expectations of different executive roles in an organization and the stature implications of the roles in question. *See* Personnel Administration.

ROLE PLAYING

A training and orientation technique in which the employee participants assume assigned roles in an organization and attempt to arrive at decisions or solve problems by imagining themselves in the positions they have temporarily assumed. When properly evaluated, the nature and quality of the individual responses reveal much about a person's capabilities. *See* Business Management, Training.

ROLLBACK

The reduction of the prices of goods and services to reflect an earlier, lower pricing structure. *See* Pricing, Retailing.

ROTARY INTERNATIONAL

An international affiliation of business and professional people, functioning as a service organization, which, among other activities, sponsors domestic and foreign community public service projects, provides funding for international student exchange programs, makes professional grants, and supports university scholarships. The name derives from the association's initial and traditional practice of periodically rotating meetings from one member's office to another's. *See* Associations.

ROTARY PRESS

A printing technique that rotates a cylindrical printing surface and an impression surface toward each other in such a way as to print type and graphics on sheets or rolls of paper fed between them. The process is known as *rotary-offset printing* when a third, rubber-covered cylinder is used to enhance the process and control the speed and quality of reproduction; a combination of rotary printing units makes it possible to print as many as four colors in a single insertion in the press, and combinations of equipment also perform related tasks, such as cutting, folding, and perforating the paper during the printing. *See* Printing, Publishing.

ROTOGRAVURE

A type of printing, produced on a rotary photogravure machine, that reproduces an image etched below the surface of a metal-plated cylinder and that is used primarily for the long-run production of magazines, as well as the printing of packaging foils, plastics, and wallpaper. The printing surface contains tiny cells of varying depths so that there are substantial differences in the amount of ink transferred to the paper, thus creating light, dark, and intermediate areas in each illustration. *See* Printing, Rotary Press.

ROYALTIES

Periodic payments made to individuals or organizations for the right to use that party's creative works, such as books or music or art, for profit. *See* Copyrights.

RUNNING COSTS

Normal, anticipated expenses incurred in the day-to-day operation of installations, machinery or equipment, and the maintenance thereof. *See* Machines, Production.

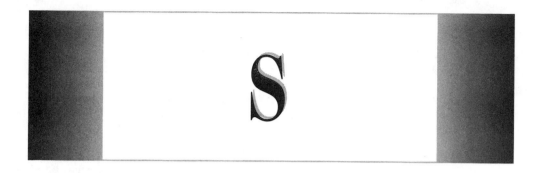

SALABILITY

The sales potential of merchandise, based on such factors as appearance, price, utility, and the interest generated among prospective buyers by advertising and promotion. *See* Marketing, Sales.

SALARY REVIEW

The periodic evaluation of the wages and salaries and other compensation of employees in light of their performances on the job, their attendance records, their attitudes, and their overall value to the organization. *See* Compensation, Personnel Administration.

SALE AND LEASEBACK

The sale of an asset that is then leased back from the new owner, a transaction that in some cases helps to increase short-term cash flow or that can have substantial tax advantages. *See* Cash Flow, Leaseback.

SALES MANAGEMENT

The administration and supervision of all aspects of selling and trade, including pricing reviews, supplier statistics, forecasts of future demand, supervision of the sales force, and sales analysis, the systematic study and comparison of sales data. Effective sales managers motivate their salespeople by developing a style that is vigorous and appealing enough for their salespeople to emulate; encourage their staffs when the market looks promising and reassure them that a situation is only temporary when sales fall off; set examples through long hours, hard work, and an avowed determination to be the best in the business; communicate regularly and lucidly with all members of their group; set realistic goals, but always leave room for the attainment of above-average performances; groom people for promotion and provide bonuses and other rewards and recognition during the interim; pass along detailed information about new products and services, sales records, and the performance of competitors; and teach and inform continuously.

The six keys to successful sales management have been presented in the following tips:

- *Think like a manager.* Maintain a top position, yet delegate authority in such a way as to encourage others to become involved to the mutual benefit of all concerned.

- *Respect time.* Establish priorities so that the right proportions of hours and days are devoted to the necessary functions of sales and related operations.

- *Work with people, not things.* A good proportion of time and effort should be three quarters with people and one quarter or less on administrative particulars.

- *Develop a management style.* Such a style should be consistent with the manager's personality, but with emphasis on those qualities and proficiencies that motivate others to follow.

- *Know your sales personnel.* Be aware not only of personal traits and personalities, but keep in mind both the strengths and the weaknesses of everyone in the department, even those who are support personnel and not directly involved in selling.

- *Act like a leader.* Good leaders have been described as those who provide guidance, rather than dictate terms; orient, rather than drive, their employees; stimulate enthusiasm, rather than arouse fear; refer mostly to "we," instead of "I"; and fix the breakdowns, rather than fix the blame.

See *Management, Marketing,* other *Sales* entries.

SALESMANSHIP

The combinations of skill, experience, and drive that make it possible for an individual or group to persuade consumers and other prospective purchasers to choose the products, services, or merchandise they are promoting and to do so in a manner that will result in buyer satisfaction and encourage repeat sales. The term has become somewhat obsolete because of the emphasis on gender and the fact that many top salespeople are women and has been replaced by such terms as *selling power* or *sales mastery.* Current titles used for selling personnel include sales agent, sales representative, account executive, sales associate, salesperson, and other terms that have neither male nor female connotations. *See* Management, other *Sales* entries.

Sales Promotion

Merchandising functions and campaigns aimed at increasing consumption and demand for a company's products or services, such as sales meetings, premium offers, consumer events, sweepstakes, trade shows, and entertainment. *See* Promotions.

Sales Tax

Any tax levied as a percentage of the selling price of products and services that are most commonly sold by a retailer or wholesaler or through a consumer catalog. *See* Taxation.

Sampling

In product and marketing research, the introduction of new products and brand lines in selected, representative regions to compile data that can be projected to larger market segments or to the entire country. Such testing takes into account *sampling error,* or the margin of error that can be expected in the resultant statistical figures. *See* Advertising, Consumers, Market Research.

Satisfacing

A colloquial management term referring to the attainment of a projected share of market, level of production, or other types of upgrading, as opposed to simply trying to maximize production or profits. *See* Marketing.

Saturation Campaign

An advertising technique whereby one or more markets are heavily inundated with print ads, promotions, and commercials in order to sell products en masse, often to introduce new products, brand names, or lines. *See* Advertising, Marketing.

Saturation Point

In marketing, the point that has been reached in sales beyond which there can be little or no significant increase in the number of prospective purchasers for the products or services in question. *See* Consumers, Marketing, Retailing.

Savings and Loan Associations (S&Ls)

Thrift institutions chartered by federal or state governments that offer savings deposit services to individual depositors an invest the bulk of their accumulated funds into real estate mortgages. The unfortunate history of S&L failures, with consequent heavy losses to depositors, was based on foolish, sometimes fraudulent, investments in seriously overpriced real estate. *See* Banking.

SCALAR THEORY

A concept of management that adheres to the belief that authority and responsibility should circulate in continuous form from the highest managers in an organization to the lowest-ranking employees, in order that an organization may function cohesively and with the greatest efficiency. *See* Management, Personnel Administration.

S CORPORATION

A corporation whose taxable income and net losses are passed through to the corporation's shareholders, thus making it possible for taxation at the corporate level to be avoided. *See* Corporation.

SCRIP

Certificates issued by corporations to represent fractional shares of stock and that can be accumulated and presented for full shares. *See* Corporations, Stocks.

SEASONAL DISCOUNTS

Price reductions applying to merchandise that is being sold off season in order to minimize the cost of maintaining large inventories or to unload products that might soon become obsolete. *See* Retailing.

SEAT

The traditional figure of speech for membership in a stock exchange, which is obtainable for a price and upon an official acceptance of membership. *See* Stock Exchange.

SECONDARY DATA

In research functions, information, statistics, and opinions compiled from earlier derivations, rather than from current original sources. *See* Research and Development.

SECURED LOAN

A debt for which some form of acceptable collateral has been pledged and that can be forfeited if the loan is in default. *See* Banking, Loans.

SECURITIES

Documents and instruments that identify the legal ownership of physical commodities and other assets, or that establish legal claim to itemized capital. *See* Bonds, Investments, Stocks.

SECURITIES AND EXCHANGE COMMISSION (SEC)

The federal agency created by the Securities Exchange Act, that is responsible for establishing regulations and supervising the issuance and marketing of securities. Among other requirements, the SEC mandates that individuals and organizations involved in the promotion or sale of securities provide public-disclosure information or statements to prospective investors. *See* Investments, Securities Exchange Act.

SECURITIES EXCHANGE ACT

A federal law, originally passed in 1934, to create the Securities and Exchange Commission (SEC) as a body, with authority to supervise and regulate the issuing and marketing of securities. *See* Securities and Exchange Commission.

SELECTIVE DISTRIBUTION

The marketing practice of choosing selected retail outlets that will have exclusive rights in their sales zones to receive certain products for sale. *See* Distribution.

SELF-EMPLOYMENT

That form of business or profession whereby individuals earn their incomes through their own private enterprise, rather than as employees of some other party. *See* Entrepreneur, Small Business.

SELF-MAILER

A direct-mail piece or product that can be sent through the mail without having to use an envelope or separate wrap. *See* Mail-Order Business.

SELLER'S MARKET

The situation that exists when the demand for a product or product line exceeds the supply. *See* Buyer's Market.

SEMICONDUCTORS

A class of memory units, consolidated in computers and other electronic equipment, composed of integrated-circuit chips mounted on printed circuit boards, whose principal application is the fabrication of solid-state, often miniaturized electronic components and integrated circuits. *See* Chips, Computers, Electronics, Integrated Circuit.

SENATE OF THE UNITED STATES

The upper house of Congress, whose membership consists of two senators from each state, elected by popular vote to serve for six years. A Senator must be at least 30 years of age, an American citizen for at least nine years, and a bona fide resident of the state that he or she represents. Under the Constitution, the Senate has certain special powers, which include the sole authority to ratify treaties proposed by the President; the power to accept or reject presidential appointments to federal judgeships at all levels, ambassadorships, cabinet posts, and the topmost positions in the executive branch of the federal government; and the right to conduct the impeachment trials of public officials. Although the Vice President of the United States serves as president of the Senate, he rarely presides over day-to-day debate in the Senate, is present only when momentous decisions are being deliberated, and has no vote unless the members of the Senate cast a tie vote. *See* Government.

SENIORITY

Regardless of an individual's age, having a longer length of service than others on the job and most often a greater tenure in the organization. *See* Tenure.

SERVICE INDUSTRIES

Those industries engaged mainly in providing services for their customers and clients, rather than selling merchandise. *See* Consumers.

SERVOMECHANISM

An automatic control device, composed of feedback amplifiers, automatic regulators, and other components, arranged in a manner so that an exterior signal can control the inner workings of the installation. Servomechanisms use mechanical motion, rather than electric or electronic signals, to activate the measures they control and are classified according to the manner in which they function. *See* Automation, Robotics.

SEVERANCE PAY

A monetary remuneration granted to an individual whose employment is to be terminated through no fault of the employee. *See* Compensation.

SEXUAL DISCRIMINATION

The illegal act of establishing different pay scales for men and women, or otherwise engaging in unequal male/female practices. *See* Civil Rights, Sexual Harassment.

SEXUAL HARASSMENT

Verbal, physical, or emotional abuse of an individual, whether male or female, heterosexual or homosexual, based solely on the sex of the victim. In the workplace in the United States, sexual harassment is a civil offense in which employers are held morally and financially liable for their own or their employees' libidinous transgressions against fellow workers, ranging from gross rudeness to intimidation and outright rape. Most legal cases involving sexual harassment are based on the Civil Rights Act of 1964, which forbids any form of discrimination in employment on the basis of gender. *See* Civil Rights, Equal Opportunity, Sexual Discrimination.

SHARED TIME

A mutual understanding in which more than one person or department shares access to a computer or other data-processing system. *See* Computers, Time Sharing.

SHARE OF AUDIENCE

The percentage of radio or television sets tuned to a specific program, calculated as a proportion of the total possible audience and often used as part of the data that determine the network's charge for commercials. *See* Advertising, Audience, Broadcasting, Media.

SHARK REPELLENT

Slang term for precautions taken by a corporation to prevent an unwanted acquisition by an industrial predator, commonly accomplished by purchasing enough shares of the corporation's stock to gain control. *See* Takeover.

SHORT RUN

A printing expression for a minimal printing production, usually on a one-time basis. *See* Printing.

SHORT-TERM LOAN

A financial obligation that must be paid off within 12 months or sooner. *See* Banking, Loans.

SHRINKAGE

Losses suffered by a company when substantial numbers of products or amounts of materials are pilfered by employees, outside handlers, and shoplifters. *See* Accounting, Business Law, Loss.

SILENT PARTNER

A participant in a partnership who provides funding or other financial assistance in expectation of eventually sharing in profits, but who takes no active part in the day-to-day functions or administration. *See* Partnerships.

SILICONES

A family of silicon-containing polymer materials, which include solids, liquids, moldable resins, and rubbers, among other elements, and which have increasingly broad use in science and industry because of their great stability. Originally perfected for the aerospace and electronics industries, they steadily began to find commercial applications in many other fields, mainly because of their stability, such as resistance to both high and low temperatures, chemicals, lubricants, or oxidizing environments. They are used in heat-resistant oils, greases, anti-foaming compounds, coatings, and paints, and have excellent properties for applications in power circuits, since they are little affected by surrounding materials and have high resistance to electrical breakdowns. Silicone rubbers have found increasing numbers and types of uses, since they can withstand a wide range of temperatures without deterioration, are inert to many chemicals that are harmful to other kinds of rubbers and plastics, and are compatible with the human body, thus making them useful for medical implants.

SILICON VALLEY

The fashionable name referring to the geographic area between San Francisco and San Jose to the south, in California, which is a focal point for industries engaged in the manufacture of semiconductors and electronic chips made out of silicon. *See* Computers, Semiconductors.

SIMULATION

The representation of a real-life system with a model to determine how changes in one or more variables will impact the rest of the system. In general, simulation relies on trial and error, as well as scientific evaluation, to reach conclusions. *See* Research and Development, Simulation Models.

SIMULATION MODELS

Models and prototypes constructed full size or to scale to be used in the testing of equipment, products, implements or other physical objects. The term also applies to prototype designs and financial charts that can be reproduced on paper or programmed into a computer. *See* Simulation.

SIMULCAST

To broadcast a commercial or program simultaneously on radio and television. *See* Broadcasting.

SINGLE PROPRIETORSHIP

See Sole Proprietorship.

SINKING FUND

A pool of liquid assets and cash set aside to provide resources for the redemption of debt or other pecuniary obligations. *See* Accounting, Assets, Bookkeeping.

SKILLED LABOR

Any classification of personnel whose qualifications include at least minimum training and experience records, along with the necessary faculties, to fill specialized jobs. *See* Labor, Training.

SLEEPER

In merchandising and sales, a product that unexpectedly reveals a strong selling potential and consumer demand, often as a result of publicity or an event that triggers unforeseen interest. *See* Consumers, Sales.

SLOAN FOUNDATION

An institution founded in 1934 by the noted American industrialist, Alfred P. Sloan, Jr., which today supports programs of research and education in the fields of social problems, science and technology, medicine, economics, and management. *See* Philanthropies.

SMALL BUSINESS

That category of business and industry that includes businesses whose gross income does not exceed $500,000 annually and whose employees total less than 100. Businesses, like humans, are born to grow to be healthy or to become sick, mature, and inevitably decline and die. This is particularly true of small businesses, a predominant number of which attain only one or two stages before passing out of the picture, and a few manage to pass through the full cycle before they, too, disappear. The concept of this business life cycle was succinctly summed up in a curriculum prospectus published by the Fuqua School of Business of Duke University, in Durham, North Carolina, which concludes, "The manager who not only understands, but accepts, this historic life cycle will hold a distinct advantage over the renegade who is determined to outsmart history." The four stages mentioned are as follows:

1. *Initial stage,* during which the concepts of the enterprise are conceived, the business is established in the location and manner intended, and the nature and offerings of the company are communicated to the public, and especially to potential customers or clients. The strength of the venture will depend upon a number of key factors, including the consumer and/or community need for it, the level of skill and experience enjoyed by the founder(s), sufficient capitalization to launch and maintain the business, the suitability of the location, the state of the local economy, and a lack of threats from competitors.

2. *Growth and expansion stage,* characterized by progress that can be measured in terms of professional achievements and financial assets and an increase in productive activity and the number of people involved. Explosive growth, when a business takes off and runs, should generally be viewed with skepticism rather than jubilation. Those with experience contend that it is much better for a new business to move gradually into the phase the founders have charted in advance, a progression that will be marked by recognition in the industry, an ascending sales or profit curve, improved financial status in the eyes of local banks and investment specialists, evidence of repeat customers or clients, and the growing need for additional employees and supervisors.

3. *Maturity,* which represents the plateau attained when the company's growth and expansion have all but leveled off and cannot realistically be expected to increase by any significant amount. Attaining maturity in the field of small business is not necessarily desirable, since it often represents a period when the founders cannot seem to move forward any longer, when managers who were formerly aggressive become docile, if not lazy, and when both growth and the attainment of goals seem more and more difficult to measure.

4. *Decline,* the final stage, which may occur abruptly or transpire over a long period of time, during which the organization as it was originally established can be anticipated only to slide downhill. This stage is marked by an increasing number of negative events and situations, such as difficulties improving the profit picture, the resignation of key managers, employee restlessness and dissatisfaction, problems in trying to recruit new personnel, and serious encroachments by competitors.

Small businesses function best when they are attuned to three major factors, sometimes referred to as *climates:* (1) the *economic climate,* an external element that represents the state of the nation, the region, and the immediate community and that can be a vital force in pushing a so-so company ahead if the market is strong or retarding an aggressive company if the market is weak; (2) the *competitive climate* which encompasses not only direct, local competitors, but indirect competitors in the region, and, equally important, any organizations, events, or situations that tend to siphon public interest and support away from the business in question; and (3) the *demographic climate,* which involves the current and changing nature of the population in the company's marketing or service area, particularly if the incomes, ages, family makeup, and other characteristics are either strengthening or weakening the company's ability to sustain business growth.

Small business is based strongly on the concept that, in a free enterprise system, anyone who has the time, the motivation, the proficiency, and the capital—from a few hundred dollars to hundreds of thousands, or a logical source of financing can embark on a chosen venture within a very reasonable period of time. It is a matter of record that entrepreneur ship is on the rise in America, since both the number and proportion of businesses with fewer than 100 employees keep growing. They number some 15 million, and they employ more people in aggregate in the United States than all of the large businesses combined. *See* business management, corporations, entrepreneurs, free enterprise, Small Business Administration.

SMALL BUSINESS ADMINISTRATION (SBA)

A federal agency, a unit of the Department of Commerce, that was established to advise the owners and managers of small businesses, provide contemporary information in their subject fields, and assist them in solving business-related problems. As an arm of the United States government, the SBA offers an extensive selection of information and counsel for owners and managers of small businesses of all kinds, or for entrepreneurs intending to start their own enterprises. SBA maintains offices throughout the country, whose locations can be found in the "U.S. Government" section of telephone directories. The organization's programs include training programs, educational seminars, counseling services, financial assistance, and professional referrals. Key units of the Small Business Administration include:

Service Corps of Retired Executives (SCORE). A national organization sponsored by SBA, whose membership includes almost 14,000 experienced volunteer business executives who provide free counseling, workshops, and seminars to small-business executives and those seeking help in starting small businesses.

Small Business Development Centers (SBDCs). Sponsored by the SBA in partnership with state and local governments, the educational community, and the private sector. SBDC provides assistance, counseling, and training to prospective and active small-business entrepreneurs.

Small Business Institutes (SBIs). Organized through the SBA for operating on more than 500 college campuses nationwide. The institutes provide counseling by qualified students and business faculty members to small-business owners and managers. *See* Consulting, Financing, Management, SCORE, Small Business.

SMALL CLAIMS COURT

A type of court established for the express purpose of settling minor claims, usually within short periods of time and at moderate costs to the parties involved. *See* Business Law.

SOCIAL ACCOUNTING

That type of personnel research and evaluation that classifies, measures, and reports on the costs and implications of social benefits and facilities in an organization. *See* Corporate Image, Employee Relations, Personnel Administration, Social Psychology.

SOCIAL PSYCHOLOGY

As it relates to business, this discipline is the study of the thoughts, feelings, preferences, and behavior of individuals and groups as they affect, or are affected by, other individuals and groups. Considerable funding is channeled by all kinds of businesses into research in the field of social psychology as a means of determining business strategies, both for the internal administration of employees and the external relationships with consumers and others who are important to the commercial success and growth of the company. Social psychology has proved to be of increasing significance in light of contemporary situations, circumstances, and problems that relate to such matters as the treatment of minorities, social bias, crime, security, and public image. *See* Employee Relations, Human Resources, Public Relations.

SOCIAL SCIENCES

Those disciplines related to the study of individuals and groups within a diverse social framework, most commonly the fields of anthropology, economics, geography, history, political science, psychology, and sociology. Aspects of these spheres of study are particularly germane to business management as a result of the increasing attention being paid to social psychology. *See* Social Psychology.

SOCIAL SECURITY

The humanitarian/social structure that evolved from the Federal Old Age Benefits law of the mid-1930s and the subsequent liberalization and extensions of its welfare benefits. The public program providing for economic security and welfare, particularly in the United States, but also in a few other countries. While programs vary from one country to another, all provide some cash payment to defray income loss or deficiency due to sickness, old age, or unemployment. (In socialist nations the insured person makes no direct contribution toward the coverage.) Germany adopted a social security program in the 1880s, and Great Britain's program, begun in 1911, was expanded after World War II. The U.S. Social Security Act (1935) established unemployment compensation, retirement insurance, and federal assistance for state welfare programs. The health insurance plans, Medicare and Medicaid and supplemental security income (SSI) for the disabled were added later. Administered principally by the Social Security Administration of the Department of Health and Human Services, the U.S. system is threatened by economic factors and by changing patterns in demography, most significantly, the increase in the number of older persons receiving benefits as compared with those persons still working and contributing to the program through taxes. Most developed countries face similar problems in funding their social security systems. *See* Department of Health and Human Services, Medicare, Social Security Administration.

SOCIAL SECURITY ADMINISTRATION

The federal agency established under the Social Security Act that is charged with mandating such domains as old-age benefits, unemployment assistance, health insurance, disability benefits, welfare, and other aid to elderly or needy persons and their families. *See* Social Security.

SOCIALISM

The form of administration and economy in which the national government owns and operates major industrial and commercial systems and controls their management and financial policies and procedures. The term refers both to the Socialist ideology and to the state of society based on that ideology, which its adherents claim stands for equality, social justice, cooperation, and progress, and a rejection of the concept of free enterprise. The Socialist concept calls for, among other things, public ownership of companies and other major organizations, state control over production and distribution, and strict adherence to the doctrines of Socialist law and belief, which originated with historic leaders like Karl Marx and Friedrich Engels. *See* Authoritarianism, *Kapital, Das.*

SOCIALIZATION

The means and procedures by which members of one generation in a society acquire their knowledge, behavioral patterns, and personal ideals from older generations, as well as through formal education. The educational process is enhanced by imitation, rewards, discipline, and any actions that register approval or disapproval. *See* Social Psychology.

SOCIETAL MARKETING THEORIES

Marketing concepts and guidance aimed at developing and producing products and services that are realistic and more in keeping with consumer demands and with broader social needs. *See* Consumer Affairs, Marketing, Supply and Demand.

SOFT CURRENCY

The legal tender and funds of a country that are controlled by monetary exchange procedures and have limited convertibility into gold and foreign currencies. *See* Foreign Currency.

SOFT GOODS

Product lines that include such items as clothing, ready-to-wear accessories, piece goods, bedding, towels, and similar merchandise. *See* Retailing.

SOFTWARE

The body of data-processing programs that are created and produced to activate computers, store information on selected subjects, and release stored data on command, in contrast to hardware, which embodies the physical components of a computer. Components of software encompass operating systems, utilities, languages, and application programs, which are controlled by a variety of operating systems such as loading, storing, executing programs, and manipulating input/output mechanisms. Personnel involved in the development of software programs are writers who create the basics, editors who review and if necessary revise the material, compilers who translate the programs into machine language, linkers who join two or more compiled programs, loaders who link programs into computer memories, and debuggers who scout out errors in programs by running through them during the course of their creation. Of fundamental significance in any software program is its *computer language.* a sequence of directions in the form of numbers that can be understood and followed by the computer. Among the most familiar software designs are those that provide educational programs for classroom instruction and home tutoring, spreadsheets, which guide users with a menu format, and word processors, which resemble electric typewriters, but which are extremely fast, can store the most complicated texts, and can be used for instant revisions, additions, and deletions. *See* Computers, Data Processing, Hardware, Spreadsheets, Word Processors.

SOLE PROPRIETORSHIP

A business enterprise that is wholly owned, managed, and controlled by one person, who is responsible for its operations and obligations. Also called a *single proprietorship.* The term relates most directly to a small- or medium-sized business that is owned and managed by one individual. To establish a sole proprietorship, you need only to obtain whatever licenses are required for that type of business and in the particular location where it will function. Because of this simple structure and minimal legal requirements, the sole proprietorship is the most common of all forms of business organization. The advantages of a sole proprietorship are:

- *Control vested in one owner.* Since there are seldom any co-owners to consult with (except possibly a spouse or other close relative), control is absolute.

- *Decision making largely handled by one person.* Owners can make all decisions themselves or are free to seek advice from paid or volunteer consultants.

- *Flexibility assured.* Owners are able to respond immediately to business needs in the form of day-to-day operating decisions not always possible with businesses whose management structure is more complex.

- *Formation simplified.* There is less formality and fewer legal or regulatory requirements associated with the founding of a sole proprietorship. Such enterprises need little or no government approval and are generally less expensive to establish than a partnership or corporation.

- *Government control minimized.* Very few sole proprietorships are subject to government control, over and beyond the reasonable demands of local environmental restrictions, fire regulations, security, and the like.

- *Profits flowing to sole owner.* Sole proprietors are not required to share profits with anyone, but may do so at their own discretion and to whatever extent they desire.

▪ *Taxation less complicated.* There are no special taxes and the tax structure is a little more intricate than it is for individual personal returns.

The disadvantages of a sole proprietorship are:

▪ *Capital less available.* Sole proprietorships can seldom count on much more capitalization than would an individual seeking funds for personal use.

▪ *Experience limited.* A single owner can seldom bring to bear the same range of experience and breadth of viewpoint that might be found in a partnership or a corporation.

▪ *Indispensability a weakness.* The success of the business hinges almost entirely on the health, alertness, and capabilities of the owner and can be severely damaged when he or she has an accident, is disabled, or dies.

▪ *Liability unlimited.* Individual proprietors are responsible for the full amount of the company's debts or adverse legal rulings in case of liability claims, which may exceed the proprietor's total business assets. Claims can be brought against their personal assets, such as residences, savings accounts, cars, or other property.

▪ *Long-term financing difficult.* As in the case of securing funds for establishing a company to begin with, sole proprietors are seldom able to secure long-term loans for improvements of future operations. *See* Corporations, Funding, Management, Ownership, Partnership, Proprietorship, S Corporations.

SOLVENCY

The ability of an individual or organization to pay debts as they become due, usually without financing. *See* Assets.

SOVEREIGN RISKS

Monetary risks that lenders gamble on when making loans to foreign governments whose administrations are shaky and where a change in the national power structure could trigger a default in repayment. *See* Foreign Trade.

SOVEREIGNTY

In foreign trade and international law, a state that is independent, free from external control, governs its own territory, selects its own political, economic and social systems, and has the power to exchange ambassadors and enter into agreements with other nations. The major restrictions to a sovereignty are international laws, duties, regulations imposed by collaborative bodies in which it holds membership, such as the United Nations, and, of course, the intimidations of stronger nations possessing more military might. Although power within the state may be vested in all the people, as in a democracy, a sovereignty can also come under the rule of one person, such as a monarchy, or a small assembly, such as an oligarchy. *See* Government.

SPACE LAW

That body of international law concerned with legislation pertaining to solar exploration and the use of outer space, a field of jurisprudence whose initial development occurred in the 1950s with the launching of the first satellites and highlighted in the mid-1960s with the creation of the international Outer Space Treaty. Participating nations agreed in effect, through this treaty, that they would not place military bases or weapons of mass destruction on the moon or in other celestial areas, that they would comply in keeping outer space free for exploration and use by all states, and that international law and the United Nations charter would apply. Further, all signatories recognized astronauts as "envoys of mankind" and agreed to assist them if they should land outside their own national borders.

SPECIALIST

Any individual with concentrated knowledge and experience in a specified field and who is enough of an authority to serve as an internal or external consultant in matters related to the subject area concerned. *See* Expert, Expertise.

SPECIALIZATION

Channeling business or commercial functions so they operate within the confines—sometimes quite narrow—of a limited field of activity or so they produce merchandise that is specialized. *See* Specialty Goods.

SPECIAL OFFERING

In the investment field, a large block of stock that becomes available for purchasing and that may require exceptional handling in its sale and processing. *See* Investments, Securities.

SPECIALTY GOODS

Merchandise designed, manufactured, and marketed that is limited in scope and application, such as dental products, cabinetry tools, or warning devices. *See* Merchandise, Specialization, Supply and Demand.

SPECULATOR

An individual investor who invests in deals that are risky, generally in the field of commodities and futures, with the hope of making big gains and profits. *See* Commodities, Futures.

SPEECH RECOGNITION SOFTWARE

Computer programs technologically oriented to the human voice that can obey oral commands as well as the more conventional ones on a keyboard, mouse, or code. *See* Computers, Programming.

SPINOFF

Detaching a department, division, or other functional unit of an organization and reestablishing it as an independent operating entity apart from the parent company or at least separate from its direct control. *See* Corporations.

SPLIT

A stock dividend whose total value remains unchanged, but which increases the number of shares and decreases the value. *See* Securities.

SPONSOR

In broadcasting, the advertiser or agency underwriting radio and TV programs and time and talent through the purchase of commercial time. *See* Broadcasting, Commercials.

SPREADSHEETS

Worksheets used in accounting as a means of summarizing an account by providing a two-way evaluation of fiscal data for a company, and used as a basis for more comprehensive financial statements. When associated with computers, spreadsheets are increasingly common and popular programs designed to facilitate the orchestration of data, often complex, in the form of words, numbers, or graphical components, automating the calculating process and making it easy for the operator to make changes and additions quickly and accurately. *See* Accounting, Computers, Data Processing, Software.

STAGFLATION

Outmoded but once popular term for the economic condition that exists when there is sluggish economic growth, rising unemployment, and inflated prices. Prior to the 1970s, inflation characterized periods of affluence when the demand for goods pushed up prices, and during economic lags unemployment and the resultant drop in consumer spending tended to have a stabilizing effect on prices. Stagflation complicates the establishment of economic policies because measures to stimulate fiscal growth often sets up other undesirable monetary conditions. *See* Depression, Inflation.

STANDARD & POORS

A leading institution in the investment world, which publishes numerous periodicals on fiscal matters and provides corporate, as well as financial data. *See* Investments, Securities.

STANDARDIZATION

In manufacturing and assembly, the accumulated procedures and implementation applied to operations in order to standardize the size, shape, caliber, and other factors of products being made and thus minimize costs and maximize quality control. *See* Manufacturing, Production, Quality Control.

STANDARD OF LIVING

The degree of physical and material affluence of citizens as evaluated by the per-capita output of a nation or other geographical entity being rated. *See* Demographics.

STANDARD OPERATING PROCEDURE

Popularly known as *SOP,* this is the kind of procedure established to identify prearranged sequences and categories of operation. *See* Business Administration.

STANDARD RATE AND DATA SERVICE (SRDS)

The most accurate and comprehensive source of information about hundreds of thousands of advertising and promotion opportunities, from consumer media to industrial publications, cable television, and more. SRDS provides more than 30 different books and electronic products covering all types of media. This vast store of information is used continuously by media buyers and planners, corporate product and brand managers, media buying services, and others, allowing them to profile the key geographic and demographic markets and industry segments in which advertisers are most interested. *See* Advertising, Media.

STAPLES

In inventory control, those goods that are continuously kept on hand for distribution and sale because of their steady demand by customers. *See* Inventory, Supply and Demand.

STATEMENT

A mandatory financial report of the assets, liabilities, and capital of a corporation, generally prepared and released quarterly and annually. *See* Annual Report.

STATE OF THE ART

The adjective applied to technological equipment and products that incorporate the latest scientific innovations in their field; more loosely and popularly, the phrase associated with almost any product—or even service—that is right up to date.

STATIC MODEL

A mode of evaluating economic occurrences and their impact without relating them to time periods or earlier or later events. *See* Economics.

STATISTICAL ERROR

An error that results from an inaccurate measure or interpretation of data in the compilation of a statistical presentation in any given subject area. *See* Advertising Research, Statistics.

STATISTICS

Data computed and presented in terms of figures and explanations for given subjects or ranges of subject matter. Also, the mathematics of compiling such information and formulating it for a variety of applications, including the census, government spending, economic and financial trends, the effects of medical research, comparisons of agricultural systems, the estimation and comparison of natural resources, determining actuarial figures for insurance coverage, the effectiveness of media when used for advertising, the extent of military operations, and trends in traffic and highway accidents. Although statistics have been in use and published for more than a century, this specialized field has come into its own only since the middle of the twentieth century. *See* Data Processing.

STATUS SYMBOLS

Products, often costly and in the luxury class, that are acquired less for utility than to impress others with the purchaser's status and lifestyle. *See* Consumers.

STATUTE OF LIMITATIONS

Laws that nullify certain types of debts as uncollectible if they are not paid within a specified period of time. This field of jurisprudence protects individuals and organizations alike from lawsuits in which evidence may not be obtainable because of the passage of time. Examples of the workings of this statute in recent times have been the cancellation of large tax delinquencies, the prosecution of World War II criminals, and the disposition of racketeering charges against mobsters who took successful evasive action. *See* Business Law, Debts, Debtors.

STEREOPHONIC

Said of audio products and electronic equipment that reproduce sounds from two or more different sources, but that are picked up by the human ear as single sounds. This effect, referred to popularly as *stereo,* is achieved by the use of multiple recording, transmission, and reproducer channels, with the original sound directed toward two or more microphones to form electrical signal channels, which are then recorded or transmitted. The reception system consists basically of the player mechanism, controls, two amplifier channels, and a pair of separated loudspeakers, while the listener can either be positioned near the speakers or wears stereo headphones. *See* Quadraphonic.

STEWARDSHIP

The responsibility of an individual or group charged with the financial management of an organization, including evaluations of assets, profits and losses, obligations, and other basic matters. *See* Financial Management.

STOCK

As used in financial and investment circles, a stock represents a share in the ownership of a corporation or other public entity and is a type of *security,* the other most common type being a *bond.* Stocks trace their origin back to seventeenth-century England, when merchants formed joint-stock companies by pooling their individual capital in order to share in the proceeds from manufacturing and trading ventures. As is true today, they received dividends that were proportionate to their original investments. *See* Bonds, Investments, Securities.

STOCKBROKER

An individual or firm certified to buy and sell securities for customers. *See* Broker, Investments.

STOCK EXCHANGE

An exchange or market that is federally regulated and authorized for the trading of securities. *See* Stock Market.

STOCK INDEX

An indicator that can be used to measure changes in value of a security or related group of securities. *See* Investments, Securities.

STOCK OPTION PLAN

An opportunity extended to employees of a corporation, through which they can exercise the right to purchase the company's stock, at a stated price and within a specified limit. *See* Compensation, Stocks.

STOCK POWER

An instrument granting power of attorney to an individual other than the owner of stock to transfer the title legally to a third party. *See* Power of Attorney, Stocks.

STOCK UNDERWRITER

The corporation or broker underwriting any given stock issue. *See* Broker.

STOP PAYMENT ORDER

A directive formally given by the drawer of a check to a bank not to honor the check. *See* Banking.

STRATEGIC PLANNING

A long-range blueprint for an organization, forecasting its fiscal and operational objectives for a period of no less than three years and as many as ten or more. *See* Management.

STRATEGY

In management, any tactic or approach that will lead to the solution of problems or the achievement of objectives, whether for an immediate crisis or long-range operations. *See* Management.

STREET NAME

The phrase used when securities are held in the name of a broker instead of a customer and when the latter wants the portfolio held by the former. *See* Portfolio.

STRIKE

In the field of labor and management, the collective actions by workers to discontinue their work for an employer or in an industry until such time as they can compel desired changes in working conditions, be assured of higher wages, or earn certain other degrees of recognition by management. Among the common forms of strike situations are *primary,* a stoppage aimed at the workers' own employer, *sympathy,* when one group of workers leaves the job out of commiseration for others, and a *sit-down,* when workers stop work, but decline to leave a company's premises in order to prevent the hiring of replacements. *See* Labor/Management, Unions.

STRONG DOLLAR

The financial condition that holds sway when the foreign exchange rate results in the U.S. dollar being able to purchase foreign goods and services more economically. *See* Foreign Exchange.

STRONG MARKET

Any market, whether for securities, commodities, or consumer goods that exists when there is a greater demand for purchasing than there is for selling. *See* Marketing.

SUBCONTRACT

A contract or agreement whose stipulations and responsibilities are passed along, in whole or in part, to parties other than the original contract holder. *See* Agreement, Contract.

SUBLEASE

A lease agreement drawn up to permit a tenant to transfer part of his or her rights to another party. *See* Lease.

SUBLIMINAL ADVERTISING

The creation of advertisements, whether commercials or in print, that are so arranged that there are hidden messages that affect readers and viewers even though they are not aware that they have received them. *See* Advertising, Media.

SUBSIDIARY

A self-contained enterprise that is owned and operated by a parent company. *See* Corporation, Management.

SUBSIDY

A monetary grant provided by a government agency as an incentive to produce more, or better, commodities or facilities, or to encourage economic growth within an industry or commercial field. Among the most common are farm subsidies, to help support farmers during lean times or after natural disasters, such as wind storms and floods. *See* Financing, Government.

SUMMATION

A briefing, whether oral or written, that reviews and outlines a larger presentation, often with the addition of conclusions and recommendations. *See* Communications.

SUPERIOR

In any organization, a person who is higher in rank or office than another employee, though not necessarily in intellectual capacity or potential. *See* Personnel Administration.

SUPPLY AND DEMAND

The proportionate balance between the supplies of products and materials and the consumer demand for them when, under competitive circumstances, the prices charged for goods and services are determined by the relationship between the demand for goods and services and the supply available. *Demand* has been defined as "a compilation of the various quantities of a particular product that can be sold at all possible prices in a given market during a given time period. The law of demand states that the relationship between price and the quantity demanded is an inverse one." In actual practice this is shown to be true, in that when retailers want to increase the sales of a product, they lower rather than increase its price. *See* Marketing, Retailing.

SWINDLE

An illegal act designed to acquire money, possessions, or property through deception, fraud, or trickery. *See* Bait and Switch, Better Business Bureau, Fraud.

SWITCH SELLING

See Bait and Switch.

SYNDICATE

An alliance of individuals who have banded together or formed a joint venture to undertake projects and operations they would have been unable to execute individually. *See* Joint Venture.

SYNERGY

An economic theory that postulates that the merging of business enterprises into a larger organization will result in more successful operations overall than was possible for the individual entities, adhering to the old adage that "the whole is greater than the sum of its parts." *See* Merger.

Systems Analysis

The scientific evaluation of a business or industrial operation to determine (a) what the accomplishment objectives are, and (b) how to achieve them. *See* Systems Management.

Systems Management

Planning and operating a business as a system or series of systems, including not only costs and objectives, but the importance of human relations in attaining the defined goals. *See* Employee Relations, Objectives.

TABLE

A presentation of statistical data to be used for reference purposes and displayed in a tabular format. *See* Chart, Graph.

TABULAR MATTER

Data presented in a table format. *See* Graph, Table.

TACIT AGREEMENT

An unwritten, and frequently unspoken, understanding that often arises not from any positive or relayed communication but from a lack of disagreement on one or more subjects under discussion. *See* Agreement.

TAFT-HARTLEY ACT

The federal statute that amended the National Labor Relations Act regulating certain union activities. *See* National Labor Relations Act.

TAKEOVER

The act of purchasing sufficient shares of the stock of a corporation to secure control of the company. *See* Corporation, Stocks.

TANGIBLE ASSET

An asset that has a physical value, such as tools and equipment, in contrast to intangible assets, such as trademarks, slogans, or customer goodwill. *See* Assets, Intangible Asset.

TAPE RECORDING

In electronic communication, the element on which words, music, or other sounds and illustrations or other graphic materials are reproduced usually in the form of a magnetic tape. The production of such tapes (or like elements) requires the use of a slender, pliant material capable of carrying articulate signals commensurate with the audio or video signals being reproduced, and a mechanism for recording and playback. Although the past two decades have seen remarkable advances in the development of tape recordings of all kinds, the system had been invented and was in limited use by the early twentieth century. *See* Audio, Communications, Videotape.

TARGET CONSUMERS

Prospective customers who typify the kinds of purchasers a manufacturer, advertiser, retailer, or service organization is hoping to reach and motivate. Also referred to as a *target market*. *See* Consumers, Marketing.

TARIFF

In international trading, the rate of price schedules for import duties and also a government-imposed tax placed on imported merchandise, either as a specific levy on each unit of an imported good or an *ad valorem* percentage of the wholesale value of the merchandise. Such assessments are often used to protect domestic industries from cheap foreign production and so-called "slave labor." Although, historically, tariffs have been used as sources of revenue in many countries, in recent years the governments of industrial nations have relied more heavily on income taxes and other forms of revenue. *See* Duty, Foreign Trade, Free Trade.

TARIFF ACTS

Legislation in the United States from the late eighteenth century to the early twentieth century that was enacted to protect domestic industry in America from foreign production and the importation of cheap products. Although these acts helped to provide the government with the greatest source of its revenues, the opening up of free markets and the increase in foreign trade brought about a decline in tariffs and other international trade restrictions. The greatest change came about in 1913 with the passage of the sixteenth Amendment to the Constitution, authorizing income taxation and thus reducing reliance on tariffs. *See* Free Trade, Tariffs.

TASK GROUP

An alliance of employees, formed either voluntarily or by assignment, to work as a unit to accomplish a goal or complete a given project. *See* Task Management.

TASK MANAGEMENT

The administration and overseeing of projects being undertaken by task groups. *See* Management, Task Group.

TAX

Any assessment or levy mandated by a government, whether federal, state, or local, to help support the government in question. At the federal level the income tax—whether for individuals or organizations—has long been one of the principal sources of revenue, while at the state level the property tax has become the fundamental source of income, along with sales taxes. Other familiar taxes are those associated with commercial trade, inheritance, excess profits, customs, and sales. While taxes have been, and always will be, among the most controversial public issues, in the end they serve as the major price paid for publicly provided benefits and services, voted on by those who are taxed in order to finance, through the public sector, services on which citizens place necessary value, but that cannot adequately be provided through commercial means. *See* Tax Accounting.

TAXABLE INCOME

The amount of personal or corporate income remaining after all allowable deductions and exemptions and losses have been subtracted.

TAX ACCOUNTING

The specialized field of accounting whose focus is on tax and compliance reporting. In the United States, tax accounting is a matter of evaluating and reporting on legal compliances with the Internal Revenue Code and various state and local tax laws and assessment regulations. Accountants in this discipline, many of whom are attorneys as well as CPAs, keep abreast of the numerous changes in tax law that apply to their organization or those of their clients, knowing that the methods they select to report assets and liabilities will determine the types and amounts of taxes to be paid. Corporations are also required to report to the Securities and Exchange Commission, which requires its own form of compliance accounting from publicly traded corporations. The SEC has a well-prescribed reporting process that a company must follow when it issues securities to be publicly traded. In addition to basic data, such reports must include disclosure of ownership, management biographies, company functions, and other information useful to investors and brokers. *See* Accounting and other *Tax* entries.

TAXATION

The procedures, actions, and systems applied by a government at any level to obtain revenue from individuals, businesses, and other organizations, specifically to support the taxing government and provide public services. Although often considered as taxes, levies for emergencies, special-service fees, and postage are not in that category. *See* Tax and other *Tax* entries.

TAXATION MANAGEMENT

The administration of tax obligations and payments in such a manner as to minimize tax burdens, penalties, and interest, even if it requires substantial modifications in an organization's business plan or method of operation. According to expert opinion, many companies—especially small businesses— overpay taxes by sums ranging from 10 percent to as much as 35 percent. One of the first steps (and one that must be taken periodically) in taxation management is a concise review of tax *accountability,* to determine the legal amount for which an organization is indebted. Concurrently, taxation management also requires careful attention to tax withholding policies, procedures, and regulations. *See* Financial Management and other *Tax* entries.

TAX EVASION

The illegal avoidance of reporting and/or paying taxes by falsifying records. *See* Business Law, Fraud.

TAX HAVEN

A country or other geographical entity that is used for certain kinds of business transactions because it imposes few, if any, taxes on the profits derived from such transactions. *See* Offshore Banking, Tax Shelter.

TAX REFORM ACT

Legislation enacted in 1986, which in effect broadened the tax base, lowered the rates of tax, lessened the number of tax brackets, and eliminated certain abuses of the tax law. The Act was then renamed *The Internal Revenue Code of 1986.*

TAX SHELTER

A business tactic whereby certain deductions for tax purposes are created without causing a corresponding decrease in cash flow. *See* Cash Flow, Deduction.

TEACHING MACHINES

Equipment used in programmed learning that is capable of storing instructional data, present information, receive responses from the user, and in turn introduce follow-up information so that students can proceed along an established course of learning. Such machines, which can teach without necessarily having the presence of an instructor, function on the principle of moving forward in sequence when students make correct responses, but requiring additional input from users when incorrect answers are given or inappropriate steps are taken. Teaching machines range all the way from simple "true or false" key-punch type instruments to highly sophisticated, computerized devices with sound and graphics, as well as vocabularies, that can be used to train airline pilots. *See* Computers, Data Processing, Training.

TEASER

An advertising gimmick that stimulates the curiosity of prospective customers by deliberately omitting essential information (such as the name of the product or source), which is promised to be revealed in a future advertisement or commercial. *See* Advertising.

TECHNICAL EDUCATION

The instructional discipline that prepares students for careers in occupations that are superior to skilled crafts, yet not necessarily at the level of the engineering and scientific professions. Technical education curricula teach the application of skills in the use of technological equipment and instruments, often in research and development, or in laboratory analysis, as well as a grasp of the basic principles of mathematics and science. Graduates of technical schools range from those who qualify as *technical assistants* after one year or less of study, those who qualify as technicians after two years of study, and those who attain the standing of *technologist* upon earning a four-year baccalaureate degree from a technical institute or college. *See* Career Education, Training, Vocational Education.

TECHNOLOGICAL UNEMPLOYMENT

A loss of jobs or a job market that can be attributed to technological advances that increase the uses of robotics and lessen the need for human control. *See* Robotics.

TECHNOLOGY

In the field of business and industry, the term has been defined as "the application of science, especially to industrial or commercial objectives, including the entire body of methods and materials used to achieve such objectives." The terms *science* and *technology,* however, are often confused because so many aspects of technology today are associated with the natural sciences, such as chemistry, biology, physics, and mathematics. In business applications, though, technology also relates to disciplines commonly thought of as "*nontechnical*," such as philosophy, psychology, or ideology. Historically, many fields of technology developed from non-scientific input, such as metallurgy, which originated with metalworking crafts, aerodynamics, which blossomed with man's attempts to fly, and ballistics, which were originally methods of determining how to aim weapons more accurately. Technological developments such as these eventually sprouted what later would be recognized as sciences, but that would also become important in such fields as economics, administration, and regulation. *See* Manufacturing, Production, Technical Education.

TELECOMMUNICATIONS

The transmission of information and communications between remotely located stations through the use of electronic units that convert data codes and control the sequences and speed of transmissions. Although telecommunications are usually transmitted over telephone lines, they can also use radio and television waves and, for very sophisticated systems, satellites. The information transmitted can be in the form of voice, sound, illustrations, or data, or a combination of media, over a carrier/signal system that includes a transmitter, receiver(s), and a physical channel of communication, even including the air. The technical procedure is referred to as *modulation* and, through a process called *multiplexing,* can transmit several signals over a single channel, each of which can be separated from the carrier signal at the point of reception. This system is sophisticated enough today so that it can transmit and, where pertinent, separate any kind of mixture of different media of communication, such as voice, music, statistics, and video symbols. The applied technology is known as *pulse-code modulation (PCM),* because the transmission works as a series of on-off pulses, and is particularly effective because the signals can be tightly compressed in order to increase the transmission capacity. Another method for expanding channel capacity is the use of electromagnetic radiation, which has a higher frequency than radio frequencies. Capacities can be expanded, too, with fiber optics, which have even greater capacity, since they make use of light waves and are literally millions of times higher than radio waves. As has been pointed out, a single glass fiber much smaller than a human hair can replace 12,000 telephone wires and is very practical for this purpose since fiber optics are rapidly increasing in telephone and other communications systems. Current telecommunications plans call for the linkage of telephone, computer, facsimile (FAX), radio, television, and mail in a single electronic system, Integrated Services Digital Network (ISDN). *See* major coverage of Communications (page 431), *E-mail, Fiber Optics, Voice Mail.*

TELECONFERENCING

Utilizing data-processing systems as a means of communication between widely scattered individuals and groups of people. *See also* Conference Calls.

TELEMARKETING

A direct-marketing program or campaign in which salespersons phone prospective purchasers, selected from prepared lists, and deliver sales pitches, followed by requests for orders. *See* Direct Sales, Marketing.

TELEMETRY

A system of communications that records calculations and measurements at remote, often almost inaccessible, positions on land or sea or in the air and transmits them to receiving stations, where they are monitored and evaluated. Examples of telemetry applications are the monitoring of solar generating stations, research instruments in the ocean depths, satellites in space, and oil pipelines frozen under the Arctic tundra. The basic units in telemetric systems include transmitters, receivers, measuring instruments, recording devices, and an alarm system for warning about equipment failures. *See* Communications, Telecommunications.

TELEPRINTER

An instrument, often controlled by a computer, that serves as a printer and uses a keyboard to set type. *See* Printing.

TELEVISION PRODUCTION

The performance of a television program or the making of that program, whether live or taped. The two major forms of production are (1) *broadcast,* which results in the wide range of subject areas covered on network stations, and (2) *nonbroadcast,* which is seen on the air as educational TV or private programming, and off the air in the form of videotaped programs presented in classrooms, assembly halls, business conference rooms, and the like. *See* Broadcasting.

TEMPLATE

An overlay or pattern cut out on a board or sheet of metal in such a fashion that it can be used as a guide in a production process. Templates also have applications in the preparation of charts and graphs, such as those that might be used to present financial data or statistics. *See* Accounting, Production.

TEMPORARY PERSONNEL SERVICE (TPS)

A TPS is not an employment agency, but a service firm that hires people as its own employees and assigns them on contract to clients who request personnel assistance, often specialized in nature. Organizations that use this kind of service are not hiring extra employees, but buying the use of their time. The temporary personnel firm is responsible for payrolls, tax withholding, bookkeeping, insurance, workers' compensation, fringe benefits, and all other similar costs connected with employees. The contracting organization is thus relieved of the burden of recruiting, interviewing, screening, testing, and, to a large extent, training. Most TPSs offer performance guarantees and fidelity bonding at no added cost to their clients. In addition, clients are relieved of the need for government forms and for reporting social security, taxes, and unemployment compensation.

The advantages of using a temporary personnel service are:

Availability. Personnel can be obtained at almost a moment's notice, usually the same day if the need is not too large or specialized.

Competitive Readiness. Personnel can be obtained in sufficient numbers to meet an unexpected surge of activity on the part of the client's competition, thus making it possible to minimize competitive inroads at significant times or in appropriate locations.

Convenience. Securing experienced help may require little more than a phone call and a description of the immediate personnel needs.

Paperwork Minimized. Since the service firm is already dealing with the paperwork required for its personnel, the client is relieved of that burden right from the start.

Qualifications. The service selects only employees who are qualified for the job at hand and guarantees their suitability and performance.

Specialization. The client has no problem finding personnel with specialized skills and experience at a moment's notice when an opportunity arises to meet a demand beyond the capability of the existing roster.

Disadvantages of using a temporary personnel service:

Morale Problems. Bringing in temporary personnel can sometimes offend regular employees who feel they could do the same job or earn overtime pay.

Cost. Users of TPS have to weigh carefully the charges and related costs. Although these may be higher per individual, some financial gain might result from not having to pay personnel various benefits or carry them on the books.

Unfamiliarity with Company. Some kinds of job assignments are best filled by people who are familiar with the company and need no further indoctrination. If a position requires close cooperation with other employees and departments, temporary personnel might be at a disadvantage in comparison with regular employees.

Long-term Needs. Generally, if individuals are to be assigned to special work for a period of more than six months, it is better to use employees already in the company or to hire full-time employees for the project at hand.
See Employees, External Services, Human Resources, Personnel.

TENANTS IN COMMON

Two or more individuals who jointly hold title to property so that each has an undivided interest that passes at death to the heirs of the deceased and not to the surviving tenant(s). *See* Title.

TENDER OFFER

An offer by one company whose objective is to gain control of another company by purchasing multiple shares of stock at a price above the current market quotation. *See* Stocks.

10-K

An annual statement filed with the Securities and Exchange Commission (SEC) by any corporation that issues stock, and containing specific information about revenues and income. *See* Annual Reports, Securities.

10-Q

A statement that must be filed with the Securities and Exchange Commission (SEC) quarterly by companies, providing interim financial data about revenues and income. *See* Assets, Corporations, Securities and Exchange Commission (SEC).

TERM INSURANCE

A policy that provides coverage only for a stated period of time, and that generally has no accumulative value. *See* Insurance.

TERMS OF TRADE

In international commerce, the number of products or units that must be given in return by the participating parties in the transaction for each unit of goods obtained. *See* Foreign Trade, General Agreement on Tariffs and Trade (GATT).

TERRITORIAL WATERS

In the field of international law, those waters situated within the jurisdiction of sovereign states, most commonly ones that are immediately adjacent to a nation's shoreline or that form commercial ports. Lakes or rivers or other bodies of fresh water situated on national boundaries come under national control to the middle of navigable channels. The most significant territorial-waters milestone came in 1982 when the United Nations Convention on the Law of the Sea was signed by 117 members, thus establishing revised rules for international water rights. This law specified, among other things, that coastal nations would enjoy a sovereignty limit of 12 nautical miles, plus economic rights for commercial fishing for 200 nautical miles offshore. *See* Foreign Trade, Water Rights.

TESTIMONIAL

In advertising, promotion, and public relations, a personal statement in praise of a product or service that is made by a satisfied user and is so reported to the public. *See* Advertising, Promotion, Public Relations.

TEST MARKET

Any sales market that has been carefully studied and selected for product testing because it represents a cross-section of prime markets for the product(s) in question, or because it has the right mix of prospective consumers. *See* Advertising Research, Marketing.

TEST MARKETING

The selective distribution and sales of a new product in a limited market area or to a limited category of consumer to determine its potential in a larger market that may be regional or nationwide. *See* Marketing, Product Testing.

T TEAM

A group of a dozen or more work-related employees or members of a profession who attend a sensitivity training program whose aim is to encourage personal development and growth, teamwork, and better applications of capabilities and skills. The teams are guided by a facilitator, who establishes certain ground rules and then stimulates group discussions and feedbacks. *See* Facilitator, Sensitivity Training.

THEORY X

A management hypothesis, somewhat tongue-in-cheek, that conjectures that people have inherent apathies toward what they consider to be "work," whether on the job or off, and will avoid it whenever possible. The theory further assumes that most job holders must be coerced or enticed into performing assignments and that the average employee prefers to be directed, avoids responsibility, and has only marginal ambitions. Another philosophy, known as *Theory Y,* takes the opposite stand and asserts that employees have a natural interest in expending time and energy working if they can be motivated and given sound objectives and goals. *See* Management.

THERMOGRAPHY

Translated as "heated printing," this is a process of raised-letter embossing that simulates engraved printing at less cost and can be used economically for such purposes as company letterheads, business cards, decorations, invitations, and other printings that require distinctive effects. The raised lettering is made possible by the use of special inks that are dusted with a powdered compound after printing and passed under heat in a way that swells the letters and simulates embossing. *See* Printing.

THESAURUS

Deriving its name from the Greek word for *storehouse,* this type of reference work is a catalog of words and phrases. Similar to a synonym dictionary, it is intended to expedite and improve the writing or speaking of the user. A typical thesaurus (Roget's is the most common and familiar) systematically groups words with their synonyms and antonyms according to subject classifications and not necessarily alphabetically. The alphabetical listings, however, will be found in a separate section, properly referenced. *See* Communications.

THINK TANK

The vernacular phrase for a high-intellect research team contracted to study issues relating to an industry or the social environment in which it functions. While think tanks are logically associated with research projects, they differ from other exploratory studies in that they tend to focus on issues that relate to policy making and are often, in fact, referred to as *policy research.* As such, this field of endeavor is considered to be part of long-range planning, directed not so much at coming to grips with technological developments as to using scientific methodologies to facilitate policy planning and decision making. Another vital characteristic is that think tanks almost invariably bring together participants from a diverse number of disciplines in such a way that their interactions help to see subjects in broad perspective. Think tanks have been used to make evaluations and recommendations in many fields, including the environment, pollution, crime, taxation, energy resources, civil rights, substance abuse, communications, weather forecasting, and military training. *See* Management, Research and Development.

THIN POSITION

The weak financial situation that applies to a business that owes a large number of debts in proportion to its assets. *See* Assets, Debits.

THIRD PARTY

An individual or group of people, or even a company, involved in negotiations with two other parties and empowered to negotiate or conclude transactions with them. *See* Contracts, Labor/Management.

THRESHOLD ENTERPRISES

A popularized reference to fledgling companies, often founded by entrepreneurs, that are proving to be successful and may be on the threshold of maturity and growth and whose future prospects look rosy. *See* Entrepreneurs, Small Business.

TIDAL ENERGY

In reference to the generation of power, this form of energy is the kind where, in more than 100 global locations, the tides rise and fall enough within a partially contained bay or basin of sea water to make the generation of electricity by tidal force commercially viable. The much-publicized Bay of Fundy, for example, lying between the State of Maine and the Provinces of New Brunswick and Nova Scotia, is said to have the energy-producing equivalent of 30 conventional power plants. However, only two tidal-energy plants are currently in use, at the mouth of the Rance River, near Normandy, France, and at Kislaya Guba, on the White Sea, north of Murmansk, Russia. As a source of consistent, usable power, tidal plants have the disadvantage of producing erratically, totally dependent upon the ebb and flow of the water. The power that could be harnessed from these tidal sources might be of great value locally, but on a global basis their combined generation could produce little more than 5 percent of the world's electricity. *See* Energy.

TIE-IN SALE

A merchandising ploy that offers consumers a bundle of related products at a discount. *See* Merchandising, Retailing, Sales.

TIGHT MONEY

Loans that are available only at high interest rates because of an economic climate in which lenders are scarce or reluctant to underwrite loans. *See* Loans.

TIME-AND-MOTION STUDIES

Studies made in manufacturing facilities, in production, on assembly lines, or in other industrial operations and functions to evaluate the relationships between work performed and the people power necessary to perform it. This field of research is also referred to as *methods design,* with the objective of coordinating methods, equipment, tools, and work situations in order that jobs and assignments may be planned with maximum effectiveness. Although time-and-motion studies are a product of the mid-twentieth century, their origins go back to the 1880s, when elementary evaluations were made of workers on factory production and assembly lines, using stopwatches and rather primitive calculating techniques. The results of the tests today are considered to be invaluable in the planning of work sequences, the scheduling of individuals and shifts, estimating costs, recruiting and controlling labor, and determining wages, benefits, and other incentives. *See* Labor/Management, Operations Research, Personnel Administration, Research.

TIME FRAME

The amount of time required, on the average, to complete a specific assignment or operation. *See* Time-and-motion Studies.

TIME SHARING

In the field of computing, a plan for using a data-processing system that permits a number of people to access the same hardware and software on a mutually agreed-upon priority basis or sequence. *See* Computers.

TIME STUDY

See Time-and-motion Studies.

TIPS

Inside information, sometimes considered illegal or unethical. *See* Investments.

TITLE

An instrument that conveys a legal right of ownership of real property, facilities, or anything of substantial value that might later be transferred or sold. *See* other *Title* entries.

TITLE INSURANCE

A policy from a title guaranty company that is underwritten for property owners to indemnify them against a defective or nontransferable title while they are listed as the owners. *See* Real Estate.

TITLE SEARCH

An investigation by a mortgage company, title guaranty firm, attorney, or other qualified party to ascertain that the title to real property is valid and in proper order. *See* Title Insurance.

TOTALITARIANISM

That system of government in which all controls and resources are monopolized by the state in such a way as to become involved in, and regulate, all segments of business and industry, public and private life, and even social affairs and religious matters. Typically in the hands of a few individuals or an organized group, this form of government strengthens and enhances its political position, influence, and clout through the extensive use of propaganda and the complete control of business, industry, the police, and the military. In practice, as well as in its political concept, totalitarianism is a form of complete bureaucracy that was almost unknown until well into the twentieth century, as an outgrowth of despotism and dictatorship. In its finite interpretation, in fact, totalitarianism saw its birth in the National Socialist (Nazi) party in Germany and later became known as a concept that rejected existing political ideologies as corrupt and disorganized and that demanded complete conformity, with the government dominated by one political party and usually by a single leader. *See* Authoritarian, Communism, Dictatorship.

TRADE ADVERTISING

Advertising directed at individuals or firms in a particular trade or field of business, such as retailers, wholesalers, technicians, or dealers, most commonly in specialized publications whose circulation is limited to their professions. Trade advertising also includes the preparation and publication of booklets, brochures, flyers, and other printed matter used in the promotion of commercial and industrial enterprises. *See* Advertising.

TRADE ASSOCIATION

Any nonprofit organization whose members are specialized in a certain field of endeavor and whose objectives are to enhance benefits and prerogatives for their common good. Commercial and industrial organizations customarily join one or more trade associations in order to act collectively to effect beneficial results that they could not expect when acting individually. Trade associations, which function in virtually every existing field of business and industry, large and small, are typically involved with the following kinds of activities:

public relations, publicity, advertising, lobbying, legislation, and recruiting. They serve as the source of information for the public and the media, provide forums for discussion and the resolution of common problems, establish appropriate policies and codes of ethics, regulate business practices, encourage healthy competition, and regularly disseminate trade news and professional information to their members and constituents. Associations whose members are producers of goods and materials also establish standards for products and processes. *See* Associations, Competition.

TRADE DEFICIT

In international commerce, the situation that exists in the economy of a country when the amounts and values of its imports exceed those of its exports. *See* Foreign Trade, Trade Surplus.

TRADE DISCOUNT

The discount or reduction in price allowed by a supplier when selling merchandise to wholesalers and others with whom it trades. "Trade discounts" are also used as a gimmick to entice consumers to pay what they think are wholesale prices. *See* Retailing, Wholesaling.

TRADEMARK

A distinguishing brand name, symbol, mark, emblem, or fancied initials that identifies a product or company, and that has been protected through registration with the United States Patent Office. Trademarks differ from copyrights and patents in that they protect the *symbol* that distinguishes products, materials, or services, and not those commodities themselves. Although, historically, trademarks go back to the Middle Ages and the formation of guilds in Europe, in America it was not until 1870 that Congress first enacted legislation for their registration and protection by the companies using them. Unprotected trademarks often become generic terms, as in the case of the word, such as *refrigerator,* and can then no longer be associated with any particular manufacturer or supplier. Trademarks exist in a number of categories, the most common of which are: *technical trademarks,* which identify the derivation of a product or service; *descriptive marks,* which feature the nature of the items being protected; *certification marks,* which authenticate the quality or origin of products and materials; *collective marks,* which associate the marketer with a trade association, union, or business *service organization; suggestive marks,* which indicate usage; and *service marks,* which are used in the sale or advertising of services. Another form of trademark is the *seal of approval,* indicating that a product or service has the blessings of an organization whose reputation is known to and respected by the public. *See* Copyright, Patents.

TRADEOFF

A deal in which one party trades an asset or other item of value with a party having something of comparable value to offer in exchange. *See* Barter.

TRADE SURPLUS

The economic situation that exists when a country's exports exceed its imports. *See* Trade Deficit.

TRADING ON EQUITY

See Leverage.

TRADING STAMP

A promotional device in the form of a stamp or small certificate that is given to purchasers as a business enticement and that can be accumulated and later used, in quantity, to buy merchandise of value. *See* Consumers, Promotion, Retailing.

TRAFFIC DEPARTMENT

The section, usually in an advertising agency, but common in a corporation as well, that schedules the job responsibilities of other units engaged in the preparation of publications and printed matter and has the primary task and accountability for seeing that timetables are prepared and deadlines are met. *See* Advertising.

TRAFFIC PATTERN

In an office, commercial establishment, factory, or other premises, the arrangement of space that facilitates the flow of personal, equipment, or goods in the course of normal operations. *See* Personnel Administration.

TRAINING PROGRAMS

Training program are conventionally internal in nature, administered by the organization on company property or in leased facilities elsewhere, or external, administered by outside specialists in a location that may or may not be owned by the company. According to a study by the National Federation of Independent Business, "the most commonly mentioned problem was the need for far more employee training than had been anticipated." A typical example was that of a financial analyst who usually required six hours to prepare a monthly report, but was spending almost triple that amount of time when "aided" by a computer, because of inadequate training.

The following questions need to be considered carefully and answered by managers who are planning training and orientation programs:

- What is the short-term goal? The long-term goal?
- What does each participant need to learn?
- What type of training is called for?
- What method of instruction is likely to be the most effective?
- How will the successful completion of a training program benefit employee performance?
- What audio-visual aids should be considered, both to expedite the learning process and to help to keep pertinent points in mind?
- What physical facilities will be needed internally? Externally?
- What cost factors are important, and how much will they add to the overall training budget?
- Will participants need job substitutes while they are enrolled?
- What about the timing and the length of the training program?
- What instructors are potential candidates?
- Which employees should be selected, and how should they be screened as qualifiers?
- What controls or checks should be used to make certain the target objectives remain valid and clear?
- Should the program be publicized, and if so, how?

Managers who have responsibilities for training programs can be more proficient if they study programs used by other organizations in their industry, or similar fields. See Career Education, Employee Qualifications, Management, Personnel Development, Specialization.

TRANSACTION

A mutual endeavor jointly undertaken by two or more parties in the conduct of business and that may or may not be specified in a contract or legal agreement. *See* Contract.

TRANSACTION TEST

A financial auditing procedure involving the examination of data relating to specific company transactions, with the objective of spotting errors or omissions in the cooperate accounting records. *See* Auditing.

TRANSDUCER

A mechanism that transforms one type of energy into another type of energy, which may be similar or different. Common examples are the electric conversion transducer, which converts electricity from one frequency to another; the electro-acoustic transducer, which transforms sound into electricity; and the ultrasonic transducer, which utilizes electricity to produce ultrasound. Another major type is the Piezoelectric transducer, composed of crystals that can generate an electric charge when they are activated by pressure or tension and that find broad applications in television broadcasting. *See* Energy.

TRANSFER AGENT

A representative of management in a corporation, often a financial officer, charged with maintaining and updating the records of socks, bonds, and other securities. *See* Financial Administration.

TRANSFER PRICE

The discounted price charged by one division of a manufacturing company when it sells products, supplies, or parts to another division, as in the case of a petrochemical corporation that produces many types of chemicals for both consumer and industrial lines of products. *See* Discount, Distribution.

TRANSIT ADVERTISING

Posters, car cards, placards, broadsides, and other forms of graphic advertising displays positioned in strategic places in subways, buses, railway cars, ferries, terminals, airports, and other mass transit areas. *See* Outdoor Advertising.

TRANSPORTATION

The movement of ground, air, or water traffic from one location to another, whether bearing cargo, passengers, freight, or other transportables. *See* Shipping.

TREASURY BILLS

Certificates sold by the U.S. government at discount through competitive bidding and usually having maturities of three months and one year. *See* Treasury Notes.

TREASURY DEPARTMENT OF THE UNITED STATES

Officially known as the Department of the Treasury, this agency oversees the nation's financial operations and answers to the executive branch of the government. The responsibilities of the department are, among other things, to advise the President on fiscal affairs, report annually to Congress on the nation's financial condition, manage the public debt, supervise monetary dealings with other nations, monitor defense lending, and coordinate law enforcement cases and functions. The operating bureaus of the Treasury Department include Comptroller of the Currency, the Customs Service, the Internal Revenue Service, the Bureau of Engraving and Printing, the Bureau of Government Financial Operations, the Bureau of the Public Debt, the United States Mint, the Bureau of Alcohol, Tobacco and Firearms, and the Secret Service. *See* Currency, Finances, Government.

TREASURY NOTES

Long-term securities, having maturities of one to five years, available to the public and issued by the U.S. government. *See* Treasury Bills.

TRIAL-AND-ERROR PRICING

A marketing research stratagem, whereby the same products are sold at different prices in selected locations to test consumer response and determine how much the price tag affects the rapidity and volume of sales. *See* Consumers, Marketing, Retailing.

TRIAL BALLOON

Vernacular for a pilot test of an administrative plan in which the procedures and approach may be modified to adjust to the initial responses acquired. *See* Research.

TRICKLE-DOWN ECONOMICS

A term associated with the manner in which federal funds flow into the economic structure of the nation and stimulate growth through their effect on business enterprises of all types and proportions. *See* Economics, Microeconomics.

TROUBLESHOOTING

Originally referring to the function of trying to find bugs and failures in mechanical, electrical, and electronic equipment and components, the expression is now commonly used in business and industry to denote the process of solving management and personnel problems, among other things. *See* Management, Personnel Administration.

TRUST

A financial establishment in which one party is appointed trustee to hold title to property on behalf of one or more other parties, called the beneficiary. The trust concept is peculiar to the United Kingdom, the United States, and other countries whose legal systems are derived from British common law. *See* Trustee.

TRUSTEE

An individual or organization assigned a legal title to property, known as the trust, for the benefit of another party, known as the beneficiary.

TRUST FUND

The assets held by one party, as trustee, for another party, as beneficiary. *See* Trust.

TRUTH-IN-LENDING LEGISLATION

The enactment of laws and the administration of restrictions to protect consumers by requiring sellers to reveal full disclosures about prices, financing terms, interest costs, and other conditions relating to purchases of goods and services. *See* Consumer Credit, Consumer Protection.

TURNAROUND

In management and administration, the procedures and approaches used in strengthening an unproductive company, failing business, or unmarketable product and tuning the situation around so that the results are positive and eventually profit making. *See* Business Administration, Management.

TURNOVER

The number of times a given stock of merchandise is sold and then replaced in an allotted period of time, generally three months, six months, or a year. The speed of movement of goods is referred to as the rate of turnover.

TYCOON

The popularized expression for an individual who has accumulated great wealth and usually power in commerce and industry. Also referred to as a *mogul* or *magnate*.

Ultimate Consumer

The consumer, not necessarily the purchaser, who eventually uses a product. Identifying the ultimate consumers, as well as prospective buyers, is important in evaluating national and regional marketing targets and directing advertising campaigns. *See* Advertising, Consumers.

Ultrasonics

That discipline that studies and applies sonic waves whose frequency is above the normal range of human hearing, whose vibrations are referred to as *ultrasound*. From the standpoint of business and industry, ultrasonics started to become an important research tool, particularly for the detection of flaws in materials and products and tools that could not be detected by X ray and other laboratory instrumentation. In use, ultrasonic waves travel through matter with about the same speed as sound waves, whether through air, liquids, or solids, and evidences most of the basic properties of sound waves. The difference is that the intensity of ultrasound diminishes much more quickly as it strikes different masses and is reflected back. Thus it can detect hidden objects that are foreign to the surrounding mass, and for this reason can, for example, detect flaws in solids, such as cracks or air pockets in a metal beam. Industrially, ultrasound has another important application—its intense vibrations will shake loose dirt, grease, and other undesirable deposits on metal products that are being readied for shipment or that need to be super-clean before being welded. *See* Manufacturing, Production.

Unbalanced Growth

The kind of irregular economic growth that transpires when capital investment expands at different rates and degrees in different geographical areas within the country or within any significant economic entity. *See* Economics.

UNCERTAINTY PRINCIPLE

The concept that profits cannot always be realistically anticipated because they are distorted by a rash of uncertainties, such as changes in the tastes of social groups, unexpected innovations, monetary fluctuations, competitive actions, and trends that cannot be foreseen. *See* Assets, Debits, Profits.

UNDERCAPITALIZED

Said of a business venture that lacks sufficient financing to fund the projects and personnel requirements necessary for its continuing operation. *See* Capital, Financing.

UNDERDEVELOPED NATION

A country in which the per-capita income and the overall economy are proportionately too weak to compete successfully with industrialized nations. *See* Third World Nations.

UNDEREMPLOYMENT

The situation that abides when employees, whether by force of circumstances or error, are assigned to jobs that are beneath their level of skill, training, and experience. This imbalance results most commonly when an employee's experience and skills are not realized by the employer, or when there is a shortage of available workers at the lower level, or when there is an oversupply of skilled workers. *See* Personnel Administration.

UNDER PROTEST

The expression used, often in writing and sometimes notarized, by an individual or business that is forced to pay for unsatisfactory merchandise or services, but that is not about to waive rights to a replacement or refund. *See* Business Law.

UNDER REVIEW

Any review of a situation, circumstance, event, program, law, procedure, policy, or the like that has not been finalized and is still being considered or refined. Such matters may be said to be *in limbo*.

UNDER THE COUNTER

Making an illegal payment or bribe, or dealing in an unethical manner.

Undervalued

Anything of worth, whether material objects such as products, documents such as stock certificates, or services whose price is less than the actual value of what has been sold or offered for sale. *See* Overvalued.

Underwriting

The financial support of a venture or monetary indebtedness, usually with the hope of making a profit or obtaining benefits, but sometimes with a high degree of risk. *See* Risk Management.

Unearned Discount

An accounting category that characterizes interest in the form of a discount that has been collected but not yet earned. *See* Accounting.

Unearned Income

An accounting category pinpointing income that has been received in advance of the period to which it is to be allocated. Also, income that has been received without having to work for it directly, as in the case of dividends from securities, real estate holdings, or bonds. *See* Accounting, Investments.

Unemployment Insurance

That class of policy that insures employees against loss of pay when they lose their jobs or are temporarily suspended because of a seasonal or economic business decline. This form of underwriting was intended to provide only short-term income and is governed by federal law that establishes guidelines and minimum standards for business programs. To be eligible for unemployment insurance, persons must have completed a minimum period in a job, have earned a specified amount in wages or other monetary compensation, and have left employment in good faith. *See* Employment, Social Security.

Unfair Competition

Any form of competition to grab a larger share of the market, such as false advertising or making misleading statements about the products of other companies, which is unethical and in some cases illegal. *See* Business Ethics, Competition.

UNFRIENDLY TAKEOVER

The acquisition of a company or business under protest from the former owners, managers, or employees. *See* Takeover.

UNIFORM COMMERCIAL CODE

A comprehensive set of laws to cover legal and ethical sales and merchandising practices in the United States as well as contracts, commercial paper, and bank deposits. *See* Ethics, Merchandising.

UNILATERAL CONTRACT

An agreement in which one party to the contract performs certain specified services in return for commitments specified, but not yet rendered, by the other party. *See* Agreement, Contract.

UNION

A recognized organization of workers who are its members, and whose primary objective is to represent these members in bargaining with employers. *See* Labor Union.

UNION LABEL

An emblem affixed to finished products or materials to identify them as having been manufactured or processed by authorized members of a trade union. The purpose of such labels is to encourage consumers to purchase items made by union labor, as well as to discourage the purchase of cheap foreign products. *See* Competition, Foreign Trade, Labor Union.

UNION SHOP

A place of business where all employees, except those considered to be at the management level, are obliged to belong to a labor union or be in the process of joining a union. The union shop differs from a *closed shop,* where all persons hired must already be union members, or from an *open shop,* where employees need not join a union. *See* Closed Shop, Labor Union, Open Shop.

UNIT CONTROL

In manufacturing, the aggregate of steps needed to assure the production of individual units that meet specifications regarding quality, durability, cost, and consumer demand. *See* Production.

UNITED NATIONS CONFERENCE ON TRADE AND DEVELOPMENT (UNCTAD)

An endeavor on the part of the United Nations and collaborating members to underwrite programs to assist the nations of the world—particularly the undeveloped ones—to improve their economies. *See* Foreign Trade.

UNITED STATES CIVIL SERVICE COMMISSION

Founded in 1883, the CSC was, until 1978, the personnel agency of the federal government, charged with recruiting, examining, training, and promoting employees of federal government agencies without regard to their age, race, religion, sex, political influence, or other factors unrelated to merit. Excluded from its compass were political appointees such as agency directors and their staff members, most federal lawyers and judges, and the employees of the legislative branch of the federal government. In 1978 the Commission was replaced by the Office of Personnel Management and the Merit Systems Protection Board. *See* Government.

UNITED STATES DEPARTMENT OF COMMERCE

Established just after the turn of the century, DOC is a business-oriented agency that promotes economic growth, providing information on international and domestic markets. It also helps to negotiate worldwide trade agreements, provides funding for businesses in depressed regions, compiles demographic statistics, sponsors commercial exploration, and keeps tabs on the weather and global meteorological conditions. *See* Foreign Trade, Free Trade.

UNITED STATES INFORMATION AGENCY

The independent agency of the executive branch of the government that was established to spread information about the United States abroad, to inform the government about foreign opinions of America, to schedule educational and cultural seminars with foreign countries, and to produce and broadcast *The Voice of America*. *See* Foreign Relations.

UNITED STATES MINT

The United States Mint, created by an act of Congress on April 2, 1792, established the U.S. national coinage system. Supervision of the Mint was a function of the Secretary of State, but in 1799 the Mint became an independent agency reporting directly to the President. The Mint was made a statutory bureau of the Treasury Department in 1873, with a director appointed by the President to oversee its operations. The Mint manufactures and ships all U.S. coins for circulation to the Federal Reserve banks and branches, which issue coins to the public and the business community through depository institutions. The Mint also safeguards the Treasury Department's stored gold and silver and other monetary assets. Mint production facilities are located in Philadelphia, PA; Denver, CO; San Francisco, CA; and West Point, NY. In addition, the Mint is responsible for the U.S. Bullion Depository at Fort Knox, KY. Proof coin sets, silver proof coin sets, and uncirculated coin sets are available annually from the Mint. The Mint also produces ongoing series of national and historic medals in honor of outstanding persons or events and sites of special meaning to the American people. Surcharges from sales of commemorative coins support teaching and graduate study of the Constitution of the United States, help fund the creation of war memorials in the United States and abroad, and assist in sponsoring scholarships and Olympic Games. The Mint offers free public tours and operates sales centers at the U.S. Mints in Denver and Philadelphia. Also, the Mint operates a museum and sales center at the Old Mint in San Francisco and a sales center at Union Station in Washington, DC.

UNITIZED LOADING

See Containerization.

UNIT TECHNOLOGY

In manufacturing, the necessity to invest a large amount of capital on labor in proportion to that spent for machinery. *See* Labor Intensive.

UNIVERSAL DESIGN THEORY

The insistent belief that there is one best way to design the sum and substance of an organization and that the ultimate blueprint can be formulated through an appropriate course of investigation and research. *See* Management.

UNLISTED SECURITIES

Those that are not listed on a regular stock exchange. *See* Over-the-counter Stock.

UNLOADING

The sale of products or materials at a loss in order to close out an inventory, often to free up personnel and facilities to introduce new, upgraded replacements, and place them on the market.

UNQUALIFIED OPINION

An opinion by an authority that is given without qualification or reservation, as in the case of a review of a corporate financial statement that is made by a CPA and given a clean bill of health.

UNREALIZED PROFITS

Proceeds that have been made by a company but are still on paper and will not be classified as actual until all payments have been processed and accounting statements have been completed. *See* Profits.

UNSECURED LOAN

A loan that has been approved on the basis of the borrower's credit viability and standing without requiring any collateral. *See* Collateral, Credit Rating.

UNWRITTEN LAWS

The assemblage of English common laws that were widely acknowledged and accepted, but that remained unwritten until the birth of the formal jurisprudence system.

UPGRADING

The term applied to any function that improves on something that already exists, ranging from manufacturing processes and equipment to real estate, management policies, and every facet of human endeavor. *See* Management, Training.

UP OR OUT

A slogan, often unstated, used to describe an employment situation or policy decreeing that executives and managers at certain levels either have to perform well enough within a certain time frame to get a promotion or else quit the company.

UPSCALE HOUSEHOLDS

Those consumer households that are considered by marketers and merchandisers to be well above average in income, education, residential lifestyle, and particularly spending money.

URBANIZATION

The steady and distinguishable movement of populations from rural areas and small towns to larger communities and cities. *See* Centralization.

URBAN RENEWAL

The refurbishment and rehabilitation of dilapidated sectors and neighbor-hoods in the central regions of a city, as well as the sociological refinements that eventually mature as a result of the physical improvements.

USEFUL LIFE

The durability of a product or material and the length of time it can realisti-cally be expected to perform the function for which it was intended. *See* Obsolescence. The expression is also applied in many instances to nonmate-rial entities, such as advertising campaigns, temporary laws, executive privi-leges, and business policies.

USURIOUS LENDING

The unethical, and usually illegal, practice of making loans with interest rates that are in excess of those authorized by law, customarily known as usury. *See* Loan Sharks.

UTTERING

Making use of a forged or counterfeit deed or other document for personal gain, with the express realization that it is fraudulent. *See* Con Artist.

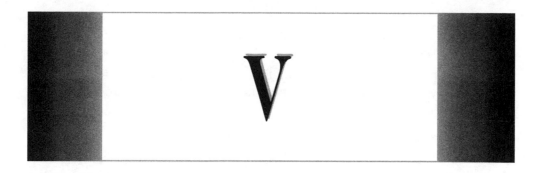

VALID

In business terminology, a statement or declaration whose substance and viewpoint are precise and reliable enough to satisfy the law or the interpretation of the authorities. *See* Business Law.

VALIDATE

To offer proof or confirmation in the case of a document or official paper, such as a passport, that must be substantiated before it can be put to use. *See* Business Law.

VALUABLE CONSIDERATION

The expression used in a contract or other legal document to imply that something other than money, or in addition to money, is binding on those signing the paper. *See* Contract.

VALUE-ADDED TAX

An assessment levied at key stages in the production and distribution cycles of a product, supposedly based on the increasing value of the product. *See* Ad Valorem Taxes.

VALUE ANALYSIS

A predetermined plan of action for studying a business or industrial function to determine the relationships of design, layout, service costs, materials, and manpower, the objectives being to upgrade efficiency, reduce costs, and become more competitive. *See* Business Administration.

VALUE JUDGMENT

An executive decision that has taken into consideration fundamental issues of fairness, morality, justice, and ethics. *See* Management.

VARIABLE ANNUITY

That style of annuity that provides lifetime retirement payments that fluctuate in amounts with the results of investments in a related account portfolio. *See* Annuity.

VARIABLE COSTS

Expenses, costs, and outlays of an enterprise that are not fixed, but vary with the amount of business handled, the volume of products manufactured, or the changes in the capital structure. *See* Accounting, Annual Report.

VENDORS

The individuals or firms from whom goods are purchased, whether directly or through an agent. *See* Distribution, Wholesaling.

VENTURE CAPITAL

Funds invested in new, sometimes speculative, enterprises that as yet have little track record, with the hope of clearing a profit. Also referred to as *risk capital,* this phrase refers basically to funds made available for investment in an enterprise of any size that has been unproven at the time of the transaction. Venture capitalists and venture capital firms lend money to new businesses, but they differ from banks and other lending institutions in that they have a longer-range vision and look to the more distant future to recoup their investment. To be sure, venture capitalists are concerned with many of the same factors that influence bankers in their evaluation of loan applications for business purposes. They want to know the past financial records of the people who will be managing the venture, the amount and intended use of the funds requested, and the objectives and projected earnings of the new organization. But venture capitalists tend to study more meticulously the features of the products, the nature of the services, and the market potential than do commercial bankers.

Venture capital firms are part owners of the organizations in which they invest. They generally hold stock in the company, adding their invested capital to its equity base. For this reason alone, they examine existing or planned enterprises and their components with great care. They invest only in organizations they believe can achieve their goals and generate desirable profits.

Venture capitalists aim at multiplying their investment at least three times in five years or five times in seven years. They may achieve capital gains of 300 to 500 percent on only a limited portion of their total investments, but their intent is to offset by a wide margin those ventures that are losses.

Most venture capital firms are interested only in potential projects that require $500,000 or more for the very simple reason that investigation, evaluation, and administration are costly and do not justify a firm's involvement at a lower financial level. While a firm may receive as many as 1,000 business proposals annually, it will typically investigate less than 10 percent and may actually follow through on only 3 or 4 percent of them and end up with one or two positive investments.

There are numerous types of venture capital firms. The following are the most prevalent:

Insurance Companies. These firms get into venture capital somewhat through the back door, often requiring a portion of equity as a condition of their loans to smaller companies as a hedge against inflation.

Investment Banking Firms. Although investment bankers usually trade in more established securities, they occasionally form investor syndicates for venture proposals.

Manufacturing Companies. A few "Fortune 500" manufacturers become involved with venture capital projects as a means of helping them keep abreast of technological innovations related to the companies being funded. Others look upon investment in smaller companies of this nature as a means of supplementing their R&D programs.

Professionally Managed Pools. Operating much like traditional partnerships, some venture capitalists solicit and pool institutional money for this kind of investment.

Small Business Investment Corporations (SBICs). Licensed by the Small Business Administration, which may provide management assistance as well as venture capital, these corporations are often interested in venture capital opportunities, as well as long-term lending.

Traditional Partnerships. Often established by wealthy families or groups of well-to-do individuals, these partnerships manage portions of their funds by aggressively investing in small companies.

In addition to these venture capital organizations, this field is composed of individual private investors and finders. Finders, who can be either individuals or firms, are often knowledgeable about the capital industry and can help entrepreneurs locate investment money, though they generally are not themselves sources of capital. *See* Commercial Loans, Entrepreneurs, Investments, Risk-Taking, Small Business, Speculator.

VENUE

The geographical legal jurisdiction in which a lawsuit or prosecution is brought for trial. *See* Business Law, Lawsuit.

VERTICAL EXPANSION

The enlargement of a company by adding depth to existing departments and divisions and retaining the same product lines, rather than broadening into new fields. *See* Horizontal Expansion.

VERTICAL INTEGRATION

The manufacturing style followed when a manufacturer or fabricator undertakes all the various stages of production in sequence, from raw materials to finished goods. *See* Horizontal Integration.

VESTED RIGHTS

In personnel administration, the rights and perquisites of an individual that take effect after that person has fulfilled a specified amount of service over a predetermined period of time. The system is particularly useful to organizations, such as public schools, that need extra incentives to ensure that employees stick with their jobs over long periods of time in order to become vested. *See* Benefits, Pensions, Perquisites (perks).

VISIBILITY

When related to products, the characteristic whereby they become more perceptible to the public—and thus more likely to be purchased—through advertising, promotion, publicity, and public relations. *See* Advertising, Retailing.

VITAL STATISTICS

Accumulated and annotated demographic information about births, deaths, and other population-related facts. *See* Demographics.

VOICE-DATA SYSTEM

A voice-mail system that is integrated to form a combination of both data exchange and voice transmission. *See* E-mail, Voice-mail.

VOICE-INPUT COMPUTER SYSTEMS

Technological data-processing equipment that is voice-activated and that can react to certain verbal commands. *See* Computers.

Voice-mail

A telephonic system that enables callers to leave voice messages, or to reply with their own voice messages. In a voice-mail network of the kind that might be active in a large business office, nonsubscribers can call and leave messages for subscribers, even though the nonsubscribers cannot receive or respond to messages in the system. Like *E-mail,* messages can be sent to one or more persons, and at any hour of the day or night. *See* E-mail.

Voice-recognition

A computer accessory that converts speech into identifiable digital signals and thus makes it possible for unskilled computer operators to communicate quickly and easily without having to use a keyboard or other command signals. The voice-activated system also facilitates the use of computers by workers who are using their fingers for other purposes, such as operating machinery on a production line, or by people who are physically handicapped and cannot use their hands. Voice-recognition mechanisms function by recognizing and decoding distinct words, diagnosing different speech waves caused by variations in frequency, pitch, and amplitude, and translating the results in a predetermined format, which is partially dictated by a period of training with the intended operator so the computer can "learn" his or her personal speech peculiarities and characteristics. *See* Communications, Computers.

Volatile Memory

That form of memory, now mostly relegated to older equipment, in which the memory (storage) is destroyed or modified when power is abruptly removed, as in the case of a utility failure. *See* Computer Memory.

Volume Discount

See Quantity Discount.

Voluntary Arbitration

See Labor Unions.

Voluntary Bankruptcy

Bankruptcy that has been initiated by the individual or business seeking relief in a bankruptcy court. *See* Involuntary Bankruptcy.

Voting Rights Act

Legislation enacted by Congress to protect the rights of minority voters, banning poll taxes in federal elections and authorizing the U.S. attorney general to send federal examiners to register minority voters in problem areas. The act also suspended literacy tests in states in which less than 50 percent of the voting-age population had been registered and was quickly instrumental in increasing the voting capabilities of minority groups. *See* Civil Rights.

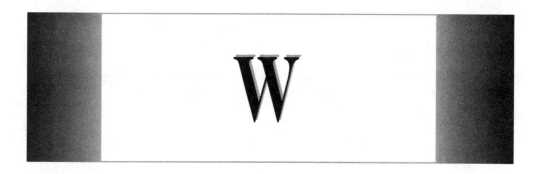

WAGE CEILINGS

Government and labor/management agreements covering the top wages payable to workers in different occupations and labor categories. *See* Wage-hour Laws.

WAGE-HOUR LAWS

Government statutes that specify and regulate minimum wages and maximum work hours for employees. *See* Wage Ceilings.

WAGNER ACT

Federal legislation passed to protect the right of workers to join unions and organize. *See* Labor/Management, Unions.

WAITING PERIOD

The time specified in certain contractual agreements that must pass before the contract will be in effect and, in some cases, before initial payments will be made.

WALKOUT

A strike that takes place after work has already been started. *See* Strike.

WANT AD

See Classified Advertisement.

WARRANT

A type of security issued by a corporation that gives holders the right to purchase a specified number of shares at a specified price and within a limited amount of time. *See* Corporation, Securities.

WASHINGTON SYNDROME

A sociopolitical phenomenon that is often regarded as myopic because it distorts a viewpoint on either grass roots issues or urban affairs.

WASTE CIRCULATION

Advertising in any medium—though traditionally associated with newspapers and magazines—that reaches a region where there is no distribution of the product(s) advertised. *See* Advertising, Media.

WATERED STOCK

Securities issued for assets that are distinctly overvalued. *See* Stocks.

WATER RIGHTS

The prerogative of making use of water bordering on, flowing through, or underneath, an owner's property. *See* Riparian Rights.

WEAK MARKET

An undesirable merchandising situation that is characterized by a greater interest in selling than there is a demand for products and services. *See* Supply and Demand, Retailing.

WHITE-COLLAR CRIME

Particularly related to the business world, this is a field of unlawfulness in which violations are committed by salaried or professional persons, usually with some direct relationship to their work or their intimate knowledge of the assets and operations of their employers. The term first appeared at the end of the 1930s during a meeting of the American Sociological Society, in which its president asserted that the popular view of criminals as lower-class citizens ignored the fact that business history was replete with accounts of "robber barons" and so-called "captains of industry" who violated the law time and again with impunity. Members of the society even went so far as to declare that deliberate violations of the rules of the SEC, the FTC, various environmental agencies, and other regulatory bodies should also be considered white-collar crimes. Among the most widely recognized white-collar crimes are embezzlement, bribery, the laundering of funds, illegal lobbying, consumer frauds, price fixing, income-tax fraud, and computer break-ins. Not until recent years, however, have law enforcement agencies and the courts really acknowledged the billions of dollars lost through this type of crime and started to crack down on white-collar criminals. *See* Business Law.

WHITE KNIGHT

The idiom used to denote a friendly suitor recruited to outmaneuver another, less desirable, bidder and thus encourage a successful company takeover. *See* Raider, Takeover.

WHOLESALE PRICE INDEX

A statistical abstract compiled monthly to compare the price changes of a large group of commodities with the prices for a selected base year. *See* Commodities, Wholesaling.

WHOLESALING

The act of purchasing products and materials from the producer and selling them to retailers and other businesses, which in turn sell them to consumers. The function of the *wholesaler,* also referred to as a *middleman* or *jobber,* is to evaluate much broader regional, seasonal, and consumer needs than those merchants at the retail level are able to do, and to anticipate supplies and demands. Among the functions that come under the responsibility of the typical wholesaler are advertising and sales promotion, warehousing, allocating inventories to locations convenient to retailers, transporting merchandise on request, servicing products and merchandise after they are purchased, extensive bookkeeping, and in many cases providing their retailer customers with financial assistance. *See* Consumers, Marketing, Retailing, Supply and Demand.

WITHOUT RECOURSE

An endorsement on a contract or other document stating that the signer is not liable for eventful changes taking place after the endorsement date, no matter how much they may affect the stipulations in the document. *See* Agreements, Contracts.

WORD-OF-MOUTH ADVERTISING

The oral communication of favorable impressions of products and services in a personal manner, rather than by formal media. *See* Advertising, Promotion.

WORD PROCESSING

The specialized function of a computer that is geared to assist the user in drafting, editing, and storing texts, and when desired preparing them for reproduction on a printer attached to the computer. *See* Computers, Data Processing.

WORKERS' COMPENSATION LAWS

Statutes and regulations, traditionally at the state level, that provide for suitable compensation for employees or their dependents in the event of work-related accidents and illnesses and that also establish the liability of an employer for such casualties, as well as specifying their responsibilities for employee benefits. *See* Employee Compensation.

WORKING CAPITAL

The surplus of current assets over current liabilities, representing therefore capital that is immediately available for the continued operation or expansion of a business. *See* Annual Reports, Assets, Liabilities.

WORK IN PROGRESS

Ongoing projects and assignments that are current, but as yet unfinished, and that have fairly dependable and anticipated due dates. Work that has been held up, placed on hold, or being substantially revised, is not considered to be "in progress."

WORK ORDERS

Written authorizations that specify types of jobs to be done, time required, personnel needs, responsibilities, and other practical details. *See* Personnel Administration.

WORLD BANK

This institution, more properly called *the International Bank for Reconstruction and Development,* was established at the end of World War II to assist European postwar recovery and has today become the single most important lending agency in international development, with operations related to some 160 nations. The responsibilities of the World Bank include loans to member governments, loans to private industries approved and also guaranteed by member governments, and counseling programs to help sustain such widespread programs as the improvement of living standards, the planning of highways and mass transportation, technological assistance for farming and other fields of agriculture, the rejuvenation of fisheries, the development of energy resources, the provision of technological and technical assistance, the enhancement of the environment, and the elimination of debt, particularly in undeveloped nations. *See* Foreign Trade, International Relations.

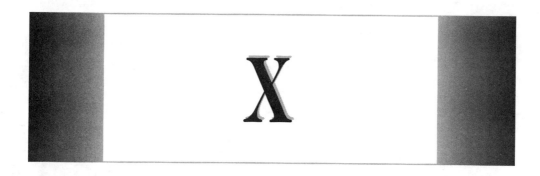

XEROX

Though commonly used as a synonym for *photocopy,* this is a copyrighted trade name. A Xerox machine makes copies through a process of depositing ink on paper by electrostatic attraction. *See* Photocopy.

X-MARK SIGNATURE

A valid and legally acceptable signature when made by persons who cannot write their own names because of illiteracy, injury, or illness. *See* Business Law.

X-RATED

The voluntary or mandatory rating given to any motion picture, videotape, or other film that is pornographic, obscene, or violent and might be viewed unsuspectingly by children or others who would not like to be exposed to it.

X-RAY

Light rays of frequencies that are higher than visible frequencies and are projected from a machine onto a special photographic film, thus producing perceptible images. In the field of business and industry, X-rays are most commonly used not only for physical examinations for employees but in the testing of materials for signs of inner flaws or stress. *See* Research and Development.

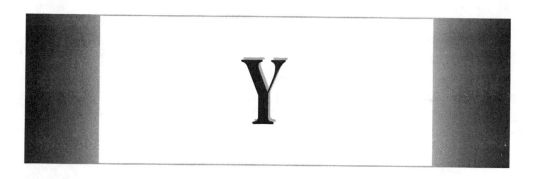

YANKEE BOND MARKET

Securities that are issued in dollars in the United States by foreign governments and corporations. *See* International Trading.

YARDSTICKS

In corporate finance, rates of one business or industry that are used as models and standards for the regulation of rates charged by others in the same, or comparable, fields. *See* Rates.

YEAR-END AUDITING

Chronological audits of a corporation that are conducted at the end of the calendar year, fiscal year, or other desired 12-month accounting period. *See* Audit.

YEAR-END DIVIDEND

A bonus paid to stockholders at the end of the fiscal year, in addition to the regular dividend. *See* Dividend.

YIELD

The return on a security based on its current earnings. *See* Return, Yield to Maturity.

YIELD TO MATURITY

A percentage figure that represents the rate of return on an investment that has been retained until maturity. *See* Maturity, Yield.

YOUTH MARKET

The consumer market composed of individuals under the age of 20, classified by marketers and merchandisers as special targets for certain types of goods and services. *See* Consumers, Target Markets.

Yo-Yo Investments

The jargon applied to volatile securities that fluctuate greatly and are generally high-priced specialty issues. *See* Speculation.

Zero-balance Account

A type of banking practice, now generally prohibited, that combines a demand-deposit account and a savings account for the same customer. *See* Banking.

Zero-base Budgeting

A system of budgetary control in which total expenditures are reassessed each time a new budget is initiated and prepared, using a planning and accounting procedure whose objectives are to reduce unnecessary spending and motivate corporate divisions and departments to anticipate and justify their budgets periodically. The zero-based system has proved to be more effective than the conventional *incremental budgeting* system, which requires computation and entries only for those sums that differ from the preceding year's budget. By contrast, ZBB requires that financial managers begin with no base (a "zero" base), and then must describe and justify the goals and expenditures of each and every program in their annual planning. *See* Accounting, Bookkeeping, Budgets.

Zero Coupon Security

A form of investment security that does not generate periodic interest payments or dividends, but instead is sold at a substantial discount from its face value. At maturity, the monetary gain, for tax purposes, is calculated as the difference between the face value of the security and the original purchase price. *See* Investments, Securities.

Zone Marketing

Also known as *zone pricing,* a pricing structure that divides a designated selling market into sectors, each of which has a different price pattern. *See* Marketing, Pricing.

ZONING

In local government and planning, that field of activity that regulates land use and building within specified zones, stating which areas can be used for business and industry, for example, and which for residences only. Zoning laws also dictate such factors as minimum lot sizes, restrictions on multifamily dwellings, and the exclusion of factories that might cause pollution or otherwise harm the environment. Zoning is traditionally a local prerogative, administered by zoning boards and backed by city or town governments and pertinent judicial bodies. *See* Business Law, Demographics.

Z RULING

Inked "Z" shaped ruled lines placed in a printed law blank when the typing on the form does not fill the space provided. The ruling protects the form from illegal alterations. *See* Business Law, Contracts.

ESSAY SECTION

PART 1: MANAGEMENT

The nature and scope of management and administration in business, industry, and commercial enterprises of all types and sizes, public and private.

Part 2: RESOURCES

An overview of the many resources available to an organization, whether profit or nonprofit, including manpower, capital, communications, research, inventory, production capability, and intangibles such as social acceptability and image.

PART 3: PROCEDURES AND REGULATIONS

The legal agenda and regulatory procedures that formalize the composition and operations of an organization, regardless of its size, areas of function, or financial structure.

PART 4: MONEY

The nature and usages of money and its many related components and derivatives, from hard cash and currency to commodities, liquid assets, securities, and intangibles such as credit ratings, appreciation, and deductibles.

PART 5: COMMUNICATIONS

The broad range of methods, equipment, and state-of-the-art research that make it possible to communicate more quickly and effectively and accurately than ever before in the history of business and industry.

Part 1

MANAGEMENT

The term *management* encompasses the multitudes of theories, policies, arts, skills, proficiencies, and techniques of running a business. Management has been defined in its simplest terms as "the art and science of getting things done through other people." It is, of course, much more complex and sophisticated than can be expressed in a single sentence. Nevertheless, those who would be successful managers could do no better than to bear this simple precept in mind, with emphasis on the absolute necessity of relying on *other people.* In free-enterprise economies, a business is both an autonomous unit in the system, run for profit, and part of an intricate political and legal system. Its administrators are obliged not only to meet wide-ranging consumer needs, but also to function within a network of government restrictions, satisfy the expectations of their employees, maintain a competitive edge, and conserve the good graces of the public at large.

The duties of management incorporate evaluating, planning, administering, communicating, and controlling, both independently and collectively. To neglect one is to neglect all. Each function is tied to the others, often in sequence. For example, no experienced managers would attempt to make plans without first evaluating the areas of need; nor would they try to put the plans into effect without communicating them or determining how they were going to control the outcomes.

FUNDAMENTAL PLANNING

The planning stage embodies those managerial functions that serve as guidelines toward the achievement of goals and objectives and is the most fluid and intangible role of management. It is essential for an effective manager to evaluate planning in three parts: *short range, long range,* and *continuing range.* The more precise the time and duration segments can be established, the easier it will be to blueprint the plans and to relate them to each component of the administration. At the top of the managerial hierarchy, planning focuses on the honing of business strategies, that is, looking at the cutting edges of the resources that will be utilized to attain the stated objectives. Planning also necessitates the establishment of policies—the day-to-day blueprints managers need to satisfy their aspirations. In planning, and in converting plans into policies, perceptive managers always contemplate what resources their organizations have available and how these resources can best be used.

One of the most essential tools in corporate management is the organizational chart, which can be created only after all plans, policies, and strategies have been established. Such charts display the relationship of the many components of the organization as well as signify who reports to whom. It is customary on the organizational chart—or any other graphic outlines—to distinguish between staff departments and line departments, the former being more advisory in nature and the latter more productive. The medical department of a large corporation, for example, is staff-oriented, while the construction department serves a line function.

Managers in large corporations tend to be susceptible to a professional deficiency: confusion over the characteristic multiplicity of levels of management. In practice, the larger the organization, the more levels of management are required, because a manager usually can supervise only a few subordinates. The number of persons one manager can oversee—the span of control—depends on the nature of the work, the training subordinates have received, and the amount of decision making required.

Most top managers have to take into consideration four major components of business in their organizations:

1. *Production.* In essence, this is the evolution of raw materials into goods and services that are to be marketed to consumers, individually and collectively, or to other commercial enterprises. In order to administer production operations as efficiently as possible, managers have to have a working familiarity with two basic specialties: *operations research* and *management science,* both of which utilize sophisticated theoretical and mathematical techniques to analyze the heart and substance of the organization's functions. On the production line itself, another discipline, *production management,* is concerned with the efficient planning and routing components.

2. *Marketing.* The ultimate objective of marketing is the transportation, distribution, and sale of products or services to consumers, each of

whom may vary from the others in needs and desires. Managers are challenged with endless choices and options in determining whom to reach, how, and when. Among the managers' best tools for accomplishing this goal are *advertising* and *promotion*.

3. *Finance.* In this area of administration, managers are most actively concerned with the search for adequate sources of capital and the management of capital already invested. Responsibilities include: estimating the amount of cash the company will need at any given time; evaluating options for trade credit and the acquisition of funds; deciding whether to turn to short-term or long-term credit; estimating the best times to underwrite securities (equity financing); providing complete reports to the SEC and other supervisory agencies; planning present and future expenditures; managing the company's surplus funds; and blueprinting budgets and details thereof. Experienced managers know that they must allocate their available funds for myriad uses on the basis of financial plans, judging that the funds spent will produce sufficient profits to discharge the interest on debt and to earn acceptable profits for the owners on their equity capital. In addition to short- and long-term financing opportunities, managers have to know about other pragmatic alternatives, such as intermediate-term financing when a company may need outside funds for longer periods, typically from one to five years. It may be vital to know whether to go after term loans, generally from commercial banks and life-insurance companies, and whether to lease certain assets rather than purchase them.

4. *Personnel.* The recruiting, selecting, and training of employees is a challenging, continuous process that has to be comprehensively administered and carefully managed in every large organization. In large corporations, personnel management also involves recruiting and training administrators, negotiating with labor unions, being knowledgeable about labor-management contracts that provide for grievance procedures to handle employees' complaints and arbitration, and supervising actions and activities regarding compensation, orientation, training, promotion, transfer, discipline, termination, layoffs, affirmative action, retirement, performance, occupational safety and health, testing, legal references, and outside personnel assistance.

In all these areas of management the element of *control* is a vital factor that too often lacks proper emphasis and scheduled follow-up programs. An effective, competent, and productive management entity is not possible without a unified system of controls for keeping all layers of administration and supervision informed as to the exact goals that are defined and how well the company is meeting its commitments. As top managers well know, flexibility is a treasure that must be consistently and continuously preserved, since no plans—even the best of them—are ever expedited exactly as conceived. It would require more than a genius to forecast and anticipate all the problems that could arise, since many of them originate far outside the corporate borders, stemming from unexpected moves made by labor unions, competitors, government regulatory agencies, changing business climates, politics, and even public opinion. Realistically, however, bright and resourceful control procedures will usually establish clear-cut standards of performance that can envision changing conditions before they become critical and then make the necessary adjustments or corrections.

MANAGEMENT BY OBJECTIVES

The essential purpose of the administrative concept of what is popularly called *MBO* is not merely to establish goals at the top level and feed them down through the ranks of managers and department heads and others in supervisory positions. Rather, it is to evolve a coordinated, participative business environment that includes all members of the organization concerned, from top administrators to middle managers, supervisors, and employees at every level, both as individuals and as members of cohesive working teams. In most instances, management by objectives also encompasses taking an overview of personnel who are outside the organization, but whose outlooks, routines, and work directly affect the fortunes of the company. These affiliates might include, for example, suppliers, agents, attorneys, independent salespersons, accountants, part-time workers, advertising executives, labor representatives, government officials, security guards, and in some cases people whose impact on the company might be only social or political.

Communicating objectives and policies, and to a certain extent strategies, to this broad audience may not necessarily guarantee management success, but the procedure does ensure that the concerns and questions of all who have enough stake in the company to raise their voices can be heard, and, when appropriate, their concerns acted upon. It is important in any MBO program that each and every objective be defined and stated as concisely as possible and incorporated into the formulation of realistic administrative plans. It is not enough, for example, for top management to declare that "state-of-the-art technology is being applied to the design and production of a new product line to outpace the competition." Such high-sounding phraseology must inform those to whom it is addressed about (1) the field of technology involved, (2) the specific product line affected, (3) the reason why products will be improved, and (4) the identity of the competition.

Furthermore, it is essential that goals and objectives be recognized in chronological terms, to answer the questions that will inevitably arise: *When* will a procedure begin? *How long* will it take? *Where* will it take place? *Who* will be affected? When the time segments fit into place, everyone concerned is more likely to move an important project along than if the dates are unclear, or, worse yet, that it seems as though management really has not come close to grips with the issues. The manager who plans ahead and whose timetables are realistic is on the right MBO track.

One other vital component of management by objectives is known as *feedback.* It is divided into a number of related classifications, most important: *inquiry feedback,* random questions that might come from various sources, whether at the management level or down the line, regarding elements of a management program that are unclear; *contradictory feedback,* questioning or even objecting to a program or parts of it; *performance feedback,* reports on the benefits and disadvantages of a program that has been in operation long enough for such judgments; and *productive feedback,* worthwhile suggestions, at almost any stage of operation, for improving or implementing a program that is in effect.

Management by objectives and all other operations and functions in management stand the best chance of present and future success when they are monitored by a formal *management control system (MCS).* Such a system may not be particularly necessary in a small- or medium-sized family-owned business, or even in a large business whose administration is autocratic and authoritarian. However, it is essential in any organization that allocates key duties and responsibilities to a number of managers and to a lesser degree to supervisors and employees down the line. Since the corporate goals will be adhered to, or changed for better or worse by the actions of these individuals, it is important to coordinate management strategies and the MCS systems established to control them.

KEY TOPICS TO REFER TO
THAT RELATE TO MANAGEMENT

accounting

advertising

affiliate

American Management
   Association

annual report

antitrust acts

assets

auditor

automation

balance sheet

bankruptcy

bar chart

Better Business Bureau

bill of sale

board of directors

bond

bond ratings

bookkeeping

breach of contract

broker

budget

bureaucracy

business administration

business climate

business communication

business council

business cycle

business index

business plan

business statistics

byproduct accounting (under
   accounting)

capability profile

capacity planning

capital

capital asset

capital gain

capital intensive

capitalism

career management

cause-and-effect evaluation

centralization

certificate of incorporation

chapter 11

chief administrative officer

chief financial officer

city manager

closed corporation

code of professional ethics

collective bargaining

common stock

competitive advantage

controlled corporation

controlling interest

cooperative venture

co-optation

corporate image

corporate planning

corporation

critical-path method
decentralization
decision theory
director
diversification
economic planning
economics
environmental economics
equity
ergonomics
ethics
executive compensation
executive orders
factory structure
finance
financial accounting
financial planner
financial risk
financial statement
fiscal policies
foundations
franchise
free trade
Gallagher's Principle
goal setting
government
heuristic
holding company
horizontal expansion
horizontal merger
human factors engineering
human rights
ideology
image

image building
incentive plan
incorporation
Index of Leading Economic
    Indicators
inductive method
industrial engineering
industrial espionage
industrial management
industrial psychology
industrial relations
intangible asset
internal control
inventory
inventory control
inventory management
investment
investment trust
iteration
job enrichment
joint agreement
joint venture
key personnel
labor agreement
Labor Management Relations
    Act
leadership
leadership training
leverage
liberalism
long-range planning
majority stockholders
management
management accounting

queue time
quota
referendum
Renaissance
reorganization
reorientation
research and development
   (R&D)
reverse takeover
reward strategy
risk
risk analysis
risk management
robotics
role discernment
role playing
sales management
scalar theory
S corporation
simulation models
small business
Socialism
social psychology
sole proprietorship
sovereignty
stewardship
stock

stock option plan
strategic planning
subsidiary
subsidy
takeover
task group
task management
tax accounting
taxation management
technology
tender offer
Theory X
think tank
time-and-motion studies
totalitarianism
training program
T team
turnaround
tycoon
uncertainty principle
undercapitalized
value analysis
venture capital
vertical expansion
vertical integration
white knight

See also the following supplements in the Appendix and elsewhere:

Part 2

RESOURCES

Whether an organization has been established as a small enterprise or as a corporation in which large numbers of people are involved so that labor and capital are combined in a single venture, the fate of the company is going to be determined by the nature and extent of the *resources*. The following resources, not necessarily in order of priority or importance, are the most universal essentials that will make the difference between success and failure, prosperity and poverty, for any business venture, large or small:

Heritage. Few organizations of any kind are likely to be fortunate enough to start off with any meaningful birthright or lineage of their own. But most can form associations with long-standing cultures in their fields of endeavor, some can tie in with local lineage, and a few can acquire affiliates whose roots go back a substantial distance in time. One of the pertinent new fields of study in the business world is *industrial archaeology,* which uses field work, supplemented by historical records, to survey the remains of industries during the past two centuries. Since the beginning of the 1970s, this new discipline has investigated the archaeology and origins of many major industries, including mining, metals, natural energy sources, manufacturing, transportation, construction, public utilities, communications, travel and recreation, foods, beverages, housing, public works, and agriculture. Faced with the destruction and disappearance of many industrial resources and production facilities, industrial archaeologists are attempting to salvage both artifacts and information that will document the trend of technology and help new businesses to establish themselves more solidly on the resources and experience of the past.

Leadership. While dominance by one or more individuals is not always integral to the formula for achievement and eventual fulfillment of goals, persevering leadership is a fountainhead that can sustain a company through hard, lean, and disruptive times. As one of the most important, yet often overlooked, resources, leadership often makes the difference between success and failure in the formation and continuation of new businesses.

403

Managerial Depth. In addition to top leaders, an organization's resources must include the availability of line, staff, and middle managers to conduct day-to-day operations or function in specialized departments and divisions. Industrial management covers not only manufacturing and production, but most of the key resources in a business, such as distribution, marketing, finance, personnel, advertising, merchandising, and research. As a resource, management serves an organization better when it includes *scientific management,* the well-founded professional concept that holds that "observation, measurement, classification, and other principles should be applied to all administrative problems, that the methods by which work was accomplished should be determined by management through the same kind of analysis, and that employees should be recruited, selected, indoctrinated, and assigned duties and responsibilities through predetermined scientific procedures." It was, in fact, through just such applications that several important management resources were perfected in recent years, including time-and-motion studies, personnel management, job identification, and quality control. Scientific management also helped to pioneer the use of *mathematical models* as a resource for analyzing repetitive problems om industrial management.

Manpower. As an indispensable resource, labor requirements are both quantitative and qualitative, requiring a proper mixture of numbers and skills. The above-mentioned concept of scientific management has had a beneficial impact on manpower, not only in the use of time-and-motion studies, but in work-efficiency control and the division of labor. The more effective use of manpower traces its evolution to the creation and development of such disciplines as industrial psychology, psychological measurement, and workplace statistics, and has been greatly enhanced by the conception of objective standards for measuring the quality and quantity of work and the level of supervision.

Manpower resources have been considerably improved since the middle of the twentieth century through the administration of *incentive systems,* which supplement wages and salaries, often by rewarding employees for improving the quality of their work or expediting their output. It has thus become common practice, for example, to disburse bonuses to workers who effect ways to save time in the performance of a task without reducing the caliber of the resultant product or function.

Social Acceptability. A little-understood and often overlooked resource is the advantage to be gained by an organization when its management recognizes the social and cultural environments and the company's many responsibilities and relationships relating to them. This area of resource management has been considerably enhanced by the evolution of *industrial relations,* which fundamentally concerns the relationships between employers and employees, but which carries over into some aspects of public relations in the building of a company's image. This kind of joint social acceptability can be traced to the endeavors of such specialists as human relations experts, psychologists, industrial engineers, and labor-relations professionals. Industrial relations plays a major role today in such areas of social acceptability as enhancing the outside recruitment of employees; classifying the status and meaning of jobs, assignments, and occupational groups; improving team efforts on the job; encouraging interior training programs and exterior adult education courses; and negotiating with trade unions. One significant spin-off has been the conception of industrial arts programs, offered at many scholastic levels, that help students to a better understanding of how mechanisms work, what materials are used in familiar commercial products, and the kinds of tools and production implements that are used in their making. Many such programs are sponsored by, or supplemented by, local industries, marketers, manufacturers, and processors and result in seminars and craft workshops that cover subjects such as mechanical drawing, metalworking, textiles, photography, and woodworking.

Capital.   Few organizations can endure for long, let alone achieve their goals, without knowing and utilizing financial resources that are available, whether internal or external, domestic or foreign. *Capital* refers to all productive assets, or the stock of goods and monies from which further goods and money are produced. In modern ideology, capital encompasses land and labor, including such intangibles as skills and education—called human capital—as well as buildings, machinery and tools, stores of raw materials and unsold finished merchandise, and even the various means of transportation. Distinctions are made between *circulating* capital, such as raw materials and parts, and *fixed* capital, such as machinery or production facilities. In financial and accounting nomenclature, capital resources refer to money invested in productive assets and therefore yielding income. As a resource, capital also refers to that part of a company's net worth that represents claims on assets.

Authority.   Almost every organization, but particularly those that are substantial in size and influence, has a wellspring of forces that can be favorably brought to bear in the matter of influencing communities and the individuals therein, for the end good of all concerned. These are those areas of authority and erudition that can activate productive company/community projects. Since people have a penchant for wanting to join in mutually beneficial activities, most organizations have plenty of internal programs that can be extended to the community at large. In this field of activity, industrial psychology also plays a part, since one of its major objectives is to help improve employee morale and working conditions and in so doing earn the respect of the community and have a more authoritarian voice in local affairs.

Legal Clout. Legal resources depend strongly on the basic structure of the organization. The law treats a corporation, for example, as a "person" entitled to enter into contracts, to sue, and to be sued. Neither the stockholders nor the employees of the corporation, however, can be held personally responsible for the acts of the corporation as a legal entity. Thus, it could be said that a corporation lacks the pass-along resource of being able to share debts and other obligations with those who own it and/or work for it. By contrast, a partnership as an entity enjoys the privilege—a resource—of sharing the burdens with the principals who manage it. See also the entry on *Business Law* on page 42 in the alphabetical dictionary listings.

Image. The very size and economic power of some industrial agglomerations has long been a controversial topic, since many of them hire thousands of employees and control billions of dollars in assets. The rapid growth of some organizations has bestowed upon their managers considerable power in shaping a region's economic policy, affecting the lifestyles of its citizens, and influencing its political trend. So it is no surprise that the corporate image is tied in with the organization's resources and its resourcefulness. These factors fall into place as a composite picture of the organization's managers' public policy, corporate accountability, and, in general, the role of business in society. In the matter of image, the organization's resources that most come into play are public relations, public affairs, industrial relations, and employee relations.

Communication Networks. These resources vary all the way from interpersonal communication, language and verbal behavior, and the anthropological aspects of communication in society to such specialized fields as cybernetics, information theory, global languages, psycho linguistics, radio and television broadcasting, motion pictures, graphics, and telecommunications. This subject area is explored in depth in the chapter on *Communications,* which starts on page 431.

Competitive Endurance. As a usable resource, the capability and clout of an organization to endure and continue in a competitive spectrum depends on its legal structure. Proprietorships and partnerships, for example, exist only as long as their owners are alive and as long as they continue the proprietorships or partnerships. By contrast, a corporation exists independently of its individual stockholders and is likely to be competing in its particular market for years to come. In all cases, the most critical competitive resource is likely to be a nonphysical one: the *planning* of products, materials, or services, and the marketing strategies used to attract consumers.

Latitude for Growth. Organizations may possess growth resources internally, externally, or both, the expansion urge prompted by the need for securing greater economies of scale, more efficient production facilities, or the need to become more competitive. Or they may want to dominate or monopolize certain markets. One of the most common exterior resources is the merger, which may take either of the following forms: (1) *Horizontal,* in which a company seeks to extend its share of the market by acquiring another firm in the same industry. Such mergers do not necessarily involve smaller companies trying to combine their resources or larger companies absorbing smaller companies to acquire specialized market niches or new technologies. (2) *Vertical,* in which a company moves up or down, say in a manufacturing business, acquiring other firms engaged in producing raw materials or in selling to the final consumer. Some mergers exemplify financial resources, motivated more than anything else by tax considerations and what are known as *asset plays,* which result in the immediate cashing in of an acquired firm's hidden assets in order to raise capital. Yet another maneuver for utilizing a growth resource is the *leveraged buyout,* the purchase of assets or stock of another company in which the purchaser uses a significant amount of debt and very little capital to negotiate the acquisition.

Control Imperatives. A striking characteristic of the modern corporation is that those who own it, the stockholders, have little say in how it is run. In most large corporations, effective control is in the hands of management, which may often select or change the board of directors as it sees fit. In the past, this control has been little challenged by individual stockholders. In recent years, however, a new kind of stockholder has emerged: the large financial institution that holds stock for its clients. So management's control resources may not be as broad or effective as in earlier times.

Property. As a resource, property is literally anything that can be possessed and disposed of in a practical manner. But in an organizational sense, property is the aggregate of legal rights of individuals with respect to objects and obligations owed to them by others, and which may be either private or public, real or personal. Real property comprises land, buildings that may be on the land, and mineral rights under the land. When a company purchases an office, that entity includes, as real property, not only the building, but the land and such facilities as are permanently attached to the buildings, such as walkways, plumbing, appliances, and fitted shelves and cabinets. Since mineral and timber rights may or may not be resources included with the land, corporate owners have to evaluate the options open to them.

Regulatory Durability. As organizations grew in size and earnings many Americans became concerned that they were becoming too powerful, a trend reflected in the passing of regulatory legislation covering such areas as anti-trust, conspiracy, restraint of trade, monopoly, environmental compatibility, product safety, unfair competition; and civil rights. More and more, the nature and extent of company resources have had to be brought to bear to counter potential charges of ineptitude or outright misconduct. Thus, to fend off claims that it was a monopoly, a company had to prove that it was engaging in open competition; to avoid pollution assertions, that its products were biodegradable; or to anticipate charges of bias, that its percentage of minority employees was well above the legal mandate. Today, each claim, or anticipated indictment, has to be balanced off by resources to disprove the allegations.

Geographical Expansiveness. Large corporations have played an important role not only in their national economies but also in the expansion of world trade and global interdependencies. In the process they have brought economic growth to large parts of the world and made possible unprecedented levels of prosperity and human welfare. But growth has been accompanied by criticism, as some companies exploit disadvantaged countries in their rush to acquire labor and commodity resources at bargain prices. This has led to a new form of international regulation of multinational corporations, which will eventually result in shortsighted management being replaced by administrators who have a keener respect for international resources—whether materials, products, or labor. Multinational corporations will face new challenges to their operational autonomy, investment security, and profitability as they evolve and adapt to meet new societal expectations. The world has also seen the emergence of global agencies and public-interest groups that monitor the performance of multinational corporations to ensure that their activities benefit all nations and parties that are involved.

KEY TOPICS TO REFER TO
THAT RELATE TO RESOURCES

adult education

arbitration

automation

binary number

blanket policy

board of trade

broker

business education

business index

business machines

capital depreciation

capital gains

capital goods

career management

cash

cash flow

cash reserves

casual labor

Certified Public Accountant

cooperative education

data

data processing

demographics

distribution

durable goods

economics

employee assistance program (EAP)

employee benefits

employee relations

environment

environmental economics

environmental health

ergonomics

European Community

extended coverage

featherbedding

focus group

foundation

franchise

fringe benefits

geothermal energy

group insurance

head hunter

health insurance

health maintenance organizations (HMOs)

holding company

homestead law

human factors engineering

no-fault insurance
observational research
observed depreciation
on-the-job training
operations research
opinion leaders
opinion polls
oral history
organizational climate
Organization of American
   States (OAS)
orientation
pace setters
pension
perceptual theory
performance evaluation
personnel administration
pilot plant
planned obsolescence
political science
population dynamics
population studies
price index
price supports
problem solving
process control
production
production control
profession
profile evaluation
profit sharing
programmed learning
public interest
public utility
quality control

reclamation
recruitment
research and development
   (R&D)
retailing
reward strategy
robotics
role discernment
role playing
silicones
skilled labor
small business
social sciences
specialist
spreadsheets
statistics
strike
subsidy
target consumers
tax accounting
teaching machines
technical education
technology
telecommunications
teleconferencing
telemarketing
telemetry
Temporary Personnel Service
term insurance
Theory X
think tank
tidal energy
time sharing
title insurance
trade association

tradeoff

trade surplus

trading stamp

training program

transducer

transportation

trickle-down economics

T team

underemployment

unemployment insurance

United States Civil Service
    Commission

upgrading

urban renewal

variable annuity

venture capital

vertical expansion

vertical integration

vested rights

voice recognition

wholesaling

work in progress

working capital

youth market

Refer also to the following supplements in the Appendix and elsewhere:

- Branches of Government of the United States (pages 451–452)
- Demographics (page 98)
- Major Business Schools in the United States (pages 444–446)
- Postal Services Abbreviations (pages 462–465)

Part 3

PROCEDURES AND REGULATIONS

In business and industry, and indeed in any kind of commercial enterprise, there are two basic procedures that must be recognized and taken into account in all of the organization's functions and operations and in management's dealing with personnel and other internal affairs and outside relationships with suppliers, consumers, and the general public. These are *legal procedures* and *government regulatory procedures.*

LEGAL PROCEDURES

Legal procedures embody the methods, individually and collectively, used in enforcing legal rights, litigation, and redress. These include rules for initiating a lawsuit, conducting a trial, and appealing to a higher court and also the processes whereby one party secures satisfaction or compensation from one or more other parties. Legal procedure in the United States has its origins in the common law of the United Kingdom, as well as in general equity law. Nations using this legal base today, which include the United States, Canada, and England, are referred to as *common-law countries* and have greatly modified and modernized the original statutes over the years.

When legal action is planned, it is customary for a lawsuit to be initiated by the attorney for the party bringing suit, known as the *plaintiff,* who prepares a *summons,* a notice to the party against whom the suit is brought, known as the *defendant,* that he or she is being sued. This agenda also specifies the time and place of the hearing and the nature of the claims being made. Also prepared at this time is a *complaint,* a brief statement of the essentials of the plaintiff's case that is made under oath before a court official who is empowered to charge people with offenses. Both the summons and the complaint are delivered to the defendant in person by a court marshal, whose action is called *servicing a process,* after which a court of law assumes further jurisdiction. If the defendant, or an authorized and acceptable representative, fails or declines to appear for the scheduled trial proceedings, the court may issue a dissenting decision, a *judgment by default*.

Under normal processing, the defendant—whether an individual or an organization— will forward the complaint to an attorney, who will then prepare the *answer,* a statement addressed to the plaintiff that generally disputes the charges made in the complaint. The plaintiff has the option of formulating a reply if new material has been introduced by the defendant. Pretrial rules allow plaintiffs and defendants to acquire more information about the case whenever new questions have been raised. The exchange of the above complaint, answer, and reply constitute what is known as the *pleading,* whose purpose is to inform each party of the concerns in the approaching trial and confine the case to the basic issues in contention.

COURTROOM PROCEEDINGS

Following the pleading, either party may request a trial by jury, but will often prefer to let the judge be the jury as well, since the case is likely to proceed more quickly. The following steps are typical of court procedure in a trial, whether with or without a jury: Both the plaintiff's and the defendant's attorneys present opening statements, which may often be waived, followed by broad outlines of what they intend to prove. The attorney for the plaintiff then presents evidence, usually supported through the direct questioning of witnesses under oath. After each witness is examined, the attorney for the defendant may cross-examine the individual to test the witness's exactness and honesty. Once this procedure has been completed, the defendant is given an opportunity to present witnesses, who are also subject to cross-examination by the plaintiff's attorney. If improper questions are asked or any witness seems to be intimidated, the opposing attorney may object, leaving it up to the judge to determine whether the objection is valid. After all evidence has been presented, the attorneys make their closing arguments in favor of their clients. If the trial is by jury, the judge then instructs the jury concerning the laws that apply in the case, and it is then up to the jury to consider all legitimate evidence and reach a verdict. The losing party may request a new trial, an appeal that can be granted if the judge believes that an error of law occurred in the original trial or if any newly discovered evidence is presented. If an appeal proves to be in order, the party effecting the appeal is called the appellant, and the opposing party the appellee or respondent. Appellate courts have no juries and are presided over by a panel of judges, usually at least three. Both parties to an appeal submit written arguments in the form of briefs. The hearing consists of oral debates, after which the court reaches a decision on the appeal, and one of the judges prepares an opinion, stating the facts of the case, the legal issues, how the case was decided, and why.

Most civil cases of the type that are frequent in the business world are brought to claim monetary damages. If the case favors the plaintiff, the court enters a judgment entitling the collection of a sum of money from the defendant. If the defendant refuses to pay, however, the plaintiff must take independent action to locate assets belonging to the defendant and call in a sheriff to seize the money or property in an execution on the judgment. If the defendant has no assets, as is often the fact of the matter in business situations, the legal procedures will all have been for naught.

GOVERNMENT REGULATORY PROCEDURES

Like the proverbial octopus, government regulatory procedures in the United States—not to mention most foreign nations as well—seem to be all tentacles without much vision or brain. Generically, these regulatory programs, individually and collectively, encompass almost any public practice that imposes constraints on individuals, associations, private or public companies, or other parties and organizations, but most especially business, commercial, and industrial entities. As a pattern of intervention, it is distinguished from taxation, subsidy, and judgment in the achievement of public goals, whether protecting citizens from hazards, shielding consumers from unfair sales practices, or assuring minorities that they have equal rights. Regulatory procedures camouflage the intensity of bureaucratic interest by giving the impression that most business decisions about compliance and conformity are left to the discretion of management. In practice, however, management is generally the underdog in a struggle that only one side can win.

Although regulations and mandates place their burdens on all industries and spheres of economic and commercial activity, administered by state, county, municipal, and other jurisdictions as well as the federal government, which alone has more than 50 regulatory agencies, a number of industries have borne special brunt in the United States. These include agriculture, banking, broadcasting, energy, insurance, securities, telecommunications, and transportation. In addition, within the various industries, certain specific classes of functions and operations have come under heavy regulatory scrutiny.

These include, for example, environmental affairs, pollution, wages and hours, labor relations, discrimination, on-the-job safety, product purity, competitive trade practices, and training.

Although there is a great diversity from state to state and region to region, the various levels of regulatory action tend to be specialized. State governments, for example, are inclined to zero in on such matters as insurance, transportation, and health services, while municipalities are likely to concern themselves with monitor such operations as water supply, sanitation, building and construction, and zoning. Regulation—whether federal, state, or local—has been a controversial subject in business and industry ever since the eighteenth century when the Industrial Revolution motivated governments in Europe to share a piece of the pie by attempting to control manufacturing, distribution, and shipping to achieve a favorable balance of trade and bolster the regulating nation's wealth. Following this era, there was a period of *laissez-faire* during the nineteenth century when many economists predominated in urging their governments to expand their international markets through free trade. However, regulations began creeping in again and had become greatly expanded by the twentieth century. The rational argument held that, while regulatory procedures were seldom welcome, they were necessary to a country's overall economy in certain specific categories. The major instances of these were to cover situations where:

- monopolies were stifling competition;
- excessive costs and/or spotty information were inhibiting consumers from making intelligent choices in their purchases;
- there were increasing instances of the sale of hazardous products;
- accident and health problems were surfacing;
- manufacturing or processing practices were causing pollution;
- operating nuisances were affecting neighboring businesses or the community.

Among the most active regulatory bodies have been the Interstate Commerce Commission (ICC), Consumer Product Safety Commission, Federal Communications Commission (FCC), Federal Reserve Board, Federal Trade Commission (FTC), Food and Drug Administration (FDA), Occupational Safety and Health Administration (OSHA), Department of Labor, National Highway Safety Administration, Environmental Protection Agency (EPA), and the Department of Transportation.

At the beginning of the twentieth century, regulatory procedures started to become an increasingly conspicuous, if not welcome, part of big business. Several major restrictive pieces of legislation were prompted by the Progressive Movement that characterized the period from 1900 to World War I, including pure food and drug laws, the Hepburn Act, aimed at governing the burgeoning railroads, the Federal Reserve Act, and several laws focused on anti-trust practices, monopolies, and trade. Further regulations were born during the Depression, which was described as a period when there was a great mistrust of capitalism in general and corporations in particular. A seeming surge of restrictions bridled institutions that had anything to do with capital and financial matters, such as banks, brokerage houses, stock exchanges, and commercial real estate agencies. Companion legislation attempted to shore up those industries that suffered most from the Depression, including agriculture, communications, travel agencies, energy resources, utilities, and transportation. The precarious balance of labor and unemployment received special attention through such legislation as the National Labor Relations Act, or the Wagner Act, at which time labor unions were guaranteed the right to collective bargaining.

Another flood of regulations washed across America as a kind of dam breaking by the liberal activism of the 1960s and 1970s, influenced by the outgrowth of citizen's organizations and consumer groups disgusted with shoddy products, overpricing, slow service, or misleading advertising. The regulatory procedures that resulted, however, were often directed as much at social objectives as at economic reform. During this period, for example, regulatory programs centered mainly on four categories areas of social concern:

1. *Consumer protection* regarding unfair trade practices, truth-in-lending, automobile hazards, product safety, price controls, and prescription drug safety.

2. *Environmental protection,* including the avoidance of pollution, pesticide safety, ecological preservation, noise control, and the recognition of toxic substances.

3. *Safety in the workplace,* especially through the Occupational Safety and Health Act of 1970 and a separate measure protecting miners.

4. *Civil rights,* and measures for dealing with discrimination in employment and access for the handicapped.

Business and industry leaders have discovered, as a result of these trends, that social regulation has become so broad and touches on so many intangibles that it is difficult to manage in the present or anticipate for the future. The Environmental Protection Agency is a prime example because of its enormous growth, its complement of some 12,000 employees, and its multibillion-dollar budget. Moreover, its mandates—unlike those for specific industries or zones of operation—are sprawling and often elusive. "Compliance with its requirements was estimated to cost billions of dollars in capital expenditures alone" reported one economist. "Partly because the environmental and the workplace-safety regulatory programs involve huge administrative tasks, such as inspecting tens of thousands of places of business, the states were given a large role in their implementation."

DEREGULATION

Since the early 1980s, the current has trended in the other direction, toward deregulation, reflecting the judgment of numerous economists that many regulations are unnecessary, excessively expensive, and even a hazard to economic health. However, because deregulation has caused some financial disasters, as in the case of banking and lax supervision of the ill-fated savings and loan industry in the early 1990s, the trend was at least temporarily interrupted. If history is any judge, government regulation and the procedures relating to it will continue its roller-coaster pattern for decades to come, affecting some industries adversely and others beneficially with each forward and backward surge.

Deregulation procedures have flourished most noticeably in industries where regulation has proven to favor certain businesses more than others, cause severe economic problems, and, in many cases, actually stifle competition. Because of evolving situations that were detrimental to free enterprise, the government was compelled to relax certain controls and/or modify legislation in a number of areas of the economy, including the trading of securities, real estate, banking, telecommunications, petroleum, railroads, trucking, and air transportation. In general, deregulation has had a beneficial effect in many ways, such as keeping the lid on prices, promoting innovation in planning and producing, and improving administrative efficiency.

KEY TOPICS TO REFER TO
THAT RELATE TO PROCEDURES
AND REGULATIONS

American Civil Liberties Union
bait and switch
Better Business Bureau
bill of lading
binder
blackmail
boycott
breach of contract
bribery
brief
business law
cease-and-desist order
civil action
civil law
civil rights
class action
Clean Air Act
Commission on Civil Rights
constitutional right
Consumer Credit Protection
    Act
Consumer Product Safety Act
Consumer Product Safety
Commission
consumer protection

conveyance
court of appeals
discrimination
double jeopardy
easement
embezzlement
eminent domain
Environmental Protection
    Agency
equal employment
Equal Employment
    Opportunity Committee
Equal Rights Amendment
estate
extradition
extra territoriality
Fair Labor Standards Act
fair market price
fair trade agreement
Federal Communications
    Commission (FCC)
Federal Housing Authority
    (FHA)
Federal Trade Commission
    (FTC)

product liability
Product Safety Commission (PSC)
proxy
proxy dispute
public domain
public sector
pyramid
right of rescission
right of survivorship
right-to-work laws
riparian rights
risk
risk analysis
risk management
royalties
S corporation
Securities Exchange Act
Securities Exchange Commission (SEC)
Senate of the United States
sexual harassment
Small Business Administration (SBA)
small claims court
Social Security
Social Security Administration
statute of limitations
sublease
tacit agreement
Taft-Hartley Act
tax evasion
tax haven
Tax Reform Act
tax shelter

tenants in common
tender offer
terms of trade
territorial waters
third party
title
title insurance
trade association
Treasury Department of the United States
trust
trustee
trust fund
truth-in-lending legislation
under protest
unfair competition
Uniform Commercial Code
unilateral contract
union label
union shop
United States Department of Commerce
usurious lending
uttering
venue
vested rights
Voting Rights Act
wage ceiling
wage-hour laws
Wagner Act
waiting period
walkout
water rights
white-collar crime
without recourse

Refer also to the following supplements in the Appendix and elsewhere:

Part 4

MONEY

Money has been defined as "an abstract unit of account in terms of which the value of goods, services, and obligations can be measured. By extension, the term may designate anything that is generally accepted as a means of payment."

Without doubt, money is one of the oldest and most important inventions of the civilized world. Without it, the very concept of economics, based on labor and the exchange of goods and services—whether international, national, regional, or local—would be totally without meaning. Although we all have an image of money when the word is mentioned, it cannot be depicted accurately as a specific article, since it has worn the widest conceivable variety of disguises, from gold and silver coins to shells, ivory tusks, furs, beads, teeth, and polished sticks. The only way money can be accurately described—and that in abstract fashion—is by the functions it serves as a vehicle of interchange and a touchstone of merit.

The very concepts of economics and the business, commercial, and industrial activities related to this discipline are concerned primarily with the *making* and *spending* of money, no matter in what form money may exist. In substance, money makes possible its transformation into *capital,* which refers to all productive assets or the goods and monies from which further goods and monies are manifested. Classical economists have defined capital, in this sense, as "the produced means of production," and have thus isolated it categorically from the other two yields of production: labor, which has been referred to as "human capital," and property. In financial terms, money is equated with capital, since the latter yields income, that is, money. Phrased a bit differently, accountants view capital as that part of a business enterprise whose net worth represents claims on assets—or money in the bank. While it can properly be said that assets are not money until they are cashed in, it can also be said that money is not money until it is actually used, since before that time it could be reduced by deflation, depleted by taxation, or even terminated by such exigencies as fraud or a bank failure.

423

In the world of modern American business, money would seem relatively easy to describe to, say, a visitor from outer space, as a medium of exchange used to make it easy to exchange things and thus aoid having to use the primitive acquisition method of bartering. Another purpose of money is to serve as a measure of worth—a very important function—so that specific values can be calculated in the abstract. The third role of money is to serve as a store of wealth without having to pay transactions costs, as would be the case in storing capital in the form of stocks or bonds. Whenever wealth is easily converted into cash, it is said to be *liquid.*

The face value of money may not always be the actual value, however, because it is not stable. People who, for example, horde large amounts of cash in their homes or elsewhere will someday realize that inflation has greatly reduced the face value of that money over the years of storage. The same is true of a monetary loan, which loses value in that the original amount is depleted by the interest that has to be paid. Money can be classified into three distinct categories:

1. *Credit (or fiat) money,* which does not have value as a commodity equal to its face value, but is established by the country of its origin. United States money is of this type.

2. *Commodity money,* which has a value as a commodity, such as gold or silver, equal to its value as money. Thus, a coin minted in a precious metal is worth its weight in that metal.

3. *Paper money* that has an actual face value because it is backed by a commodity and is freely convertible.

No matter what type of money is commonly in use in the United States, or in any nation, its practical value hinges on the fact that the currency must be promptly and readily acceptable by other consumers and everyone in trade or commerce. The same is true of all the other commonplace and easily convertible monetary instruments, such as postage stamps, certificates, or certified checks. The supply of money in the United States is controlled by the Federal Reserve, which issues paper money, and the Treasury, which issues coins. The Federal Reserve system functions by providing banks with as much currency as is needed through purchases and sales of securities, which directly affect bank reserves and the entire structure of deposits, loans, and the supply of money.

MONEY DEFINED

Although currency, cash, coins, and the like form our immediate and familiar image of "money," they are really just the tip of the iceberg. The underlying mass of the dollar value of payments is made by consigning bank deposits, rather than by currency.

The real key to the working economy is the *supply of money,* since changes in supply of money activate changes in prices, yield, and income. The Federal Reserve System established three categories of money: (1) "narrow money," which included currency and checking deposits, (2) "broad money," which included the above, plus savings deposits in banks, and (3) all of these, plus deposits held in savings and loan associations and savings banks. Although these have been modified in the past and will continue to be in the future, as banks offer new kinds of accounts to their customers, they illustrate the difficulties of delineating "money" in its various forms and establishing businesslike definitions.

EXCHANGE RATES

History does not clarify the birth of the exchange rate, since it started far back in time and was local in nature long before it became truly international. However, it is safe to assume that some form of exchange took place in China, where coinage was probably invented, as well as in ancient Greece and Rome, when those countries did business with other nations in their broadening economic spheres. In modern usage, an exchange rate is the price at which one nation's currency can be replaced for the currency of another country. The rates fluctuate constantly, dictated essentially by the law of supply and demand, depending upon the major sources that use exchange rates frequently, such as importers and exporters, military units, international marketers, or travel agents.

Why do rates vary so markedly, and who benefits most? A typical example would be that of an import firm in the United States that deals in French wines and arranges for its bank to pay French vineyards in francs. At the same time, a nearby exporter is shipping American computers to Paris and being paid in dollars through a French bank.

An American businessperson who imports automobiles from Japan may have his or her bank pay the Japanese exporter in yen. At the same time, an American exporter of typewriters may receive a check for dollars from a Japanese bank. If the demand for francs in the money market is greater than that for dollars, the value of the franc inclines to rise. If the reverse is true, the dollar takes a stronger position. And thus the exchange rate seesaws back and forth over a period of time. In the mid-1940s the International Monetary Fund was established in an effort to stabilize exchange rates, while at the same time fostering a continuing growth of trade. Under current international monetary systems, the major industrial nations allow their currencies to float, which in simplified terms means that they seek their own value levels in relation to one another. This procedure is monitored by central banks, such as the Federal Reserve Bank, the Bank of England, and the German Bundesbank, to prevent or at least minimize undesirable short-term fluctuations. The advantages of the floating rate system is that it encourages an international free-market system and establishes currency prices more on the basis of supply and demand. Even so, floating rates may vacillate sharply over short periods as a result of speculation, a situation that leads many international traders to favor fixed exchange rates, which make financial planning a great deal simpler.

MONETARY AND FISCAL POLICIES AND THEORIES

Policies and principles relating to money are formally established by monetary authorities, and in particular the Federal Reserve System, in a manner calculated to stabilize currency and stimulate the country's economy during excessive circumstances, such as periods of recession or inflation. The objective is to attain situations whereby loanable funds are available to businesses at reasonable cost and commercial investment is encouraged. The right policy at the right time can promote the enlargement of the available money supply, lower the interest rate, and encourage companies to invest in capital facilities that will increase their productivity. In a nutshell, "easy" money alleviates a recession, while "tight" money minimizes inflation. Somewhere between the two lies the balance that economists strive for.

Through the application of *monetary theory,* economists explain the levels of income in terms of current dollars, pinpoint the price levels, and communicate their interpretations of the value of money and the supply/demand situation within any given national economy. A common objective is to convince the general public that when people try to hold onto their money too tightly they divert it from production, labor, and capital, with the result that, while the inflation rate declines, so does employment. This kind of situation relates to what is known as the *quantity theory* of money: if the quantity of money increases, spending raises prices and thus reduces the real quantity of money. The evolution continues until prices have risen proportionately to the rise in the nominal quantity of money, and then the real quantity of money returns to its former desired level.

Where money is concerned, there is always a balancing act that keeps governments and economists constantly on their toes trying to maintain stability and avert unpleasant financial surprises.

KEY TOPICS TO REFER TO
THAT RELATE TO MONEY

accounting

assets

audit

auditor

backdoor financing

bad debt

balance of payments

balance of trade

balance sheet

bank draft

bank statement

bankruptcy

banks and banking

barter

bearer bond

beneficiary

bill of exchange

bill of sale

blue chip

boiler room

bond

bond redemption

bookkeeping

Bretton Woods Conference

budget

capital

capital asset

capital depreciation

cash flow

cash management

central bank

certificate of deposit (CD)

certified check

Certified Public Accountant (CPA)

commercial paper

cost of living

debt

devaluation

direct selling

National Bank
negotiable instrument
net
net asset value
net earnings
net loss
net price
net worth
New York Stock Exchange (NYSE)
New York Stock Exchange Common Stock Index
ordinary income
out-of-pocket expenses
overhead
paper money
paper profits
parity
parity policy
pension
portfolio
precious metals
price control
price fixing
price index
prime rate
profit
profit-and-loss statement
profit sharing
real income
recession
retailing
sales tax

savings and loans
securities
soft currency
spreadsheets
stagflation
stock
strong dollar
subsidy
tangible asset
tariff
tax
taxable income
taxation
tight money
trade deficit
trade discount
trading on equity
transfer price
treasury notes
trial-and-error pricing
trickle-down economics
undercapitalized
United States mint
unrealized profits
value-added tax
variable costs
warranty
working capital
year-end discount
yield
yield to maturity
zero-balance account
zero-base budgeting

Refer also to the following supplements in the Appendix and elsewhere:

- Banks and Banking (page 439)
- Foreign Currencies (pages 446–448)
- Investment Terms and Phrases (pages 458–459)
- Mutual Funds (pages 460–462)
- Tax Forms (pages 465–467)

Part 5

COMMUNICATIONS

Communication has been described as "a variety of behaviors, processes, and technologies by which meaning is transmitted or derived from information describing such diverse activities as: verbal conversation, the exchange of data between computers, the courting behavior of birds, the emotional impact of a work of art, the course of a rumor through a school, and the complex network of nervous and metabolic systems that comprise the body's immune system."

Challenged by such divergent uses of the term, it is no wonder that "communication," when used in the business world, overwhelms many a manager who realizes full well that the success or failure of an enterprise may depend on how completely communications are established among all the people involved. How does one cope with a situation in which no sharply defined boundaries narrow the field, no clearcut terrains are within it, and no professionally accepted prototype of the nomenclature functions as a serviceable guideline?

Historically, until well into the twentieth century, concepts of communication were the bailiwick of writers on philosophy, language, and elocution. And even these theories were derived from ancient times when philosophers like Aristotle taught that rhetoric was a study of every possible means of communication and that its practitioners had to evaluate the speaker, classify the message, and weigh the audience in order to understand the cause and effect of the rhetoric and determine what it had achieved. Later philosophers and scientists accepted the rhetoric theory, but attempted to universalize the concept by interpreting communication in terms of the "global language," mathematics. Their dream was to create an artificial language that would serve as the basis for worldwide communication. Mathematics was thought to be the answer to better communication for a threefold reason: Meaning could be transmitted through symbols; symbols could carry intended meanings; and the meanings could then motivate action, as desired.

Psychologists engaged in the study of behavior also focused on communication as a strong factor in patterns of deportment and attempted to determine the elements that enhanced the communicative process. Surprisingly, however, it was not until the middle of the twentieth century that there was anything like a pragmatic theory of communication that would be meaningful in the business world. At that time, a number of major studies were published, typified by two that were influential: *The Mathematical Theory of Communication,* by Claude Shannon, and *Cybernetics,* by Norbert Weiner. Cybernetics referred to the general analysis of control procedures and communication systems in both living organisms and machines and drew analogies between the functioning of the brain and nervous system and the computer and other electronic data-processing networks. A significant element in communication was *feedback,* the manner in which organisms of all kinds, no matter how simple or how sophisticated, could modify their own behavior to adjust malfunctions. In communication, feedback has been described as "a verbal or visual clue that indicates whether the message has been received and correctly interpreted." This concept has become increasingly pivotal in the development of every form of business communication where the credibility of the source is vital, such as advertising, promotion, public relations, speech-making, graphic presentations, publishing, films, or general correspondence. Further studies in this field focused increasingly not just on the media of communications but on the ultimate interaction, the response to the message. In its extreme form, this is Marshall McLuhan's contention that "the media is the message," that the medium itself exerts so strong an influence on the recipients that it virtually controls what is communicated.

A working knowledge of interpersonal communication is an essential for managers who have to communicate, even to a minimal degree, with their peers and employees. This informational exchange has been defined as the manner in which people influence one another, even in many cases inadvertently, and includes such factors as nonverbal communication and body language. Since the response of the receiver is activated not only by words or conversation, it includes the total environment of social behavior rather than just specific acts or utterances. As for those positive, recognizable acts of communication, they succeed or fail because of certain specific factors: the relationship of those involved in the communication, the significance of what is being communicated, the implied intentions, the order of presentation of facts or contentions, the credibility of the sources, the role of selective perception, and pressures to conform to group norms.

MASS COMMUNICATION

The mid-twentieth century saw a historic escalation of mass communication, what with television and other developments in broadcasting, the wildfire spread of computers, and the evolution of state-of-the-art telephonic equipment—to name a few catalysts in the electronics revolution. Mass communication is described as "any medium of communication that reaches a significantly large number of people with one or more messages that are timely and relevant, and potentially of interest to a substantial percentage of the recipients." In practice, a message that reached thousands of people but caught the attention of only a few hundred would not fit this category: nor would a message that interested 100 percent of the recipients, but was delivered to only a very small group. As for the nature of the medium, it has no restrictions and can range all the way from the most sophisticated computer internets and databases down to a throbbing network of jungle drums. Since the advent of communications satellites and the proliferation of electronic online systems, mass communication has taken a quantum leap and can reach not only the farthest corners of the globe, but can do so instantly, and frequently in a multitude of languages at the same time. This information revolution is all the more startling when it is realized that as recently as one generation ago mass communication was limited largely to broadcasting, which was instantaneous, but fleeting, and the print media, which, though lasting, were delayed in reaching their recipients. The print media—chiefly newspapers, magazines, and books in that order of audiences—were lessened in impact by the fact that their shots were scattered, that newsworthy contents seldom reached readers at the same time, and that the impact of any particular message depended to a great degree on the skill and fluency of the writer and the comprehension level and experience of the reader. As for radio and television, their credibility often suffered in that they had from the beginning established themselves as *entertainment,* and consequently it was often difficult for listeners and viewers to comprehend where fiction left off and fact began—classifications that are more clearly specified in the printed media.

Mass communication in its present concept thus has strong electronic elements, which in effect combine the plausibility advantages of newspapers and magazines, the graphic appeal and duration of books, and the instantaneous clout of radio and television. Electronic communication is popularly considered to be "broadcasting" in the sense that it originates in a single source and then fans out to its recipients, either en masse or, far more often, in controlled demographic segments. Even when electronic communication is directed at moderate-sized, specialized groups, it can often be considered a "mass" medium because it is, in effect, reaching a large percentage of the specialized public intended. The very swiftness of such communication multiplies its impact rating many times over, since the message can reach a person in the United States and persons in Europe or Asia or the upper reaches of the Amazon before any of them can draw a breath. If the news is shocking, such transmissions can heighten the emotional tempo far more effectively than the most telling account in print.

VERBAL PERFORMANCE AND LANGUAGE

In the practical field of business communications, verbal performance and language are major concerns in operations dominated by psychology, linguistics, and anthropology, where the objectives emphasize the potential of language to transmit meaning. Language, in this context, includes not only rhetoric but gestures, graphic arts, symbols, numbers, colors, euphonics, and semantics, the relationship between sounds and visualization and meaning. A related phenomenon is that all of these communications concepts can be expressed by, if not translatable into, other languages, of which there are more than 3,000 around the globe. Psychologists and anthropologists, as well as experienced business managers, interpret communication as the ultimate channel through which human relations exist and develop.

It is readily apparent to those researching and developing mass communications that language, not technology, is the most stubborn obstacle in the effort to project the voice beyond the eye and ear. For this reason, research and development (R&D) programs in the field of mass communication have necessarily focused on trying to overcome the language barrier.

ARTIFICIAL LANGUAGES

Artificial languages have been defined as "those which have been expressly conceived for the purpose of communication in media that are the brainchildren of global state-of-the-art technology, and can be universally understood, regardless of the nationality or language of the recipient." Unlike natural tongues, which evolved culturally and historically without conscious planning, the new artificial languages are as calculated as the tracings on a blueprint. With applications in computer science, mathematics, and research deduction, artificial languages make use of symbols, characters, numerals, and ciphers to denote such elements as categories, commands, controls, and other precise and specific classifications relating to functions that are familiar to both the senders and the recipients. This form of communication has obvious limitations and is not intended to describe ranges of human experience or attempt the subtle nuances of common speech. Nevertheless, it can be intensive and productive and can accomplish as much as, or even more than, traditional language in its specialized sector of collaborative endeavor.

Also, in the research stage, are less limited prototypes of artificial languages that incorporate selective vocabularies of words, phrases, abbreviations, and acronyms that are generally familiar and recognized worldwide. These provide more extensive vehicles of thought and understanding than can be found in the basic artificial languages, yet at the same time avoid the barriers caused by the multiplicity of natural languages that exist in the international business world. Historically, attempts to overhaul an existing natural language have failed because the vocabulary has had to be pared until it is almost ineffectual, and meanings are too oversimplified for use in professional and business applications. The fabricated language that enjoyed the greatest success was *Esperanto,* with roots drawn from English, French, Spanish, and German. However, its most practical use proved to be for social and cultural, rather than for business, communications. In a more limited way, a Latin-based artificial language called *Interlingua,* based on an international vocabulary of scientific and technological terms, has found functional applications during scientific and medical conferences and in some cases in reporting research and data in professional journals.

KEY TOPICS TO REFER TO
THAT RELATE TO COMMUNICATION

---

advertising
American Newspaper
    Publishers Association
    (ANPA)
automation
bar chart

bibliography
Books in Print
braille
brochure
business communication
byte

captive audience
circulation
commercial
computer
computer graphics
computer hardware
computer language
computer network
computer programming
computer software
copyright
corporate image
cybernetics
depth interview
desktop publishing
digital computer
direct mail
electronic mail (E-mail)
electronic publishing
facsimile (FAX)
Federal Communications
    Commission (FCC)
fiber optics
FORTRAN
fourth estate
Government Printing Office
    (GPO)
graph
graphic arts
handbill
hardware
hidden offer
human-oriented language
identifier

image
image building
industrial espionage
industrial psychology
industrial relations
information retrieval
inquiry testing
institutional advertising
integrated circuit
integrated commercials
integrated software
internal memory
International Press Institute
internet
journalism
key brand
language
laser technology
Library of Congress (LOC)
linear programming
lobbyist
logotype (logo)
loop
loop modification
magnetic tape memory
mailing
mail-order advertising
mail-order business
main frame
marketing
market research
mass communications
mass medium
masthead

media
media industry
memory
microcomputers
microelectronics
microprocessor
modem
multiple brands
multiple listing
multiprocessing
national brand
network
newsletter
Nielsen ratings
nomenclature
numerical control
online
online computer
online system
open letter
optical computing
optical reader
optimization
organizational chart
outdoor advertising
output
package advertising
package engineering
password
patent
patent office
peripherals
personal computers
point-of-purchase (POP)
    advertising

postal services
preferred position
prime time
probability
processor
programmed learning
programmer
programming
promoter
promotion
proofreading
proposal
prospectus
public opinion
public relations
public service advertising
quadraphonic sound
radial transfer
random access memory (RAM)
random sampling
rate card
readership
rotary press
rotogravure
royalties
sales promotion
saturation campaign
semiconductor
share of audience
short run
social psychology
software
speech-recognition software
Standard Rate and Data
    Service (SRDS)

stereophonic
subliminal advertising
table
tabular matter
tape recording
teaching machine
teaser
telecommunication
teleconferencing
teleprinter
television production
testimonial
test market
thermography
thesaurus

time sharing
trade advertising
trademark
transit advertising
ultrasonics
union label
United States Information
Agency (USIA)
visibility
voice-input computer systems
voice-data system
voice mail
voice recognition
word-of-mouth advertising
X-ray

Refer also to the following supplements in the Appendix and elsewhere:

- Abbreviations (pages 468–471)
- Computer Terms and Phrases (pages 442–444)
- Copyright (page 83)
- Foreign Words and Phrases (pages 448–450)
- Investment Terms and Phrases (pages 458–459)
- Postal Services Abbreviations (pages 462–464)

APPENDIX

LARGEST COMMERCIAL BANKS IN THE UNITED STATES

Bank and Headquarters	Deposits
Citibank (New York)	$162,044,000
Bank of America (San Francisco)	$132,166,000
Chemical Bank (New York)	$107,615,000
Chase Manhattan Bank (New York)	$ 59,662,000
Security Pacific National Bank (Los Angeles)	$ 45,376,676
Wells Fargo Bank (San Francisco)	$ 42,716,399
Manufacturers Hanover Trust (New York)	$ 41,384,000
Morgan Guaranty Trust (New York)	$ 37,847,005
Bank of New York (New York)	$ 33,466,870
Chemical Bank (New York)	$ 30,667,000
Bankers Trust (New York)	$ 28,844,000
NCNB Texas National Bank (Dallas)	$ 26,593,824
First National Bank (Chicago)	$ 25,289,561
First National Bank (Boston)	$ 20,079,100
NBD Bank (Detroit)	$ 16,864,551
Continental Bank (Chicago)	$ 16,455,000
Marine Midland Bank (Buffalo, NY)	$ 16,356,546
First Interstate Bank of California (Los Angeles)	$ 15,831,927
Republic National Bank (New York)	$ 15,750,448

Source: American Bankers Association

MEASURING INSTRUMENTS

Name of Instrument	Action, Condition, or Object Measured
actinometer	intensity of radiation
altimeter	height of an aircraft above ground
anemometer	wind speed; flow rate of a liquid
baroscope	atmospheric pressure
bathometer	depth of water
calipers	diameter of rods, tubes, pipes
calorimeter	degrees of heat
chronometer	time in hours, minutes, seconds
clinometer	angle of inclination
colorimeter	colors and shades
cryometer	very low temperatures
cyclometer	distance, on map or ground
densimeter	density
electroscope	presence of an electrical charge
Geiger counter	radiation
gavimeter	gravitational field
hydrometer	relative density of liquids
hygrometer	humidity
interferometer	wavelengths of light
machmeter	ultra-high speeds beyond speed of sound
magnetometer	strengths of magnetic fields
manometer	pressures of gases and liquids
micrometer	precise dimensions of small objects
ondometer	frequency of radio waves
optometer	refraction of the eye
pedometer	distance traveled by a pedestrian
photometer	light magnitude and intensity
pluviometer	rainfall, dew level
potentiometer	electrical voltages
protractor	angles and corners
psychrometer	humidity

pyrheliometer	solar and celestial radiation
pyrometer	high temperature
psychrometer	humidity
pyrheliometer	solar and celestial radiation
pyrometer	high temperature
radio-micrometer	heat radiation
sclerometer	hardness of materials
seismograph	earthquakes and earth tremors
sextent	altitude of celestial bodies
spherometer	curvature of a sphere or cylinder
tachometer	rotational speed of a shaft
tensiometer	tensile strength, stretchability
velocimeter	acceleration or velocity
voltameter	electrical voltage

ROMAN NUMERALS

I	1	XVIII	18	DCCC	800
II	2	XIX	19	CM	900
III	3	XX	20	M	1000
IV	4	XXX	30	MC	1100
V	5	XL	40	MCC	1200
VI	6	L	50	MCCC	1300
VII	7	LX	60	MCD	1400
VIII	8	LXX	70	MD	1500
IX	9	LXXX	80	MDC	1600
X	10	XC	90	MDCC	1700
XI	11	C	100	MDCCC	1800
XII	12	CC	200	MCM	1900
XIII	13	CCC	300	MM	2000
XIV	14	CD	400	MMM	3000
XV	15	D	500	M$\bar{\text{V}}$	4000
XVI	16	DC	600	$\bar{\text{V}}$	5000
XVII	17	DCC	700	$\bar{\text{V}}$M	6000

Note: A line over the top of a roman numeral indicates that the original value of the numeral is multiplied by 1,000. Thus V, which is five, becomes 5,000 when topped by a line.

COMPUTER TERMS AND PHRASES

ALGOL. *A*lgorithmic *O*riented *L*anguage, a mathematical data-processing language.

Analog Computer. A form of computer, now outdated, that was activated by different voltages, keyed by number.

BASIC. A computer language evolved from its terminology: *B*eginner's *A*ll-Purpose *S*ymbolic *I*nstruction *C*ode.

Binary System. The numbers system used by computers, in which all numbers are represented by the two digits O and 1.

Bit. The smallest unit in a computer's memory system.

Bugs. Flaws or faults in an electronic—or any other—system.

Byte. The name for a standard unit used to describe a computer's memory and functional capacity.

Central Processing Unit (CPU). The heart of a computer's functional components.

COBOL. A computer language evolved from its terminology, *C*ommon *B*usiness *O*riented *L*anguage.

Compact Disk Read-only Memory (CD-ROM). A prepared and programmed disk that can be "played" on a special computer installation and that can be excerpted, but not changed or erased. A CD-ROM may also have illustrations and other graphics, as well as music, speech, and a wide variety of sounds, such as those made by animals, birds, machinery, or railroad trains.

Cursor. A point of light, usually in the form of an arrow, which moves back and forth across a computer screen, as activated by the operator using a *mouse* or other controlling device.

Digital. The term for a computer using numbers (digits) or displays of symbols as it is activated by user commands.

Disk (or disc). A data-storage component that consists of a flat, rotating circular unit, usually contained in a square sheath, which has a magnetic surface that records inputs and provides outputs of information on command.

Disk Drive. The component of a computer that transfers data to or from any form of disk compatible with the computer and its peripheral equipment.

Diskette. A form of *disk,* often called a *floppy disk,* that can store, retrieve, and dispense data on command.

Format. The arrangement and blueprint whereby computers and other data processors arrange information in usable patterns and applications.

FORTRAN. A mathematical computer language that takes its name from the term, *formula translation.*

Hacker. A person who has the experience and skill to access data from a computer system, but does so without authorization, and usually unlawfully.

Hardware. The physical, mechanical parts of a computer and its components, in contrast to *software,* the independent programming elements used to operate the equipment and provide commands.

Interface. Any form of connection or link between the hardware and software and related components of a computer or data-processing system.

Internet. The name for a broad network, which can join thousands of computers together in mutual communication around the globe.

Mainframe. A large and powerful computer of the types needed for far-ranging, instantaneous, and reliable information gathering and dissemination, as found in commercial telephone systems or the compilation and application of financial data on a global basis.

Modem. A device that is built into, or attached to, a computer in order to receive and transmit data over a telephone line or other vehicle of communication.

Mouse. A small, compact, hand-operated instrument used to activate and move a cursor on the computer screen, to give directions for storing and retrieving data from the disks.

Optical Character Reader (OCR). A device for scanning printed texts and graphics and converting them into a format that can be stored in disks and later retrieved or printed.

Peripherals. Items of hardware that are not part of the basic computer, but are attached to it, such as a modem, a printer, or sonic speakers.

Program. The *software* used to activate a computer, provide directions, and store and retrieve data. The function of preparing this material is known as *programming* and the specialists who prepare such programs are known as *programmers.*

Random Access Memory (RAM). Sets of data that can be utilized by a computer, stored, retrieved, changed, and erased.

Read-only Memory (ROM). Sets of data that are fixed and can be excerpted, but that cannot be changed or erased.

Scroll. The function of a computer that permits the image on the screen to be moved vertically or horizontally for viewing.

Software. Components that are not part of the main body of a computer, but are inserted or attached to it and used to program the *hardware* components and provide instructions for the computer's operation.

Visual Display Unit (VDU). The computer screen, generally the slightly bowed face of a cathode-ray tube, much like a television screen.

MAJOR BUSINESS SCHOOLS IN THE UNITED STATES

The following business schools, associated with leading universities, are considered to be the finest in the country. They are listed alphabetically, by university:

Carnegie Mellon University
Graduate School of Industrial Administration
Schenley Park
Pittsburgh, PA 15213

Columbia University
Columbia Business School
New York, NY 10027

Cornell University
Johnson Graduate School of Management
Ithaca, NY 14853

Dartmouth University
Amos Tuck School of Business Administration
Hanover, NH 03755

Duke University
The Fuqua School of Business
Durham, NC 27706

Harvard University
Graduate School of Business Administration
Boston, MA 02163

Indiana University
Graduate School of Business
Bloomington, IN 47405

Massachustts Institute of Technology
Sloan School of Management
Cambridge, MA 02139

New York University
Graduate School of Business Administration
New York, NY 10006

Northwestern University
Kellogg Graduate School of Management
Evanston, IL 60208

Purdue University
Kellogg Graduate School of Management
Evanston, IL 60208

Stanford University
Graduate School of Business
Stanford, CA 94305

University of California at Berkeley
Graduate School of Business Administration
Berkeley, CA 94720

University of California at Los Angeles
John E. Anderson Graduate School of Management
Los Angeles, CA 90024

University of Chicago
Graduate School of Business
Chicago, IL 60637

University of Michigan
School of Business Administration
Ann Arbor, MI 48109

University of North Carolina
Graduate School of Business Administration
Chapel Hill, NC 27599

University of Pennsylvania
The Wharton School
Philadelphia, PA 19104

University of Pittsburgh
Joseph M. Katz Graduate School of Business
Pittsburgh, PA 15260

University of Rochester
William E. Simon Graduate School of Business
Rochester, NY 14627

University of Southern California
Graduate School of Business Administration
Los Angeles, CA 90089

University of Texas
Graduate School of Business
Austin, TX 78712

University of Virginia
Darden Graduate School of Business Administration
Charlottesville, VA 22906

Vanderbilt University
Owen Graduate School of Management
Nashville, TN 37203

Yale University
Yale School of Organization and Management
New Haven, CT 06520

FOREIGN CURRENCIES

Names of some of the major currencies of the world and the countries with
which they are associated:

austral	Argentina
baht	Thailand

balboa	Panama
bolivar	Venezuela
colon	Costa Rica, El Salvador
cordoba	Nicaragua
cruzado	Brazil
deutsche mark	Germany
dinar	Algeria, Kuwait, Yugoslavia
dirham	Morocco, United Arab Emirates
dong	Vietnam
drachma	Greece
escudo	Portugal
forint	Hungary
franc	France, Switzerland, Senegal, others
gourde	Haiti
guarani	Paraguay
guilder, gulden	Netherlands, Suriname
inti	Peru
kina	New Guinea, Papua
koruna	Czechoslovakia
krona	Iceland, Sweden
krone	Denmark, Norway
kwacha	Malawi, Zambia
kwanza	Angola
kyat	Burma
lek	Albania
lempira	Honduras
leu	Romania
lev	Bulgaria
lira	Italy, Malta, Turkey
marka	Finland
metical	Mozambique
naira	Nigeria
ouguiya	Mauretania
pa'anga	Tonga

peseta	Spain
peso	Chile, Mexico, Philippines, others
pula	Botswana
quetzal	Guatemala
rand	South Africa
rial	Iran, Saudi Arabia, Yemen
riel	Cambodia
ringgit	Malaysia
riyal	Qatar, Saudi Arabia
ruble	Russia
rupee	India, Pakistan, others
rupiah	Indonesia
schilling	Austria
shekel	Israel
shilling	Kenya, Tanzania
sucre	Ecuador
taka	Bangladesh
tala	Western Samoa
tugrik	Mongolia
won	North Korea, South Korea
yen	Japan
yuan	China
zaire	Zaire
zloty	Poland

FOREIGN WORDS AND PHRASES

ad hoc.	For the purpose at hand
ad hominem.	To the person.
ad infinitum.	Endless.
ad lib.	Improvised.
aficionado.	Fan or devotee.
appropos.	Appropriate, to the point.
a priori.	Self-evident, from experience.

au fait.	Familiar with.
bona fide.	Genuine, in good faith.
carte blanche.	Without restriction.
caveat emptor.	Let the buyer beware.
chutzpah.	With a show of fortitude or audacity.
compos mentis.	Of sound mind.
coup d'etat.	Forceful overthrow of a person or body in power.
cum laude.	With praise or honor.
curriculum vitae.	Course of life; resume.
dacha.	Country house; modest dwelling.
de facto.	In reality.
de jure.	In accordance with the law; by right.
demode.	Out of fashion.
de rigeur.	According to convention.
detente.	Easing strained relations.
en masse.	In a large body.
entre nous.	Between us; in confidence.
ergo.	Therefore.
esprit de corps.	Cameraderie; in the spirit of the group.
ex gratia.	Out of decency; as a favor.
ex post facto.	Explanation after the event.
fait accompli.	An accomplished fact, or deed.
faux pas.	A social or political blunder.
hoi polloi.	The illiterate masses.
in loco parentis.	In place of a parent.
in memoriam.	In memory of.
in situ.	In the original terms.
in toto.	Totally, in total.
ipso facto.	By that fact; as a consequence of a fact, or act.
joie de vivre.	Joy of living.
karma.	Fate, destiny.
laissez-faire.	Let be; noninterference.
mantra.	Sacred word or living code.

mea culpa.	My fault, or error.
modus operandi.	Method of operating.
modus vivendi.	Manner of living.
ne plus ultra.	Perfection.
nizam.	Ruler
noblesse oblige.	Obligation of the nobility.
non compos mentis.	Demented, not with it.
non sequitur.	It does not follow; illogical.
nouveau riche.	The recent rich.
per capita.	By the head; per person.
perestroika.	Restructuring.
per se.	By, or in, itself.
persona non grata.	Unacceptable or unsuitable individual.
post mortem.	Evaluation after an event or function has occurred.
prima donna.	Conceited individual.
prima facie.	At first sight; on the face of it.
pro bono.	For the public good; voluntarily, without cost.
quid pro quo.	That which is given, or gotten, for something else.
raison d'etre.	Reason for being, or happening.
samizat.	Underground, or secret, members of the press.
savoir-faire.	Social dexterity and poise.
semper fidelis.	Always faithful.
sine die.	Without a day; at no set date.
status quo.	State of being.
sub rosa.	Secretly.
sui generis.	Unique; of its own kind.
tour de force.	Feat of strength or virtuosity.
tout court.	Plainly and simply.
tovarich.	Comrade.
terra firma.	Solid ground.
verbatim.	Word for word.
vis-a-vis.	Compared with.
volte-face.	About face; change of mind.
vox populi.	Voice of the people.

BRANCHES OF GOVERNMENT OF THE UNITED STATES

LEGISLATIVE
CONGRESS

House   Senate

General Accounting Office

Government Printing Office

Library of Congress

Congressional Budget Office

Unites States Tax Court

Office of Technology Assessment

Capitol Architect

United States Botanical Garden

JUDICIAL

Supreme Court of the United States

Courts of Appeals

Court of Appeals for the Federal Circuit

Court of Military Appeals

Court of Veterans Appeals

Court of International Trade

District Courts

Claims Court

Territorial Courts

Federal Judicial Center

Administrative Office of the Courts

EXECUTIVE

President

Executive Office of the President

Vice President   Cabinet

White House Office

Office of Management and Budget

Council of Economic Advisors

EXECUTIVE
(cont'd)

National Security Council
National Economic Council
Office of United States Trade
Council on Environmental Quality
Office of Policy Development
Office of Administration
Office of National Drug Control Policy
Office of Science and Technology Policy
National Space Council
National Critical Materials Council

GOVERNMENT SYSTEMS

Absolutism. Ruled by a dictator or absolute monarch.

Aristocracy. Governed by a hereditary ruling class, family, or empowered minority.

Autocracy. Under the iron thumb of an individual ruler who is all-powerful.

Despotism. The state or condition of being dominated by a tyrannical individual or close-knit band.

Dictatorship. A country ruled by a single strongman, zealously supported by hand-picked subordinates.

Dyarchy. A government in the hands of two dominant individuals or parties.

Gerontocracy. A state whose leaders are customarily persons who are elderly or considered to be senior citizens.

Hierocracy. A state under the dominion of the clergy or other church-related leaders.

Matriarchy. A government largely controlled by women, both as leaders and as members of the administering body.

Monarchy. A kingdom, whose head of state is a king, queen, or other hereditary ruler.

Oligarchy. A government under the control of one family or a small faction.

Pantisocracy. A government in which all citizens have equal say in the administration of the laws and customs.

Patriarchy. A government largely controlled by men, both as leaders and as members of the administering body.

Plutocracy. A government in the control of persons of wealth, to the exclusion of those who have lesser means.

Stratocracy. Government by an army or other military entity, generally enforced in nations that have been subjugated and taken over by an enemy.

Technocracy. A state in which the ruling classes, if not the leaders themselves, are composed of scientific and technological professionals.

Theocracy. A state or nation whose government is dominated by a priesthood or religious figures who represent gods or deities.

Totalitarianism. The name for a governmental situation that is completely controlled by a dictator, or at most a compact group of authoritarians.

Triumvirate. A country governed by three rulers, each of whom is equally powerful, although perhaps in charge of different segments of administration.

UNITED STATES GOVERNMENT
INDEPENDENT AGENCIES
(In Washington, DC, unless otherwise listed)

ACTION: 1100 Vermont Ave., NW, 20525.

Administrative Conference of the United States: Suite 500, 2120 L St. NW, 20037.

African Development Foundation: 1400 I St. NW, 20005.

Central Intelligence Agency: DC 20505.

Commission on Civil Rights: 624 9th St. NW, 20425.

Commodity Futures Trading Commission: 2033 K St. NW, 20581.

Consumer Product Safety Commission: East West Towers, 4340 East West Hwy., Bethesda, MD 20814.

Environmental Protection Agency: 401 M St., SW, 20460.

Equal Employment Opportunity Commission: 1801 L St. NW., 20507.

Export-Import Bank of the United States: 811 Vermont Ave. NW 20571.

Farm Credit Administration: Farm Credit Administration Board, 1501 Farm Credit Drive, McLean, VA 22102.

Federal Communications Commission: 1919 M St. NW, 20554.

Federal Deposit Insurance Corporation: 550 17th St. NW, 20429.

Federal Election Commission: 999 E. St. NW, 20463.

Federal Emergency Management Agency: 500 C St. SW, 20472.

Federal Housing Finance Board: 1777 F St. NW., 20006.

Federal Labor Relations Authority: 607 14th St. NW, 20424.

Federal Maritime Commission: 800 N. Capitol St. NW, 20573.

Federal Mediation and Conciliation Service: 2100 K St. NW, 20427.

Federal Mine Safety & Health Review Commission 1730 K St. NW, 20006.

Federal Reserve System: 20th St. & Constitution Ave. NW, 20551.

Federal Retirement Thrift Investment Board: 1250 H St. NW, 20005.

Federal Trade Commission: Pennsylvania Ave. at 6th St. NW, 20580.

General Accounting Office: 441 G St. NW, 20548.

General Services Administration: 18th & F Sts. NW, 20405.

Government Printing Office: North Capitol and H Sts. NW, 20401.

Inter-American Foundation: 901 N. Stuart St., Arlington, VA 22203.

Interstate Commerce Commission: 12th St. & Constitution Ave. NW, 20423.

Library of Congress: 101 Independence Ave. SE, 20540.

Merit Systems Protection Board: 1120 Vermont Ave. NW, 20419.

National Aeronautics and Space Administration: 300 E St. SW 20546.

National Archives & Records Administration: 7th St. & Pennsylvania Ave. NW, 20408.

National Credit Union Administration: 1776 G St. NW, 20456.

National Foundation on the Arts and the Humanities: 1100 Pennsylvania Ave. NW, 20506.

National Labor Relations Board: 1099 14th St. NW, 20570.

National Mediation Board: Suite 250 East, 1301 K St. NW, 20572.

National Railroad Passenger Corporation (Amtrak): 60 Massachusetts Ave. NE, 20002.

National Science Foundation: 1800 G St. NW, 20550.

National Transportation Safety Board: 490 L'Enfant Plaza SW, 20594.

Nuclear Regulatory Commission: 1717 H St. NW, 20555.

Occupational Safety and Health Review Commission: 1120 20th St. NW, 20036.

Office of Personnel Management: 1900 E St. NW, 20415.

Peace Corps: 1990 K St. NW, 20526.

Postal Rate Commission: 1333 H St. NW, 20268-0001.

Railroad Retirement Board: 844 N. Rush St., Chicago, IL 60611.

Securities and Exchange Commission: 450 5th St. NW, 20549.

Selective Service System: National Headquarters, 20435.

Small Business Administration: 409 Third St. SW, 20416.

Smithsonian Institution: 1000 Jefferson Dr. SW, 20560.

Tennessee Valley Authority: 400 W. Summit Hill Dr., Knoxville, TN 37902, and Room 300, 412 1st St. SE, Washington, DC 20444.

United States Arms Control & Disarmament Agency: 320 21st St. NW 20451.

United States Information Agency: 301 4th St. SW, 20547.

United States International Development Cooperation Agency: 320 21st St. NW, 20523.

United States International Trade Commission: 500 E St. SW, 20436.

United States Postal Service: 475 L'Enfant Plaza SW, 20260.

Source: National Archives & Records Administration

PROMINENT AMERICAN BUSINESS LEADERS OF THE PAST

Philip D. Armour, 1832–1901, meat packing entrepreneur

John Jacob Astor, 1763–1848, fur trader, banker, and real estate magnate

Francis W. Ayer, 1848–1923, advertising agency trailblazer

Adolphus Busch, 1839–1913, founder of a brewery empire

Andrew Carnegie, 1835-1919, industrialist, founder of U.S. Steel, who personally helped to finance 2,900 libraries

William Colgate, 1783–1857, founder of a soap-making empire

Ezra Cornell, 1807–1874, businessman, philanthropist; headed Western Union and established Cornell University

Walt Disney, 1901–1966, motion-picture animation pioneer

James Duke, 1856–1925, founder of the American Tobacco Company and Duke University

Eleuthere I. du Pont, 1771–1834, gunpowder and chemical manufacturer, who established one of world's largest industrial empires

William C. Durant, 1861–1947, industrialist and founder of the General Motors Corporation

George Eastman, 1854–1932, inventor and pioneer in the manufacture of photographic equipment

Marshall Field, 1834–1906, merchant and founder of one of America's largest department stores

Harvey Firestone, 1868–1938, tire and rubber pioneer

Henry M. Flagler, 1830–1913, co-founder of the Standard Oil Company and the man who developed Florida as a resort state

Henry Ford, 1863–1947, automobile manufacturer, developer of the assembly line and America's first popular low-priced car

Henry C. Frick, 1849–1919, steel magnate and philanthropist

Jean Paul Getty, 1892–1976, founder and head of a petroleum empire

Amadeo P. Giannini, 1870–1949, founder of the Bank of America

Jay Gould, 1836–1892, railroad baron and financier

Hetty Green, 1834–1916, financier who became America's richest woman

Meyer Guggenheim, 1828–1905, a mining entrepreneur and philanthropist who built a merchandising conglomerate

William Randolph Hearst, 1863–1951, American journalist who built an enormous publishing domain

Henry J. Heinz, 1844–1919, top pioneer in merchandising food products

Conrad N. Hilton, 1888–1979, hotel chain founder

Walter L. Jacobs, 1898–1985, founder of the first rental car business, which later became Hertz

Howard Johnson, 1896–1972, ice cream, restaurant, and motel entrepreneur

Henry J. Kaiser, 1882–1967, industrialist, who established his domain in aluminum and steel

Minor C. Keith, 1848–1929, a railroad pioneer who developed Central America commercially and founded United Fruit Company

Will K. Kellogg, 1860–1951, founder of the breakfast food company bearing his name

Richard King, 1825–1885, a cattleman who parlayed a few acres of farmland into the half-million-acre King Ranch in Texas

Ray A. Kroc, 1902–1984, founder of McDonald's fast-food chain

Andrew W. Mellon, 1855–1937, financier, industrialist, and one of America's top philanthropists

John Pierpont Morgan, 1837–1913, America's most commanding figure in finance and industry in his day

William S. Paley, 1901–1989, pioneer in broadcasting

George Peabody, 1795–1869, merchant, financier, and leading philanthropist

William C. Procter, 1862–1934, co-founder of one of the world's largest soap and detergent manufacturing corporations

John D. Rockefeller, 1839–1937, founder of the Standard Oil Company and in his day the world's wealthiest individual

John D. Rockefeller, Jr., 1874–1960, philanthropist, founder of the Rockefeller Foundation

David Sarnoff, 1891–1971, broadcasting pioneer, established America's first radio network

Richard W. Sears, 1863–1914, founded mail-order business

Alfred P. Sloan, 1875–1966, industrialist, head of the General Motors Corporation

A. Leland Stanford, 1824–1893, railroad official and founder of Stanford University

Gustavus Swift, 1839–1903, pioneer meat-packer who developed refrigerated railroad cars

James Walter Thompson, 1847–1928, advertising executive

Theodore N. Vail, 1845–1920, established Bell Telephone system and headed AT&T

Cornelius Vanderbilt, 1794–1877, financier, who built steamship and railroad conglomerates

Lila Wallace, 1890–1984, who with her husband, DeWitt Wallace, 1890–1981, founded *The Reader's Digest* magazine and a vast publishing empire

Sam Walton, 1918–1992, founder of Wal-Mart stores

John Wanamaker, 1838–1922, pioneered department-store merchandising

Aaron Montgomery Ward, 1843–1913, entrepreneur who founded the first mail-order firm

John Hay Whitney, 1905–1982, publisher, sportsman, philanthropist

Frank W. Woolworth, 1852–1919, merchandiser who inaugurated the five- and ten-cent store

William Wrigley Jr., 1861–1932, parlayed chewing gum into a major industry

Source: American Management Association

INVESTMENT TERMS AND PHRASES

AMEX. American Stock Exchange.

Arbitrage. The purchase of shares, commodities, and currencies with the objective of making a quick resale at a higher price.

Bear. An investor who speculates that stock-market prices will fall and sells certain securities with the hope of rebuying them more cheaply at a later date.

Blue Chip. Stocks and other securities that have a long record of stability and reliability and are considered safe to purchase and likely to be profitable in the long run.

Bull. An investor who speculates that stock-market prices will rise and buys certain securities with the expectation of selling them later at a higher price.

Collateral. Property or other things of value pledged as security for a loan against the purchase of securities.

Debenture. A fixed-interest bond, with a long-term outlook and guarantee, issued by a government body or private organization.

Discount Rate. The rate of interest that is deducted in advance, as in the case of the purchase of treasury bills.

Dow Jones Index. The listing of prices on the New York Stock Exchange, based on the average prices of shares.

Fiscal Year. An accounting period of 12 months for financial and investment purposes, which is instituted arbitrarily and may differ from the calendar year.

Floating. The adjective applied to any currency whose exchange rate is determined by supply and demand, without government mediation or intervention.

Futures. Securities, especially commodities, that are purchased or sold at an agreed-upon price on one date for future delivery on another date.

Gilt-edged Securities (gilts). Fixed-interest securities, generally having a low price, that are government-issued.

Letter of Credit. Authorization in letter form that permits the person(s) named to draw a stated sum from the institution or another party so specified.

Mutual Fund. A securities portfolio containing selections made and sold as a package by a mutual fund brokerage firm.

NYSE. New York Stock Exchange.

Par Value. Also called *nominal value,* the face value of a stock or other security.

Portfolio. The combined lists of securities held by an investor.

Preferred Stock. A fixed-interest security, whose issuer guarantees payment of dividends to holders before any are assigned to ordinary shares.

Securities. The general name applied to stocks, bonds, shares, certificates, or other evidence of ownership or entitlement of worth, whether fixed or fluctuating in market value and price.

Stock Split. The issuance of one or more extra shares of stock to stockholders for each share they already own.

Treasury Bill. An obligation of the United States Treasury, which bears no interest, but is sold at a discount and matures within one year.

Underwriter. An individual or firm that guarantees the value of an issue of a security by endeavoring to purchase any shares that are left over.

Valorize. To maintain or raise the price of a commodity artificially, most commonly through intentional government action.

LEGAL OR PUBLIC HOLIDAYS

When a holiday falls on a Sunday or a Saturday it is usually observed on the following Monday or the preceding Friday. For some holidays, government and business closing practices vary. In most states, the office of the Secretary of State can provide details for holiday closings. The following are legal or public holidays in most states:

Jan. 1	New Year's Day
Jan., third Monday	Martin Luther King Day
Feb. 12	Lincoln's Birthday
Feb. 22	Washington's Birthday
Third Monday in February	Presidents' Day, or Washington-Lincoln Day
May, last Monday	Memorial Day, or Decoration Day
July 4	Independence Day
Sept., first Monday	Labor Day
Oct., second Monday	Columbus Day, Discoverers' Day, or Pioneers' Day
Nov., second Tuesday	Election Day
Nov. 11	Veterans' Day
Nov. fourth Thursday	Thanksgiving Day
Dec. 25	Christmas Day

MUTUAL FUNDS AS A LONG-TERM INVESTMENT PROGRAM

Despite the comings and goings of the financial market and the ups and downs of investing, mutual funds continue year after year to be regarded as the most secure form of investment for the average person who has neither the desire nor the ability to evaluate the offerings of Wall Street on a daily basis. Below are listed 18 categories of mutual funds:

1. *Short-term Treasury Bonds.* The most rock-solid funds buy U.S. Treasury securities with short-term maturities of up to three years, taking almost no risk of default.

2. *Short-term World Income.* These funds prefer bonds with maturities of under three years by corporations and governments around the world, subject to fluctuations in interest rates and the value of the dollar against foreign currencies.

3. *Municipal Bonds.* These funds hold bonds issued by states and cities, which provide tax-free income and have low default rates. Prices fluctuate, based on movements of interest rates.

4. *Mortgage-backed Securities.* Funds backed by quasi-governmental agencies such as Ginnie Mae, Fannie Mae, and Freddie Mac, which have almost no risk of default, although they are subject to fluctuations caused by interest-rate changes.

5. *Corporate High-quality Bonds.* Although interest-rate changes cause fluctuations, these bonds issued by highly rate corporations rarely default.

6. *World Bonds.* Issued by governments and corporations around the world, these bonds seldom default, but they are subject to fluctuations with the movements of interest rates and foreign currencies.

7. *Income Funds.* These cover a wide variety of income-producing investments chosen by fund managers, including corporate and government bonds, mortgage-backed securities, foreign bonds, and convertible issues. Funds are affected by a variety of movements in the market because of the diverse nature of the holdings.

8. *Convertible Bonds.* Funds that contain hybrid securities that pay higher yields than common stocks and have more appreciation potential than bonds and that rise less with a rising market, but fall less in a down market.

9. *Corporate High-yields.* High-yielding bonds issued by companies with below-investment grade ratings, commonly known as *junk bonds*. Inherently riskier than high-quality corporate or government bonds because the default risk is greater, they nevertheless have potential for high current income and capital gains.

10. *Asset Allocation Funds.* For investors who are not sure where to put their money, the managers of these funds move around among socks, bonds, and cash in order to provide the highest return with the least amount of risk.

11. *Balanced Funds.* These funds always keep a certain sum in both stocks and bonds, in order to get the high income from bonds and the poten-

tial capital gains from stocks, weighting one side or the other more heavily as the outlook changes.

12. *Equity Income.* Capital appreciation is emphasized, while still providing a relatively high level of current income, dividends that cushion the fund's fall when stock prices tumble.

13. *World Stock Funds.* High-risk funds made up of stocks from around the world, including emerging foreign markets, for investors willing to gamble, with the objective of seeking large capital gains.

14. *Foreign Stocks.* For investors who want to diversify their portfolios outside the United States—Europe, Asia, Latin America, and elsewhere—and hope that the dollar and the movement of stock markets abroad will produce winning combinations.

15. *Specialty Stocks.* Instead of diversifying, as most mutual funds do, this type chooses to put all the eggs in one basket, industrially speaking, such as energy, electronics, or real estate. If the selected industry is hot, the funds soar, but if it grows cool, the funds can nose dive.

16. *Growth Stocks.* These funds select stocks the managers feel have the strongest long-term growth potential, generally the large, familiar blue chips, which are more stable than small companies.

17. *Aggressive Growth Stocks.* By taking more risk on smaller and less well known corporations, these funds seek to achieve above-average returns. Such shares generally outperform market averages during a bull market, but fall harder during a bear market.

18. *Small-company Growth Funds.* These portfolios are built on the theory that solid gains can be made by betting on companies that have not yet been discovered, but seem ready to take off. A few success stories can make all the difference between wealth and poverty.

Source: Morningstar mutual fund rating service.

AUTHORIZED POSTAL ABBREVIATIONS

Alabama	AL
Alaska	AK
American Samoa	AS
Arizona	AZ

Arkansas	AR
California	CA
Colorado	CO
Connecticut	CT
Delaware	DE
District of Columbia	DC
Federated States of Micronesia	FM
Florida	FL
Georgia	GA
Guam	GU
Hawaii	HI
Idaho	ID
Illinois	IL
Indiana	IN
Iowa	IA
Kansas	KS
Kentucky	KY
Louisiana	LA
Maine	ME
Marshall Islands	MH
Maryland	MD
Massachusetts	MA
Michigan	MI
Minnesota	MN
Mississippi	MS
Missouri	MO
Montana	MT
Nebraska	NE
Nevada	NV
New Hampshire	NH
New Jersey	NJ
New Mexico	NM
New York	NY
North Carolina	NC
North Dakota	ND

Northern Mariana Islands	MP
Ohio	OH
Oklahoma	OK
Oregon	OR
Pennsylvania	PA
Puerto Rico	PR
Rhode Island	RI
South Carolina	SC
South Dakota	SD
Tennessee	TN
Texas	TX
Utah	UT
Vermont	VT
Virginia	VA
Virgin Islands	VI
Washington	WA
West Virginia	WV
Wisconsin	WI
Wyoming	WY

Authorized, too, for addressing mail are the following abbreviations of common locations:

Alley	Aly
Arcade	Arc
Avenue	Ave
Boulevard	Blvd
Branch	Br
Bypass	Byp
Causeway	Cswy
Center	Ctr
Circle	Cir
Court	Ct
Crescent	Cres
Drive	Dr
Expressway	Expy

Extension	Ext
Freeway	Fwy
Gardens	Gdns
Grove	Grv
Heights	Hts
Highway	Hwy
Lane	Ln
Manor	Mnr
Place	Pl
Plaza	Plz
Point	Pt
Road	Rd
Rural	R
Square	Sq
Street	St
Terrace	Ter
Trail	Trl
Turnpike	Tpke
Viaduct	Via
Vista	Vis

Source: United States Postal Service

TAX FORMS

706: U.S. Estate Tax Return. Used for the estate of a deceased U.S. resident or citizen.

709-A: U.S. Short Form Gift Tax Return. Used by married couples to report nontaxable gifts of more than $10,000 but less than $20,000.

1040: U.S. Individual Income Tax Return. Used by citizens and residents of the U.S. to report their income tax. (Some taxpayers may also use the short 1040A or 1040EZ.)

1040-ES: Estimated Tax for Individuals. Used to make estimated income tax payments required during the year.

1040NR: U.S. Nonresident Alien Income Tax Return. Used by all nonresident alien individuals who file a U.S. tax return.

1040X: Amended U.S. Individual Income Tax Return. Used to correct errors, omissions, and other adjustments on Forms 1040, Form 1040A, or 1040EZ tax returns that have already been filed.

1041: U.S. Fiduciary Income Tax Return. Used by a trustee for a domestic estate or domestic trust.

1065: U.S. Partnership Return of Income. Used by partnerships as an information return.

1120: U.S. Corporation Income Tax Return. Used by a corporation to report their income, deductions, and payment of taxes.

1120S: U.S. Income Tax Return for an S Corporation. Used by S corporations to report income and deductions under Subchapter S of the IRS code.

1139: Corporation Application for Tentative Refund. Used by corporations that have loss and credit carrybacks and would like a quick refund of taxes.

1310: Statement of Person Claiming Refund Due a Deceased Taxpayer. Used by a claimant to secure a refund on behalf of a deceased taxpayer.

2106: Employee Business Expenses. For use by employees and outside salespersons to support deductions from income for travel, transportation, and other business expenses.

2119: Sale of Your Home. For use by individuals who sold their principal residence. Also used by persons age 55 or older who elect to exclude gain on the sale of their principal residence.

2441: Child and Dependent Care Expenses. Used to figure the credit for child and dependent care expenses.

2848: Power of Attorney and Declaration of Representative. Used as an authorization for one person to act for another in certain tax matters.

3903: Moving Expenses. For optional use to support deductions from income for expenses of travel, transportation, and certain expenses of selling an old residence and buying a new residence, for employees or self-employed individuals moving to a new job location.

4562: Depreciation and Amortization. For use by individuals, estates and trusts, partnerships, and corporations claiming depreciation, amortization, and expense deduction.

4684: Casualties and Thefts. For use by all taxpayers for reporting gains and losses from casualties and thefts.

4868: Application for Automatic Extension of Time to File U.S. Individual Income Tax Return. Used to apply for an automatic four-month extension of time to file Form 1040 or 1040A.

5329: Return for Additional Taxes Attributable to Qualified Retirement Plans, Annuities, and Modified Endowment Contracts. Used to report tax on excess contributions, premature distributions, excess distributions, and excess accumulations.

5500EZ: Annual Return of One-Participant (Owners and Their Spouses) Pension Benefit Plan. Used to report on a pension or profit-sharing plan covering an individual, partner, or an individual and spouse or partners and spouses who own a business.

6251: Alternative Minimum Tax Individuals. Used by individuals to report tax preference items and to figure their alternative minimum tax liability.

7004: Application for Automatic Extension of Time to File Corporation Income Tax Return. Used by corporations and certain exempt organizations to request an automatic extension of six months to file their returns.

8283: Noncash Charitable Contributions. Used by taxpayers to report noncash contributions of property in which the total claimed fair market value of all property contributed exceeds $500.

8606: Nondeductible IRA Contributions, IRA Basis, and Nontaxable IRA Distributions. Used to report the nondeductible amount of IRA contributions and distributions.

8615: Tax for Children Under Age 14 Who Have Investment Income of More than $1,200. Used to figure the tax on unearned income of more than $1,200 belonging to a child under age 14.

8815: Exclusion of Interest from Series EE U.S. Savings Bonds Issued After 1989. Used to figure the amount of interest on post-1989 Series EE U.S. Savings Bonds that can be excluded from income when the bonds are cashed and approved higher education expenses are paid.

COMMON ABBREVIATIONS FOR GENERAL TERMS

AA	Alcoholics Anonymous
AAA	American Automobile Association
AAAL	American Academy of Arts and Letters
AAAS	American Academy of Arts and Sciences, American Association for the Advancement of Science
AARP	American Association of Retired Persons
AAU	Amateur Athletic Union
AAUP	American Association of University Professors
ABA	American Bar Association
ABC	American Broadcasting Company
AC	alternating current
ACLU	American Civil Liberties Union
ACP	American College of Physicians
ACRA	American Car Rental Association
ACS	American Chemical Society
AD	*Anno Domini* ("in the year of the Lord")
ADA	American Dental Association, Americans for Democratic Action
AEA	American Electronics Association
AEC	Atomic Energy Commission
AFC	American Football Conference
AFL-CIO	American Federation of Labor-Congress of Industrial Organizations
AFM	American Federation of Musicians
AFSCME	American Federation of State, County, and Municipal Employees
AFT	American Federation of Teachers
AFTRA	American Federation of Television and Radio Arts
AHA	American Heart Association, American Historical Association, American Hospital Association
AHMA	American Hotel and Motel Association
AIA	American Institute of Architects
AIAA	American Institute of Aeronautics and Astronautics
AIBS	American Institute of Biological Sciences

AIC	American Institute of Chemists
AIP	American Institute of Physics
AL	American League (baseball)
ALA	American Library Association
A.M.	ante meridiem (before noon)
AMA	American Management Association, American Medical Association
AMEX	American Stock Exchange
ANA	American Nurses Association
anon.	anonymous
ANPA	American Newspaper Publishers Association
ANTA	American National Theater and Academy
AP	Associated Press
APO	Army Post Office
APS	American Physical Society
ASAP	as soon as possible
ASTD	American Society for Training and Development
B.A.	Bachelor of Arts
bbl	barrel(s)
B.C.	before Christ
bu	bushel
CBT	Chicago Board of Trade
CEA	Council of Economic Advisors
CEO	chief executive officer
CFP	certified financial planner
COD	cash on delivery
CPA	Certified Public Accountant
CST	Central standard time
DA	district attorney
dc	direct current
DJIA	Dow Jones Industrial Average
DOA	dead on arrival
DWI	driving while intoxicated
e.g.	*exempli gratia* (for example)
EPA	Environmental Protection Agency
esp.	especially

ESP	extrasensory perception
EST	Eastern standard time
ETA	estimated time of arrival
et al.	and others
etc.	et cetera (and so forth)
fax	facsimile
FCC	Federal Communications Commission
FDA	Food and Drug Administration
FDIC	Federal Deposit Insurance Corporation
FICA	Federal Insurance Contributions Act
ft.	foot
FTC	Federal Trade Commission
FYI	for your information
GDP	gross domestic product
GI	government issue
GNP	gross national product
GPO	Government Printing Office
HMO	health maintenance organizations
Hon.	the Honorable
HQ	headquarters
ICBM	intercontinental ballistic missile
ICC	Interstate Commerce Commission
IMF	International Monetary Fund
Inc.	incorporated
IOU	I owe you
IQ	intelligence quotient
IRA	individual retirement account
IRS	Internal Revenue Service
kg	kilogram
km	kilometer
kw	kilowatt
LL.B	Bachelor of Laws
M.A.	Master of Arts
M.D.	doctor of medicine

ms	manuscript
MPAA	Motion Picture Association of America
NAM	National Association of Manufacturers
NASD	National Association of Securities Dealers
NASDAQ	National Association of Securities Dealers Automated Quotations
NEA	National Education Association
NIRA	National Industrial Recovery Act
NTSB	National Transportation Safety Board
NYSE	New York Stock Exchange
OPRC	Organization of Petroleum Exporting Countries
OSHA	Occupational Safety and Health Administration
oz.	ounce
PAC	political action committee
PD	police department
PO	post office
PS	postscript
POW	prisoner of war
PST	Pacific standard time
R&D	research and development
REIT	real estate investment trust
Rev.	Reverend
RFD	rural free delivery
RICO	Racketeer-Influenced and Corrupt Organizations Act
RSVP	*répondez s'il vous plaît* (French for "please reply")
SAT	Student Aptitude Test
SBA	Small Business Administration
SEC	Securities and Exchange Commission
SOP	standard operating procedure
TLC	tender loving care
TKO	technical knockout
UFO	unidentified flying object
USS	United States ship
yd.	yard

METRIC CONVERSION TABLE

	To Convert:	To:	Multiply by:
LENGTH:	inches	millimeters	25.0
	feet	centimeters	30.0
	yards	meters	0.9
	miles	kilometers	1.6
	millimeters	inches	0.04
	centimeters	inches	0.4
	meters	yards	1.1
	kilometers	miles	0.6
AREA:	square inches	square centimeters	6.5
	square feet	square meters	0.09
	square yards	square meters	0.8
	square miles	square kilometers	2.6
	acres	square hectometers	0.4
	square centimeters	square inches	0.16
	square meters	square yards	1.2
	square kilometers	square miles	0.4
	square hectometers	acres	2.5
MASS:	ounces	grams	28.0
	pounds	kilograms	0.45
	short tons	metric tons	0.9
	grams	ounces	0.035
	kilograms	pounds	2.2
	metric tons	short tons	1.1
LIQUID VOLUME:	ounces	milliliters	30.1
	pints	liters	0.47
	quarts	liters	0.95
	gallons	liters	3.8
	milliliters	ounces	0.034
	liters	pints	2.1
	liters	quarts	1.06
	liters	gallons	0.26

25.31